W9-AVR-303

Prices, Reproduction, Scarcity

In this exhaustive and definitive study, Christian Bidard develops a theory of prices of production. This theory, of classical inspiration, breaks down the symmetry between producers and consumers and gives more importance to reproduction than scarcity. In his analysis of multiple-product systems, Bidard focuses on the notion of an all-engaging system which elucidates the link with von Neumann's theory; examines the notions of sector and vertical integration which make possible an elegant treatment of fixed capital; clarifies the status of the internal rate of return (IRR); and proposes a general theory of rent. In the discussion of capital theory and marginal equalities – or, more specifically, the treatment of exhaustible resources – Bidard compares and contrasts different readings of Sraffa's work and revisits the question of the relationships between classical theory (Smith, Ricardo and Marx) and the general equilibrium theory (Walras, Arrow and Debreu).

CHRISTIAN BIDARD is Professor of Economics at the University of Paris X-Nanterre. He is the editor or author of several books on Sraffa's theory – *Prix, reproduction, rareté* (1991), *La rente* (1987), *La production jointe* (1984) and its relationship with Keynesian theory. He is the author of over sixty papers in economic journals and books largely devoted to the theory of long-term competitive prices.

Prices, Reproduction, Scarcity

Christian Bidard

PUBLISHED BY THE PRESS SYNDICATE OF THE UNIVERSITY OF CAMBRIDGE
The Pitt Building, Trumpington Street, Cambridge, United Kingdom

CAMBRIDGE UNIVERSITY PRESS
The Edinburgh Building, Cambridge, CB2 2RU, UK
40 West 20th Street, New York, NY 10011–4211, USA
477 Williamstown Road, Port Melbourne, VIC 3207, Australia
Ruiz de Alarcón 13, 28014 Madrid, Spain
Dock House, The Waterfront, Cape Town 8001, South Africa

http://www.cambridge.org

Originally published in French as *Prix, reproduction, rareté* by Editions Dunod S.A. 1991.

First published in English by Cambridge University Press 2004.

Printed in the United Kingdom at the University Press, Cambridge

Typeface Plantin 10/12 pt. *System* LaTeX 2_ε [TB]

Library of Congress Cataloguing-in-Publication Data
Bidard, Ch. (Christian)
[Prix, reproduction, rareté. English]
Prices, reproduction, scarcity/Christian Bidard.
p. cm.
'First published in French by Editions Dunod S.A. as Prix, reproduction, rareté, 1991.'
Includes bibliographical references and index.
ISBN 0 521 47283 0
1. Production (Economic theory) 2. Prices. 3. Scarcity 4. Rent (Economic theory) I. Title
HB241.B5313 2004
338′.001 – dc21 2003055140

ISBN 0 521 47283 0

Contents

Part II Joint production

Preface

In 1968, when we undertook the study of political economy by reading *Capital* and *Theory of Value*, two books each inspiring in their own way, the ambition was to gain an understanding of the ways in which society works. We thus began with the essential issues. The present work is rooted in a profound perplexity in the face of the incompatibility between these constructs. The impossibility of linking labour value with capitalist competition, as opposed to the formal rigour of the general equilibrium theory, should have led us to abandon our quest, but the reading of *Production of Commodities by Means of Commodities* encouraged us to continue. In this book, a theory of prices of production is developed: the symmetry between producers and consumers is broken and more importance is given to reproduction than to scarcity, thereby reviving the accents of classical theory. Sraffa's construct must be situated in the context of a radical programme that aims to establish the primacy of the classical way of thought. To reflect on this ambition seriously is to measure the scope of the critique and the long road still ahead. The project explains the structural analysis developed here in both its analytical and methodological aspects.

Our discourse keeps a varying, yet calculated distance from Sraffa's. Part I, Single production, deals with familiar matters. Its innovations concern the study of relative prices and the interpretation of Ricardo's theory of value. The economic properties referred to here are used as landmarks, but their real understanding requires the possibility of eluding them. This is the main interest of part II, Joint production. The study is centred on a few concepts: the notion of an all-engaging system elucidates the link with von Neumann's theory; the notions of sector and vertical integration make possible an elegant treatment of fixed capital; and the theoretical status of the internal rate of return (IRR) is specified. Finally, a general theory of rent is proposed. The permanent principle is that of identification of the frame where such a property is true and its association with either a central concept or a small core of irreducible hypotheses.

Capital theory and marginal equalities are analysed in part III, Questions of method. The issue of the choice of technique illustrates our methodological and analytical effort. Two approaches to Sraffa's work are contrasted. Either it outlines an original theory which we develop in a resolutely 'fundamentalist' perspective and which endeavours to define principles while considering their limits, or it constitutes a variant of the general equilibrium model, which has to be explicitly recognized. Implicitly orienting itself in the second direction without acknowledging the change of theoretical status or accepting its consequences, the post-Sraffian analytical literature, whose contributions are remarkable in other respects, has rendered the identification of fundamental problems more difficult. If this interpretation were to be retained, the critique of economic theory would be significantly different from the one initially contemplated. To become conscious of this discordance is an intellectual prerequisite for economists interested in classical thought and in the pursuit of an ambitious programme: 'We should regret that the truth only progresses slowly, but it shall surely triumph at last' (Ricardo, letter to *Morning Chronicle*, 4 November 1810).

The book is an updated version of *Prix, reproduction, rareté* (Editions Dunod, 1991), which has been simplified and extended. It is our choice not to attempt to drown the reader in calculations. The most significant changes result from a stimulating and friendly cooperation with Guido Erreygers. I have shared the joys and the torments of research with many colleagues, but disclaiming their responsibility in the views and the opinions defended here is by no means conventional. My nearest and dearest have had the patience to bear a consuming intellectual passion – sustained thanks to Piero Sraffa.

Acknowledgements

The book presents adapted versions of papers published in the following journals: *Actualité Economique*, *Analisis Economico*, *Bulletin of Economic Research*, *Cahiers d'Economie Politique*, *Cambridge Journal of Economics*, *Comptes rendus de l'Académie des Sciences*, *Econometrica*, *Economic Issues*, *Economic Systems Research*, *Economic Theory*, *Economie Appliquée*, *European Journal of Political Economy*, *International Economic Review*, *International Journal of Applied Economics and Econometrics*, *Journal of Economics*, *Journal of Economic Theory*, *Journal of Mathematical Economics*, *The Manchester School*, *Metroeconomica*, *Oeconomica*, *Oxford Economic Papers*, *Operations Research*, *Political Economy*, *Review of Political Economy*, *Revue Economique*, *Revue d'Economie Politique*, *Ricerche Economiche*, *Rivista di Matematica per la Scienze Economiche e Sociale* and *Studi Economici*.

Part I

Single production

1 Principles

It has been economists' long-standing conviction that, in a competitive state, there is a long-term tendency towards uniformity of rates of profit. This is why, after having studied the formation of short-term equilibria, Walras attempted to incorporate this law into his grand construction. The nature of his project should not be eclipsed by its failure in the treatment of time. But it is in the works of the classical economists, who elaborated the concept of the long run, that the most profound developments of the idea are found. In a circular conception of production, the outputs become the inputs of a new cycle. Since the rate of profit links the price of inputs to that of output, the uniform profitability hypothesis implies a consistency within the set of prices. When the number of operated processes and commodities are equal ('square' economic systems) the prices are determined by distribution and the technical coefficients: they are called *prices of production*. The present book is mainly devoted to the study of these prices and the behaviour of long-run equilibria. For economists accustomed to think in terms of the equilibrium of demand and supply, the surprising fact is that demand is apparently missing. However, demand matters for the determination of activity levels and affects prices in a twofold fashion: either because distribution is involved (as illustrated by the treatment of land in classical economics), or because the operated processes are those which comply with demand (in this respect, the distinction between single and joint production is significant). After the marginalist revolution, less attention has been devoted to these aspects but the reference to the rate of profit and long-term equilibria survives under different headings (discount rate, turnpike) in the modern formulations of the neoclassical tradition.

This study refers to such great economists as Ricardo, Marx, Jevons, Böhm-Bawerk, Wicksell, von Neumann, Hicks, Leontief, Arrow, Debreu, Malinvaud, Samuelson, Solow and Morishima. Above all, it is inspired by Sraffa's work. The publication of *Production of Commodities by Means of Commodities* (hereafter, *PCMC*) marks the renewal of that field of research in modern economics. The interesting ideas of the present book, when not directly borrowed from Sraffa, derive from an elaboration of his model, sometimes in a critical way. However, we should like to be explicit from the very beginning regarding a principle. Simply put, the reader is invited not to interpret our work as being faithful to Sraffa's ideas before it has been scrutinized and compared with Sraffa's own conception. In fact, we never hesitate to plunder every tree in the garden of economic knowledge: our analytical approach is flexible and looks at connections among ideas from diverse horizons. On the contrary, the chapters devoted to economic thought or methodology draw particular attention to the specificity of an approach. They presuppose that a 'school' is not a gentlemen's club and is characterized by adhesion to a global conception and basic principles.

If the greatest economists are those who have defined a project that illuminates their choice and their methodology, then Sraffa is one of them. First, as an historian: while many marginalists considered that it suffices to extend Ricardo's analysis of rent to all factors and forget his absurd theory of value to make him comprehensible, i.e. to make him a precursor of their own approach, Sraffa rendered justice to Ricardo's own conception and restored the working of his logic by destroying the puppet in marginalist clothes. Secondly, as an economist: Sraffa's strong convictions are reflected in *PCMC*'s sub-title 'Prelude to a Critique of Economic Theory'. *PCMC* intends to be a radical critique of marginalism. It points towards its logical inconsistencies and, simultaneously, constitutes a first step towards a reconstruction of economic theory on classical principles. No pages are more significant for this project than the foreword. Remember that Sraffa spent thirty years elaborating the one hundred pages that he considered worth publishing (compare that with my own shameless participation in the deforestation process). The foreword of *PCMC* stresses that no assumptions on returns are made because no change, either finite or infinitesimal, is contemplated. Prior to any judgement on its validity, the very existence of this position must be recognized. It would be paradoxical to treat Sraffa himself in the very way he critiqued others for giving Ricardo short shrift.

Many analyses in this book derive from Sraffa's model but do not necessarily claim to be Sraffian. Some readers may find the dichotomy somewhat schizophrenic. This choice is dictated by our desire for methodological caution. Opinions and feelings are less important than the endeavour to grasp ideas and evaluate their originality, consistency and validity.

Constant returns are assumed.

2 The corn model

1 A simple economy

Let us consider an extremely simple society which produces wheat by means of wheat and labour.[1] Our aim is to introduce some concepts and obtain results which will later be extended to more complex economies. The production process (or method) of b units of wheat by means of a units of wheat (seeds) and l units of labour ($a > 0, l > 0, b > 0$) is written

$$a \text{ wheat} + l \text{ labour} \rightarrow b \text{ wheat}. \tag{1}$$

The notation $(a, l) \rightarrow b$ will also be used. A certain time period (a 'year') separates the inputs (or advances) from the product. Constant returns prevail. In sections 2 and 3, only one method is deemed available. For more complex technologies, the question of the selection of the operated production method will be addressed (section 4).

2 Duality

The economy is *viable* in a strict sense if its net product is positive ($b > a$). The economy is viable in a broad sense if $b \geq a$. When the surplus is completely consumed, the economy reproduces itself at the same level (simple reproduction). Otherwise, a part of the surplus is invested in order to enhance production. Let g be the rate of investment and c the surplus per labourer for final consumption. The division between consumption and investment is written $b - a = cl + ga$, hence

$$c = (b - (1 + g)a)/l. \tag{2}$$

Relation (2) shows that:

[1] The organization of the very first chapters is close to that of *Theory of Production* (Kurz and Salvadori 1995). This similarity is explained by the pursuit of a common project with Neri Salvadori in the 1980s, which did not come to fruition.

- Consumption per head $c = c(g)$ is a continuous and decreasing function of the rate of investment: there is a trade-off between consumption and the rate of growth.
- There exists a maximum rate of growth $G = (b - a)/a$, which is attained in investing the totality of the product. Consumption is then nil.
- The economy is strictly viable if $G > 0$.

The net product is the source of incomes. Let there be two classes in society: workers who receive a real wage w per labour unit, and capitalists who advance the seeds required for production, employ and pay the workers, then sell the final product. Let r be the rate of profit on these operations. If the workers are paid at the end of the period, the division of the net product between profits and wages is written $b - a = ra + wl$, hence

$$w = (b - (1 + r)a)/l. \tag{3}$$

The economy is said to be *profitable* in a strict sense if it is possible to obtain a positive rate of profit (resp. profitable in a broad sense if the maximum rate of profit is positive or zero). According to (3):

- The real wage $w = w(r)$ is a continuous and decreasing function of the rate of profit: there is a trade-off between the wage and the rate of profit
- These exists a maximum rate of profit $R = (b - a)/a$ to which corresponds a zero wage
- The economy is profitable if $R > 0$.

The parallel with the previous conclusions is striking. In particular:

- The maximum rates of growth and profit are equal: $G = R$
- The properties of viability and profitability are both equivalent to $G = R > 0$.

These results are explained by the formal similarity of (2) and (3): the curves $c = c(g)$ and $w = w(r)$ coincide. The reason is that, when the capitalists reinvest all the profits and the workers consume all of their wages (the 'golden regime'), profit and investment on the one hand and wage and consumption on the other are identified ($r = g$ and $w = c$). Outside the 'golden regime', the c variable given by (2) no longer represents consumption per worker since the capitalists consume as well.

The identity of curves $c = c(g)$ and $w = w(r)$ disappears when 'the classical idea of a wage "advanced" from capital' (*PCMC*, § 9) replaces the hypothesis of wages paid at the end of the period. If w^M denotes the real wage, the total advances made by capitalists rise to $a + w^M l$ and the sharing of the net product between profits and wages leads to a rate of profit r such as $b = (1 + r)(a + w^M l)$, hence

$$w^M = (b - (1 + r)a)/l(1 + r). \tag{4}$$

Even though (4) differs from the relation obtained for a wage paid *post factum*, the main conclusions remain unchanged. In particular, the maximum rate of profit is not modified, since it does not matter whether a zero wage is advanced or paid *post factum*. We generally follow the Sraffian tradition of a wage paid *post factum* but we shall assure ourselves that the principal conclusions do not depend on this choice.

3 Expressions of price

The wage expresses the exchange ratio between labour and wheat. Its inverse p defines the price of wheat in wage units. With a wage paid *post factum*, (3) shows that the price of wheat amounts to $p(r) = l/(b - (1 + r)a)$. This price is positive, rises with the rate of profit and tends towards infinity when r tends to its maximum level R. These conclusions constitute an alternative reading of previous results: it is equivalent to say that the wage decreases with the rate of profit and vanishes at the limit or that the wage price of wheat rises indefinitely. When the choice of the numéraire is left open, the fundamental equation is written

$$(1 + r)ap + wl = bp \tag{5}$$

and the relative prices of wheat and labour are

$$p(r) = wl/(b - (1 + r)a). \tag{6}$$

Let us choose the gross product as the measurement unit of wheat ($b = 1$). Relation (6) is developed as:

$$p(r) = wl + (1 + r)wal + (1 + r)^2wa^2l + ... + (1 + r)^twa^tl + R_t \tag{7}$$

with

$$R_t = (1 + r)^{t+1}a^{t+1}p(r). \tag{8}$$

Equality (7) admits an economic interpretation: in order to produce one unit of wheat today (date 0), the capitalists pay wl to the workers and have invested a units of seeds at date -1. These seeds have themselves been obtained as products of the preceding period for which the capitalists have paid wal to the workers and advanced a^2 units, etc. In pursuing the reduction over t periods, the capitalists have successively paid the wages $wa^tl, \ldots, wal, wl$ on dates $-t, \ldots, -1, 0$, whose total present value is the second member of (7). They have also made a 'primitive advance' of a^{t+1} units of wheat, whose present value R_t is given by (8). Despite the compounded interests, the present value of the primitive advance is negligible when t is great (because $(1+r)a < (1+R)a = 1$). The formula of infinite reduction to dated wages

$$p(r) = \sum_{t=0}^{\infty} w(1+r)^t a^t l \tag{9}$$

holds for all admissible values of r ($r < R$). If the wage is advanced, (5) and the reduction formula are written

$$(1+r)(ap + wl) = bp. \tag{10}$$

$$p(r) = \sum_{t=0}^{\infty} w(1+r)^{t+1} a^t l. \tag{11}$$

In relation (1) describing technology, we have assumed that the coefficients a and l are positive. What happens if one of them is nil? Let us exclude a land of plenty where there is production without input. If the production of wheat requires labour but not wheat ($a = 0, l > 0$), a simple case of the Austrian model, then the rate of profit has no upper bound ($R = +\infty$) and the reduction is exact from the very first period onwards, with a nil residue. Inversely, the hypothesis ($a > 0, l = 0$) is that of production without labour. Nature alone renders possible the growth of the product, the 'physiocratic' polar conception of the former. Sraffa's conception of wage (*PCMC*, § 8) is intermediary. A part of it, corresponding to minimum level that is historically and socially determined, is incorporated into the input of production: the socio-technical coefficient 'a' is the sum of the pure technical coefficient and the guaranteed real wage. Sraffa denotes as w the part of the real wage that exceeds the minimum level and depends on the force relations between workers and capitalists.

From an economic standpoint, the positivity of profit ($r > 0$) is necessary to the survival of a capitalist economy. Formally, it is the value -1 and not 0 which constitutes the lower limit (the *factor* of profit $1 + r$ is positive even though the rate of profit is not) and the algebraic properties mentioned previously hold in the extended range $]-1, R]$. Similarly, negative rates of growth cover cases of disaccumulation. The values $g = 0$ (simple reproduction) or $r = 0$ (labour value) have no particular property.

4 Choice of techniques

Until now, technology has been reductively thought of as one method. The presence of m methods $(a_i, l_i) \rightarrow b_i$ ($i = 1, \ldots, m$) raises the question of the choice of the operated method. We presuppose the absence of *a priori* constraints on the available quantities of wheat and labour, therefore a method is not abandoned because of the scarcity of an input. The choice of a technique depends on the objective of the decision maker. If the rate of profit is set at a long-term level r, the capitalists will look for innovation rents that yield temporary extra profits. Let i be the currently employed method at the ruling rate of profit r. The nominal price p_i and nominal wage w_i are such that

$$(1+r)a_i p_i + w_i l_i = b_i p_i. \tag{12}$$

There is no incentive to change the present method if any alternative method j is more costly:

$$\forall j \ (1+r)a_j p_i + w_i l_j \geq b_j p_i. \tag{13}$$

When (12) and (13) are met, the method i is said to be *cost-minimizing* or *dominant*. Conversely if, when the prices are (p_i, w_i), inequality

$$\exists j \ (1+r)a_j p_i + w_i l_j < b_j p_i \tag{14}$$

holds, the first contractor who innovates by using method j obtains a positive extra profit equal to the difference between the two members of (14). By assumption, this extra profit is temporary: once this entrepreneur is imitated the rate of profit will return to the ruling rate r, but the substitution of method j for i leads to new prices (p_j, w_j)

$$(1+r)a_j p_j + w_j l_j = b_j p_j. \tag{15}$$

The existence of transitory extra profits is therefore compatible with the stability of the long-term rate of profit. An alternative hypothesis consists in assuming that, instead of the long-term rate of profit, the real wage is fixed. The capitalists will then choose the method yielding the maximum rate of profit.

For a given rate of profit, does a dominant method exist? How is it determined? Relations (12)–(14) suggest an algorithm that can be seen as a stylization of the process of technical change. Let us start from the price and the wage (p_i, w_i) associated with the current method i and defined by (12). If this method is not dominant, a certain method j yields extra profits. Once this is substituted for i and the temporary extra profits have disappeared, new prices (p_j, w_j) emerge. The procedure is repeated until a dominant method is obtained, for which (12)–(13) hold.

The simplicity of this 'market algorithm' conceals a difficulty: the decision to choose the more profitable method j is taken on the basis of existing prices (p_i, w_i); but the basis will change and become (p_j, w_j) after the adoption of method j. It is *a priori* conceivable that method i that has just been set aside becomes profitable for the new prices. The algorithm would then lead, indefinitely, from i to j and then to i. The consistency property stipulates that such a situation is excluded. Consistency is the noteworthy equivalence whereby method j is cheaper than i on the basis of prices (p_i, w_i):

$$(1+r)a_j p_i + w_i l_j < b_j p_i \tag{16}$$

if and only if method i is more costly than j on the basis of prices (p_j, w_j):

$$(1+r)a_i p_j + w_j l_i > b_i p_j. \tag{17}$$

Let us prove the equivalence between (16) and (17). Prices (p_i, w_i) associated with the use of method i verify (12). By calculating p_i/w_i in (12), (16) can be written

$$(b_i - (1+r)a_i)/l_i < (b_j - (1+r)a_j)/l_j. \tag{18}$$

The same transformation can be carried out in relation (17), with prices (p_j, w_j) defined by (15). Then (17) is also written as (18). Therefore, (16) and (17) are both equivalent to (18).

Consistency is a 'local' property of the algorithm: if method j is substituted for i, then the algorithm does not immediately revert from i to j (symbolically: $i \to j$ implies $j \nrightarrow i$). Since consistency alone does not exclude successive substitutions $i \to j \to k \to i$ and the algorithm progresses in a cyclical way, a supplementary argument is necessary to conclude to convergence. The argument is that, according to (18), there is technical change $i \to j$ if and only if the r-net product per worker $(b - (1 + r)\, a)/l$ is higher for method j than for i. Cycles are therefore excluded, the algorithm converges and the dominant technique is the one for which the r-net product is maximum.

According to (3), the r-net product per worker represents the real wage associated with method i when the rate of profit is r. Therefore method j is preferred to i if it pays a higher wage and the dominant technique is the one which maximizes the real wage. An application of the property is the graphic selection of the methods. For any method i, let us draw in figure 2.1 the associated wage–profit curve $w = w_i(r)$, which is a segment ((3) with $w \geq 0$, $r \geq 0$ or $r \geq -1$). For a given rate of profit the selected technique is located on the upper envelope. When the rate of profit varies the set of dominant techniques is represented by the bold curve in figure 2.1. The rates of profit r^* and r^{**} correspond to switch points when r varies. At these points, two methods are equally profitable and the corresponding price and wage vectors are identical, up to the numéraire.

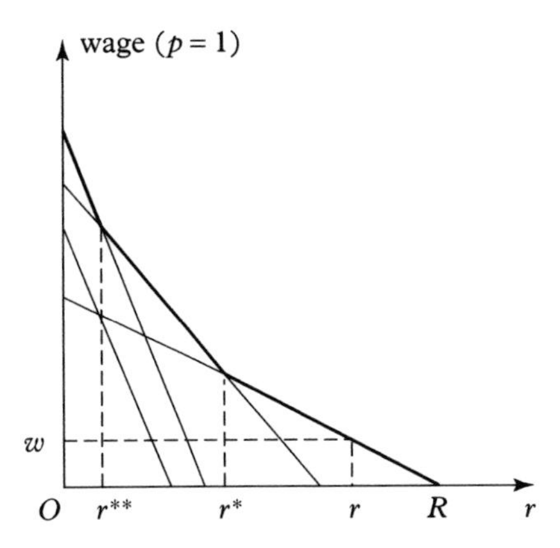

Figure 2.1 Choice of technique: graphical solution

The wage-maximization property results from technical choices. It is not a norm governing the selection of techniques (capitalists do not aim at maximizing wages!) but a manifestation of the good done by the 'invisible hand'. The change of technique is undertaken by the entrepreneur who comes across an opportunity to obtain extra profits. Because of the *hypothesis* of a profit returning to its initial level in the long run, the surplus is ultimately transferred to the workers as a wage increase.

For a given rate of profit but an advanced wage, the choice of technique is identical to that of the wage paid *post factum*. This results from the equivalence of (12) and (19) on the one hand and (13) and (20) on the other:

$$(1 + r)(a_i p_i^M + w_i^M l_i) = b_i p_i^M \tag{19}$$

$$(1 + r)(a_j p_i^M + w_i^M l_j) \geq b_j p_i^M \tag{20}$$

Alternatively, let us suppose that the choice of technique is made under the hypothesis of a given real wage. The dominant technique maximizes the rate of profit. According to figure 2.1, the introduction of a new method can lead only to an increase in the rate of profit. This result, known as the Okishio Theorem, is famous because it seems to contradict the 'law of the falling rate of profit' formulated by Marx. We will examine this law in chapter 8, section 3. Finally, thanks to duality and the golden rule, the market algorithm can also be referred to in a totally different framework, that of a 'socialist' economy in which the planner aims at maximizing consumption per head for a given rate of accumulation.

5 Scope and limits of the model

The essential properties of the corn model for a given rate of profit are:

- Let R_i be the maximum rate of profit for the technique i. The choice of technique is possible for all rates lower than $R = \max_i R_i$. In particular, R is positive as soon as one of the techniques is profitable.
- For $r < R$ the algorithm converges to the dominant technique.
- The nominal price and the nominal wage are positive and unique up to a factor.
- The real wage decreases continuously when the rate of profit grows; it cancels itself out when the maximum rate of profit is reached.
- The dominant technique maximizes the real wage.
- The dominant technique at the rate r maximizes consumption per head when the rate of accumulation is $g = r$ (the golden rule).

The corn model constitutes a powerful heuristic tool and these properties will later be extended to multisector economies. It is not the case that all properties of the corn model have a large range of application, as the discussions on capital theory demonstrate. Of a given property, it is *a priori* impossible to say whether it is peculiar or general: the relevant criterion is the very test of its extension. In pointing at the 'good' (= general) properties and ignoring the 'bad' (= specific) properties of the corn model, we have anticipated results on multisector models, but the selection of properties has been influenced and inspired just as much by the future conclusions of the generalization. Our presentation (for instance, the stress on the consistency property) is also an initiation to the approach that will be subsequently elaborated in more detail.

Other reasons have led us to omit the properties that are called 'marginal', such as the equality of the real wage and the marginal productivity of labour. Sraffa does not know of such relations and many post-Sraffians purport to refute them. The deferment of this question until part III of the book is intended to preserve the reader's pleasure and permit a serene reflection on questions relevant to classical theory.

3 A two-commodity economy

1 A basic two-good economy

Let there be an economy with two goods, wheat and iron, which are produced by means of themselves and labour. The two processes (or methods) of production are written

$$\begin{aligned} a_{11}\text{ wheat} + a_{12}\text{ iron} + l_1\text{ labour} &\rightarrow b_1\text{ wheat} \\ a_{21}\text{ wheat} + a_{22}\text{ iron} + l_2\text{ labour} &\rightarrow b_2\text{ iron} \end{aligned} \qquad (1)$$

($a_{ij} \geq 0$, $l_i \geq 0$, $b_i > 0$). The set made of the two methods is called the *technique of production*. Constant returns to scale prevail. The inputs are invested at the beginning of the period (date t) and the outputs obtained at date $t+1$, which is the end of the present period and the beginning of the next. The economy is *basic* when every good enters into the production of the other commodity ($a_{12} > 0$ and $a_{21} > 0$). Many concepts and properties of the corn economy can be extended to a basic two-sector economy. The general plan is the same as in chapter 2, except for the choice of technique which will be examined in chapter 9. We also introduce a geometrical illustration as a support for the intuition and which will prove to be especially fruitful for the study of joint production.

Let us introduce the benign restriction that every process requires labour ($l_1 > 0$, $l_2 > 0$). As the unit activity level of the ith process, we choose the level corresponding to the employment of one worker ($l_1 = l_2 = 1$). Then the activity level y_i of the ith process is identical to the employment $y_i l_i$ in this industry. These conventions aim at facilitating the geometrical representations. Finally, a matrix A, or a vector l, is called:

- non-negative if $\forall(i, j)$ $a_{ij} \geq 0$ (resp. $l_i \geq 0$), the notation being $A \geq 0$ (resp., $l \geq 0$)
- semi-positive if $A \geq 0$ and $A \neq 0$ (resp. $l \geq 0$ and $l \neq 0$), the notation being $A > 0$ (resp., $l > 0$)
- positive if $\forall(i, j)$ $a_{ij} > 0$ (resp., $l_i > 0$), the notation being $A \gg 0$ (resp., $l \gg 0$).

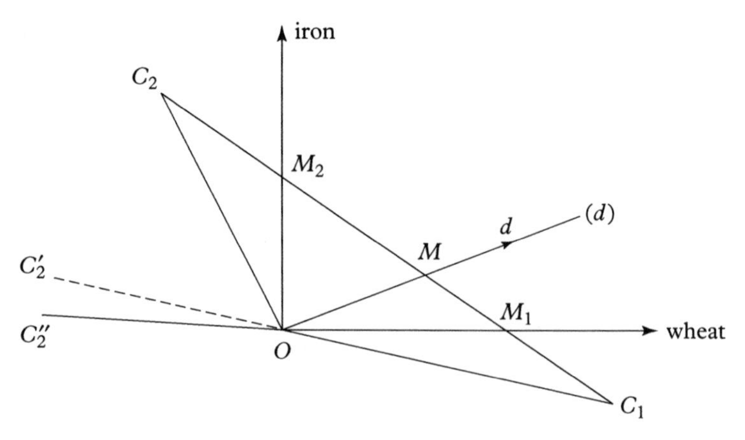

Figure 3.1 The feasible surpluses ($g = 0$)

2 Viability

The economy is (strictly) viable if there exist semi-positive activity levels $y = (y_1, y_2)$ such that the net products of wheat and iron are strictly positive:

$$\begin{aligned} y_1 a_{11} + y_2 a_{21} &< y_1 b_1 \\ y_1 a_{12} + y_2 a_{22} &< y_2 b_2. \end{aligned} \tag{2}$$

The net product is also called the *surplus*. The economy is just viable if the surplus is zero: the inequalities (2) are replaced by equalities. We will refer to viability in the broad sense to cover the two cases. These notions are natural generalizations of those introduced for the corn model. Though the viability property depends only on the coefficients (a_{ij}, b_i), the effective production of a positive surplus requires an adequate choice of the activity levels y_1 and y_2. Since only the relative levels matter, we assume $y_1 + y_2 = 1$, i.e. one unit of labour is employed in the economy.

In figure 3.1 the vectors $c_1 = OC_1 = (b_1 - a_{11}, -a_{12})$ and $c_2 = OC_2 = (-a_{21}, b_2 - a_{22})$ represent the net products of each method. For $(y_1, y_2) > 0$ and $y_1 + y_2 = 1$, the surplus is represented by the vector $y_1 c_1 + y_2 c_2$, whose extremity M belongs to the segment $[C_1 C_2]$. The geometrical interpretation of inequalities (2) is that at least one point of $C_1 C_2$ admits positive coordinates. This is the case in figure 3.1 for any point M on $M_1 M_2$. If the second method had been represented by C_2'' instead of C_2, the economy would not be viable. The limit case of a just-viable economy corresponds to position C_2' when the points C_1, O and C_2' are aligned: the surplus is nil for the activity levels such that $y_1 c_1 + y_2 c_2' = 0$.

Since the economy is basic, the second component of c_1 and the first of c_2 are negative. The segment C_1C_2 cuts the interior of the positive orthant (strict viability condition) if and only if C_1 and C_2 are located in the fourth and second quadrants ($b_1 - a_{11} > 0$ and $b_2 - a_{22} > 0$) and the angle (OC_1, OC_2) is smaller than the flat angle. These conditions are translated in algebraic terms by the Hawkins–Simon (1949) inequalities

$$b_1 - a_{11} > 0, b_2 - a_{22} > 0, \Delta = \begin{vmatrix} b_1 - a_{11} & -a_{12} \\ -a_{21} & b_2 - a_{22} \end{vmatrix} > 0 \qquad (3)$$

which therefore characterize the viability property. The second inequality is a consequence of the other two and may be ignored. The economy is just viable if the determinant is zero.

In a viable economy, which are the feasible surpluses? Let us notice that the point M_1 in figure 3.1 corresponds to a net product made of wheat only, and M_2 to a net product in iron. This amounts to saying that there exist activity levels $y_w > 0$ (resp. $y_i > 0$) for which the surplus is reduced to one unit of the first (resp. second) good. In Sraffa's terms, the activity levels y_w define the wheat sub-system and y_i the iron sub-system. An arbitrary semi-positive surplus is then obtained by combining the two sub-systems. We call this noteworthy result *the adjustment property*: an economy which can produce *some* surplus can generate *any* surplus thanks to an adequate choice of its activity levels. If social demand has direction $d > 0$, the surplus per worker is represented by the point M (figure 3.1) and its level per worker is characterized by the scalar c such that $OM = cd$.

3 Accumulation and consumption

3.1 *Feasible rates of growth*

An examination of the case of extended reproduction ($g > 0$ instead of $g = 0$) generalizes the results of section 2. The gross product $(y_1 b_1, y_2 b_2)$ at the end of the period, obtained by means of the advances $(y_1 a_{11} + y_2 a_{21}, y_1 a_{12} + y_2 a_{22})$, is shared among investment and consumption. Let g be a rate of accumulation common to both industries. This rate is strictly feasible if some positive surplus is obtained:

$$\begin{aligned} &(1+g)(y_1 a_{11} + y_2 a_{21}) < y_1 b_1 \\ &(1+g)(y_1 a_{12} + y_2 a_{22}) < y_2 b_2. \end{aligned} \qquad (4)$$

From a formal point of view, system (4) is identical to system (2) after replacement of coefficients a_{ij} by $(1 + g)a_{ij}$. According to the

Hawkins–Simon conditions, the accumulation at rate g ($g > -1$) is strictly feasible if and only if

$$b_1 - (1+g)a_{11} > 0 \quad \text{and}$$
$$\Delta(1+g) = \begin{vmatrix} b_1 - (1+g)a_{11} & -(1+g)a_{12} \\ -(1+g)a_{21} & b_2 - (1+g)a_{22} \end{vmatrix} > 0. \tag{5}$$

Let us note $\alpha = 1 + g$ the growth factor and study the determinant $\Delta(\alpha)$ which is a polynomial of degree two in α. The inequalities $\Delta(0) > 0$, $\Delta(b_1/a_{11}) < 0$ and $\Delta(b_2/a_{22}) < 0$ imply that Δ admits exactly one root, denoted $1 + G$, between 0 and $\min(b_1/a_{11}, b_2/a_{22})$ and that the conditions (5) are met if and only if $0 < 1 + g < 1 + G$. The feasible growth factors are therefore characterized by their upper bound G which is the smallest positive root of $\Delta(\alpha)$. Moreover, let $q = (q_1, q_2)$ be a positive row vector proportional to $((1 + G)a_{21}, b_1 - (1 + G)a_{11})$. Equality $\Delta(1 + G) = 0$ shows that these activity levels sustain a regular growth at the maximum rate G. Following Sraffa, the ratio $q_1 : q_2$ is called the *standard ratio.* A normalization of q defines 'the' *standard activity levels.* For $g < G$, the economy can produce any given g-net basket $d > 0$ (adjustment property) and all methods must be operated (this 'g-all-engagingness' property is equivalent to the positivity of the matrix $(I - (1 + g)A)^{-1}$).

3.2 Consumption

The above results are again found by means of a geometrical representation, which generalizes that of figure 3.1. For a given rate of accumulation, let us draw in figure 3.2 the vector $OC_1(g) = c_1(g) = (b_1 - (1 + g)a_{11}, -(1 + g)a_{12})$ that we call the g–net product of the first method and, similarly, $OC_2(g) = c_2(g) = (-(1 + g)a_{21}, b_2 - (1 + g)a_{22})$. At activity levels $(y_1, y_2) > 0$ such that $y_1 + y_2 = 1$, the g-net product of the economy is represented by the vector $OM(g) = y_1c_1(g) + y_2c_2(g)$ whose extremity $M(g)$ belongs to the segment $[C_1(g)C_2(g)]$. The length $c = c(g)$ of $OM(g)$ represents the available surplus per head after accumulation at rate g, for a given direction d of final demand. When the rate of accumulation increases, the points $C_1(g)$ and $C_2(g)$ go down and slide along the half-lines Δ_1 and Δ_2 whose directions are $(-a_{11}, -a_{12})$ and $(-a_{21}, -a_{22})$. Then the segment $[C_1(g)C_2(g)]$ intersects d closer to the origin: the surplus per worker decreases.

The following properties derive from geometrical considerations:

- The maximum rate G of accumulation corresponds to the case when the surplus is no longer positive. The points O, $C_1(G)$ and $C_2(G)$ are then aligned and the standard proportions $(q_1, q_2) > 0$ are such that $q_1c_1(G) + q_2c_2(G) = 0$.

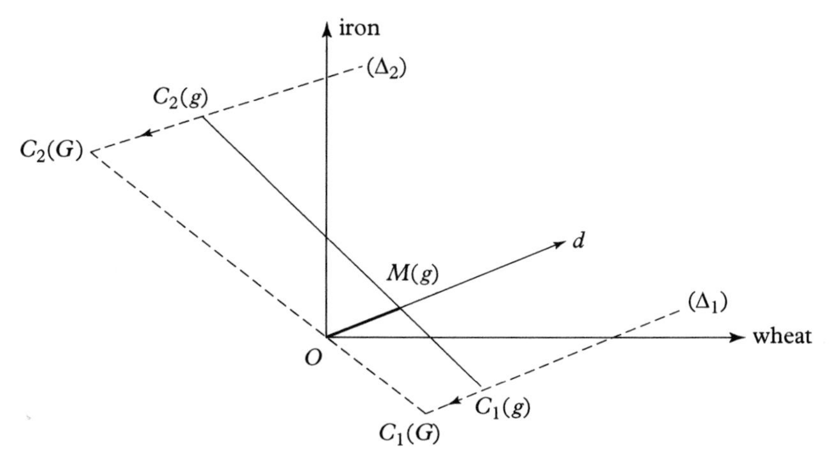

Figure 3.2 Accumulation and consumption: the g-space

- For $g < G$ the segment $[C_1(g)C_2(g)]$ cuts the whole positive orthant, which means that *any* g-net product is feasible: this is the *adjustment property*. Let $d = (d_1, d_2)$ be the direction of the surplus and $c = c(g) = OM(g)$ its level per worker after accumulation. The algebraic translation of the adjustment property is that the system

$$\begin{aligned}(1+g)(y_1 a_{11} + y_2 a_{21}) + c d_1 &= y_1 b_1 \\ (1+g)(y_1 a_{12} + y_2 a_{22}) + c d_2 &= y_2 b_2\end{aligned} \tag{6}$$

admits a positive solution (y_1, y_2) for any $g < G$.
- For $g < G$, the surplus per worker is a continuous and decreasing function of the rate of accumulation.

4 Profit and wage

4.1 Profitability and prices

The economy is strictly *profitable* if there exist positive prices $p = (p_1, p_2)$ and a non-negative wage w such that every industry yields profits. This condition is easier to fulfil when the wage is zero. It is written

$$\begin{aligned}a_{11} p_1 + a_{12} p_2 &< b_1 p_1 \\ a_{21} p_1 + a_{22} p_2 &< b_2 p_2.\end{aligned} \tag{7}$$

Formally, systems (7) and (2) are identical after permutation of a_{12} and a_{21}. Profitability is therefore equivalent to the Hawkins–Simon conditions (3) after permutation. Since the Hawkins–Simon conditions are invariant by permutation, profitability is equivalent to viability. In economic terms, viability is a physical property. It is because the economy reproduces itself with a physical surplus that the capitalist class can obtain a real profit. The profitability property ensures that prices permit the distribution of the net product in such a way that *every* entrepreneur obtains a positive profit, and it is even possible to have a uniform rate of profit. This condition is essential to the working of a decentralized economy in order that 'competition effects an operating fraternity of the capitalist class' (Marx, 1894 [1972], III ch. 15).

The norm of perfect competition is the uniformity of the long-run rates of profit. The prices of production are prices associated with a wage which ensure the norm is met. With a wage paid *post factum*, the prices of production are defined by

$$\begin{aligned}(1+r)(a_{11}p_1 + a_{12}p_2) + wl_1 &= b_1 p_1 \\ (1+r)(a_{21}p_1 + a_{22}p_2) + wl_2 &= b_2 p_2.\end{aligned} \tag{8}$$

For a given rate of profit r, (8) admits one solution (p_1, p_2, w), defined up to the numéraire. A rate of profit is admissible if (8) admits a semi-positive solution (p, w). The algebraic study of this condition can rely on the formal analogy between the systems (6) relative to quantities and (8) relative to prices: they are identical when one reads p for y, l for d, w for c, r for g and when indices 1 and 2 are permutated. According to the results of section 3 and the invariance of $\Delta(g)$ by permutation, we obtain the conclusions:

- The maximum profit factor $1 + R$ is equal to the maximum growth factor $1 + G$. Profitability is equivalent to $R > 0$.
- For any r in $]-1, R[$ and any labour vector, the prices and the wage are positive. The real wage is a continuous and decreasing function of the rate of profit and vanishes at the maximum rate of profit R.
- At the maximum rate of profit R, there exist positive prices $\pi = (\pi_1, \pi_2)$ such that

$$\begin{aligned}(1+R)(a_{11}\pi_1 + a_{12}\pi_2) &= b_1\pi_1 \\ (1+R)(a_{21}\pi_1 + a_{22}\pi_2) &= b_2\pi_2.\end{aligned} \tag{9}$$

When a basket $\delta > 0$ is chosen as numéraire, the wage in terms of this basket is a function $w = w(r)$ whose analytical expression is obtained by eliminating p_1 and p_2 between (8) and the numéraire equation $\delta_1 p_1 + \delta_2 p_2 = 1$. In contradistinction to the corn model, there exist as many w–r curves as baskets, so that any reference to 'the' wage–profit curve presumes a preliminary definition of the basket δ. The w–r curve, which is convex for the corn model, is convex or concave for a two-commodity economy, depending on the numéraire. When the numéraire

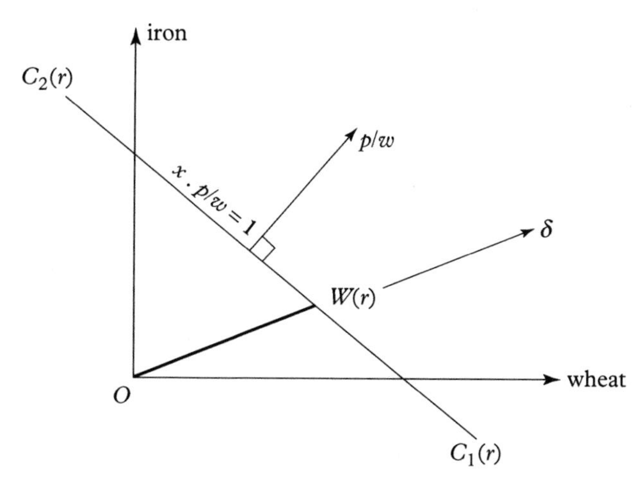

Figure 3.3 Wage and prices: the r-space

is in the standard proportions, the w–r curve is affine: $w = w_0(1 - r/R)$; the scalar w_0 measures the level of the wage for a zero profit, i.e. the net standard product. After adequate normalization of the standard basket, one can set $w_0 = 1$.

4.2 *Geometrical representation*

The duality between prices and quantities is also found in a geometrical approach. The methods being normalized by condition $l_1 = l_2 = 1$, let us consider the r-net products of the two processes – the vectors $OC_1(r) = c_1(r) = (b_1 - (1 + r)a_{11}, -(1 + r)a_{12})$ and $OC_2(r) = c_2(r) = (-(1 + r)a_{21}, b_2(1 + r)a_{22})$. Because of the choice $l_1 = l_2 = 1$, (8) is reduced to

$$c_1(r)p/w = 1$$
$$c_2(r)p/w = 1. \tag{10}$$

The price vector in terms of wage p/w is therefore orthogonal to the segment $[C_1(r)C_2(r)]$. The wage $w(r) = 1/\delta p(r)$ in terms of basket δ is measured by $OW(r)$ in figure 3.3. (In this book, notation δ is used when we refer to magnitudes linked to prices and the rate of profit, such as the real wage, whereas notation d refers to magnitudes linked to quantities or the rate of accumulation, such as the social final demand.) Figure 3.3 permits us again to find the properties of prices by geometrical means. For instance, when the rate of profit increases, the points $C_1(r)$ and $C_2(r)$ move in a south-west direction and W comes closer to the origin, i.e. the real wage decreases. In the vicinity of the maximum rate, the vector $p(r)/w$ increases indefinitely with r and, at the limit R, its direction is orthogonal to the segment $[C_1(R)C_2(R)] = [C_1(G)C_2(G)]$. The limit direction π_1/π_2 is reached for a zero wage and defined by (9). In the golden regime ($g = r$), figures 3.2 and 3.3 coincide and the level of surplus per head $OM(g)$ is identified with the wage $OW(r)$. In the general case when the rates of growth and profit differ the two figures must be set side by side: the g-space of figure 3.2 is concerned with quantities, consumption and activity levels, the r-space of figure 3.3 with prices, wage and profits.

The results of the corn model have been adequately generalized to a basic two-commodity economy. This extension suggests the type of properties expected for more general models. The tools used in this chapter also have an intrinsic value: the matricial calculation is privileged in single production but the geometrical approach will be useful for the theory of the choice of technique and the study of joint production.

4 A basic multisector economy

1 A complex economy

Our aim is to extend the laws established in chapters 2–3 to basic multisector economies. Their generalization to an arbitrary number of commodities also permits us to deal with different periods of production: Assume that the production of wine requires T years. Then, one can introduce $T - 1$ intermediary goods and decompose the ageing process as a sequence of T successive one-year processes in which the output of the tth one-year process is an input of the next. Wine is the output of the last one-year process. In the associated price equations, the rate of profit applied to the value of the inputs dated t gives the value of the liquid of age $t + 1$. This reduction of an intertemporal process to a sequence of short processes shows the flexibility of the multisector approach, which is able to take both the interindustrial and the intertemporal aspects into account.

Let there be n commodities, reproduced by means of commodities and labour. Without loss of generality, it is assumed that all of them are produced in one period. There are as many methods as goods (no choice of method). By convention, the unit activity level of the ith method produces one unit of i. In matricial notation, the productive system is then written $A = [a_{ij}]$, $l = (l_i) \rightarrow B = I$, where A is an $n \times n$ semi-positive matrix, l an $n \times 1$ semi-positive vector and I the identity matrix. The ith process is represented in the ith row as $(a_{i1} \ldots, a_{in})$, $l_i \rightarrow (0, \ldots, 1, \ldots, 0)$. That normalization facilitates the algebraic treatment (it differs from the convention $l_i = 1$ adopted in chapter 3, which was more adapted to the geometrical approach).

The main questions we address concern the solutions of (1) and (2) below. Equation (1)

$$\exists ? y > 0 \quad (1 + g)yA + cd = y \tag{1}$$

determines the activity levels y which sustain accumulation at rate g and produce c units of the given basket d (y and d are semi-positive row vectors). For which rates g does the system admit a solution? Does there exist a maximum rate compatible with constraint $c \geq 0$? What is the shape of the c–g relationship? Similarly, the prices of production with a wage paid *post factum* are solutions to

$$\exists ? p > 0 \quad (1 + r)Ap + wl = p \tag{2}$$

where w is the wage (p and l are column vectors). If the wage is advanced, prices p^M and the wage w^M are solutions to

$$(1 + r)\left(Ap^M + w^M l\right) = p^M \tag{3}$$

Except when otherwise mentioned, we retain the hypothesis of a wage paid *post factum*. Which are the admissible rates of profit? What is the shape of the w–r curve?

2 Properties of indecomposable matrices

The technical coefficient a_{ij} is positive when j is an input of good i. If there exists a chain $i_0, i_1, \ldots, i_k$ such that any good enters directly in the production of the previous one, the good i_k enters indirectly into i_0. These relationships can be visualized by means of a graph: each good $i, j, \ldots$ is represented by a point, an arrow is drawn from vertex j to vertex i if a_{ij} is positive. The good i_k enters directly or indirectly into i_0 if there exists an oriented path starting from i_k and going to i_0. Good j is called *basic* if it enters directly or indirectly into the production of all goods. The economy is called *basic* if all goods are basic and matrix A is then called *indecomposable* or *irreducible* (these terms are synonymous for single-product systems but we will distinguish them in joint production). The properties of basic economies are obtained by translating those of indecomposable semi-positive matrices in economic terms. That procedure has been proposed by Newman (1962), but Besicovitch had already informed Sraffa of the parallel.[1] The mathematical properties are well known after Perron's (1907) and Frobenius' (1908, 1909, 1912) works. Let us first characterize indecomposability:

Theorem 1. Let A be an $n \times n$ square and semi-positive matrix ($n \geq 2$). A is *indecomposable* (or *irreducible*) if it satisfies anyone of the following

[1] Entry 'Sraffa', in *The New Palgrave* (Eatwell and Panico 1987). The post card sent by Besicovitch has apparently disappeared from the Sraffa fund at the Wren Library (from a correspondence with H. D. Kurz). Our conjecture is that the card might have referred only to the uniqueness of the eigenvectors. Its content would then be reflected in *PCMC*, § 41 which is the mere transcription of a mathematical proof. The more striking existence result would have been rediscovered by Sraffa by means of economic reasoning.

Table 4.1 *Properties of indecomposable matrices*

Let $A > 0$ be a square irreducible matrix. Then:

A $\exists\,\Lambda > 0$	$\exists\,\pi \gg 0 \quad A\pi = \Lambda\pi$	A$'$. $\exists q \gg 0$	$qA = \Lambda q$

B, B$'$. Vectors π and q are unique up to a factor. Let $p(\lambda) = (\lambda I - A)^{-1} l$ and $q(\lambda) = d(\lambda I - A)^{-1}$

$\forall l > 0$	$\pi = \lim_{\lambda \to \Lambda^+} p(\lambda)/\|\|p(\lambda)\|\|$	$\forall d > 0$	$q = \lim_{\lambda \to \Lambda^-} q(\lambda)/\|\|q(\lambda)\|\|$
C $\exists\, x > 0$	$Ax \geq \lambda x \Rightarrow \Lambda \geq \lambda$	C$'$. $\exists\, y > 0$	$yA \geq \lambda y \Rightarrow \Lambda \geq \lambda$
$\exists\, x > 0$	$Ax > \lambda x \Rightarrow \Lambda > \lambda$		
$\exists\, x > 0$	$Ax \leq \lambda x \Rightarrow \Lambda \leq \lambda$	(etc.)	
$\exists\, x > 0$	$Ax < \lambda x \Rightarrow \Lambda < \lambda$		

D, D$'$ Λ is the only eigenvalue associated with a (left or right) semi-positive eigenvector

E Λ is a simple root of the characteristic polynomial $|\lambda I - A|$

F Λ has maximum modulus among the eigenvalues of A

G $\Lambda = \Lambda(A)$ is a continuous and strictly increasing function of A

H $\forall \lambda > \Lambda \quad (\lambda I - A)^{-1} \gg 0 \quad$ and $\quad (I - A/\lambda)^{-1} = \sum_{t=0}^{\infty} A^t/\lambda^t$

I (Hawkins–Simon) $\lambda \geq \Lambda \Leftrightarrow \det(\lambda I - A_{ii}) > 0 \;\; \forall i = 1, \ldots, n-1$ and $\det(\lambda I - A) \geq 0$

equivalent properties:

(*i*) $\forall (i, j) \;\; \exists t \;\; (A^t)_{ij} > 0$

(*ii*) $I + A + \cdots + A^{n-1} \gg 0$

(*iii*) $\{x;\, x > 0$ and $\exists \lambda > 0 \;\lambda x \geq Ax\} \subset \{x;\, x \gg 0\}$.

Conversely, A is decomposable if and only if there exists a proper subset I of $\{1, \ldots, n\}$ such that $A_{I\bar{I}} = 0$, $\bar{I}$ being the complementary subset of I.

Table 4.1 summarizes the main properties of indecomposable semi-positive matrices. Row and column vectors are not distinguished: letters y, q, d (activity levels, standard basket, basket) always designate row vectors whereas p, π, l, x (prices, prices at the maximum rate of profit, labour vector, vector) are column vectors. The transposed matrix is denoted $\tilde{A}$. Other notations are: Λ and λ are scalars; $|\lambda I - A|$ is the $n \times n$ determinant of the matrix $\lambda I - A$; $|\lambda I - A_{ii}|$ is the $i \times i$ determinant of the matrix made of the first i rows and columns. Scalar Λ, also denoted $\Lambda(A)$ or *PF*(A), is the Perron–Frobenius (hereafter, *PF*) eigenvalue, associated with the column eigenvector π and the row eigenvector q. After normalization, the vector q is called the standard basket.

3 Economic properties

Sraffa's arguments for establishing the economic properties of single-product systems are attractive. Let us recall one of them: the price vector is positive for the zero rate of profit (labour values) and a continuous variation of r does not allow any price to vanish first, because the value of its inputs should then be negative and a contradiction would be obtained (*PCMC*, § 39). Therefore, the price vector remains positive until a first root of $det(I - (1 + r) A)$ is reached. Or consider this other reasoning: assume that the wage in terms of some commodity i increases with the rate of profit. When i is chosen as numéraire, the price equation of that good shows that there exists another good j whose price with respect to i decreases. When the good whose price decreases the most is chosen as numéraire, a contradiction is obtained. The conclusion is that the wage in terms of any commodity decreases when the rate of profit increases (*PCMC*, § 49). Examined in detail, these delicious arguments are sometimes dubious and Sraffa will be mistaken when he extends some of them to joint production. This justifies the mechanical translation, that we sketch below, of the mathematical properties into economic terms.

Let us set $\lambda = (1 + g)^{-1}$ for the study of (1) and $\lambda = (1 + r)^{-1}$ for that of (2) or (3). The *PF* value Λ corresponds to G or R defined by $\Lambda = (1 + G)^{-1} = (1 + R)^{-1}$. Property ($A$) of table 4.1 states that, for the rate of profit R, there exist positive prices π associated with a zero wage. Property (H) implies that, for $r < R$, the price vector in terms of wage is positive and is obtained by means of the infinite reduction formula

$$p = \sum_{t=0}^{\infty} w(1 + r)^t A^t l \tag{4}$$

which generalizes the result obtained for the corn model. The formula shows that the prices in terms of wage are increasing: the real wage is decreasing (the Ricardian trade-off). The real wage in terms of a basket δ amounts to

$$w(r) = 1/\delta(I - (1 + r)A)^{-1}l. \tag{5}$$

Similarly for the quantity side:

Definition 1. Let g be a strictly feasible rate of growth ($g < G$). The economy has the *adjustment* property if, for any basket $d > 0$, there exist semi-positive activity levels which sustain the production of the surplus d after accumulation at rate g.

Definition 2. The economy is called *g-all-engaging* if, in order to obtain a semi-positive g-net basket, all processes must be operated.

The activity levels which sustain the production of the g-net product d are $y = d(I - (1 + g) A)^{-1}$. Since, for $g < G$, the generalized Leontief inverse is positive, a basic single-product system has the adjustment property and is g-all-engaging. The economy working at activity levels such that the net product amounts to one unit of commodity i is called the ith *sub-system*. If g is a strictly feasible rate of growth, the ith *g-sub-system* produces one unit of commodity i after accumulation at rate g. The surplus per worker in terms of a given basket d amounts to

$$c(g) = 1/d(I - (1+g)A)^{-1}l. \tag{6}$$

The curve $c(g)$ is continuous and decreasing and, when the rate of growth comes close to the maximum rate G, the g-surplus per worker tends to zero. In a vicinity of G, the influence of final demand on the activity levels fades: the relative activity levels come close to the standard proportions and their absolute level increases indefinitely.

The main economic properties can be summarized in two parts: the partition is based on the distinction between non-basic systems (properties (*i*)) and basic systems (properties (*i*) and (*ii*)) and will be clarified in chapter 5:

(*i*) Let the economy be represented by a square matrix A and $1 + G = 1 + R$ be the smallest positive root of $det(I - (1+r)A) = 0$. The set of strictly feasible rates of growth is $[-1, G[$. For activity levels proportional to the standard proportions the economy accumulates at the maximum rate G, with a zero surplus. The economy is strictly viable if G is positive. For any $g < G$, any desired net surplus $d > 0$ is obtained exactly for some adequate choice of the activity levels (adjustment property). The economy is g-semi-engaging, i.e. all methods are operated if $d \gg 0$. The surplus per worker $c = c(g)$, which is also the consumption per worker under the golden rule hypothesis, is a non-increasing function of the rate of growth. Similarly, the strictly admissible rates of profit are $]-1, R[$ with $R = G$. The economy is strictly profitable if and only if it is strictly viable. For any $r < R$, the prices of production are positive if labour is necessary to production. The prices in terms of wage are given by the reduction formula (4) and increase with the rate of profit. Therefore, the wage $w(r)$ measured in terms of any commodity is decreasing. The $w(r)$ and $c(g)$ curves coincide when the wage and the surplus per head are measured in terms of the same basket.

(*ii*) More precisely, a basic economy corresponds to an indecomposable (= irreducible) input matrix. The value $1 + G = 1 + R$ is finite and is the only root of $det(I - (1+g)A)$ associated with a positive standard basket q and/or a positive price vector π; q and π are unique up to a factor. A semi-positive surplus (resp. wage) is excluded for $g \geq G$ (resp. $r \geq R$). For $g < G$ any semi-positive surplus can be obtained (adjustment property) and all methods must then be operated

(g-all-engagingness). At rate G the only possible surplus is zero and is obtained for the relative activity levels q. In a left neighbourhood of the maximum rate the activity levels orient themselves in the direction of the standard proportions. Similarly the real wage is zero at the maximum rate of profit R and, in a left neighbourhood of R, the relative prices are close to their limit proportions π.

4 Sensitivity analysis

The input matrix A determines the maximum rate of profit R and its attached vectors q and $\pi : R = R\,(\ldots, a_{ij}, \ldots)$. For practical (the coefficients a_{ij} are derived from observation) and theoretical reasons, we would like to know how these elements vary with A, at least locally. This is the aim of the sensitivity analysis. It is simpler to consider the variations of $\Lambda = (1 + R)^{-1}$ instead of R. The result is that the partial derivatives of Λ are given by

$$\partial \Lambda / \partial a_{ij} = q_i \pi_j \Big/ \sum_k q_k \pi_k. \tag{7}$$

An equivalent statement is (8) below. As for the variations of prices, vector π must first be defined precisely. The normalization adopted here assumes that a *PF* row eigenvector q of A is first chosen and does not change when A is replaced by $A + \Delta A$.

Theorem 2. Let π be normalized by setting $q\pi = 1$, q being the standard basket of A. Following an infinitesimal change dA, the change in Λ is

$$d\Lambda = q\,[dA]\pi \tag{8}$$

while $d\pi$ is the unique solution to the system (9):

$$q(d\pi) = 0 \tag{9.1}$$

$$[\Lambda I - A]d\pi = [dA]\pi - (q\,[dA]\pi)\pi. \tag{9.2}$$

5 Linear models

5.1 Sraffa and Leontief

Sraffa's model belongs to the linear analysis of production, a notion which refers to a type of formalization rather than a school of economic thought. Another well-known linear model is Leontief's (1941). Leontief's model refers to an input-output matrix A^L. Disregarding a difference in notations (the methods are usually written in columns in the Leontief matrix, but we retain their description in rows here), an essential difference comes from the very nature of the 'technical' coefficients. Sraffa's coefficients a_{ij} are physical magnitudes (amount of j entering into the production of one unit of i) and one of the theoretical objectives is to determine prices. On the contrary, the Leontief coefficients are expressed in terms of value: a^L_{ij} is the value spent on the input j to obtain one unit of value in good i. The magnitudes a_{ij} and a^L_{ij} are not immediately comparable.

Starting from Sraffa's physical matrix, let us estimate the values by means of an *arbitrary* positive price vector (at this stage, the only required property is that the price of a commodity remains the same whether it is considered as an input or an output). The relationship between the Sraffa and the Leontief coefficients is then written $a^L_{ij} = a_{ij}\, p_j/p_i$. In more compact terms, we have

$$A^L = \hat{p}^{-1} A \hat{p} \tag{10}$$

where $\hat{p}$ is the diagonal matrix made up of the components of vector p. Formula (10) links the properties of A with those of A^L. Since similar matrices have the same eigenvalues we have $R(A) = R(A^L)$, therefore the maximum rate calculated on the Leontief matrix is identical to the maximum rate in Sraffa's sense. However, the passage from the physical matrix to the value matrix leads to a loss of information on the structure of production. Consider an arbitrary diagonal matrix $\hat{d}$ and the two economies represented by the physical data (A, l) and $(A' = \hat{d}A\hat{d}^{-1}, l' = \hat{d}l)$. Their respective price vectors are written (p, w) and $(p' = \hat{d}p, w)$ since the two equations $(1 + r)Ap + wl = p$ and $(1 + r)A'p' + wl' = p'$ hold simultaneously. An application of (10) to these economies

$$A'^L = \hat{p}'^{-1} A' \hat{p}' = (\hat{p}^{-1}\hat{d}^{-1})(\hat{d}A\hat{d}^{-1})(\hat{d}\hat{p}) = \hat{p}^{-1} A \hat{p} = A^L$$
$$w\hat{p}'^{-1} l' = w\hat{p}^{-1} l$$

shows that they have the same Leontief coefficients. An interpretation of relationship $A' = \hat{d}A\hat{d}^{-1}$ is that, after a change in the physical units (a new unit of good i represents d_i old units), the same coefficients appear in the methods of production. For instance the economies

$$0.2 \text{ litre} X + 0.4 \text{ ton} Y + 1 \text{ labour} \rightarrow 1 \text{ litre} X$$
$$0.3 \text{ litre} X + 0.5 \text{ ton} Y + 1 \text{ labour} \rightarrow 1 \text{ ton} Y$$

and

$$0.2\ \text{hl}X + 0.4\ \text{kg}\,Y + 1\ \text{labour} \rightarrow 1\ \text{hl}X$$
$$0.3\ \text{hl}X + 0.5\ \text{kg}\,Y + 1\ \text{labour} \rightarrow 1\ \text{kg}Y$$

remain indiscernible when only data in value terms are contemplated. An economy might switch from one technique to another with no visible effect on its input–output tables. Let us retain that:

- An economy admits the Leontief matrix A^L if, for some choice of the physical units, its physical matrix is written $A = A^L$ (take the amount of i corresponding to one unit of value as the physical unit of good i).
- Two economies have the same Leontief matrices if one of the equivalent conditions is satisfied: (*i*) for the same physical units, the relationships between the physical coefficients are written $A' = \hat{d}A\hat{d}^{-1}$ for some vector d, or (*ii*) for adequately chosen physical units specific to each economy, the physical coefficients are identical.

The irremediable loss of information when the value coefficients are substituted for the physical coefficients is easily explained: a Leontief coefficient is a pure number (it is a ratio of values), whereas a Sraffa coefficient has a dimension. The physical units, which are necessary to describe the economic reality, cannot be recovered from the Leontief coefficients. Keeping this simple point in mind may avoid certain misuses of I-O analysis.

5.2 *A taste of von Neumann's theory*

Von Neumann built a theory which deals with joint production and choice of method simultaneously. A first approach in the simplified frame of basic single production with no choice of technique permits us to introduce the main concepts and clarify the relationships with the *PF* theorem.

The von Neumann theory relies on two concepts – those of the rate of growth and the rate of interest. The notion of the rate of interest derives from neoclassical theory which distinguishes the *owners of the factors* (capital goods and/or labour) on the one hand and the *entrepreneurs* on the other. In von Neumann's formalization, each unit of labour is replaced by the wage basket, so that labour does not appear explicitly in the input matrix A. The entrepreneur, who owns no factor, organizes production. He borrows money, rents the means of production, combines them and sells the product. His personal income, or pure profit, is equal to the value of the product less the expenses, including the financial costs which depend on the interest rate. If an entrepreneur could obtain a positive income his example would be soon imitated and competition would reduce the pure profits to zero. (The idea that newcomers can replicate the experiment under the same conditions relies on a constant returns hypothesis at the industry level.) That is why Walras (1874) concludes that, at equilibrium, there is 'neither profit nor loss'. In order to reduce the pure profits to zero, the interest paid to the bankers must be *high* enough. That is the meaning of the following definition:

Definition 3. The scalar r ($r > -1$) is a rate of interest if

$$\exists p > 0 \quad (1+r)Ap \geq p. \tag{11}$$

In view of that inequality, any rate greater than a rate of interest is itself a rate of interest. The rates of interest are therefore characterized by their *lower* bound R_N, whereas the rates of profit admit an *upper* bound R. It follows from a comparison between Definition 3 and that of rate of growth that any rate of interest is greater than any strict rate of growth, hence $R_N \geq G$. But (11) is satisfied for $r = G$ when p is the *PF* vector of A. Therefore, G is the minimum rate of interest. Equality $1 + R_N = 1 + G$ constitutes von Neumann's main result and will be generalized later to a fairly general framework.

6 Proofs

Some significant proofs have been selected. Further results are available on the web (christian-bidard.net).

Proofs of properties (A)–(H) in Table 4.1. Indecomposable matrices A can be viewed as particular case of all-engaging pair of matrices (A, B) with $B = I$. The properties follow from those established in (chapter 12, section 9). Note that the semi-positivity of A is not required in chapter 12 but guarantees existence results.

Proof of Theorem 2. By differentiating equality $A\pi = \Lambda\pi$ one obtains

$$[dA]\pi + A(d\pi) = (d\Lambda)\pi + \Lambda(d\pi). \tag{12}$$

A pre-multiplication of both members of (12) by the row vector q, with $q\pi = 1$, implies equality $d\Lambda = q[dA]\pi$. Then (12) is also written

$$[\Lambda I - A](d\pi) = [dA]\pi - (q[dA]\pi)\pi. \tag{13}$$

By differentiation of $q\pi = 1$, it turns out that $q(d\pi) = 0$, therefore $d\pi$ belongs to the hyperplane H orthogonal to q. This hyperplane is stable by A ($x \in H$ implies $Ax \in H$, because $qx = 0$ implies $qAx = 0$). Consider the restriction A_H of A to H. The kernel of $\Lambda I - A_H$ is the trace on H

of the kernel of $\Lambda I - A$. Since the kernel of $\Lambda I - A$ is generated by the positive vector π, which is not orthogonal to q, the kernel of $\Lambda I - A_H$ is reduced to $\{0\}$. Therefore $\Lambda I - A_H$ is bijective on H. This means that, given a vector z such that $qz = 0$, there exists a unique vector x in H such that $(\Lambda I - A)x = z$. Since the vector on the right-hand side of (13) is indeed orthogonal to q, there exists a unique vector $x = d\pi$ which is both orthogonal to q and solution to (13): the system (9) admits one solution. ■

Deutsch and Neumann's (1985) formulas, which are substantially equivalent to Theorem 2, remain involved because they do not take the standard basket as numéraire. Dietzenbacher (1988) explores the sensitivity to non-marginal changes, when A is replaced by $A + \Delta A$. The notion of Hilbert distance (see chapter 6, section 3) should play a part in this field. For instance, the inequality between Hilbert distances

$$2\,d(\pi, \pi + \Delta\pi) \geq d(\pi, (A + \Delta A)\pi) \tag{14}$$

provides a lower bound to the variation of the *PF* eigenvector after a perturbation of A.

The notion of primitive matrix matters for the calculation of the *PF* eigenvectors and the convergence of short-term Walrasian prices towards long-term prices (see chapter 23, section 2). The main result is:

Theorem 3. Let A be a semi-positive and irreducible square matrix. The following properties are equivalent:

(*i*) There exists a partition of $\{1, \ldots, n\}$ into proper subsets $I_0, \ldots, I_{T-1}, I_T = I_0$ such that $A_{I_{t+1}\bar{I}_t} = 0$;

(*ii*) $\forall k\ A^k$ is not positive;

(*iii*) $\exists T\ A^T$ is reducible.

Matrix A is then called *imprimitive*; otherwise it is *primitive*. If A is primitive, we have $\lim_{t\infty} A^t x / ||A^t x|| = \pi$ for any vector $x > 0$.

If the coefficients of the input matrix A are chosen at random, Bródy's (1997) conjecture is that the speed of convergence increases statistically with n. This is counter-intuitive since the speed is governed by the ratio between the subdominant and the dominant eigenvalue, which should be close to one when the number of eigenvalues increases. But, unexpectedly, the non-dominant eigenvalues tend to accumulate towards zero (Bidard and Schatteman 2001).

5 Non-basic economies

1 Nested systems

When some goods do not enter directly or indirectly into the production of other commodities, the input matrix is decomposable and the economy is called *non-basic*.The economic system is then not fully integrated: it is obtained by nesting a self-reproducible sub-economy into a greater economy. The peculiarities of non-basic economies come from the indeterminacy of the level of the relevant properties, which may refer either to the global economy or only the sub-economy. The point of view privileged in this chapter is to take the whole economy into account. In spite of its peculiarities, the decomposability hypothesis can sometimes be seen as a simplification and, for instance, the Austrian model has great historical and theoretical importance.

2 Relevant notions

The notion of *strict viability* illustrates the difficulties linked to the study of non-basic economies. Two alternative definitions may be considered: strict viability can be defined as the possibility of obtaining either a semi-positive surplus (a surplus for some commodities) or a positive surplus (a surplus for all commodities). In a basic system, these definitions are equivalent. Let us indeed assume a net surplus in commodity i. A slight reduction of the activity level of the ith industry maintains a positive surplus of i and saves on all inputs of that good. Therefore all commodities which enter directly into the production of i now appear in the surplus. By repeating the operation for these inputs, a positive surplus is obtained for all commodities which enter directly or indirectly into commodity i. In a basic economy, the surplus becomes positive. In a nested economy, on the other hand, the existence of a surplus in the sub-economy does not ensure that of a global surplus: the two notions of viability are no longer equivalent. The one we retain considers the working of the economy as a whole and refers to a surplus in all commodities (Definition 1). This notion is suited to the extension of the properties of basic economies.

Definition 1. An economy is (strictly) viable if a surplus in all commodities can be obtained. More generally, g ($g > -1$) is a strictly feasible rate of growth if

$$\exists y > 0 \quad (1+g)yA \ll y. \tag{1}$$

Similarly, the scalar r is a (strictly) admissible rate of profit if all industries can yield a positive extra profit at this rate:

$$\exists p > 0 \quad (1+r)Ap \ll p. \tag{2}$$

An economy is said to be (strictly) profitable if $r = 0$ is an admissible rate of profit.

Theorem 1. The set of the strictly feasible rates of growth is $]-1, G[$, where $(1+G)^{-1} = \Lambda$ is the greatest eigenvalue of A in terms of a modulus (dominant root). The economy is strictly viable if and only if G is positive. The set of the strictly admissible rates of profit is $]-1, R[$, with $R = G$. R and G are continuous and non-decreasing functions of A.

A two-good economy is non-basic if one commodity does not enter into the production of the other. With $a_{12} = 0$, the model is written

$$\begin{array}{llll} a_{11} \text{ wheat} & & + l_1 \text{ labour} & \rightarrow 1 \text{ wheat} \\ a_{21} \text{ wheat} & + a_{22} \text{ iron} & + l_2 \text{ labour} & \rightarrow 1 \text{ iron.} \end{array}$$

The wheat industry can reproduce itself autonomously. The properties established for basic economies – for instance, the duality property $R = G$ and the positivity of prices – would not hold if other notions of viability and profitability had been retained. By reference to appendix B of *PCMC*, let us call 'case of beans' the case when the reproduction of the non-basics is more difficult than that of basics. In our example, this occurs if $a_{11} < a_{22}$, e.g. $a_{11} = 0.5$ and $a_{22} = 0.8$ ('beans' is the new name for 'iron' when $a_{11} < a_{22}$). The maximum rate of growth of the corn sub-economy is 100 per cent but that of the whole economy is limited to $G = 25$ per cent in the presence of beans. A zero surplus is obtained at rate G for the standard activity levels q defined by $(1 + G)qA = q$. But is also possible to obtain a wheat surplus at this rate by operating the corn sub-economy alone. Sraffa assumes that the maximum rate of profit R_S is always determined by the basic part ($R_S = 1$ when $a_{11} = 0.5$). With wheat as numéraire, the price equation for beans $(1 + r)(a_{21} + 0.8p) + wl_2 = p$

implies that beans have a negative price as soon as $0.8(1 + r) > 1$ $(0.25 < r < R_S)$. The solution of this paradox does not consist in referring to 'accounting values' (*PCMC*, appendix *B*) or in considering the case as unrealistic (Sraffa, 1962 [1970]), but in adopting the adequate definitions. When Definition 1 is followed, the maximum rate of growth and profit is $G = R = 0.25$ and the apparent paradoxes disappear.

3 Properties

For any rate of growth smaller than G, the economy has the adjustment property, i.e. it can produce exactly any desired g-net surplus d $(d > 0)$. However, if the surplus is reduced to wheat, it suffices to let the corn sub-economy work, without using the iron process. The economy is semi-engaging in the following sense: in order to obtain a *positive* g-net basket, all processes must be operated (the generalized Leontief inverse $(I - (1 + g)A)^{-1}$ is semi-positive). In viable non-basic economies, it is assumed that the production of any good i requires direct or indirect labour or, equivalently, that any surplus requires labour:

$$\forall i \quad \exists t \ (A^t l)_i > 0 \qquad (T')$$

$$\{y > 0, y(I - A) > 0\} \Rightarrow yl > 0. \qquad (T)$$

Then the production per worker is finite and the surplus per head at the rate of growth g amounts to $c(g) = 1/d(I - (1 + g)A)^{-1}l$. Some important properties of basic systems still hold. A difference, however, is that the wage and the consumption in terms of wheat do not necessarily vanish at the maximum rate R or G. From a formal point of view, the properties of non-basic economies result from those of semi-positive square matrices, as summarized in Table 5.1 that parallels the one given in chapter 4, section 2.

Theorem 2. Under assumption (T) or (T'), the $c = c(g)$ curve is positive, continuous and decreasing. The prices in wage units are positive, continuous and increasing with r. The curves $c = c(g)$ and $w = w(r)$ coincide when the wage basket is chosen as numéraire.

In table 5.1, note a curious asymmetry between two properties: the first property (C) or (C') holds, but the reverse inequalities may not hold for decomposable matrices $(yA \leq \lambda y \nRightarrow \Lambda \leq \lambda)$. In economic terms, some non-basic economies can obtain a semi-positive g-net product even if $g \geq G$. Symmetry reappears in the presence of strict inequalities, when all commodities and industries are involved.

Table 5.1 *Properties of semi-positive matrices*

Let $A > 0$ be a square matrix. Then:				
A	$\exists \Lambda \geq 0$	$\exists \pi > 0 \quad A\pi = \Lambda\pi$	$A'. \exists q > 0$	$qA = \Lambda q$
C	$\exists x > 0$	$Ax \geq \lambda x \Rightarrow \Lambda \geq \lambda$	$C'. \exists y > 0$	$yA \geq \lambda y \Rightarrow \Lambda \geq \lambda$
	$\exists x > 0$	$Ax \gg \lambda x \Rightarrow \Lambda > \lambda$	(etc.)	
	$\exists x > 0$	$Ax \ll \lambda x \Rightarrow \Lambda < \lambda$		
F	Λ has maximum modulus among the eigenvalues of A			
G	$\Lambda = \Lambda(A)$ is a continuous and non-decreasing function of A			
H	$\forall \lambda > \Lambda$	$(I - A/\lambda)^{-1} = \sum_{t=0}^{\infty} A^t/\lambda^t > 0$		
I	$\lambda > \Lambda \Leftrightarrow det(\lambda I - A_{ii}) > 0$ for $i = 1, \ldots, n$			
J	$\Lambda = 0 \Leftrightarrow \exists t\ A^t = 0 \Leftrightarrow A^n = 0 \Leftrightarrow$ after a permutation on the rows and columns, A is written $A = [a_{ij}]$ with $a_{ij} = 0$ for any couple (i, j) with $j \geq i$			

The definitions have led to an extension of the equality between the maximum rates of growth and profit. Another question concerns the generalization of the von Neumann equality between the maximum rate of growth and the minimum rate of interest (see chapter 4, section 5). Let us retain the notion of strict rate of growth as given in Definition 1 and the same definition of a rate of interest as in chapter 4 (section 5, Definition 3). Let matrix A be one with no zero row or column. Then the set of strict rates of growth is defined by its upper bound G, $(1 + G)^{-1}$ being the dominant root of A, and the set of the rates of interest is defined by its lower bound R_N, with $R_N = G$. These definitions depart from a literal reading of von Neumann's pioneer paper without betraying its general spirit. The idea illustrated here is that the indecomposability hypothesis is useless when the right definitions are chosen.

Finally, the geometrical interpretation illustrated by figures 3.2 and 3.3 (pp. 17 and 19) can also be adapted. For a non-basic economy, the peculiarity is that the vectors $c_1(g)$ and $c_1(r)$, which represent the g-net product and the r-net product per worker, have a zero iron component. The representative points $C_1(g)$ and $C_1(r)$ are on the horizontal axis and move towards the origin when g or r increases. The constructions of the surplus per worker, the price vector and the real wage are unchanged. A rate of growth is strictly feasible if the segment $[C_1(g)C_2(g)]$ cuts the *interior* of the positive orthant (because of the strict inequality $\ll$ in Definition 1).

4 The Austrian economy

The Austrian school neglects the interindustrial relationships and privileges the intertemporal dimension of production. A project is conceived as a flow of dated labours which give birth to a final product after T periods:

flow $(l_0, l_1, \ldots, l_{T-1})$ of dated labours $\rightarrow$ 1 unit of good X at date T.

The matricial representation does take into account the intertemporal aspects of production: it suffices to introduce intermediary goods $M_1, \ldots, M_{T-1}$ which correspond to the state of elaboration of the final product X, then decompose the Austrian project into T one-period processes:

$$\begin{array}{l} l_0 \rightarrow 1M_1 \\ 1M_1 + l_1 \rightarrow 1M_2 \\ \ldots \\ 1M_{T-1} + l_{T-1} \rightarrow X \end{array} \qquad A = \begin{bmatrix} 0 & 0 & 0 & 0 \\ 1 & 0 & 0 & 0 \\ 0 & 1 & 0 & 0 \\ 0 & 0 & 1 & 0 \end{bmatrix}, \quad l = \begin{bmatrix} l_o \\ \cdot \\ \cdot \\ l_{T-1} \end{bmatrix} \rightarrow B = I_T$$

Let us notice that:

- The first row and the last column of the input matrix are zero.
- The Austrian matrix A is reducible in multiple ways: the matrix made up of the first t rows and the last $T - t$ columns of A is zero for $t = 1, \ldots, T - 1$. Since A is sub-triangular, we have $A^T = 0$ and the maximum rates R and G are infinite. These properties of the Austrian matrices reflect the lack of interindustrial exchanges.
- The price of the commodity is the present value of the wages. In a general basic model, the reduction formula to dated labours (chapter 4, section 3, formula (4)) has a non-zero residue $(A^t l \neq 0)$ and the infinite series of dated wages converges only for bounded values of r. On the contrary, the Austrian reduction is finite $(A^T = 0)$ and the rate of profit is unbounded. This specificity is due to the absence of 'primitive advance'. It is useful to remember this point when one reads Smith and the criticisms addressed by Marx to Smith concerning the resolution of the price into wages and profits. The convolutions of Marx's thought should not hide the accuracy of his intuition. Sraffa (*PCMC*, appendix *D*) discovers a reappearance of it in chapter 15 of *Capital* (vol. III), in which the rate of profit is bounded 'even if the workers could live on air'. The Austrian model is the exception.

To sum up, the presuppositions of the Austrian conception have often let it be perceived as contradictory to the multisector approach. We prefer to look at the Austrian model as characterized by a peculiar configuration of the input matrix. The status of the model becomes similar to that of the corn model: because of their simplicity both are powerful heuristical tools, but their properties must be validated by an extension to multisector basic economies. Some economic properties have indeed been discovered in an

Austrian framework before being generalized (see chapter 15). These are the properties which should retain our attention.

5 Tax and tribute

Among the peculiarities of non-basic economies, Sraffa underlines the incidence of a tax: a tax levied on a non-basic good does not affect the price of the goods into which the taxed commodity does not enter directly or indirectly. More generally, Sraffa considers that only the basic goods determine the economic behaviour of the system – for instance, the maximum rate of profit. We consider, on the contrary, that no absolute hierarchy is defined between the two types of goods. Let us call *essential* a good which *uses* directly or indirectly all goods in its production. The notion is dual to that of a basic good (= a good which is used in the production of all goods). In an indecomposable system all goods are simultaneously basic and essential. In a decomposable wheat–iron economy, wheat is basic but inessential, whereas iron is non-basic and essential. The concept of 'essential good' has already been implicitly referred to at the beginning of section 2: the reasoning shows that a physical surplus in an essential good can be transformed into a positive surplus after adaptation of the activity levels.

In order to make a parallel with taxation, let us imagine that some industry is committed to the additional production of a physical tribute. The economic incidence of the tribute is partial if it concerns an inessential good like wheat (it suffices to increase the activity level of the wheat industry alone); but the whole economy is affected if the good is essential (an increased production of iron requires an increased production of wheat). It turns out that the economic impacts of a tribute and a tax are reversed.

6 Conclusion

Though the notion of a non-basic good was not formalized by the classical economists, it is historically linked to that of a luxury good, which is consumed by the capitalist class. Sraffa's definition refers to production. By considering that the rate of profit is determined in the basic sector, he separates himself from Marx, for whom all industries do play a role in the extraction of the surplus value and the transformation of values into prices. More generally, Sraffa gives a logical priority to the basic industries: When he finds out that the maximum rate of profit can be limited by the conditions of reproduction of the non-basic goods, he looks for some way to reestablish the primacy of the basic goods.

The main conclusions of the study are:

- The *non-basic economies* are those for which the productive system is not fully integrated: a sub-economy can work autonomously. Then any property becomes ambiguous because it may concern either the system as a whole or the sub-economy only. Hence the stake of the definitions. Those retained here extend the properties of basic economies in an adequate way.
- The notion of a *decomposable system* is usually linked to the idea of a polarized asymmetry between commodities, going from the basic to the non-basic goods. The example of the tribute shows that the incidence of the effects depends on the economic problem: there is no absolute hierarchy between commodities. The distinction between basic and non-basic *goods* (or essential and inessential goods) is less important than between basic and non-basic *economies*. For the latter, an asymmetry exists and the impact of some economic changes remains local, but its nature depends on the perturbation one considers.
- The *economic properties* of basic and non-basic economies are compared in chapter 4, section 3: The properties stated under head (*i*) hold for all economies, those referred to under head (*ii*) for basic economies only. The von Neumann equality holds for all economies.
- The *Austrian approach* considers that the products are obtained by means of labour and time and breaks the physical relationships between industries. The model has a heuristic value but only the generalization of its properties to multisector basic economies can give them a solid foundation.

7 Proof

The following result will be used in chapter 12. $\bar{I}$ denotes the complementary subset of I.

Theorem 3. Let A_{np} and B_{np} be semi-positive matrices such that AB is decomposable: $(AB)_{I\bar{I}} = 0$. Then there exists $J \subset \{1, \ldots, p\}$ such that $A_{IJ} = 0$ and $B_{\bar{J}\bar{I}} = 0$. Moreover, if A and B are square ($n = p$) and B regular ($B = C^{-1}$), then $A_{IJ} = C_{IJ} = 0$ with $\text{card}(I) + \text{card}(J) = n$.

Proof. Let K be a maximal subset such that $A_{IK} = 0$. Equality $0 = (AB)_{I\bar{I}} = A_{IK}B_{K\bar{I}} + A_{I\bar{K}}B_{\bar{K}\bar{I}} = A_{I\bar{K}}B_{\bar{K}\bar{I}}$ implies that any element $b_{\bar{k}\bar{i}}$ of $B_{\bar{K}\bar{I}}$ is null, otherwise the $\bar{k}$th column of $A_{I\bar{K}}$ would be null, contrary to the maximality of K. Therefore $A_{IK} = B_{\overline{K}\,\overline{I}} = 0$. Let $\overline{J}$ be a maximal subset containing $\overline{K}$ (hence, $J \subset K$ and $A_{IJ} = 0$) such that $B_{\overline{J}\,\overline{I}} = 0$. Assume moreover that $n = p$ and $B = C^{-1}$. Since $B_{\overline{J}\,\overline{I}} = 0$, equality $0 = (CB)_{I\overline{I}} = C_{IJ}\, B_{J\overline{I}} + C_{I\overline{J}}\, B_{\overline{J}\,\overline{I}} = C_{IJ}\, B_{J\overline{I}}$ implies that any element c_{ij} of C_{IJ} is zero, otherwise the jth row of $B_{J\overline{I}}$ would be null, contrary to the maximality of $\overline{J}$. Hence $A_{IJ} = C_{IJ} = 0$. Because $B_{\overline{J}\,\overline{I}} = 0$ and $C_{IJ} = 0$, with B and C regular, we have $\text{card}(\overline{I}) + \text{card}(\overline{J}) \leq n$ and $\text{card}(I) + \text{card}(J) \leq n$. Hence, the conclusion. ■

6 Relative prices

How do relative prices vary with the rate of profit? The exceptional case of uniform organic composition apart, all prices interact in a complex way because commodities enter into the production of other commodities. Our aim, however, is to show that, from several points of view, the relative prices vary monotonically (sections 2–3). The rehabilitation of an old idea allows us to link the price variations with the characteristics of production (section 4). When the operated technique is not given *a priori* and depends on distribution, these monotonicity laws do not hold. It will be shown that the relative prices then vary arbitrarily, an important negative result for capital theory (section 5).

1 Price and payment of wages

For a given rate of profit, the price equation with an advanced wage is written $(1 + r)(Ap^M + w^M l) = p^M$. When it is developed as $(1 + r)Ap^M + [w^M (1 + r)]l = p^M$, it can be identified with the price equation $(1 + r) Ap + wl = p$ with a wage paid *post factum*. Hence:

Theorem 1. For a given rate of profit, the relative prices are independent of the payment of wages *ante* or *post factum*. More precisely, the relationships are written $p = p^M$, $w = w^M(1 + r)$, or $p = p^M/(1 + r)$ and $w = w^M$.

The economic reason for this result is that it is equivalent for an entrepreneur to pay w^M at the beginning of the period or $w^M(1 + r)$ at its end. Theorem 1 allows an easy transposition of the results from one system to the other. For instance, the wage–profit equation with the standard basket as numéraire, which is written $w = 1 - r/R$ for a wage paid *post factum*, becomes $w^M = (1 - r/R) : (1 + r)$ if wages are advanced. The reason why Sraffa assumes 'that the wage is paid *post factum* as a share of the annual product, thus abandoning the classical economists' idea of a wage "advanced" from capital' (*PCMC*, § 9) is unclear.

2 Price curves

2.1 *Price space*

The ratio between the cost $c_i = \sum_j a_{ij}p_j$ of capital and that $v_i = wl_i$ of labour is called the *organic composition* of the *i*th industry. If this magnitude is identical for all industries, a 1 per cent increase of the factor of profit is exactly compensated by a c/v per cent decrease of the wage, with no change in the relative prices. Since the prices are proportional to the labour vector for $r = -1$ and to the *PF* vector for $r = R$, the invariance of relative prices requires that these vectors coincide:

Theorem 2. Two relative prices $p(r_1)$ and $p(r_2)$ are equal if and only if $Al = l/(1 + R)$. Then the organic composition is uniform and the prices are always proportional to the labour vector.

If the organic composition differs across industries, the relative costs are affected by a change in distribution and a deformation of the price structure is necessary to restore the uniformity of the rates of profit. Our aim is to study this deformation. The price vector describes a curve (C) in R^n when the rate of profit varies. A first question concerns the space in which the prices move. The reduction to dated labour (chapter 4, section 3) shows that if the vectors l, Al, . . . , $A^s l$ are linearly dependent, the price vector belongs to the subspace E they span. Hence:

Definition 1. Let $s = \deg(A, l)$ be the greatest integer such that the s vectors $l, \ldots, A^{s-1}l$ are independent. The system (A, l) is called *regular* if $s = n$, *irregular* if $s < n$.

Theorem 3. A system is irregular if and only if $yl = 0$ for some row eigenvector y of A. If A admits a non-semi-simple eigenvalue (that is, the associated eigenspace has a dimension greater than one), the system (A, l) is irregular whatever the labour vector l is.

Let us study the relationship between the system (A, l) and the solutions $(p_t, w_t) \in R^{n+1}$ of the price equation $(1 + r_t)(Ap_t + w_t l) = p_t$ for different levels of the rate of profit (the advanced wage hypothesis simplifies the statement of the results). In the case of a regular system, a noteworthy property is that *any* set of n price vectors (the wage component being omitted) is independent in R^n, and *any* set of $n + 1$ price and wage vectors is independent in R^{n+1}. The property is characteristic in the following sense: given $n + 1$ vectors in R^{n+1} satisfying the property, there exists a system (A, l) which generates these vectors as price vectors, and this system is unique. Therefore $n + 1$ points on (C) determine the whole curve (C). However this characterization takes into account only the formal equality $(1 + r)(Ap + wl) = p$, not the additional constraints implied by the semi-positivity of (A, l) which, for instance, require that prices in terms of wage are increasing. In other terms, the price behaviour is identified only from the standpoint of linear structures.

If the system (A, l) is irregular, these statements must be adapted: the prices belong to the subspace E spanned by $l, \dots, A^{s-1}l$; in this subspace, any s price vectors are independent and the movement of prices is similar to that of a regular system (Theorem 4). $s + 1$ prices determine the whole curve (C), but the underlying system (A, l) is no longer unique and admits $n(n - s)$ degrees of freedom (Theorem 5).

Theorem 4. Let there be $s + 1$ scalars $1 + r_t$ and $s + 1$ vectors (p_t, w_t). There exists (A, l), with $l \neq 0$ and $\deg(A, l) = s$, such that (p_t, w_t) is the solution, unique up to a factor, of the equation $(1 + r_t)(Ap_t + w_t l) = p_t$ for $t = 0, \dots, s$, if and only if the properties (i) and (ii) hold:

(*i*) The $s + 1$ vectors p_t are linearly dependent and any s out of them are linearly independent.

(*ii*) The $s + 1$ vectors (p_t, w_t) are linearly independent.

Theorem 5. Let $s = \deg(A, l)$. Another system (A', l') generates the same curve of prices in terms of wage if and only if both systems generate the same prices for $s + 1$ levels of the rate of profit. Then $l' = l$ and $A' = A + H$ where H is any matrix such that $Hl = HAl = \cdots = HA^{s-1} l = 0$ or, alternatively, $Hp(r_0) = \cdots = Hp(r_{s-1}) = 0$. If the system is regular $(s = n)$, then $H = 0$ and (A, l) is unique.

If the only relative prices, not the prices in terms of wage, are known, two more reasons for the indetermination of the underlying technique appear, even for regular systems: first, replacing the labour vector by a proportional vector does not alter the relative prices; second, replacing the input matrix A by $A + l\delta$ amounts to incorporating the (row) basket δ into the necessary wage. For a given rate of profit, the remaining part of the wage decreases by an amount equal to the value of δ but the relative prices are not affected:

Theorem 6. Let there be $s + 1$ vectors of relative prices associated with technique (A, l) of degree s. Another technique (B, m) admits the same relative prices at the same rates of profit if and only if it is written $B = A + l\delta + H$, $m = \mu l$ (any $\mu > 0$ and δ), the matrix H being defined in Theorem 5. The relative prices then coincide for any rate of profit.

The geometrical interpretation of the next result is that the price curve always turns clockwise or anti-clockwise:

Theorem 7. In the space E, $det(p(r_0), \ldots, p(r_{s-1}))$ has a constant sign for any increasing sequence of admissible rates of profit, the sign being that of $det(l, Al, \ldots, A^{s-1} l)$.

We now look at the price curves from the standpoint of quadratic structures. The very definition of the prices of production shows that the three vectors Ap, p and l are linearly dependent. Any 3×3 determinant extracted from the matrix $[Ap, p, l]$ is zero. The corresponding equation being homogeneous of degree two in p, we obtain that the curve $p = p(r)$ is located on quadratic cones. For $n \geq 3$ there are $n - 2$ independent cones of this type. For $n = 3$, the equation of the quadratic cone is $det(Ap, p, l) = 0$, therefore the labour vector and any (real or complex) eigenvector of A belong to it. A conic is obtained when the cone is intersected with a plane (normalization of prices). Its type depends on the plane. In case of normalization by the standard basket, the geometrical characterization is:

Theorem 8. Let there be $n = 3$ goods and the standard basket be chosen as numéraire. When distribution changes, the prices describe a part of a conic. That conic is an ellipse, parabola, or hyperbola, according to the number 0, 1, or 2 of real non-*PF* eigenvalues of A.

2.2 *Visualization*

In order to visualize the relative prices for $n = 3$ goods, the simplest way is to normalize them, for instance by setting $p_1 + p_2 + p_3 = 1$. The price vector is then represented by a point P in the unit simplex and the relative prices are proportional to the distances from P to the three sides of the triangle. For a given matrix A and any labour vector l, the curve $p = p(r)$ starts from the labour vector (for $r = -1$) and ends at the Frobenius vector (for $r = R$). The curves in figures 6.1a and 6.1b correspond to various positions of l. The system (A, l) has degree 1, 2 or 3 according to the choice of l:

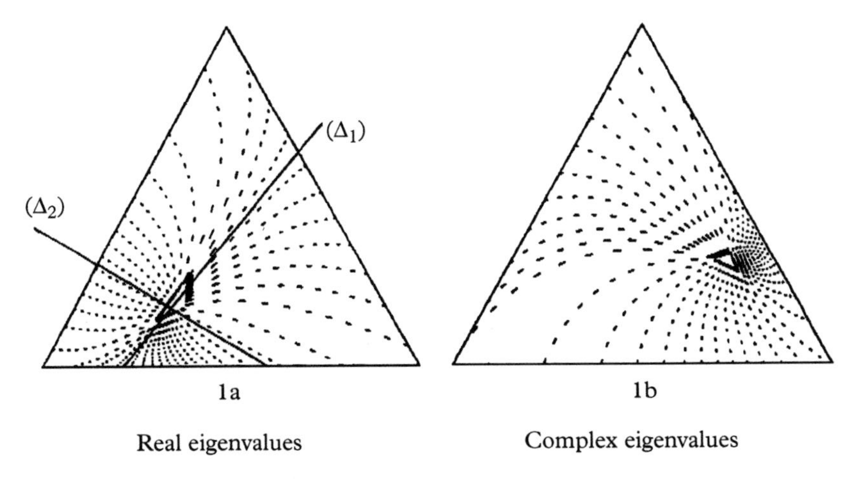

Figure 6.1 Two plates of spaghetti

- The degree of irregularity $s = 1$ is obtained when $l = \pi$. The organic composition of capital is uniform and the curve of relative prices is reduced to point π.
- The degree of irregularity $s = 2$ is obtained when l is a linear combination of π and another eigenvector π_2 or π_1 of A: the equality $yl = 0$ mentioned in Theorem 3 holds for the row eigenvector associated with the third eigenvalue. Two 'critical lines' $\Delta_1 = \pi\pi_2$ and $\Delta_2 = \pi\pi_1$ appear in figure 6.1a and define four critical zones within the simplex.
- The system is regular when $s = 3$ ($l \notin \Delta_1 \cup \Delta_2$). The curve $p = p(r)$ remains inside the critical zone containing l and turns either clockwise or anti-clockwise, with opposite curvatures in neighbouring zones.

That classification assumes that the other two eigenvalues of A are real (figure 6.1a). If they are complex, the critical lines (Δ_1) and (Δ_2) disappear and the degree of regularity is either one (if $l = \pi$) or three (if $l \neq \pi$). All the curves have the same type of curvature (figure 6.1b).

When matrix A moves continuously from the first (three real eigenvalues) to the second (two complex eigenvalues) type, the limit case is that of a double eigenvalue. Two types of transition exist according to whether the eigenspace associated with the double root has dimension one (semi-simple eigenvalue) or two. They differ by their behaviour in the vicinity of the transition. In the first case, the critical lines become closer and closer and almost all curves turn in the same way. At the limit the critical lines coincide with the direction $\pi\pi_1$, where π_1 is the unique eigenvector associated with the semi-simple root, then disappear. In the second case the critical lines remain apart from each other but all trajectories are straighter and straighter, then become segments in the limit case.

3 Distances between relative prices

For two goods, calculation shows that the relative prices vary monotonically with the rate of profit. The rule does not hold for more commodities. However, we would like to state that the movement of vector $p(r)$ towards $\pi = p(R)$ is monotone when r increases. How can the distance between relative prices be measured? The answers are not unique, but all of them rely on the notion of attractive cones. A first idea is to calculate the Euclidean angle between price vectors, but the reference to the Hilbert distance is more relevant.

3.1 Attractive cones

For a given input matrix but an arbitrary labour vector, let $\pi = p(R)$ be the limit price. Consider an infinite family $\mathcal{F}$ of cones, one included into the other $(\ldots \supset C_\delta \supset C_\gamma \supset C_\beta \supset \ldots)$ and which have π as their common intersection. The family is said to be 'attractive' for the relative prices if a price curve which has entered into a cone remains inside it when the rate of profit increases, whatever the labour vector is. Since the price curves enter into narrower and narrower cones, the movement of the relative prices towards π is monotone relatively to family $\mathcal{F}$. The monotonicity property depends upon the point of view, i.e. upon the choice of family $\mathcal{F}$. The most immediate – though not necessarily the best – idea is to consider the circular cones, i.e. the cone C_γ is made of vectors which have the Euclidean angle γ with π. Before contemplating this family, Theorem 9 states a simple monotonicity property which is at the basis of further results.

Theorem 9. Let q_i be a row eigenvector other than the standard basket q. The ratio $|q_i p(r)|/qp(r)$ decreases monotonically to zero when r increases up to R.

The result can be translated in geometrical terms. Assume first that q_i is real. Consider the hyperplane whose equation is written $q_i x = k\, qx$, where the constant $k = q_i p(r_0)/qp(r_0)$ is chosen in order that the hyperplane contains $p(r_0)$. The hyperplane splits the space into two half-spaces.

According to Theorem 9, the half-space containing π is attractive. If q_i is a complex vector, the surface defined by the equation $|q_i x| = k\ qx$ is a quadratic cone and the corresponding family is attractive for the price curve.

The origin of the difficulty in understanding the movement of prices lies in the interaction between industries. Let us first eliminate this phenomenon. When every commodity is produced only by means of itself and labour, simple calculations show that the angle between $p(r)$ and its limit direction π decreases when r increases, i.e. the family of Euclidean cones with axis π is attractive. This result is more general:

Theorem 10. If the input matrix is symmetric ($A = \tilde{A}$) or normal ($A\tilde{A} = \tilde{A}A$), the Euclidean angle between $p(r)$ and $\pi = p(R)$ decreases when r increases.

The conclusion is satisfactory . . . but not the assumptions! There is no economic reason for the input matrix to be symmetric or otherwise normal. Nor may one hope to obtain significant extensions of the conclusion. It is the very idea of Euclidean angle which is at stake: assume a change in the physical unit of the ith commodity, say, the new unit is half of the previous one. The economic system itself is not affected, but the ith component of every price vector is halved and the Euclidean angle between the vectors modified. But the Euclidean angle, even if it is of common use, is not an absolute reference. Theorem 11 introduces the notion of N-angle:

Theorem 11. Let A be diagonalizable and p_i $(i = 1, \ldots, n)$ be a basis of eigenvectors of A. Let the N-angle $(x, y)_N$ between vectors $x = \sum_{i=1}^{n} x_i p_i$ and $y = \sum_{i=1}^{n} y_i p_i$ be defined by

$$cos(x, y)_N = \sum_i x_i \bar{y}_i \Big/ \Big(\sum_i |x_i|^2 \cdot \sum_i |y_i|^2 \Big)^{1/2}.$$

The N-angle between $p(r)$ and $p(R)$ decreases monotonically as r increases.

When A is a normal matrix, the N-angle is the usual Euclidean angle and Theorem 11 reduces to Theorem 10. But Theorem 11 is general (almost any matrix is diagonalizable), which was not the case for Theorem 10. What is its meaning? Mathematicians tell us that the cones which make a constant N-angle with $\pi = p(R)$ look circular through distorting glasses.

For Euclidean readers, these attractive cones are quadratic cones, which are ‘elliptic’ instead of being ‘circular’.

3.2 *Hilbert distance*

The main weakness of the notion of Euclidean angle is that the angle between vectors depends on the physical units of measurement. This was not the case for the ratio of values considered in Theorem 9. Similarly:

Definition 2. The Hilbert distance $d(x, y)$ between positive relative price vectors x and y is defined as $d(x, y) = \ln [\max_i (y_i/x_i) : \min_i (y_i/x_i)]$. It is independent of the physical units of measure.

The distance is zero if and only if the relative prices coincide. A change in the physical unit of commodity i modifies the ith component of x and y but not $d(x, y)$. The Hilbert measure is not as exotic as it seems: for two positive vectors with no component coming close to zero, the ratio between their Euclidean angle and their Hilbert distance is bounded from below and from above by positive scalars. This means that the Hilbert distance is a rough approximation of the Euclidean angle. Therefore, a monotonicity law on the Hilbert distance excludes important irregularities in the variations of the angle.

Theorem 12. For $r \leq t$, the Hilbert distance between $p(r)$ and $p(t)$ decreases when r increases.

Theorem 12 is the most general simple law on relative prices. Other results are:

- For $r < s < t < R$, the expected symmetric property $d(p(r), p(s)) < d(p(r), p(t))$ holds if $n = 3$, but not for $n > 3$ (Bidard and Krause 1996).
- For $r < t$, the segment $[p(r), p(t)]$ does not cut the interior of the Hilbert circle of centre π going through $p(t)$. This implies that a price curve does not turn ‘too much’.
- When r is close to R, the speed of convergence of $p(r)$ towards π is finite (except in case of uniform organic composition) and depends on the relative position of π and the tangent to the curve at π.

Let us conclude on a numerical example. For the data

$$A = \frac{1}{1000}\begin{bmatrix} 498 & 1 & 1 \\ 498 & 1 & 1 \\ 1 & 1 & 498 \end{bmatrix}, \quad l = \begin{pmatrix} 0.1 \\ 1 \\ 1 \end{pmatrix}$$

and the normalization $p_1 + p_2 + p_3 = 1$, the *PF* vector π is located at the centre of the unit simplex. For $r = -1$, the price curve starts from the labour vector which is close to the middle of a side of the simplex. When r increases, the price curve comes close to a corner and, finally, rushes towards the centre of the triangle. We have heroically shown that this movement to the centre is monotone from several points of view.

4 The golden sub-system

When the organic composition is not uniform, the relative prices vary with distribution. Let the rate of profit increase. Intuition suggests that the cost of the more capital-intensive industries increases more and, therefore, the relative price of the more capital-intensive product increases. This result seems to be confirmed by a simple calculation: with the notations of sub-section 2.1, equality $p_i = (1 + r)c_i + v_i$ suggests that $\Delta p_i/p_i = c_i\Delta r/((1 + r)c_i + v_i)$ and, therefore, that inequality $c_i/v_i > c_j/v_j$ implies $\Delta p_i/p_i > \Delta p_j/p_j$. What is wrong with this calculation? It omits the variations induced in the value of capital by the price changes. Taking these Wicksell price effects into account can reverse the inequality, so that the more capital-intensive product is not necessarily the one whose price increases the most: 'The reason for this seeming contradiction is that the means of production of an industry are themselves the product of one or more industries which may in their turn employ a still lower proportion of labour to means of production' (*PCMC*, §19). It is the very idea of a ranking of industries according to their capital intensity which is at stake: the ranking is local and varies with the rate of profit. In spite of these discouraging observations, Theorem 13 rehabilitates the notion of organic composition. The reference, however, is not to the composition of the ith industry, but that of the ith 'r-sub-system' defined in chapter 4, section 3. The basket made of one unit of commodity i is denoted e_i:

Definition 3. For a commodity i, the r-sub-system $rss(i)$, or 'golden sub-system', is the productive system working at the activity levels $y(i) = e_i(I - (1 + r)A)^{-1}$ which sustain the production of one unit of commodity i after accumulation at rate $g = r$.

Theorem 13. In a neighbourhood of r, the relative prices of two commodities vary according to the relative organic compositions of their associated r-sub-systems.

5 Wicksell price effects

Up to now, it has been assumed that only one technique is available. The previous laws do not withstand the choice of method. For instance, with two goods, the relative prices can increase for some technique then decrease when another technique is operated because it is cheaper at a higher rate of profit. The question concerns the existence of laws on prices which are robust to the change of technique. It presumes a theory of choice of technique. For the time being, it suffices to generalize the principle seen in chapter 2 for the corn model: For a given set of methods and a given rate of profit, the dominant price-and-wage vector is such that, in every industry, some operated process yields exactly the ruling rate of profit at these prices and no alternative process yields more. The relative prices are obtained by leaving the wage component aside. In the context of capital theory, the variations in the relative prices are called the Wicksell price effects. If the relative prices were invariant, the input items might be aggregated by using them as relative weights and many properties of the corn model would still hold for multisector models. Knowing some properties of relative prices would permit us to take them under control, so that the behaviour of multisector models would not deviate too much from that of the corn model. Theorem 14 aims to state laws on relative prices and does find all of them: it claims that, unfortunately, there are none! Like the Debreu (1974) – Mantel (1974) – Sonnenschein (1973) Theorem on the dynamics of the Walrasian tâtonnement, it is basically a negative result. The Wicksell price effects cannot be monitored and the anarchy of the relative prices condemns capital theory to remain basically a blank page (however, this prospect will not prevent us from returning to the topic).

Theorem 14. Given T arbitrary rates of profit and T arbitrary positive vectors, there exists an economy in which these vectors are the relative prices at these rates.

In conclusion, some laws on the monotonicity of relative prices have been found for a given technique, but the movement of relative prices is unforeseeable in the presence of choice of methods.

6 References

Schefold (1976) introduced the notion of regular system and established Theorem 4(i) and Theorem 5 in this case. The extension of Theorem 4 to irregular systems has been studied by Raneda and Reus (1985). The statements follow Bidard and Salvadori (1995, 1998). For $n = 3$, the fact that the prices belong to a quadratic cone (Theorem 8) was noticed by Steedman (1997). The results relative to Euclidean and N-angles (Theorems 9, 10, 11) come from Bidard and Steedman (1996, 2001). Bidard and Krause (1996) introduced the notion of Hilbert distance and proved Theorem 12. Theorems 1, 7, 13 and 14 come from Bidard (1991, 1998c). My collaboration with Hans Ehrbar (sections 2 and 3) has been especially enjoyable even if, following Hans' practice, the results remain unpublished.

7 Proofs

Proof of Theorem 3. If y is a row eigenvector of A such that $yl = 0$, equalities $0 = yl = yAl = \cdots = yA^{n-1}l$ show that the n vectors $l, Al, \ldots, A^{n-1}l$ are linearly dependent. Conversely, if they are dependent, the subspace $F = \{y;\ 0 = yl = yAl = \cdots = yA^{n-1}l\}$ is not reduced to the zero vector and is stable by A ($y \in F$ implies $yA \in F$). A admits an eigenvector y in F, hence $yl = 0$. When the eigenspace attached to an eigenvalue has dimension two at least, it admits a vector y orthogonal to l, therefore (A, l) is irregular. ■

Hint on the proof of Theorem 4. Let $w_t = 1$ without loss of generality. The key argument for establishing properties (i) and (ii) is the following procedure: let us assume a first linear relationship between the s vectors l, $Al, \ldots, A^{t-1}l, p(r_{t+1}), \ldots, p(r_s)$ $(0 \le t < s)$; take its image by A, replace $Ap(r_i)$ by $\lambda_i p(r_i) - l$ and, finally, eliminate $p(r_{t+1})$ between the first relationship and the new one. A dependence is found between $l, \ldots, A^t l$, $p(r_{t+2}), \ldots, p(r_s)$. Therefore:

(i) Any s vectors $p(r_t)$ are independent: if not, start from $p(r_1), \ldots, p(r_s)$ and repeat the procedure s times: a dependence between $l, \ldots, A^{s-1}l$ will then be obtained.

(ii) $s + 1$ vectors $(p(r_t), w = 1)$ are independent: if not, the s vectors $p(r_t) - p(r_{t+1})$ are dependent and a dependence between $p(r_1), \ldots, p(r_s)$ will be obtained by applying the procedure once. ■

Proof of Theorem 7. Since $det_E(p(r_0), \ldots, p(r_{s-1}))$ is non-zero for any sequence of increasing rates, its sign is the one obtained at $r_0 = -1$: it is the sign of $det_E(l, p(r_1), \ldots, p(r_{s-1}))$ for any increasing rates. When $r_1 = -1 + \varepsilon$, we have $p(r_1) = l + \varepsilon Al + o(\varepsilon)$. It is therefore the sign of $det_E(l, Al, p(r_2), \ldots, p(r_s))$, etc. By induction, the Taylor formula shows that the sign is that of $det(l, Al, \ldots, A^{s-1}l)$. (It is also the sign of $det(p(r), Ap(r), \ldots, A^{s-1}p(r))$ for any r.) ■

Proof of Theorem 8. The non-normalized prices satisfy $F(p) = det(Ap, p, l) = 0$ and, therefore, belong to a quadratic cone in R^3. Consider its intersection with the plane $\{x; qx = 1\}$. In order to recognize the type of the conic, we look at the values of function F on a line of this plane going through π. The calculation of $F(\pi + tu)$ for a real vector u such that $qu = 0$ and the scalar t gives $F(\pi + tu) = t^2\, det(Au, u, l) + t\, det(Au - \Lambda u, \pi, l)$, whose sign at infinity is that of $det(Au, u, l)$. Since the sign indicates whether the point is inside or outside the conic, we obtain:

- If $det(Au, u, l)$ has the same sign whatever u, the conic is an ellipse.
- If $det(Au, u, l)$ is positive for some values of u and negative for other values, the conic is a hyperbola. The asymptotic directions are those of real vectors u such that $det(Au, u, l) = 0$ and $qu = 0$. Therefore, they are the two distinct eigenvectors π_1 and π_2 of A associated with the real non-*PF* eigenvalues λ_1 and λ_2.
- In the limit case where $det(Au, u, l)$ vanishes in one direction, the conic is a parabola. The unique other eigenvector indicates the direction of its axis. ■

Hint on the proof of Theorems 10 and 11. If matrix A is diagonal, the cosine of the angle between $p(r)$ and π is calculated by means of the inner product and the monotonicity result follows. If A is symmetric (respectively, normal), it is diagonalizable in an orthogonal (resp. unitary) basis made of eigenvectors (Horn and Johnson 1990). Since an orthogonal transformation does not affect the angle between vectors, the angle between any two price vectors is the same as if the input matrix were diagonal: hence, Theorem 10. If A is diagonalizable, any vector x can be decomposed as $x = \sum_{i=1}^{n} x_i p_i$ in a basis made of eigenvectors, one of them being the *PF* eigenvector. The sesquilinear form defined by $< x, y >_N = \sum_{i=1}^{n} x_i \overline{y}_i$ is a Hermitian inner product. For this N-metric, the basis is unitary and the N-angle $(x, y)_N$ is defined as stated in Theorem 11. Therefore, the calculations are the same as for Theorem 10. ■

Lemmas 1–3 state some important properties of the Hilbert function $d(x, y)$:

Lemma 1. The Hilbert measure is a distance between positive directions.

Lemma 2. The Hilbert distance is additive on lines:

$$d(x, (1-\lambda)x + \lambda y) + d((1-\lambda)x + \lambda y, y) = d(x, y).$$

Lemma 3. Let H be a square matrix with semi-positive rows. Then d is a contraction for H:

$$d(Hx, Hy) \leq d(x, y).$$

Lemma 4. For $A > 0$ and $r \leq s \leq t < R$, let us define the matrix

$$H(s, r) = (I - (1 + s)A)^{-1}(I - (1 + r)A).$$

- The two matrices on the right-hand side commute, and two matrices H also commute.
- Any eigenvector of A is an eigenvector of H.
- $p(s) = H(s, r)\, p(r)$, where $p(u) = (I - (1 + u)\, A)^{-1}l$.
- $H(t, s)\, H(s, r) = H(t, r)$
- $(t - r)\, H(t, r) = (s - r)\, H(s, r) + (t - s)\, H(s, r)\, H(t, r)$.
- $H(s, r)$ is semi-positive.

Proof of Theorem 12. Let $r < s < t < R$. According to the lemmas, we have:

$$\begin{aligned} d[p(t), p(s)] &= d[H(t, r)p(r), H(s, r)p(r)] \\ &= d\left[H(s, r)\left(\frac{s - r}{t - r}p(r) + \frac{t - s}{t - r}H(t, r)p(r)\right), H(s, r)p(r)\right] \\ &\leq d\left[\frac{s - r}{t - r}p(r) + \frac{t - s}{t - r}p(t), p(r)\right] \\ &\leq d[p(t), p(r)]. \end{aligned}$$

The result is extended to $t = R$ by continuity; or, directly:

$$d(p(s), \pi) = d[H(s, r)p(r), H(s, r)\pi] \leq d(p(r), \pi). \quad \blacksquare$$

Proof of Theorem 13. Let labour be chosen as numéraire. As $p_i = e_i[I - (1 + r)\, A]^{-1}l$, we have:

$$\begin{aligned} dp_i/p_i dr &= e_i[I - (1 + r)A]^{-1}A[I - (1 + r)A]^{-1}l/p_i \\ &= y(i)Ap/p_i \end{aligned}$$

where $y(i)$ are the activity levels in $rss(i)$. The magnitude $y(i)Ap/p_i$ is the value of capital per unit of net product in the golden sub-system. Therefore $dp_i/p_i > dp_j/p_j$ if and only if $rss(i)$ is more capital-intensive than $rss(j)$. The ranking of two systems according to their capital intensity or their organic composition is the same. $\blacksquare$

Proof of Theorem 14. Theorem 7 in chapter 9 states that a sufficient condition for T positive vectors (p^t, w^t) to be price-and-wage vectors associated with the rates of profit r^t $(r^1 < \ldots < r^T)$ is property (P): Whatever the commodity i chosen as numéraire is, the points $(r^t, w_i^t = w^t / p_i^t)$ belong to a decreasing and convex r–w curve. Let T positive arbitrary vectors p^t be given. When $w^1, \ldots, w^{t-1}$ have been chosen in order to have property (P) for the first t points, there exists a small enough level of w^t such that, for any numéraire, the straight line joining the points (r^{t-1}, w^{t-1}) and (r^t, w^t) is decreasing and cuts the horizontal axis before r^{t+1}. Then property (P) holds for one more point. By induction, it holds for the given T prices, which are therefore the relative prices for some economy. ■

7 Ricardo's theory of value

In this Edition, I have endeavoured to explain more fully than in the last, my opinion on the difficult subject of VALUE.

(Ricardo (1817 [1951] 3rd edition, 1821)

1 The theory of value as a stake

This chapter proposes an interpretation of Ricardo's theory of value that is illustrated and complemented by the construction of a standard commodity of Ricardian inspiration. Ricardo's theory of value has been the subject of numerous studies by theorists and historians. These readings are rarely innocent and are inscribed in different legitimization strategies which use opposing means: some early marginalists present themselves as heirs to the Ricardian tradition, wherein an overdevelopment of the rent theory occupies the entire space devolved to value; other marginalists are opponents of the classical school and underscore the break provoked by the new science. The vivacity of these debates until today highlights the richness of Ricardo's thought, which remains sufficiently provocative to nourish our own investigations.

Sraffa's merit as an historian of economic thought is to propose a reading of Ricardo that breaks with the marginalist approach. In the analytical field, the *ex post* study of the relations between the classical and the neoclassical constructions is a legitimate one. Here, every possible means is deemed to be adequate to the task of tracing parallels or oppositions, even if their use requires the disruption of chronological references and familiar intellectual categories. The task of the historian is of another nature, however, proceeding from an internal reading of texts whose inner logic he wishes to reconstitute.

The Marxist theory is the other pole to which the Ricardian theory is attracted. The evolution of Ricardo's thought before 1817, throughout the three editions of the *Principles* and the notes of 1820 and 1823, has been analysed on the basis of the frame of reference constituted by labour value. One of the implicit stakes here is the interpretation of Marxian and Ricardian constructions. It is chiefly a question of underscoring the traces of an eventual weakening of the reference to labour value. Sraffa situates himself in this perspective whilst disputing this thesis:

The theory of edition 3 [of *Principles*] appears to be the same, in essence and in emphasis, as that of edition 1. (1951, I, p. xxxviii)

[N]o essential change was made in the successive editions about the rule which determines value. (1951, I, xl)

[In several respects, Ricardo's] last paper on value reverts to a position similar to that of edition 1. (1951, I, xlvii)

Dobb, who collaborated in the edition of Ricardo's works, is more straightforward (even though he expresses himself in the context of a private correspondence and not that of an academic publication):

In particular I think we conclusively establish (in opposition to the traditional Hollander–Marshall–Cannan view) that there was no 'weakening' of Ricardo's enunciation of the labour theory as time went on: that in fact he reached at the end of his life a position rather close to that of Marx, so that the true line of descent is certainly from Ricardo to Marx, and not from Ricardo to cost-of-production theory as in Mill to Marshall as the bourgeois tradition has it. A minor scoop is the unpublished (and unfinished) final paper which he was writing just before his death on 'Absolute Value and Exchangeable Value', showing that he was at the last still exercised with a notion of an Absolute Value (= embodied labour) as something distinct from, but underlying, exchange-value; in fact the notion and the distinction is *more* explicit in this last paper than in the *Principles*. (Correspondence, M. H. Dobb to Th. Prager, 23 December 1950, quoted from Pollitt, 1990)

This reading orients the Ricardian system towards a centre of gravity that is the theory of labour value. Our analysis is influenced by Sraffa and his Introduction to the *Works and Correspondence of David Ricardo* (hearafter, *WCDR*). The divergences with this interpretation concern chiefly the following points:

- We uphold the thesis of the fundamental unity of Ricardo's thought despite variations that are attributed to the difficulty of grasping the concept of absolute value
- We reject the identity 'Absolute Value = embodied labour' which does no justice to Ricardo's thought.

In particular, we see in the notes of 1823 a return to a reflection on the standard commodity, even if the apparent conclusion is a defence of labour value, for want of anything better. We will illustrate this by proposing an analytical construction of a standard commodity. Ricardo distinguished two causes of variation of relative values: changes in the distribution or in the conditions of production. Of these, the second is the more important. Sraffa endeavours to define an invariable standard that is independent of changes affecting distribution. We, on the contrary, construct a standard for technical changes which is derived from (a critical reappraisal of) Ricardo's reflections on value.

2 Difficulty of production and absolute price

From 1809 until 1823, Ricardo had only one general approach of value and defended only one fundamental thesis. Let us retain a formulation which is reproduced almost identically throughout his work: *the value of a commodity is a reflection of its difficulty of production*. This assertion draws attention to two questions. One concerns the very notion of 'difficulty of production' and the other its measurement (value is conceived as a measurable magnitude). Ricardo varies in his responses which we will subsequently examine. However, the essential founding principle, which confers its unity and specificity on his approach, is found elsewhere: in the sentence 'The value of a commodity is [. . .]', the important word is 'a' (= one).

Ricardo's statement seems senseless: value in itself does not exist and a commodity does not have value outside of its relation with another. The concept nowadays posited as first is that of exchange value, which is established in the confrontation of *two* commodities. By interrogating the value of *one* commodity, Ricardo posits the concept of absolute value. Once this concept is elaborated, the exchange value does not appear in ideal conditions as anything other than a derivative concept (the ratio between two absolute values) whose concrete manifestation is the long-run exchange ratio. One understands the radical opposition between, on the one hand, Ricardo's reflections centred on the concept of absolute value and the related notion of invariable standard (whose aim is the identification of the origin of variations of absolute value when the conditions of production change) and, on the other hand, any theory which knows only of the notion of relative price.[1]

What can be expected from measuring the difficulty of production? In his moments of discouragement or when faced with the objections of his correspondents, Ricardo reassures himself: the theoretical stake is worth the trouble of delimiting the concept. Its range of application is operational since the exchange ratios, as they emerge beyond temporary fluctuations, can be described as value ratios. Assuredly, a theory of relative prices would be sufficient here. The irreducibly significant contribution of absolute value consists in *elucidating the cause* of the variation of

[1] '[The invariant standard of value] has something to do with Ricardian theory but to a modern theorist it is almost incomprehensible' (Hahn 1982).

relative prices. A variation, whether spatial or temporal, of the exchange ratio between wheat and iron from 2:1 to 1:1 reflects a change in the conditions of production. But it can be due either to a deterioration in the conditions of agricultural production (it has become twice as difficult to produce wheat), or a technical progress in metallurgy (it is twice as easy to produce iron), or a combination of these two causes. The economic implications of these phenomena are radically different for the dynamics of accumulation, while remaining indistinguishable as long as one does not have anything other than a theory of relative prices. This is why

> No one can doubt that it would be a great desideratum in Political Economy to have such a measure of absolute value in order to enable us to know, when commodities are altered in exchangeable value, in which the alteration in value has taken place. (Ricardo, *Value*, 1823b, 399)

The theory of value possesses an explanatory rather than a purely descriptive function. The same is true for the whole discourse of Political Economy of which it constitutes the centrepiece. By means of a process of abstraction, Ricardo's methodology endeavours to shed light on causal relations and hierarchical structures whose effects (and only these effects) can be observed in the markets. Ricardo's (1810b) early critiques of the merchants' pretensions ('[merchants who] are notoriously ignorant of the most obvious principles of political oeconomy') highlight an epistemological rupture with the common discourse. This ambitious conception, which founds the hypothetico-deductive approach and draws upon thought experiences, had disconcerted those at the time who had anchored economics within the moral and historical sciences:

> I am accused of stating an impossible case and it is asked 'what confidence can be placed upon such an hypothesis? it is a mode of reasoning as unusual as it is unavailing'. (Ricardo, The Price of Gold, a Further Reply [to Trower], 1809, *WCDR*, III, 45)

Ricardo is the first to have ever applied this method systematically to the domain of political economy. He has thus oriented the discourse of economics on pathways that have never since been abandoned, even if certain segments of its initial ambition have been left aside. In this respect, the very form of Ricardo's statement is symptomatic: the high price of wheat, writes Ricardo, is the cause of the high level of rent, and not the opposite; the distribution of national income is to be thought of as that between wages and profits, once rents have been eliminated by taking account of the marginal land, etc. In other words, Ricardo attempts to unravel the maze of reciprocal interdependencies and identify the thread that leads from one magnitude to another. He brings about the decomposition which permits the tracing of the impact of each parameter: 'The profits made by the farmer regulate the profits of other trades' (Ricardo, letter to Trower, 8 March 1814, *WCDR*, IV, 104).[2]

Far from being an anomaly in Ricardo's thought, his reflection on absolute value, understood as explanation of relative values, participates in this effort by highlighting the causal structure and constitutes a methodologically inseparable element of the object assigned to economic theory. This is why it runs the entire breadth of his works. The unity of Ricardo's questioning is not contradicted by the multiplicity of his attempts at defining the concrete forms of value. Ricardo's dissatisfaction with his own answers leads him to return time and again to the question itself. The final step of his quest is the manuscript of 1823: which ideal characteristics should a commodity possess in order for its invariability of value to be recognized as such?

3 The embodiments of value

Once the concept of absolute value is posited, what meaning can be attached to the difficulty of production? How can it be measured? This question appears early in Ricardo's work, in conjunction with the concept of standard commodity. The answers evolve. The position initially defended by Ricardo is that precious metals have a permanent value, an advantage that has made them adopted as universal means of exchange. That is why the nominal rise of the price of gold indicates a depreciation of the value of the banknotes resulting from their excessive issuance by the Bank:

> Experience has indeed taught us, that though the variations in the *value* of gold or silver may be considerable, on a comparison of distant periods, yet for a short time their value is tolerably fixed. It is this property, among their other excellencies, which fits them better than any other commodity for the uses of money. Either gold or silver may therefore, in the point of view in which we are considering them, be called a measure of value. (1810a, 63, emphasis in the original)

If precious metals constitute a permanent measure of value, this is however only a first approximation:

> Strictly speaking, there can be no permanent measure of value. A measure of value should itself be invariable; but this is not the case with either gold or silver, they being subject to fluctuations as well as other commodities. (*Ibid.*, 65)

[2] The exact quotation is: 'To this proposition Mr. Malthus does not agree. He thinks that . . . the profits of the farmer no more regulate the profits of other trades than the profits of other trades regulate the profits of the farmer.'

Gold and silver, like other commodities, have an intrinsic value, which is not arbitrary, but is dependent on their scarcity, the quantity of labour bestowed in procuring them, and the value of the capital employed in the mines which produce them. (*Ibid.*, 52)

If, upon the discovery of mines, the nominal prices rise, should one say that the value of commodities has increased when in fact it is the decline of the value of gold that should be pointed out? Moreover, even if the reference to gold is deemed desirable and the stability of the currency's value protects the activity of all the inhabitants, the wealth of a nation relies on the abundance of commodities and not upon the means of circulation. Thus, the invariance property of the value attributed to gold is predominantly conventional and will remain so as long as the concept of value is not clarified. This is precisely what Ricardo undertakes from the *Essay* (1815) onwards. He dissociates the search for a standard from monetary questions. The variations in exchangeable value are explicitly connected to the conditions of production: 'The exchangeable value of all commodities rises as the difficulties of their production increase' (1815 [1951], 19).

Sraffa's idea that the *Essay*'s reasoning is based on a model where agriculture constitutes the basic sector is illuminating. The corn model eliminates relative prices and makes possible a physical measurement of distribution. However, must we identify the question of value with that of relative prices and conclude that value itself is removed from the corn model? We claim, on the contrary, that the corn model is typical of value models. It makes the difficulty of production, measured by the stock of seeds required to obtain a given product, immediately visible. Ricardo's argument is that the cultivation of low-grade land leads to a drop in agricultural profits to the advantage of rents. Therefore, the general level of profits decreases. The difficulty of the production of wheat, that is the very question of value, is at the heart of his reasoning. This is what Malthus fails to understand. In the controversy that followed the publication of the *Essay*, Malthus maintained, rightly, that if the relative price of wheat rises, the same must happen to the rate of profit of the farmer. Ricardo's answer (letter dated 14 March 1815) must be read with care:

I cannot hesitate in agreeing with you that if from a rise in the relative value of corn less is paid for fixed capital and wages, – more of the produce must remain for the landlord and farmer together –, this is indeed self evident, but is really not the matter in dispute between us, and I cannot help thinking that you overlook some of the circumstances most important connected with the question. (*WCDR*, VI, 189)

Ricardo follows through the phenomenon (that is, the rise in the relative price of wheat) to its cause, which is the increasing difficulty of production:

My opinion is that corn can only permanently rise in its exchangeable value when the real expences of its production increase. If 5000 quarters of gross produce cost 2500 quarters for the expences of wages &c., and 10000 quarters cost double or 5000 quarters, the exchangeable value of corn would be the same, but if 10000 quarters cost 5500 quarters for the expences of wages &c., then the price would rise 10 pc[t] because such would be the amount of the increased expences. (*WCDR*, VI, 189)

Ricardo's reasoning is based on the notion of value, which is the meaning of the word 'price' in this quotation. The exchange value of wheat grows because its real price rises by 10 per cent between economies represented respectively by the production relationships 5,000 qr. wheat → 10,000 qr. wheat and 5,500 qr. wheat → 10,000 qr. wheat:

[T]he cause of the rise of the price of corn is solely on account of the increased expence of production. (*WCDR*, VI, 189)

The abandonment of the corn standard after the *Essay* results from the specific character of the corn model, as Malthus argued: even in agriculture, the product and the capital are heterogeneous. The theory of labour value that Ricardo elaborates in preparing the *Principles* (1817) frees itself from the homogeneity hypothesis and constitutes a general answer to the problem of value. This time, value is not embodied in a reference commodity and the measure provided by incorporated labour is theoretically self-sufficient. The theme of the invariable standard is therefore withdrawn.

The common point between the second and the third stages (corn standard and labour value) of the evolution of Ricardo's thought is that of measuring the difficulty of production by a volume of inputs which is, as the case may be, a quantity of seeds or labour. Of course, the reduction to a commodity or to labour are distinct operations, which also differ by their degree of generality. The problem for Ricardo was that of conceiving a *mode of reduction*. His successive answers allow us to distinguish different phases in his evolution while revealing their common backdrop: value as an estimation of the difficulty of production.

In the third edition of the *Principles* (1821), the chapter *On Value* is reorganized, reformulated and developed. This return is necessary after the publication of Malthus' book to which Ricardo reacts first through his *Notes on Malthus' Principles* (1820 [1951]). Similarly, it is in reaction to *The Measure of Value* that Ricardo drafts *Absolute Value and Exchangeable*

Value (1823). He is then fully aware of the analytical defects of labour value: (*i*) the prices are not proportional to the labour contents, (*ii*) for a given quantity of labour, the price depends on the delay of production and, (*iii*) relative prices, but not labour values, are affected by changes in distribution. The theory of labour value is henceforth expressed in terms of the best possible approximation. Depending on whether one insists on the imperfection of approximation or its quality, the last writings of Ricardo seem to distance him from or draw him close to the notion of labour value. The third edition of *Principles* and *Absolute Value* must be viewed as elements of the same process. The opinion of Sraffa and Dobb, who identify value and incorporated labour and therein believe to have established Ricardo's attachment to labour value, finds some support in the literally formulated conclusion of *Absolute Value*. However, in our view, the essential point is not the conclusion but rather the approach adopted in the 1823 manuscripts. In this last examination of the problem of value, one can see Ricardo attempting an analysis *ab ovo* of the question of value, while embarking on a path that is reminiscent of the *Essay*'s. Though Ricardo's failure is usually attributed to the impossibility of resolving the jigsaw of heterogeneity, the thesis we uphold is that it is explained by another, more profound reason that has not until now been identified.

4 A Ricardian standard of value

Ricardo identifies two distinct causes of variation of prices: a change either in the conditions of production or in distribution. He considers the first cause as more significant in practice as well as in theory. This section proposes the construction of a Ricardian standard, i.e. a standard of value when the conditions of production change. In order to neutralize the effects of distribution, the real wage is given and incorporated into the input matrix (the operation also eliminates any possible reference to labour value). We therefore compare two economies represented by the respective input matrices A_1 and A_2, where E_1 is the initial economy and E_2 the economy after technical change. The construction of a standard basket with respect to change of technique is developed in three successive steps. The first two stages are concerned with the corn model and the last with multisector economies.

4.1 Corn as an absolute standard

Consider two economies in which corn (= commodity C) is the only basic commodity, commodity X being non-basic. There is a technical change in the production of the non-basic ('non-basic' technical change):

E_1	E_2
0.5 qr. corn $\to$ 1 qr. corn	0.5 qr. corn $\to$ 1 qr. corn
$0.4\ C \oplus 0.3\ X \to 1\ X$	$0.2\ C \oplus 0.2\ X \to 1\ X$

Its difficulty of production being constant, corn is the invariable standard of value. Let us set, by convention, that a quarter of corn represents one unit of value (this is but a normalization). In view of the production relationships, commodity X is easier to produce in the second economy. As a matter of fact, a calculation of relative prices in both economies leads to $(p_X/p_C)_1 = 2 > (p_X/p_C)_2 = 2/3$. The decrease in the difficulty of production of X is reflected in the decline of its relative price with respect to corn. However, as long as only the relative prices are known, the fall of the price ratio p_X/p_C from 2 to 0.67 provides no hint as to the origin of the change: it might stem from an improvement in the production of X, or a deterioration in the production of C, or a combination of the two causes. A measure of values aims at rendering visible the cause of the variation. In the present case, since the conditions of production of corn are unchanged, let us set:

$$V_1^C = 1,\ V_2^C = 1 \quad \text{and} \quad V_1^X = 2,\ V_2^X = 0.67.$$

(V is for value, the upper index for the good and the lower index for the economy.) An economist who has no direct knowledge of the conditions of production can read in these figures the evolution of relative prices, from $(V^X : V^C)_1 = 2$ to $(V^X : V^C)_2 = 0.67$, *and* the reason for their variation: since the value of corn is unchanged, whereas that of X has decreased, commodity X is easier to produce in the second economy. Note that:

- The construction adopts the Ricardian hypothesis that the relative prices reflect the relative difficulties of production. Once the values of one commodity (here, corn) have been determined in both economies, the values of the other commodity(ies) are calculated by means of the relative prices. By construction, relative prices and relative values are identical.
- In the above numerical example, the production of X in E_2 requires less of every input, so that the technical change is an unambiguous and clear technical progress. One might as well imagine that the second process requires more of one input and less of another. The principle of calculation of the values remains unchanged. The reader can verify the following property: if and only if the value of X is smaller for the second method, an entrepreneur who currently employs the first

method but has access to the new technology will indeed switch to the second method.

4.2 *Ricardo on measure*

We consider now a change in the production of corn ('basic' technical change). Assume first that corn is the only commodity, which leaves no room for variations of relative prices. Let the economy E_1 be described by relationship 5000 $C \rightarrow$ 10000 C, whereas E_2 is described by 5500 $C \rightarrow$ 10000 C. The question we are interested in is that of giving an expression, in terms of *value*, to the fact that corn is more difficult to produce in E_2. This is achieved by stating that the value of corn is higher in E_2 ($V_2^C > V_1^C$). As such, an economist who has no direct knowledge of the conditions of production can learn, from the values, that corn has become more difficult to produce.

In quantitative terms, how many times is corn more difficult to produce after technical change? The simplest proposal is to identify the difficulty of production with the amount of seeds necessary to obtain a given product, say two quarters of corn (the reference to 'two quarters' is artificial and reminds us that the definition of the unit of difficulty of production is conventional). Then $V_1^C = 1$ and $V_2^C = 1.1$, so that the difficulty of production, or value, rises by 10 per cent. These data fit with Ricardo's numerical example (letter to Malthus, quoted above). However, a contradiction in Ricardo's thought becomes apparent at this stage.

Ricardo (1823 [1951]) identifies the problem of the absolute measure with that of the definition of an absolute standard. The measure of value is not distinguished from the search of a commodity whose difficulty of production is constant:

> The only qualities necessary to make a measure of value a perfect one are, that it should itself have value, and that that value should itself be invariable, in the same manner as in a perfect measure of length the measure should have length and that that length should be neither liable to be increased or diminished; or in a measure of weight that it should have weight and that such weight should be constant. (Introductory sentence, *Absolute Value and Exchangeable Value*, 1823a, 361)

In this manuscript, the problem of value is reconsidered from its very foundations. This is why Ricardo states a general epistemological principle in the introductory sentence. The principle itself corresponds to Ricardo's permanent conviction ('A measure of value should itself be invariable', *The High Price of Bullion* (1810, 65), quoted above) and is in accordance with the physical (Galileo, Newton) and philosophical

(Kant) conceptions of his time. Our point is that the principle *is* and *must* be violated for the measure of value, even in a one-commodity economy: after a technical change, corn has *not* an invariable value. By extension, in a multicommodity economy with generalized technical progress ($A_2 < A_1$), all commodities become easier to produce, so that none is an invariable standard.

Sraffa's contribution has made clear that the passage from one to several commodities is a serious obstacle in the search for a standard. Most economists tend to believe that the main difficulty in Ricardo's quest is located here. Our opinion, on the contrary, is that the origin of Ricardo's failure is to be traced back to the very definition of its object: namely, the search for an absolute value is unduly identified with that of an invariable standard. This approach leads Ricardo to make reference to activities such as shrimping (which is not affected by technical progress) and, finally, accept a measure of value in terms of everlasting elementary labour.

Is an alternative way of thinking conceivable? Yes, when the idea of absolute value is dissociated from the search for an *invariable* standard. In a world of generalized technical progress, what is required for a standard is a commodity for which change in the difficulty of production is measurable. This commodity is a *sliding* standard (sliding, because its value need not be constant). Then the variations of the other commodities are obtained by comparing their value with that of the sliding standard. In more grandiloquent terms, one can say that the approach is based on a *relativity principle*: in order to calculate the speed of a cyclist observed from a boat, it suffices to know the drift of the boat (the change in the standard) and the speed relative to the boat (the change relative to the standard). That procedure is the only possibility in the absence of an observer on the mainland.

Let us apply this strategy to the corn model. We consider a non-basic economy with technical change in the production of the unique basic commodity (corn):

E_1	E_2
$0.5\ C \rightarrow 1\ C$	$0.55\ C \rightarrow 1\ C$
$\alpha C + \beta X \rightarrow 1\ X$	$\gamma C + \delta X \rightarrow 1\ X$

As in sub-section 4.1, the initial and final values of corn are measurable: corn is the sliding standard, with $V_1^C = 1$ and $V_2^C = 1.1$. Even in the absence of technical change in the production of the other commodity ($\alpha = \gamma$ and $\beta = \delta$), it could not be said that its difficulty of production is constant: commodity X is indirectly affected by the change concerning its corn input. The calculation of the values of X in both economies is based on Ricardo's hypothesis that the relative values and the relative prices coincide. The relative prices p_1^X/p_1^C and p_2^X/p_2^C can be calculated. Knowing V_1^C and V_2^C, the values V_1^X and V_2^X are then obtained by means of equalities $V_1^X/V_1^C = p_1^X/p_1^C$ and $V_2^X/V_2^C = p_2^X/p_2^C$. The absolute values of all commodities are well defined, in spite of the absence of an absolute standard.

4.3 *Multisector economies*

The construction can be extended to the comparison of multisector basic economies. The economies E_1 and E_2 that we compare are represented by $A_1 \to I$ and $A_2 \to I$. The relative values in every economy being determined by the relative prices, it remains to superimpose the two scales of value, one upon the other. This result will be achieved if we can identify a *sliding standard*, i.e. a commodity or a basket of commodities whose difficulty of production changes but can be followed precisely. Sraffa's (*PCMC*, ch. 4) device can be adapted to this problem. Let us consider the inputs required in both economies to produce a given basket s. Normally, these input vectors sA_1 and sA_2 are not comparable. However, it may be the case that the input vectors are proportional for some adequately chosen basket s: $sA_1 = \alpha\, sA_2$. Since the production of basket s requires α times less inputs in the second economy, it can be said that basket s is α times easier to produce in E_2. This basket plays a role analogous to corn in the previous example and is the sliding standard. The absolute values are then calculated by means of the properties:

- The value of corn in the first economy is equal to one (normalization convention)
- V_1 and p_1 are proportional; V_2 and p_2 are proportional
- $V_1^s = \alpha V_2^s$ (the value of the standard s decreases by factor α).

The construction can be illustrated by a numerical example. Let there be two economies represented by the input matrices A_1 and A_2:

$$A_1 = \begin{bmatrix} 4/18 & 6/18 \\ 7/18 & 3/18 \end{bmatrix}, \quad A_2 = \begin{bmatrix} 0.56 & 0.3 \\ 0.17 & 0.15 \end{bmatrix}.$$

By convention, the value of the first commodity is equal to one in the first economy. Then the absolute values are written $V_1 = \binom{1}{1}$ and $V_2 = \binom{3\lambda}{\lambda}$, where the components of these vectors reflect the relative prices 1:1 and 3:1 in both economies. It remains to determine the scalar λ. As the inputs required to produce basket $s = 1\,X + 2\,Y$ amount to $sA_1 = 1\,X + 2/3\,Y$ and $sA_2 = 0.9\,X + 0.6\,Y$, respectively, equality $sA_2 = 0.9\,sA_1$ shows that the basket s is a sliding standard. Its value in the second economy is 0.9

times its value in the first. Hence, $\lambda = 0.54$ and $V_2 = \binom{1.62}{0.54}$ follow. This result once obtained, a comparison of V_1 and V_2 shows that the difficulty of production of X has increased by 62 per cent while that of Y has decreased by 46 per cent.

5 Range of the construction

The apparent difficulties encountered in defining a standard of value in the presence of a change of technique stem from the interindustrial relationships and the heterogeneity of commodities. However, the direct cause of Ricardo's failure in his quest is to be found elsewhere. Given his epistemological premises on measurement, Ricardo associates the notion of absolute value with that of an invariable standard, but such a standard cannot exist when all commodities have become easier to produce. This is why Ricardo, after having examined several theoretical alternatives, finally reverts to a measure in terms of labour. Our proposal is to abandon Ricardo's premises: a sliding standard can be used to measure absolute values. We recognize that the construction does not totally fulfil Ricardo's ambition: it defines a standard for a pair of economies, not a 'universal' standard valid simultaneously for all economies. But the fact that it is concerned only with technical change, not distribution, is secondary for Ricardo's approach (or, one might alternatively sustain that the variation of relative prices with distribution is unthinkable if value is rooted in the difficulty of production). As it is, it constitutes the closest attempt to formalize Ricardo's conception of value.

Some theorists refer to the problem of value as an example of the classical economists' mistakes. The approach is deeper than may appear to a superficial examiner and constitutes the archetype of most problems concerning the measurement of change. The difficulty in understanding Ricardo is that his level of abstraction is higher than is the norm in economics.

6 Notes on Sraffa's interpretation

The two elements of Sraffa's interpretation that have been most discussed are the reading of the *Essay* on the one hand and that of Ricardo's last writings (1821–3) on the other. In his Introduction to Ricardo's works, Sraffa (1951) attributes a multisector model with agriculture as the basic sector to Ricardo's *Essay* (1815). Since the seeds and the crop consist of the same commodity, the agricultural rate of profit is obtained as a ratio between homogeneous physical quantities, with no reference to prices:

> [In the trade of corn] no value changes can alter the ratio of product to capital, both consisting of the same commodity. (Sraffa, 1951, I, xxxi)

Because of the uniformity of the rates of profit, the rate of profit in the remainder of the economy cannot differ from that in agriculture. The argument gives a logical basis to Ricardo's assertion that the profits of the farmer regulate the profits of other trades. *Se non è vero è ben trovato.* The opponents to Sraffa's interpretation have stressed the weakness of textual proofs sustaining that reading. However, the following quotation from Marx, anterior to the modern disputes on compared Ricardology, shows that Sraffa's interpretation is not an *a posteriori* rationalization:

> It leaps to the eye, particularly in the case of agriculture, that the causes which raise or lower the price of a product, also raise or lower the value of capital, since the latter consists to a large degree of this product, whether as grain, cattle, etc. (Ricardo). (Marx 1894 [1972], ch. 6)

The striking similarity of the two formulations gives rise to the question of knowing whether Sraffa's interpretation is not directly inspired by Marx. Sraffa's discretion regarding his sources does not permit us to answer the question.

Our principal divergence with Sraffa concerns our claim that the general notion of absolute value possesses both conceptual predominance and chronological priority in Ricardo's writings. It is already at work in the *Essay* (whereas Sraffa considers that the corn model eliminates the question of value) and Ricardo's last writings represent an attempt at deepening his understanding of it. It is thus not to be identified with labour value. Nor does Sraffa clarify his view on an apparent contradiction: if labour value is the measure of value, then the concept is deemed as operational and suffices in formulating precise laws as have been established by the *Principles*. What then would the object of a reflection on the question of standard be? No necessity as such is seen in the embodiment of labour value in a commodity (this is why the very theme of an invariable standard is absent from the work of Marx).

Finally, Sraffa constructs an invariable standard with respect to distribution-related changes. This construction is, as far as I am concerned, unclear. The above construction of a standard when a technological change occurs takes up Sraffa's idea of looking for proportional vectors, which constitutes a device for extending the properties of the corn model to multisector economies. But the principle of excluding the variations of relative prices in order to isolate the real value had already been propounded by Ricardo in 1810:

A varying circulation medium, though injurious to every class of the community, is least so to mercantile men; as the prices of their commodities will undergo the same variations as the price of all others, their comparative value will, under all circumstances, be the same, and their nominal, not their real value, will be affected. (First letter on the Bullion Report, *WCDR*, III, 136)

7 Mathematical discussion

This section briefly discusses the existence and the uniqueness (up to a factor) of a standard basket relative to technical progress. The initial system is written

$$\exists ?\alpha \quad \exists ? s > 0 \quad sA_1 = \alpha s A_2. \tag{1}$$

Scalar α is a root of $det(\alpha A_2 - A_1) = 0$; if $detA_2 \neq 0$, it is an eigenvalue of $A_1(A_2)^{-1}$. The equation may have no positive solution α. Symmetrically, up to n positive solutions may coexist, n being the number of commodities. In order to state existence and/or uniqueness results, we introduce additional hypotheses on A_1 and A_2 and/or modify (1) slightly.

(*i*) Consider first a technical change restricted to a unique method of production, say the last one (only the last row of A_1 and A_2 differs). For s equal to the ith unit vector ($i = 1, \ldots, n-1$), (1) holds formally with $\alpha = 1$. However, in basic economies, the difficulty of production linked to an unchanged method does change, because the last commodity is used as an input. Therefore, the input basket of the ith method ($i = 1, \ldots, n-1$) cannot be considered as constant in terms of value: these $n-1$ candidates, all corresponding to $\alpha = 1$, are thus eliminated. The only remaining solution is the nth eigenvalue of $A_1(A_2)^{-1}$, which is also equal to the product of all eigenvalues. We conclude that the standard basket, if any, is the one associated with $\alpha = detA_1/detA_2$. A significant solution to (1) is excluded if the determinants have opposite signs.

(*ii*) The difficulty of production has been measured by the amount of seeds (corn model) or inputs (multisector models) necessary to obtain a given gross product. Why not refer to the *net* product? Let us modify (1) and set that s is a sliding standard if the corresponding net products are proportional in the two economies. Formally (1) is replaced by

$$\exists ?\alpha \quad \exists ? s > 0 \quad s(I - A_1) = \alpha s(I - A_2). \tag{2}$$

Assume a change of method in the nth industry. Then the standard basket, if any, is associated with scalar $\alpha = det(I - A_1)/det(I - A_2)$, which is positive. As α is usually different from 1, it is a simple root, so that s is uniquely defined. The only remaining question is whether the basket s is indeed positive. The same conclusion holds if the change concerns the *use* of one commodity, i.e. A_1 and A_2 differ by one column: scalar 1 being a root of multiplicity $n - 1$, scalar $\alpha = det(I - A_1)/det(I - A_2)$ is the only remaining candidate. This conclusion allows us to identify the next two simple cases in which a standard basket defined by (2) is unique and semi-positive:

(*iii*) *Generalized progress.* There is generalized technical progress if $\Delta = A_1 - A_2$ is positive. Then matrix $M = (I - A_2)\ (I - A_1)^{-1} = I + \Delta\ (I - A_1)^{-1}$ is semi-positive. The sliding standard basket solution to (2) is its row *PF* eigenvector.

(*iv*) *Change in the use of one input.* Matrices A_1 and A_2 differ by their nth column. Let s be the nth row of $(I - A_1)^{-1}$. As s is orthogonal to the first $n - 1$ columns of $I - A_1$ and $I - A_2$, the vectors $s(I - A_1)$ and $s(I - A_2)$ are proportional. Therefore, they are equal up to a positive factor.

8 The labour value

1 A measure of absolute value

This chapter examines a few analytical aspects of Marxian theory. The theory of labour value is historically tied to that of prices of production. In a viable economy, the labour value of a commodity is the quantity of direct and indirect (that is, incorporated into the inputs) labour used in its production. By following the chain of successive inputs, the vector $\hat{V}$ of values is written

$$\hat{V} = l + Al + A^2 l + \cdots + A^t l + \cdots \qquad (1)$$

Under the form $\hat{V} = l + A\hat{V}$, the value of a commodity appears as the sum of direct labour and the value of the consumed means of production. There is an infusion of the value of the circulating capital in the product, together with an increase through living labour: this is a substantialist conception.

Labour value is a measure of the absolute value in the sense clarified in chapter 7. Its task is that of defining the value of a commodity on the basis of the difficulty of its production. It precedes the comparisons of commodities as well as the exchange ratios, which it is meant to explain. To say that a commodity incorporates eight hours of labour has an intrinsic signification that goes beyond the fact that it is exchangeable (or would be exchangeable . . .) with two units of a commodity which incorporates four hours of labour. Similarly, stating that the values shift from ($\hat{V}_1 = 8h$, $\hat{V}_2 = 4h$) to ($\hat{V}'_1 = 4h$, $\hat{V}'_2 = 4h$) is more than just observing an evolution of the exchange ratio. It accounts for this change by means of a technical progress in the production of the first commodity. The situation is economically different from the one resulting from a degradation of the conditions of production of the second commodity ($\hat{V}''_1 = 8h$, $\hat{V}''_2 = 8h$). The theory of labour value thus constitutes a typical example of a theory of absolute value, and the most developed within the classical approach. The definition of the essence of value was a far-reaching ambition, meant to discover some fundamental laws and resolve a number of problems related to comparative economics.

2 The problem of transformation

Marx uses the theory of labour value in order to ground his theory of exploitation as the origin of all profit. The labour values $\hat{V} = (I - A)^{-1}l$ formally coincide with the prices in terms of wage when the rate of profit is nil. In this case, the exchange ratio and the value ratio are equal. But, contrary to labour values, the relative prices depend on distribution. The reference to labour values, as far as they aim to explain the exchange ratios, poses the analytical problem of the 'transformation' of values into prices.

2.1 From values to prices

The exchanging of commodities according to their value should not leave any possibility of making a profit. For Marx, the paradox of profit is resolved by the existence of a specific commodity, the *labour power*, whose use creates more value than it represents itself. As in the case of any commodity, the value of labour power is defined by the quantity of labour necessary to its reproduction, that is to say, the production of the wage basket. By setting at five hours the necessary time needed for the production of this basket, a worker who rents his force for eight hours to the possessor of the means of production creates a surplus value of three hours, corresponding to three hours of surplus labour. The rate of exploitation (or rate of surplus value) is the ratio of surplus labour to necessary labour (here $e = 3/5 = 60$ per cent). It is therefore the exploitation of workers, a quantifiable magnitude, which is at the origin of surplus value and, so, of profit. Let us introduce a few notations:

- c: the *value of material capital consumed in production*. Let us posit the simplificatory hypothesis according to which all capital is circulating (if the life span of capital exceeds one period, the value is transmitted *pro rata temporis*). The value c is said to be constant since it goes from the input to the product without a modification of its magnitude.
- v: *the value of the capital used for employment*. Marx denotes this factor as the variable capital since the capital invested in the labour force is the one which makes possible the exploitation of workers and, thereby, increases the value of the entire capital thanks to surplus value.
- $C = c + v$: the *value of total capital*.

- s: *surplus value*; $e = s/v$ the rate of surplus value (or exploitation) which is assumed to be uniform among the industries.

The equation $\hat{V}_i = c_i + v_i + s_i$ makes visible the decomposition of the total value among intermediary consumptions, wages and surplus value in the *i*th industry. The highlighting of the analytical difficulties leads us to distinguish the space of values from that of prices. The surplus value extracted by the capitalists manifests itself in the form of profit. Let us call 'the rate of profit in the space of values' the ratio between the surplus value and the value of the total capital used in the industry i:

$$r_i = s_i/(c_i + v_i) = e/(\chi_i + 1) \tag{2}$$

where $\chi_i = c_i/v_i$ is the organic composition in the *i*th industry. According to (2), the exchange of commodities for their value leads to a rate of profit that is higher in labour-intensive industries than in capital-intensive ones. This state being incompatible with the competitive uniformity of the rates of profit, Marx imagines the following answer: commodities are in fact not exchanged for their value but for a 'price of production' which is higher than the value for capital-intensive commodities and lower for labour-intensive commodities. This distortion operates a process of socialization and levelling of surpluses by means of the mechanism of competition. By dividing the sum of surpluses by the total value of invested capital, the average rate of profit $\hat{r}$ in the economy amounts to

$$\hat{r} = \sum_i y_i s_i \Big/ \Big(\sum_i y_i c_i + \sum_i y_i v_i \Big) \tag{3}$$

where y_i designates the activity level of the *i*th industry. In the ideal and yet never fully realized conditions of perfect competition, the 'price of production' p_i of the good i would be

$$p_i = (1 + \hat{r})(c_i + v_i). \tag{4}$$

The exchange of commodities at these prices, instead of their labour values, ensures that a uniform rate $\hat{r}$ of profit is attained in all the industries. These 'prices of production' depend on distribution whereas this was not the case for labour values. The space of prices and the space of values are moreover linked by two conservation relations: the total product in terms of value is equal to the total product in terms of prices, and the total surplus values are equal to the total profits. In Marx's view, the 'prices of production' and the profits constitute the apparent forms adopted on the market by the values and the surplus values.

2.2 *The impossible transformation*

Marx, however, was aware of the imperfections of his formal solution to the problem of the transformation of values into prices: on the right-hand side of (4), the costs should be accounted for in terms of prices and not of values, since the inputs are bought on the market (von Bortkiewicz 1906–7 [1952]). Hence, the use of quotation marks for the Marxian style 'prices of production', which differ from the veritable prices *à la* Sraffa.

The problem is that of examining the possibility of improving Marx's approximative solution: can his intuition that labour values are the basis of prices of production be fully justified? There is no difficulty in two cases: the one in which the organic composition is uniform (since the problem lies in the differences of organic composition) and the one in which the rate of profit is nil. It is to the second case that Smith's (1776) reference to the 'primitive and rough state of society' applies: a deer and a beaver are exchanged according to the direct and indirect labour required in hunting for them. However, in the general case, the transformation from values to prices of production is impossible. Of course, it would be possible to correct the above-mentioned imperfection by repeating the procedure of which Marx described only the first stage. But, in this algorithm, the influence of the initial vector of values vanishes progressively. Any starting point p_0 other than the labour values would reach the same result, without p_0 'explaining' the prices of production. The basic reason for the insolvability of the transformation is that, from a theoretical standpoint, the productive systems $(A, l) \rightarrow I$ are intermediary terms between systems that use only direct labour ($A = 0, l > 0$) and those which do not use it ($A > 0, l = 0$). These polar cases are unrealistic but theory should in principle be able to account for them. Manifestly, the reference to labour values cannot be adapted to the second case: in this 'physiocratic' economy, the growth of the product is due exclusively to the goodness of Nature (according to the physiocrats, labour is unproductive and modifies only the form of the goods). The same argument holds if the economy is automated – or, more simply, if the real wage basket is given. Prices, which also exist in this case, defy all attempts at their evaluation in terms of labour (see Steedman 1977, for a detailed study).

One can ask oneself whether, given the lack of a complete transformation, there exist relationships between the space of values and that of prices. If the rates of profit are close to zero, the prices of production are almost proportional to values. But the distortion can be significant because of differences in capitalistic intensity and in the length of various processes. To specify and shed light on this distortion is tantamount to studying the deformation of relative prices with distribution (that was the subject of chapter 7). Another type of relation between values and prices has been explored by Morishima (1973, 1974). Morishima's 'Fundamental Marxian Theorem' consists in the following statement: the rate of profit is positive if and only if the rate of exploitation is positive as well. This result can be seen as linking the space of prices of production to that of values, but it does no more than state a primary truth: there shall be profit if workers do not receive the totality of the incomes. But this can be observed by a measure in terms of labour value or by any other means. The necessity of a formal proof appears only because Morishima does not assume the reproduction of quantities.

3 The falling rate of profit

3.1 Statement of the law

Does capitalism give rise to such acute contradictions that its development is doomed in the long run? The law of the 'tendency of the rate of profit to fall' expresses the internal contradictions of a mode of production which its very dynamism condemns to perdition. This prediction clashes with the collective imagination of a society founded on the belief in indefinite expansion and progress. The fascination exerted by this statement is explained by its quasi-mechanical character, formulated in the implacable statement of a quantitative law.

We would like to re-examine these mechanics under the hypothesis retained by Marx (1894 [1972], vol. III, chs. 13 and 14). Let us follow in Marx's steps. The general rate of profit amounts to $r = s/(c + v) = e/(\chi + 1)$ (magnitudes s, c, v relate to the entire economy and $\chi = c/v$ is the average organic composition). Let us assume that the rate of exploitation e is stable in time. Then the rate of profit varies in the opposite direction to that of the organic composition. Marx affirms that the organic composition $\chi = C/V$ grows with technical progress: competition encourages the substitution of machines for workers since this is the way in which the entrepreneur creates an advantage for himself in the short run. But in the long run this evolution will turn against the capitalist class as a whole: the surplus value is extorted on a reduced basis and remunerates a greater amount of capital and, therefore, the average rate of profit declines. This reasoning ignores the fluctuations of the rate of exploitation and unusual forms of technical progress: the law in question does no more than express a trend. Moreover, Marx expressly states 'counteracting influences' to the law, which 'give it merely the characteristic of a tendency'. The cheapening of elements of constant capital will retain our attention: the value of goods that compose the constant capital decreases because of the very effects of the technological improvement. Therefore, the organic composition $\chi = c/v$ grows less rapidly than the technical composition $k = K/L$ where capital K is measured in the real units: 'The value of the constant capital does not increase in the same proportion as its material volume.' Therefore, the drop in the rate of profit $r = e/(\chi + 1)$ is not as sharp as it might seem, were one to consider only the physical quantities. This is why 'the same influences which tend to make the rate of profit fall, also moderate the effects of this tendency'.

It is often written that the law has been refuted by Okishio (1961): the Okishio Theorem states that, for a given real wage, the rate of profit cannot decrease when new methods are invented (the existence of a positive standard plays an implicit role in this result, cf. Bidard 1988). But this statement is not an appropriate answer to Marx's problem since it assumes that the real wage is constant when production per worker increases and, therefore, the rate of exploitation increases. It is true that Marx imprudently widens the application of the law in ch. 15 by envisaging the extreme case of workers 'who could live on air and hence did not have to work for themselves at all'. This daring extension is contradicted by the Okishio Theorem. Nevertheless, the law should be discussed under the hypothesis of a constant rate of exploitation as initially conceived by Marx.

A serene discussion seems impossible because of the articulation of the law with the theory of labour value. To those who have 'faith' in this theory, the law is irrefutable; to others, it lacks any logical foundation. The dilemma encourages its study outside the context of Marx's hypothesis. We claim that the discussion is possible when one refers to a corn economy: then the question of transformation is avoided since the rate of profit is indeed equal to $r = s/(c + v)$. The law can thus be studied in a Marxian framework with no bias regarding the theory of labour value.

3.2 *A Marxian study*

Let us start with a numerical example in a corn model. The initial method is represented by $(a_i, l_i) \rightarrow b_i$ with $a_i = 10$ qr, $l_i = 1$ and $b_i = 14$ qr. The net product per labour unit being four quarters, the value of the quarter is $\hat{V}_1 = 0.25$. For a rate of exploitation $e = 100$ per cent, the real wage represents half of the net product, i.e. two quarters. The profit amounts to two quarters and so the rate of profit r_1 is $2/12 = 16.7$ per cent (in accordance with the classical tradition, the real wage is a part of the advanced capital). Let $(a_2, l_2) \rightarrow b_2$ be a new method of production with $a_2 = 12$ qr, $l_2 = 1$ and $b_2 = 20$ qr. The choice $l_1 = l_2$ simply reflects the convention that all magnitudes are reduced to quantities per worker, while the growth of the physical capital per head is reflected by the inequality $a_1 < a_2$. The new method is adopted by the capitalists only because it is profitable at the present level of wages. When we retain the constancy of the long-run exploitation rate, the two phenomena by Marx are confirmed:

- The increase in the real wage which, contrary to Okishio's hypothesis, shifts from two qr. to four qr. The reason is that the net product per worker becomes eight qr., of which half returns as wages when the rate of exploitation remains at level $e = 100$ per cent.
- The devaluation of wheat which, owing to the rise in productivity per head, drops from $\hat{V}_1 = 0.25$ to $\hat{V}_2 = 0.125$.

However, we observe that the rise of 20 per cent in the technical composition of capital (from $k_1 = a_1/l_1 = 10$ to $k_2 = a_2/l_2 = 12$) is accompanied by a fall in the organic composition (from $\chi_1 = k_1\hat{V}_1 = 2.5$ to $\chi_2 = k_2\hat{V}_2 = 1.5$) because of a decline of 50 per cent in the value of wheat. Then the rate of profit $r = e/(\chi + 1)$ grows from $r_1 = 16.7$ per cent to $r_2 = 25$ per cent, contrary to the prediction of the law.

Are the numerical data of the example to be questioned here? Let us keep the same data a_1, l_1, b_1, a_2, l_2 and e and let the b_2 parameter vary. A simple calculation shows that: (*i*) the inequality $b_2 > 16.3$ ensures that the new technique is profitable in the short run, i.e. with an unchanged real wage (otherwise, the capitalists will not change the actual method of production); (*ii*) despite the rise of wages in the long run (constancy of e), the rate of profit grows as soon as $b > 16.8$. Therefore, it is only in the interval $16.3 < b_2 < 16.8$ that the law of the falling rate of profit holds.

For a general discussion, let us write the rate of profit as

$$r = \frac{e}{(c/l) : (v/l) + 1}$$

This expression invites us to evaluate the evolution of the variable and the constant capital per head for a constant rate of exploitation:

- Let the net product per worker be doubled. Two consequences follow: on the one hand, the real wage is doubled because the rate of exploitation is constant; on the other, the value of each wheat unit is halved. These two effects compensate for each other exactly and so the value v/l of variable capital per worker is constant.
- Therefore, the variable which determines the variation of the rate of profit is the amount c/l of capital per worker. In the corn model $(a_i, l_i = 1) \rightarrow b_i$, the constant capital per head amounts to a_i physical units and the value of the wheat unit is $1/(b_i - a_i)$, hence $c/l = a_i/(b_i - a_i)$. The conclusion is that the level of r depends only on the ratio b_i/a_i.

Theorem. For a constant rate of exploitation, the rate of profit varies like the product per unit of capital b_i/a_i (measured in volume or value).

The noteworthy phenomenon is the elimination of labour. Under the retained hypotheses, the evolution of the rate of profit depends on the type of technical change, but it is the product per unit of capital which, ultimately, is the significant magnitude. More precisely, the rate of profit remains stable if the technical change is neutral in Harrod's (1948) sense. If not, it increases or falls depending on the technical bias.

To sum up, Marx correctly identified the factors that act on the rate of profit but failed to appreciate their relative importance adequately. If depreciation overcomes the rise in technical composition, the rate of profit increases in the long run. Marx had the right to make mistakes, but not his successors.

9 Choice of technique

1 The question

This chapter generalizes the theory of the choice of technique, which has already been examined for the corn model, to multisector economies. The emphasis is on the market algorithm and its properties. The terminology (e.g. the distinction between the insertion and consistency 'properties' and the 'theorems') and the organization obey a strict logic, which will come to light with the later extension of the theory to joint production. Section 5 introduces a new problem to economic literature, that of laws on prices which are robust to changes of technique. Section 6 considers whether the approach put forward in the present chapter is faithful to Sraffa's intent. The questions relative to marginal equalities and capital theory will be examined in part III of the book.

2 Dominant technique and market algorithm

Let there be n commodities, each produced in a specific industry. Several methods are available in industry i ($1 \leq i \leq n$). The returns to scale are constant. A *technique* is a set of n methods (or n-set), one in every industry, which satisfies a certain constraint. The only constraint retained in the present chapter is that the n-set must be compatible with the level of the given rate of profit r. Let A be the input matrix made of the m available methods, B the output matrix (every row of B has $n-1$ zeros and one 1) and l the labour vector. The choice of one method per industry defines an extracted square matrix of inputs A_t, an output matrix B_t and a labour vector l_t. The pairs (A_t, B_t) for which $r \leq R_t$ constitute the family $\boldsymbol{T}$ of techniques, which is non-empty by assumption. For any technique, the solution (p_t, w_t) to

$$(1+r)A_t p_t + w_t l_t = p_t \tag{1}$$

is positive, with $w_t = 0$ if $r = R_t$. The technique (A_t, l_t) is called *dominant* if no available method yields extra profits at its associated prices, i.e. if

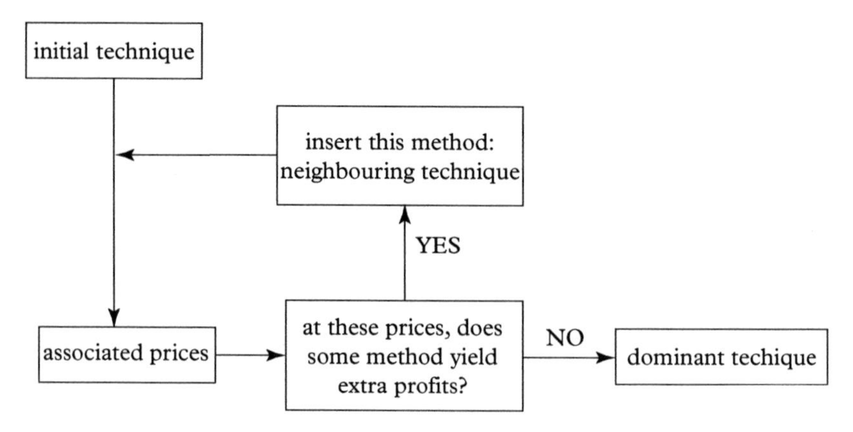

The market algorithm

(1) and inequality

$$(1 + r)Ap_t + w_t l \geq Bp_t \tag{2}$$

hold. The research concerns the existence, the uniqueness and the properties of the dominant technique.

Even though prices vary according to whether the wage is advanced or paid *post factum*, the dominant technique at a given rate of profit is independent of this feature. The reason is that, if the wage is advanced, the prices and the wage (p^M, w^M) are modified according to the formulas $p = p^M$, $w = w^M(1 + r)$ seen in chapter 6, section 1. The equivalence between the inequalities $(1 + r)Ap + wl \geq p$ and $(1 + r)(Ap^M + w^M l) \geq p^M$ shows that the dominant technique is the same in both cases. Except when otherwise mentioned, we choose the rate of profit as the exogenous variable and retain the hypothesis of a wage paid *post factum*.

The starting point of the analysis is an arbitrary square initial technique (A_t, l_t), which is compatible with the given long-term rate of profit r. If the technique is not dominant, there exists at least one method which yields extra profits at its associated prices (p_t, w_t). The first entrepreneur who innovates by using it pockets a technological rent. When his example has been widely followed the rent disappears, with a uniform rate of profit back again to level r. The final effect is twofold: the technique has switched from (A_t, l_t) to the neighbouring technique (A_{t+1}, l_{t+1}) ('neighbouring' means that only one method is changed) and the prices have moved from (p_t, w_t) to (p_{t+1}, w_{t+1}). A similar procedure is repeated for the new technique, until a dominant technique is found. The numéraire does not matter, since the profitability inequalities are independent of it. The organigram above represents the working of this 'market algorithm'.

Only one method is modified at each step. If several methods are profitable simultaneously, a complete description of the algorithm would require a rule to define the new one to insert at the next step. It will turn out that the properties of the algorithm do not depend on this rule, which is therefore left aside. The algorithm stops on a dominant technique. Since the only possibility of infinite working would be the existence of a cycle $T_1 \rightarrow T_2 \rightarrow \cdots \rightarrow T_s \rightarrow T_{s+1} = T_1 \rightarrow \cdots$, the convergence of the algorithm is equivalent to the absence of a cycle. Though the concept of a dominant technique is independent of the algorithm, the convergence property is richer than a mere existence result because of its interpretation as stylized economic dynamics.

3 Convergence and existence

By assumption, labour is directly or indirectly necessary. The geometrical representation is simplified if we assume that the labour vector is positive. As in chapter 3, each process is normalized by setting $l_i = 1$. For the moment, the economy is assumed to be basic.

A geometrical study of the problem permits us to follow the working of the algorithm and discover its properties. Figure 9.1 generalizes the illustration given in chapter 3, section 4 for two goods and introduces other methods of production for wheat (odd methods) and iron (even methods). Each method is characterized by its r–net product per worker $c_i = c_i(r) = (b_i - (1 + r)a_i)/l_i$ or the extremity C_i of this vector (we will loosely refer to 'method c_i' or 'C_i' instead of 'method i'). The jth component of c_i is negative or zero for $j \neq i$. With $n = 2$ goods, a technique is defined by a pair of methods such as (c_1, c_2). The assumption that the given rate of profit is admissible means that the segment $[C_1C_2]$ admits at least one point in the positive orthant. It then cuts the whole orthant. The prices $p = (p_1, p_2)$ in terms of wage satisfy equalities $c_1p = c_2p = 1$ and, therefore, the vector p is orthogonal to $[C_1C_2]$. The straight line C_1C_2 separates the plane in two half-planes: a 'lower' half-plane containing the origin and an 'upper' half-plane. A method 3 represented by C_3 in the upper half-plane satisfies $c_3p > 1$, i.e. $(1 + r)\, a_3p + l_3 > b_3p$. In economic terms, the methods above C_1C_2 are profitable at prices associated with technique $(1, 2)$, whereas the methods under C_1C_2 pay extra costs.

Let us follow the working of the algorithm. After the substitution of the profitable method 3 for method 1, the new combination $(2, 3)$ is a technique (the segment $[C_2C_3]$ cuts the positive orthant). Method 1, which has just been excluded, is located under C_2C_3 and, therefore, pays extra costs at the new prices. We see in figure 9.1 that point C_4 is above C_2C_3. A new technique $(3, 4)$ is obtained by replacing method 2 by 4.

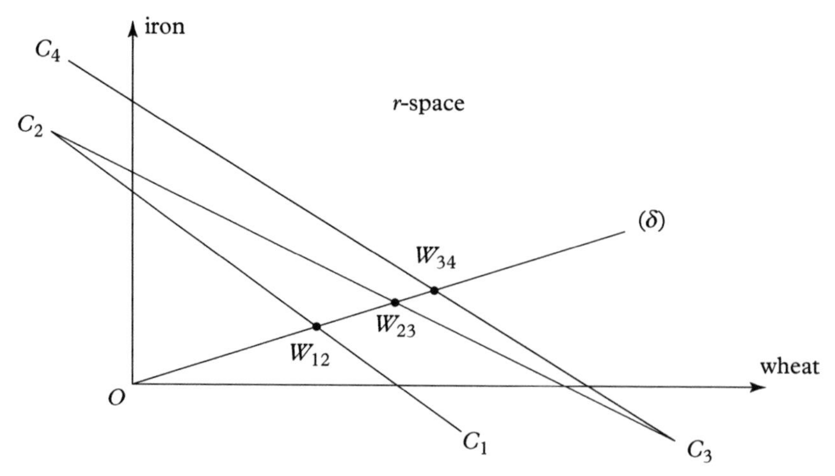

Figure 9.1 Algorithm and dominant technique

Now, all points C_i are under the straight line C_3C_4, i.e. no available method yields extra profits: the technique (3, 4) is dominant. Let us notice that:

- The dominant technique is represented on the outside frontier.
- The real wage increases at each step of the algorithm: According to (chapter 3, p. 19), the level of the real wage for the composition (δ) of the wage basket is measured by OW in figure 9.1. The dominant technique is wage-maximizing for any wage basket.

The conclusions suggested by the geometrical study are general. The main two properties of the algorithm are:

Insertion property. Given a technique T_1 and a method c_2 which yields extra profits at prices (p_1, w_1) associated with T_1, a new technique T_2 is obtained by substituting c_2 for the old method producing the same good.

Consistency property. The old method c_1 which has just been excluded is not profitable at the new prices (p_2, w_2) associated with T_2.

Sraffa states the consistency property explicitly: 'While the *extent* of the cheapness of one method of production relatively to the other will vary according as the comparison is carried out in system *I* or in system *II*, the *order* of the two methods as to cheapness must be the same in the two systems' (*PCMC*, § 93). From a formal viewpoint, the property is implied by lemmas 1 and 2:

Lemma 1. Let T_1 and T_2 be two neighbouring techniques, p_1 and p_2 their associated prices in terms of wage and δ an r-net product common to these techniques. Then technique T_2 is preferred to technique T_1 if and only if δ has become cheaper ($\delta p_2 < \delta p_1$).

Lemma 2. There exists some r-net product δ common to all techniques.

It follows from lemmas 1 and 2 that the value of δ decreases at each step of the algorithm and, therefore, cycles are excluded and the algorithm converges. Note that lemma 2 is a minimalist statement since, in fact, *any* semi-positive basket is an r-net product common to all techniques. The statement has been chosen for methodological reasons and aims at delineating the arguments leading to the existence, convergence and uniqueness results. This choice will be fully justified by the analysis of multiple-product systems, when two cases are distinguished: if lemmas 1 and 2 still apply, the same reasoning leads to the same results as in single production; otherwise, the arguments are of a different nature.

Theorem 1. The market algorithm converges towards a dominant technique.

The structure of relative prices is modified after the introduction of a new method. The intuition is that the difficulty of production decreases more in the industry which initiates the change, since the benefit for other industries is only indirect:

Theorem 2. After a change of method in the ith industry, the relative price of good i with respect to any other commodity decreases.

The working of the algorithm requires the calculation of the price vector associated with the new technique. Theorem 3 avoids this operation and provides an algebraic criterion relative to the sign of a determinant. Since the determinant is a polynomial of degree n in $\lambda = (1 + r)^{-1}$, it also follows from it that the number of switches between two techniques when r varies is at most equal to that of commodities (Bharadwaj 1970).

Theorem 3. Let (A, l) be a technique, (a_1, l_1) being the present method in the first industry. A new method $(a_1 + \Delta a_1, l_1 + \Delta l_1)$ is cheaper than (respectively: indifferent to, more costly than) the present one if and only if the determinant

$$\begin{vmatrix} (1+r)^{-1}I - A & -l \\ -\Delta a_1 & -\Delta l_1 \end{vmatrix}$$

is positive (respectively: nil, negative).

4 Properties

The argument used to establish the convergence of the algorithm is that the value of a basket decreases at each step: a minimum is ultimately reached. But is it an absolute minimum? The algorithm might stop in a local 'hollow'. This, however, is excluded if any two techniques are connected by stairs which permit us to continue the descent as long as the *minimum minimorum* is not reached. In the present case, the staircase is:

Robustness property. Any two techniques have some r-net product in common.

This property, which is a weak form of lemma 2, implies that the dominant technique is unique, up to indifference: if the points C_1, C_2 and C_3 are aligned, the techniques represented by (C_1, C_2) and (C_2, C_3) are associated with the same price vector and simultaneously dominant. A strong form of lemma 2 is:

r-adjustment property. Any semi-positive basket δ is an r-net product of all techniques.

In conjunction with lemma 1, the adjustment property shows that the dominant technique minimizes the price in terms of wage of any semi-positive basket – or, in other words, that it is wage-maximizing. Wage-maximization, in its turn, implies uniqueness. In multiple-product systems these properties will be dissociated.

Theorem 4 (uniqueness). For a given rate of profit, the competitive price vector in terms of wage is unique. The dominant technique itself is unique, up to indifference between equally costly methods.

Theorem 5 (maximization). A dominant technique maximizes the real wage.

The wage-maximization property justifies an alternative procedure to determine the dominant technique. Let us take an arbitrary basket as

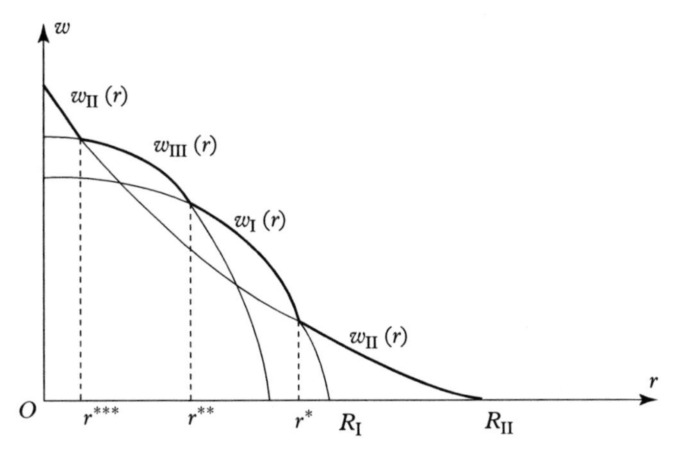

Figure 9.2 Choice of technique and wage

numéraire and draw the corresponding wage–profit curves for all techniques. For a given rate of profit, the dominant technique is associated with the highest wage. Therefore, when distribution varies, the upper envelope of the w–r curves defines the w–r relationship for the economy with choice of technique. As each curve is decreasing, so is the envelope (figure 9.2).

The Okishio Theorem takes the real wage as the exogenous distribution variable and states that the long-run rate of profit can increase only when new methods are introduced. This result follows from two properties: every isolated w–r curve is decreasing and their envelope is the w–r curve for the family of techniques. Then, when a new method is introduced and given the wage, the envelope can move to the right only: the abscissa r therefore increases.

When the rate of profit varies, a dominant technique at rate r retains the property in a neighbourhood of r. In order to build the set of dominant techniques when r varies, it suffices to identify the switch points r^*, r^{**}, r^{***} when $n + 1$ methods are compatible. At these points two dominant techniques coexist, with a unique price vector. A *reswitching* occurs when the same technique is dominant at low and high rates, while being dominated at intermediate levels (Champernowne 1953–4; Robinson 1953–4). This phenomenon, which does not occur in the corn model, plays a major role in the debates on capital theory. Part III of the book will go into the subject in greater depth. It will also satisfy the desire for an expression of the cost-minimization property in terms of marginal equalities (the friends of truth are patient).

In a non-basic economy, the properties of the algorithm still hold if any good enters directly or indirectly in the production of basket δ. Otherwise:

- When the technical change concerns a non-basic (iron), the prices are unchanged for all commodities, other than iron itself, in which the good does not enter directly or indirectly.
- Consider a decomposable dominant technique and a non-dominant technique obtained by modifying the method of production of a non-basic good, iron, which does not enter into the production of wheat. The wage in terms of wheat is the same for both techniques at any rate of profit. Therefore the w–r curves associated with the two techniques, one being dominant and the other not, coincide.
- The number of operated methods depends on demand: if wheat and iron are demanded, the unique dominant technique must produce both commodities; if the final demand is reduced to wheat, the operated technique is reduced to the corn method.

Decomposable systems herald some difficulties which will become more visible with multiple-product systems: demand matters, whereas basic economies fall within the range of validity of the non-substitution theorem.

Let us return to basic single-product systems. The non-substitution property (Arrow 1951; Georgescu-Roegen 1951; Samuelson 1951) states that the dominant technique depends only on the rate of profit, not on demand. This result attracted attention because it contradicts the common idea that a change in demand induces a change in prices. In fact, the composition and the level of demand do not matter if distribution is not affected. In the long run, the rate of profit governs the choice of methods and the prices, whereas the demand regulates the activity levels. The non-substitution property relies on three hypotheses: single production, constancy of returns and uniqueness of the primary factor (here, labour). It permits us to conceive a theory of prices of *production*. Demand matters for short-term prices, such as the price of black cloth when public mourning occurs (Smith 1776 [1976], vol. I, ch. 7), and for the relative importance of the main three sectors: production of capital goods, consumption goods and luxury goods. Its role becomes crucial when the limits of reproduction appear, which affect distribution (rent theory), or when the commodities are produced jointly.

5 Laws on prices

How do long-term prices vary with distribution? The laws examined in chapter 6 assumed a given technique. Our present aim is to study the variations of the price-and-wage vector as a function of distribution, in the presence of a choice of methods. For instance, one general law is the Ricardian trade-off property: it means that prices in terms of wage increase with the rate of profit. Can additional properties be found? Their existence is suggested by the corn model: it was shown in chapter 2 that the $w - r$ curve for a corn economy is the upper envelope of the straight lines $w^t - r^t$ associated with every available technique. The envelope is decreasing (this is the Ricardian property) *and* convex (additional property). In a multisector economy the shape of the $w - r$ curve depends on the numéraire, but some weak form of convexity is maintained.

Let us be ambitious. We would not only like to find some properties of the price vectors, but to derive all of them. This will be achieved when, considering T arbitrary rates of profit and T arbitrary positive vectors, we can recognize whether these vectors can be identified with price-and-wage vectors for some economy. Theorem 6 proposes such a characterization. The notation becomes slightly involved: the upper index t refers to the dominant technique at rate r^t, the lower index i to a commodity or an industry. Consider an economy with Tn methods $(a_i^t, l_i^t) \to 1i$ (without loss of generality, the methods are restricted to those selected at some rate of profit and some of them may coincide). Condition (3) below means that method (a_i^t, l_i^t) is cost-minimizing in industry i at the rate of profit r^t.

Definition 1. Let there be T scalars r^t $(-1 < r^t)$ and T positive vectors $p^t \in R_+^n$ $(t = 1, \ldots, T)$. These vectors are *a set of price vectors* (in terms of wage) if and only if there exist semi-positive vectors (a_i^τ, l_i^τ) such that inequality

$$(1 + r^t)a_i^\tau p^t + l_i^\tau \geq p_i^t \tag{3}$$

holds for any triple t, τ, i of indices $(t, \tau = 1, \ldots, T; i = 1, \ldots, n)$, with equality for $t = \tau$.

The method followed to characterize a set of price vectors is to transform (3) by duality (the Theorem of the Alternative). The approach explains why a set of price vectors admits a characterization in terms of linear programming problems:

Theorem 6. For a given set of T positive vectors p^t, let (P_i^t) be the linear programming problem $(i = 1, \ldots, n;\ t = 1, \ldots, T)$ with the $T - 1$ non-negative variables $\{x^\tau; t = 1, \ldots, T, \tau \neq t\}$:

$$(P_i^t) \quad V_i^t = \max_{x \geq 0} \sum_{\tau \neq t} p_i^\tau x^\tau$$

subject to

$$\sum_{\tau \neq t} x^{\tau} \leq 1, \tag{4.1}$$

$$\forall j = 1, \ldots, n \quad \sum_{\tau \neq t} (1 + r^{\tau}) p_j^{\tau} x^{\tau} \leq (1 + r^t) p_j^t. \tag{4.2}$$

The set $\{p^{\tau}, \tau = 1, \ldots, T\}$ is a set of price vectors if and only if the value V_i^t of programme (P_i^t) is at most equal to p_i^t for any i and any t.

In order to clarify the scope of Theorem 6, let us apply it to the 3-sets of price vectors ($r^1 < r^2 < r^3$). It implies that, for any commodity i such that $p_i^2 \neq p_i^1$, inequality

$$\frac{p_i^3 - p_i^2}{p_i^2 - p_i^1} \leq \sup_j \frac{(1 + r^3) p_j^3 - (1 + r^2) p_j^2}{(1 + r^2) p_j^2 - (1 + r^1) p_j^1} \tag{5}$$

holds. This relation is typically a property which is easy to check directly once it is written down but difficult to guess by other means than the dual method. The method is also useful to establish more appealing properties. Its main synthetic result is:

Theorem 7. For a set of T positive vectors to be price vectors, a sufficient condition is that, whatever is the commodity i chosen as numéraire, all points (w_i^t, r^t) belong to a non-increasing convex curve.

6 Sraffa on switches

The theory of choice of technique set out in sections 2–4 is inspired by *PCMC* (ch. XII). Several clues suggest the existence of significant differences between the two presentations:

- Chapter XII is entitled 'Switch in Methods of Production'. The problem of 'switch' is close to that of 'choice', but Sraffa's argument does consider the effect of changes in distribution and follows their incidence in quasi-dynamic terms.
- The main concepts in Sraffa's construction are those of the non-basic commodity and switch point, which play no role in the post-Sraffian literature on the topic.
- Sraffa considers that the problem concerns the system of production as a whole (there are two systems, I or II, depending on which method 1, or 2, is operated). Hence his reference to method I and system I, while we use different notations for the method and the system.

These differences justify a closer reading of chapter XII in order to identify its logic. For Sraffa, the choice of technique is complex because the system *and* the numéraire (called standard) both affect the price vector. There exist, however, two cases in which the interference between these effects is limited. First, in the case of a non-basic change: then the price vectors of both systems are identical except for the non-basic commodity (the standard is made of basic goods only), and the selected system is the one which produces the non-basic good at the lower cost. Second, in the case of a switch point: then the price vectors are identical and the choice of the system does not matter. Sraffa's reasoning reduces the general problem to an extension and combination of these special cases. Confronted with the choice between two methods of production 1 and 2 of a basic good (copper), Sraffa adds non-basic uses to their basic uses. Let us imagine that copper 1 and copper 2 are perfect substitutes for basic uses (electric wires), but not for non-basic uses: copper 1 is required for statues and copper 2 for shields. Will an economy which produces wires, statues and shields choose system I (the one for which copper 1 is basic and copper 2 non-basic) or system II (with the opposite characteristics)? Let the prices in system I be written (p_I, p_2), in which the last component of p_I is the price of the basic copper 1, while p_2 the price of the non-basic copper 2. Starting from system I and its associated prices, the criterion of choice is that, if the price of copper 2 is smaller than that of copper 1 (the property is independent of the standard), the capitalists substitute copper 2 for copper 1 in the basic uses and the economy switches to system II.

The criterion requires us to prove the consistency property – that the order of the prices of copper 1 and 2 is the same in systems I and II. The argument relies on a change in distribution. (From a methodological point of view, one may notice the parallel between this way of reasoning and the 'dynamic' approach used in *PCMC*, §§ 39 and 49, in order to establish the positivity of prices and the Ricardian trade-off.) Let R_I and R_{II} be the maximum rates of profit in systems I and II, with $R_I < R_{II}$. Sraffa starts from the fact that, for a rate of profit in interval $]R_I, R_{II}]$, there is no ambiguity on the choice of technique since only system II can be operated. By continuity, system II is also selected for r slightly below R_I. When the rate of profit decreases, a switch point corresponds to a state in which the two systems are associated with the same price vector and the prices of copper 1 and copper 2 are equal. In a dynamic interpretation, a switch occurs when, following a continuous change in distribution, both ratios $(p_1: p_2)_I$ and $(p_1: p_2)_{II}$ cross the value one simultaneously. Therefore, the signs of $(p_1: p_2)_I - 1$ and $(p_1: p_2)_{II} - 1$ have two properties: they are identical for high rates of profit and, when the rate of profit decreases and reaches a switch point, they change simultaneously. The conclusion is that $(p_1 : p_2)_I$ and $(p_1 : p_2)_{II}$ are simultaneously greater or smaller than one for any rate of profit. In other words, the consistency property holds.

Finally, Sraffa establishes the wage-maximization property. His argument is once more of a dynamic nature. Let us draw both curves $(w, r)_I$ and $(w, r)_{II}$ in the same figure (figure 9.2, p. 83). For a rate of profit between R_I and R_{II}, only system II is admissible and, when the rate of profit becomes smaller than R_I, it is not before the first (i.e. the greatest) switch point r^* that a switch from system II to system I occurs. Two phenomena happen when r becomes slightly smaller than r^*. First, the dominant system switches from II to I; second, since the curves $w_I(r)$ and $w_{II}(r)$ intersect at r^*, the upper curve, which was w_{II} for $r > r^*$, becomes w_I. The conjunction of both phenomena shows that the wage associated with the selected system is always on the upper curve. The argument can be repeated at the next switch points, therefore the wage-maximization property is general.

A delineation of Sraffa's reasoning (Bidard and Klimovsky 2004) aims at understanding its nature, as well as the cause of its failure for multiple-product systems according to Sraffa's own logic (*PCMC*, ch. XIX, §8).

7 Proofs

Proofs of Theorems 1, 4 *and* 5. See the text (pp. 81–82).

The next proof is inspired by an argument used by Sraffa (*PCMC*, § 49) for another purpose.

Proof of Theorem 2. Let us choose as numéraire the commodity j whose relative price decreases the most after the technical change in industry i. Then the prices of all other commodities increase. Consider the price equation for commodity j. If $j \neq i$, the costs of the material inputs increase, therefore the wage in terms of j should decrease in order to maintain equality $p_j = 1$. This contradicting with the wage-maximization property of the dominant technique, we have $j = i$. ■

Proof of Theorem 3 (Bidard 1981). If two methods are indifferent, the column vector $((1 + r)p_1, w_1 = 1)$ belongs to the kernel of the matrix M considered in the statement of Theorem 3, therefore $det(M) = 0$. If method (a_2, l_2) is preferred to (a_1, l_1) one may increase l_2 by $\Delta l > 0$ in order that $(a_2, l_2 + \Delta l)$ becomes as costly as (a_1, l_1) and, therefore, indifferent to that method. In the operation the determinant decreases because the coefficient $-det(\lambda I - A)$ of Δl_1 in $det(M)$ is negative. Therefore the determinant was positive before the change. ■

Proof of Theorem 6 (Bidard 1998c). Let indices i and t be given and $R^t = 1 + r^t$. Conditions (3) are a set of inequations (the equality for $\tau = t$ once replaced by two inequalities with opposite signs $\geq$ and $\leq$) which, being affine in coefficients a_{ij}^{τ} and l_i^{τ}, is written

$$(a_i^{\tau}\ l_i^{\tau})[Q] \geq b$$

with

$$Q = \begin{bmatrix} R^1 p^1 \ldots R^t p^t, & -R^t p^t \ldots R^T p^T \\ 1 \quad \ldots 1 & -1 \quad \ldots 1 \end{bmatrix} \text{ and } b = (p_i^1, \ldots, p_i^t, -p_i^t, \ldots, p_i^T).$$

By the Theorem of the Alternative, the existence of a semi-positive row vector $(a_i^{\tau}\ l_i^{\tau})$ satisfying such a relationship is equivalent to the non-existence of a semi-positive column vector z, whose components are $(z^1, \ldots, z^t, \bar{z}^t, \ldots, z^T)$, such that $Qz \leq 0$ and $bz > 0$. Let the variables x^{τ} $(\tau = 1, \ldots, T)$ be defined by $x^{\tau} = z^{\tau}$ $(\tau \neq t)$ and $x^t = z^t - \bar{z}^t$. Conditions $Qz \leq 0$ and $bz > 0$ are written

$$\forall j = 1, \ldots, n \quad \sum_{\tau=1}^{T} R^{\tau} p_j^{\tau} x^{\tau} \leq 0, \tag{6.1}$$

$$\sum_{\tau=1}^{T} x^{\tau} \leq 0, \tag{6.2}$$

$$\sum_{\tau=1}^{T} p_i^{\tau} x^{\tau} > 0. \tag{6.3}$$

Condition (6.2) with $x^{\tau} \geq 0$ $(\tau \neq t)$ shows that the component x^t is negative. After homothety on x, we set $x^t = -1$ without loss of generality. The non-existence of a solution to (6) amounts to saying that, when the non-negative variables x^{τ} $(\tau \neq t)$ are subject to the $n+1$ constraints (6.1) and (6.2), the value of $\sum_{\tau \neq t}^{T} p_i^{\tau} x^{\tau} - p_i^t$ is at most equal to zero. Theorem 6 is another expression of the same property. ■

As an application of Theorem 6, choose $n = 3$, $t = 2$ and (x^1, x^3) such that (4.1) and one of the inequalities (4.2) hold as equalities: relation (5) is obtained.

Proof of Theorem 7. Assume that, for some i, the points $(w_i^t = 1/p_i^t$, $R^t = 1 + r^t)$ belong to a convex decreasing curve. For any $t = 1, \ldots,$

T, consider the programme (Q_i^t):

$$(Q_i^t) \qquad \max_{z \geq 0} \sum_{\tau \neq t} z^\tau$$

$$\text{subject to} \quad \sum_{\tau \neq t} w_i^\tau z^\tau \leq w_i^t,$$

$$\sum_{\tau \neq t} R^\tau z^\tau \leq R^t.$$

Let $aw + bR = 1$ ($a > 0$, $b > 0$) be the equation of a tangent at point (w_i^t, R^t) to the w–R curve. By the convexity assumption, the curve is above its tangent, therefore $aw_i^\tau + bR^\tau \geq 1$. Therefore:

$$val(Q_i^t) = \max_{z \geq 0} \sum_{\tau \neq t} z^\tau \leq \max_{z \geq 0} \sum_{\tau \neq t} (aw_i^\tau + bR^\tau) z^\tau$$

$$\leq a \max \sum_{\tau \neq t} w_i^\tau z^\tau + b \max \sum_{\tau \neq t} R^\tau z^\tau \leq aw_i^t + bR^t.$$

Hence, $val(Q_i^t) \leq 1$. Let us proceed to the change of variable $z^\tau = p_i^\tau x^\tau / p_i^t$ in (Q_i^t) with $p_i^\tau = 1/w_i^\tau$. It turns out that the value of programme $(\overline{P}_i^t)$:

$$(\overline{P}_i^t) \qquad \max_{x \geq 0} \sum_{\tau \neq t} p_i^\tau x^\tau$$

$$\text{subject to} \quad \sum_{\tau \neq t} x^\tau \leq 1,$$

$$\sum_{\tau \neq t} R^\tau p_i^\tau x^\tau \leq R^t p_i^t,$$

is at most equal to p_i^t. Since the programme (P_i^t) considered in Theorem 6 differs from $(\overline{P}_i^t)$ only by the existence of more constraints, its value is also p_i^t at most. Therefore, when the initial assumption on i holds for any i, Theorem 6 implies that the set $\{p^t; t = 1, \ldots, T\}$ is a set of price vectors. ■

Part II

Joint production

10 Joint production: a theoretical object

1 A grain of sand

A method of *joint production* provides several goods simultaneously. A well-known example is that of wool and mutton. Production with fixed capital also belongs to this category: an agricultural process uses a tractor which, besides corn, gets out older from the annual cycle until it is worn out. The land itself constitutes another joint product of agriculture.

Our interest in joint production comes less from its relevance in applied economics (Steedman 1984) than from the intellectual challenges it raises. The accountants come up against the imputation issue: What are the rules for allocating refining costs, whether for gas or other joint products? How should the prices for travellers and for freight be determined? But we are interested mainly in economic properties and laws. We believe that the economic laws of single production remain obscure because they cannot be isolated from each other. Joint production is a laboratory for a wealth of experiments. Its formalism enables us to introduce some grains of sand *ad libitum* in the construction: the creaks give information about the internal mechanisms – that is to say the links between a property and an hypothesis, or between two properties. The study of multiple-product systems is a means to reach a deeper understanding of economic laws, each one being associated with the larger frame where it is valid. In the same way that the geometry of the circle is enriched through the study of deformations permitting the classification of the properties, joint production aims to become acquainted with the properties of single production by going beyond them.

2 The project

The economic laws of single production are violated in pure joint production (chapter 11). This statement is the starting point for our reflection, not its end. The longer-term purpose is to identify the hypotheses and the situations where some laws hold, in order to link the properties and the concepts.

The notion of an all-engaging system (chapter 12) constitutes a natural generalization of single production. The associated mathematical properties can be understood as an extension of the *PF* theorem – even if our formal study goes from the general to the particular. The all-engaging systems share a lot of the properties of single production, such as the adjustment to demand. Surprisingly enough, almost all the economic systems are all-engaging after an adequate analytical treatment. This statement is based on a reinterpretation of Sraffa's equations that permits a theoretical rapprochement with von Neumann's construct (chapter 13). The concept of a sector generalizes that of an industry, taking into account pure capital goods and the choice of technique (chapter 14). Though production with fixed capital is a type of joint production, a unique good is produced over the lifetime of a machine, as in single production. These dual aspects explain the paradoxes first examined, before they are resolved by truncation theory in an Austrian-type model and a multisector model, with one machine in every industry or sector. In the absence of the truncation hypothesis, the theoretical foundations of internal rate of return are established (chapter 15). This is the starting point for a more ambitious construction centred on the concept of vertical integration, which extends the results of the truncation theory. The conclusions are reached with a great economy of means (chapter 16). We finally elaborate a general theory of rent. An indeterminacy theorem which seems to contradict Ricardo's project to explain the laws of distribution invites us to go back over the characteristics of Ricardo's approach (chapter 17).

The topics treated in these chapters almost correspond to those considered in the second part of *PCMC*. The parallel is not perfect: Sraffa had the idea of studying each economic system in isolation before comparing them; we consider, on the contrary, that this methodology does not apply to joint production, where the choice of methods is done inside the multiple-product system. The main focus is on the concepts. Such notions as those of sector or vertical integration introduce a form of refined thinking which attains a more profound degree of comprehension of the problem. The ultimate aim is to understand the deviations from single production and to search for conditions sustaining similar properties. The study of joint production is also intimately linked with methodological issues. This programme will be carried on in part III, in both its analytical and its methodological dimensions. A comparative study of the approaches to joint production will be a significant element of the debate.

11 Paradoxes and tools

1 Not amused

In the study of joint production, a paradox signals the absence of one of the economic properties established for single production. We are not amused by these paradoxes. The best starting point, however, is to consider that virtually no property of single-product systems holds in pure joint production. This assertion is close to the truth and, moreover, any success in recovering some properties then appears as a great achievement. How can these properties be recovered, if they are not here from the very beginning? In two ways: either by a specification of the model or by a deeper economic analysis that makes the apparent paradoxes disappear. Both aspects (multiplicity of paradoxes, possibility of eliminating some of them) are illustrated in this chapter. An important place is given to the geometrical representations as support for economic intuition.

Except when choice of methods is explicitly taken into account, it is assumed that the number of operated methods is equal to that of produced goods. Without this squareness hypothesis, prices cannot be determined when only distribution and production methods are known: the notion of the price of production is linked to the idea of the square system. The squareness hypothesis will be established as a property in some specific contexts. Its discussion will take place in part III.

2 Some catastrophes

In basic single-product systems, the maximum rate of growth and profit is characterized by the existence of an attached positive standard basket. For multiple-product systems, a formal extension of the definition leads us to consider that a standard basket is a non-zero solution q to the equation $qB = (1 + G)qA$. In single production ($B = I$), there exists a unique scalar G such that q is positive and, for a viable system, it is the smallest positive root of $det(I - (1 + g)A) = 0$. In joint production, Sraffa recognizes that all baskets q may have negative components and proposes to select the one associated with the smallest positive root of $det(B - (1 + g)A) = 0$. The proposal relies on a hasty transposition and is untenable. As a matter of fact, it fails when the equation has only complex solutions (Manara 1968). The methodological point is to consider the properties of single production as guidelines, not to impose them as arbitrary rules. The notion of a standard commodity is hidden in multiple-product systems: the main goal of chapter 13 will be to restore local properties of single production after an adequate construction. To get over the appearances and re-establish some order requires an elaborated approach to the problem.

Assume that the maximum rate G has been identified. For $g < G$, the usual equation relative to quantities is written $yB = (1 + g)yA + d$. The system (A, B) has the adjustment property if there exist semi-positive activity levels y sustaining the production of any given g-net product d $(d > 0)$. The formal solution $y = d(B - (1 + g)A)^{-1}$ assumes that the matrix $B - (1 + g)A$ is invertible. The difference with single production is that the generalized Leontief inverse $L(g) = (B - (1 + g)A)^{-1}$ may have negative entries, and the same for the row vector y. Similarly for the price space: the prices of production, which are the solution to $(1 + r)Ap + wl = Bp$, are defined up to a normalization by the numéraire as $p = w(B - (1 + r)A)^{-1}l$ and their positivity is not ensured. Even if the prices are positive, the rate of profit and the real wage may vary in the same direction.

Another important paradox concerns the comparison of neighbouring n-sets in terms of profitability. Assume that, for a given rate of profit, a system made of $n - 1$ methods of production must be completed by one among two methods j and k. When some method is inserted, its associated price and wage vector is well defined (assume that it is positive) and one can check if the alternative method yields extra profit or pays extra costs. In single production, the consistency property states that method k yields extra profits at j's prices if and only if method j pays extra costs at k's prices. In joint production, it may occur that each method yields extra profits at the other's prices. In such a configuration, the market algorithm oscillates perpetually between the two n-sets and the existence of a long-term equilibrium is questionable. This is the most important problem: existence must be established before wondering if the usual properties of single-product systems are preserved.

3 The price space

3.1 A geometrical approach

A geometrical approach confirms the paradoxes. It also suggests some ways to analyse the nature of these difficulties and solve some of them.

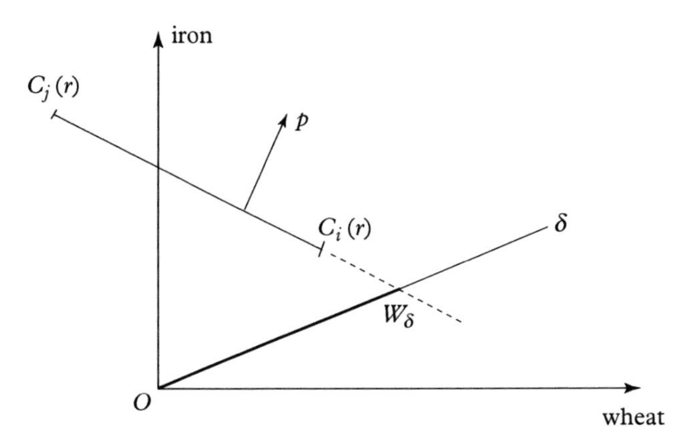

Figure 11.1 r-space, prices and wage

The geometrical representation in the price space (or r-space, the rate of profit being given) was introduced in part I. It is assumed that every process makes use of labour and is normalized by setting $l_i = 1$ (the properties are easily extended to the case when labour is only indirectly necessary for production). The process i is then represented either by its r-net product per worker $c_i(r) = b_i - (1+r)a_i$ or by the extremity $C_i(r)$ of the vector. The difference with figure 3.3 (p. 19) is that the r-net product is arbitrary in joint production, whereas it has $n - 1$ negative or zero components in single production. Let there be two commodities ($n = 2$) and two methods i and j. Thanks to the normalizations $l_i = 1$ and $w = 1$, the price vector in terms of wage is such that $c_ip = c_jp = 1$, therefore it is orthogonal to the segment $[C_i(r)C_j(r)]$. For a given composition δ of the wage basket, the level of the real wage is $\overline{OW_\delta}$ (figure 11.1).

When the number of available methods exceeds that of commodities, a process k represented by a point C_k 'above' the straight line C_iC_j (i.e. in the half-plane not containing the origin) yields extra profits at the prices p_{ij} associated with system (i, j). The process k will be included in a new competitive system. The paradox mentioned at the end of section 2 occurs when C_k is above C_iC_j and, simultaneously, C_j is above C_iC_k ($C_jC_iC_k$ has a 'bird' configuration).

Definition 1. A *candidate*, or *dominant* n-set, is an n-set of methods such that, at its associated prices, no available process yields extra profits.

In order to identify the candidates, it suffices to look at the convex envelope of the origin and all points $C_i(r)$: the candidates are the n-sets defining the facets (the frontier) of this convex hull. In figure 11.2 (for the

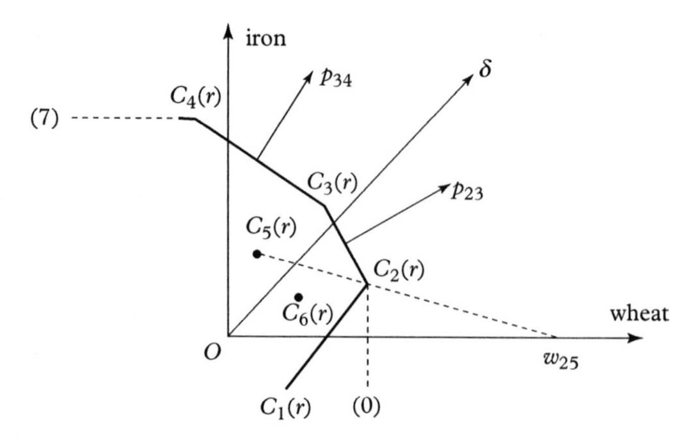

Figure 11.2 The candidates (r-space)

moment, ignore the dotted lines) with six methods from 1 to 6, where i stands for $C_i(r)$, there are three candidates: (1, 2), (2, 3) and (3, 4). Competition excludes methods 5 and 6 and any other combination of methods.

In the algebraic formulation, the price vector (p, w) associated with a candidate satisfies (1) with complementarity relationships

$$(1+r)Ap + wl \geq Bp \quad [y]. \tag{1}$$

These inequalities mean that every operated method belonging to the candidate yields the rate of profit r, whereas the non-operated methods do not yield more (generally, they pay extra costs). The profitability conditions are common to all systems we consider: the candidates – i.e. the n-sets on the frontier – are the only ones that can be elected, independently of the still missing part of the system of equations. Figure 11.2 illustrates several paradoxes:

- For the dominant 2-set (1, 2), the price of iron is negative.
- In terms of corn, the real wage w_{25} associated with the non-dominant 2-set (2, 5) is greater than for any candidate. Nevertheless, competition eliminates the use of method 5.
- (2, 3) and (3, 4) are dominant 2-sets, with two different price vectors and two different real wages. How can we choose among several candidates? In joint production, there is no reason to imagine that the selected candidate is associated with the maximum wage but further requirements, that will be written down later to complete the system, play a role. Then three cases may occur: first, if exactly one dominant 2-set satisfies these additional requirements, the problem is solved.

Second, if several candidates satisfy the requirements, the dynamics of the economic system matter for the selection. And, third, the hope is that at least one candidate does meet the requirements: this is the existence problem.

- When the rate of profit increases from r to r', condition $r' > r$ implies $c_i(r') < c_i(r)$, so that the representative points slip towards the southwest. However, the real wage in terms of corn, as represented by the intersection of the horizontal axis with the line $C_i(r)C_j(r)$, may be higher for r' than for r: the trade-off property is violated. We also see that the real wage may increase in terms of corn and decrease in terms of iron, therefore the shape of the wage–profit curve depends on the wage basket.

3.2 *Some properties of the candidates*

Let us look at the geometrical representation with the idea of discovering economic properties. Figure 11.2 shows that two candidates (= dominant n-sets) do not overlap, i.e. they have no common direction (δ) in the r-space, corners excepted.[1] The exception occurs when three points on the frontier are aligned. In algebraic terms:

Theorem 1. Two n-sets I and $\mathcal{J}$ with an interior common r-net product δ cannot be simultaneously dominant, except if they are associated with the same price and wage vector.

In figure 11.2, the 2-sets (2, 3) and (5, 6) have an interior common r-net product δ: both segments $]C_2(r)C_3(r)[$ and $]C_5(r)C_6(r)[$ intersect the half-line (δ). Among all 2-sets having this property, the dominant 2-set (2, 3) is the one with the higher intersection with (δ). The property means that the real wage, *if* measured in terms of basket δ and *within* this family, is maximum for the candidate. When labour is chosen as numéraire ($w = 1$), the value of δ is minimum. Definition 2 and Theorem 2 constitute an algebraic translation of the property.

Definition 2. For a given r, a price vector π *supports* basket δ if δ is an r-net product of a subset of n processes which yield at least the rate of profit r for the price vector π:

$$\exists z > 0 \quad \delta = z(B - (1 + r)A)$$
$$z_i > 0 \Rightarrow (B\pi - (1 + r)A\pi - l)_i \geq 0.$$

[1] Notations δ or (δ) are used for a vector, resp. a direction, in the r-space. In the g-space (section 4), notations d or (d) are adopted.

Theorem 2. Consider a candidate and its associated price vector p ($w = 1$), and let δ be an r-net product of its processes. Vector p satisfies properties

$$\delta p = \min_{\pi} \{\delta\pi, \pi \text{ supports } \delta\}$$

and

$$\delta p = \min_{\pi} \{zl; z > 0 \text{ and } z(B - (1+r)A) \geq \delta\}.$$

The algebraic formulation is more complicated than the original geometric observation. The reader, if not aware of the origin of the statement, may be lured by its superficial complexity. We will avoid a perverse use of mathematics: most properties of joint production result from the combination of elementary geometrical facts and a correct handling of a few concepts.

3.3 *Restoration of semi-positive prices*

The geometrical representation is a tool for analysing the nature of the problems and elaborating new results. The endeavour concerns the understanding of the paradoxes as a step towards their solution. The example of negative prices illustrates the approach followed (which will hopefully lead to more original considerations).

A first reaction consists in identifying the systems for which the phenomenon occurs. Figure 11.2 shows that the price vector associated with the candidate (1, 2) has a negative component. Then a change in the distribution of employment between the two methods (a move on the segment $[C_1(r)C_2(r)]$) can increase the r-net product of the system: this criterion characterizes the conditions allowing for the paradox. Another approach consists in imagining a construction that eliminates the paradox. Let us introduce the free disposal hypothesis. The free disposition of a commodity is the process whose input is reduced to that commodity, with no output. The free disposal of a negatively priced good is profitable. Once it has been performed, the price of that good becomes equal to zero. The restoration of semi-positive prices then relies on an assumption (the free disposal hypothesis) and a theory (that of choice of technique, which is only sketched here). These arguments invite us to go beyond the original data (A, l, B) and the mechanical calculation of prices: the effective economic system is obtained by replacing some of the initial processes by free disposal.

In the r-space, the free disposition of commodity i is represented by its r-net product per labourer (since $l_i = 0$, this case is an exception to the convention that every process uses labour), hence the r-net product is

$(0, \ldots, -\infty, \ldots, 0)$. The convex hull of the $C_j(r)$s is modified accordingly and becomes 0–2–3–4–7, as indicated by the dotted line in figure 11.2. The price of iron becomes non-negative.

Definition 3. The system (A, B) is strictly r-viable (or r-productive) if

$$\exists y > 0 \quad y(B - (1 + r)A) \gg 0. \tag{2}$$

The geometrical interpretation of (2) is that the origin is located 'below' the frontier of the candidates (figure 11.2). The free disposal hypothesis is frequently combined with the strict r-viability hypothesis and the hypothesis that labour is indispensable for production. These assumptions ensure the existence of a price and wage vector (p, w) with p semi-positive and $w = 1$, such that (1) holds.

4 The quantity space

The price inequalities (1) refer to the competitiveness of a set of methods, but they are only the first part of a greater system. The missing part defines the economically permitted n-sets and expresses, in Sraffa's words, that the 'requirements for use' are met by the operated methods. The n-sets satisfying the requirements for use are called the *techniques*. The present study is mainly concerned by the usual (in *post*-Sraffian analyses) specification of the requirements (Lippi's definition), and constitutes a first step towards the general theory developed in chapter 19.

Following Lippi (1979), the post-Sraffian economists have paid attention to the economic systems characterized by a given rate of growth g ($g \leq r$) and either a given final demand basket d or a rigid direction (d) of demand, these alternatives being equivalent under the constant returns hypothesis. Only the n-sets able to produce a g-net product equal or proportional to d are acceptable: they are the techniques for Lippi's problem. In single-product systems, the adjustment property states that a g-viable system can produce any semi-positive g-net product. The property does not hold in joint production: a multiple-product system in which every method produces more corn than iron is unable to produce a basket with equal quantities of corn and iron, whatever its activity levels are. The effectiveness of the additional constraint explains why the notions of requirements for use (the constraint) and techniques (n-sets satisfying the constraint) must now be explicitly introduced.

Let method i be geometrically represented by its g-net-product $c_i(g) = (b_i - (1 + g)a_i)/l_i$ per worker, or the extremity $C_i(g)$ of that vector (figure 11.3). In the g-space, a Lippi technique is an n-set such that d is a positive combination of the $C_i(g)$s. For two goods, when a unit of labour is

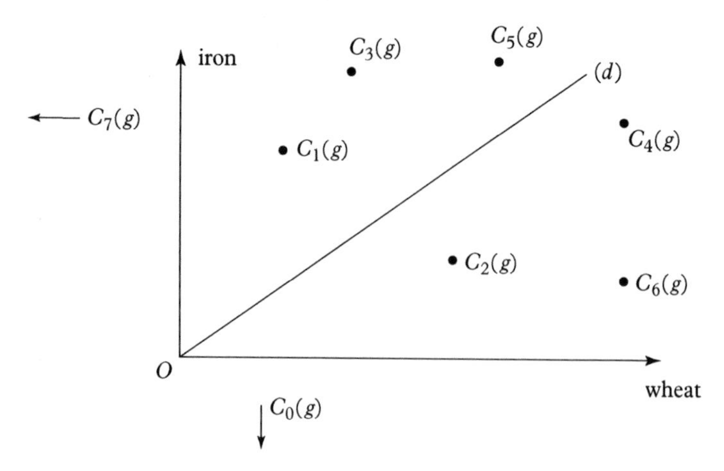

Figure 11.3 g-space and Lippi's techniques

shared among two methods i and j, the g-net product is a point on segment $[C_i(g)C_j(g)]$. Therefore, the Lippi techniques, i.e. the 2-sets which satisfy the requirements for use as defined by Lippi, are the 2-sets (i, j) such that segment $[C_i(g)C_j(g)]$ intersects the half-line (d). The presence of the free disposal methods increases the number of techniques, because the desired composition d can be obtained by eliminating a commodity in excess. This eases the search for a solution on the quantity side, but imposes a constraint on the price side since the disposed good receives a zero price. Free disposal and the g-viability condition (which is implied by the r-viability condition (2) and assumption $g \leq r$) play a role in the existence results.

When the direction of (d) varies, basket d is sometimes produced by less than n methods: the system is not square when d has the direction of some $d_i = c_i(g)$. The case is exceptional, so that squareness (the number of operated methods = the number of commodities) is a generic property. But it is important: when either (d) or g varies, the kinks indicate a change in the collection of techniques. We call a 'Stiglitz point' a change in the dominant technique due to a change in the rate of growth, to distinguish it from a switch point, when the reason of the change is the rate of profit. When the phenomenon does not occur, a technique for some given demand is also a technique for any other demand, as in single production. The joint production systems which have the same specific property will be studied in chapter 12. In the following analysis, direction (d) is definitely fixed and degeneracies are excluded.

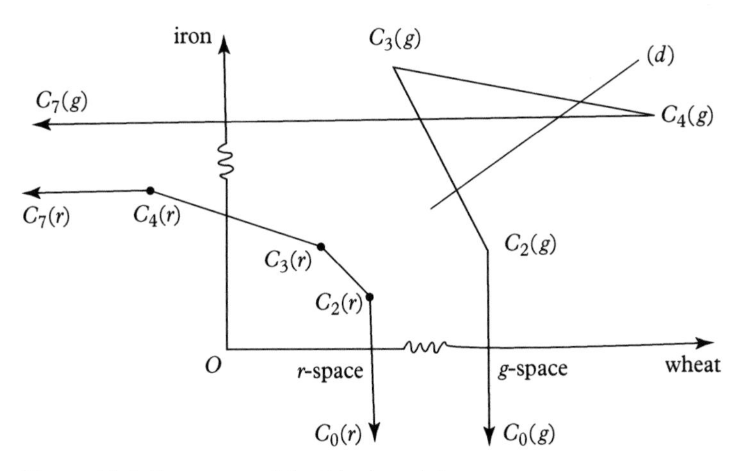

Figure 11.4 Geometry of the Lippi model

5 The Lippi problem

5.1 *Rigid demand, in particular*

The Lippi model is made up of two parts: one deals with the notions of prices, profitability and candidates in the r-space, the other with those of quantities, requirements for use and techniques in the g-space. We are looking for an n-set which is simultaneously a candidate and a technique. Figure 11.4 is obtained by superimposing figure 11.2 (in the r-space, method i is represented by point $C_i(r)$) and figure 11.3 (in the g-space, method i is represented by point $C_i(g)$). As $g \leq r$, the only relationship between the r- and the g-spaces is inequality $c_i(r) \leq c_i(g)$, which does not matter since we are interested only in the relative positions of the points in each space separately.

The geometrical analysis (Bidard and Erreygers 1998a) identifies the candidates first (r-space). Free disposal being admitted, the family of candidates is $\{(0, 2), (2, 3), (3, 4), (4, 7)\}$. Then we move to the g-space and draw the counterpart of the frontier of candidates by connecting the $c_i(g)$ points in the same order 0–2–3–4–7. This typically results in a kind of 'folded frontier'. Since the dominant techniques (i, j) are candidates as well as techniques, the solutions of the Lippi problem are found by looking at the intersections of the folded frontier with (d). In figure 11.4 we see that the 2-sets (2, 3), (3, 4) and (4, 7) are the three dominant techniques. The existence result is known as Lippi's Theorem:

Theorem 3 (Lippi). Let $(A, l) \to B$ and $-1 < g \leq r$ be such that:
- (r-strict viability): $\exists\, y > 0 \quad y(B - (1 + r)A) \gg 0$;
- (indispensability of labour): $\{y > 0, y(B - (1 + g)A) \geq 0\} \Rightarrow yl > 0$;
- (free disposal): all goods can be freely disposed.

Then there exists at least one solution to system (L):

$$\begin{aligned} yB &= (1+g)yA + d \\ Bp &\leq (1+r)Ap + l \qquad [y] \\ y &> 0,\, p > 0. \end{aligned} \tag{L}$$

Flukes apart, any solution is square.

'Squareness' means that the number of commodities equals that of the operated methods. There are two ways to count the commodities and the operated methods: either all produced goods and all operated methods, including free disposal; or the non-overproduced goods and the operated production methods, excluding free disposal. The two counts are different but, flukes apart, the squareness property is independent of the procedure.

Lippi's result can be stated more precisely. Consider the folded frontier in figure 11.4 as a one-way road and build a lane on its right side, starting from the south. By following the frontier, the reader can see that the number of times that (d) cuts the road first, then the lane, exceeds by one the intersections of type 'lane then road'. The type, or 'colour', of a solution to (L) results from its relative orientation as a candidate and as a technique:

Theorem 4 (Colour Theorem). Let a square solution Y to system (L) be dubbed 'white' if $det(\ldots, c_i(r), \ldots)$ and $det(\ldots, c_i(g), \ldots)$, $i \in Y$, have the same sign, 'black' if they have opposite signs. Flukes apart, the number of white solutions exceeds that of black solutions by one.

Has the solution other properties? If $g < r$, inequality $c_i(r) < c_i(g)$ is the only connection between the r-space and the g-space, therefore the relative positions of the points $C_i(r)$, which determine the candidates in the r-space, and the points $C_i(g)$, which determine the techniques in the g-space, are independent. The paradoxes encountered in section 2 may occur: even if the dominant technique is unique, there is no reason why it should be wage-maximizing or why the real wage and the rate of profit should vary in the same direction. The reader is invited to build counter-examples by superimposing the g-space and the r-space. Figure 11.5 illustrates a Lippi problem for which the market algorithm does not

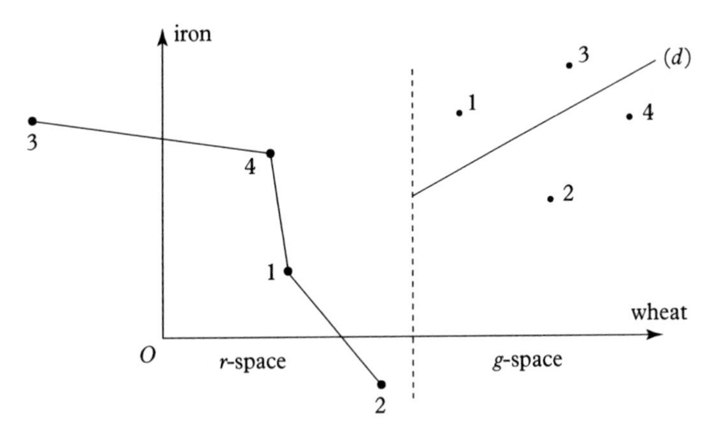

Figure 11.5 Non-convergence of the market algorithm

converge towards a dominant technique. In the g-space the odd methods are located above (d), the even methods below. Since a technique is a 2-set which generates direction (d) in the g-space, it is made of any pair (i, j) with i and j of different parities. The technique is dominant if, in the r-space, $[C_iC_j]$ is an edge of the convex hull of the $c_i(r)$s. The free disposal methods play no role and are ignored for simplicity. Let 1, 2, and 3 be the three initial methods; then (1, 2) is the dominant technique. A new method 4, which yields extra profits at prices p_{12}, is now introduced. The unique dominant technique becomes (3, 4). But no sequence of neighbouring techniques connects the old and the new solutions, with profit increasing at each step, because the algorithm is blocked by a 'bird' configuration (1, 2) → (1, 4) → (1, 2).

5.2 *The golden rule*

If all profits are accumulated and the workers do not save ($g = r$), the g-space and the r-space coincide and Figure 11.6 suffices. A unique dominant technique (2, 3) is obtained. It is defined by the intersection of the line $(d) = (\delta)$ and the frontier, and none of the paradoxes encountered above occurs. The only significant difference with single production is that, for a given $g = r$, the dominant technique depends on the wage basket δ. For a given rate g of accumulation, the consumption–maximization property of the technique selected at the rate of profit $r = g$ is called the 'golden rule' (Allais 1947; Desrousseaux 1961; Phelps 1961).

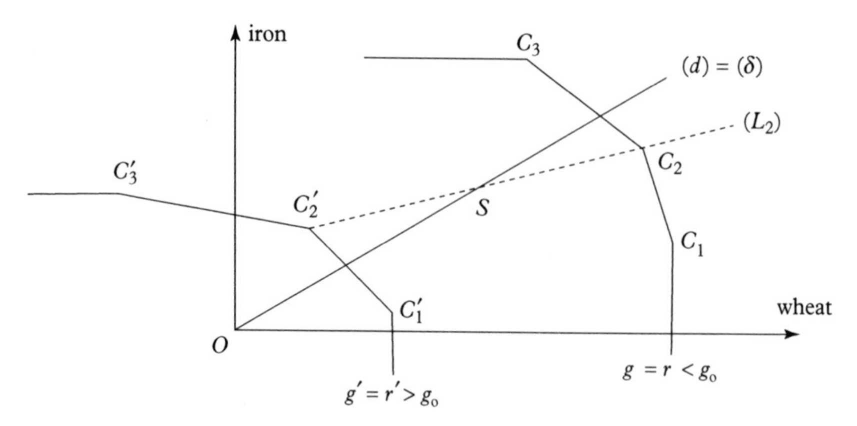

Figure 11.6 The golden space

Theorem 5 (golden rule). Let (A, l, B) be a joint production system satisfying the assumptions of Lippi's Theorem. Assume $g = r$. Then, for any demand vector (= wage basket), the dominant technique is wage-maximizing and consumption-maximizing. It is generically square, unique and obtained by means of the market algorithm. When $g = r$ increases, the real wage decreases continuously (the Ricardian trade-off).

The range of application of Theorem 5 (Schefold 1978a) can be extended beyond its initial framework: for a given rate of profit, assume that the n-sets satisfying the requirements for use (for the moment, we do not want to clarify what this more general constraint is) coincide with the n-sets able to produce a given r-net product δ. This amounts to saying that the techniques coincide with the Lippi techniques under a golden rule hypothesis. Then a dominant technique exists and is δ-maximizing (Salvadori 1982). The hypothesis that the economy mimics a golden rule is artificial but illustrates the more general notion of technique that will be defended in chapter 19.

6 Conclusion

The analysis of pure joint production systems presents many paradoxes. Some of them are partially or totally eliminated by introducing some more assumptions: for instance, free disposal eliminates the occurrence of negative prices. We have studied Lippi's problem and sketched a more general approach to the choice of techniques. The alternative explored in chapters 12–17 consists in studying specific joint production systems.

7 References

Sraffa's analysis of joint production exhibits a certain number of methodological features that will be examined in part III. The difficulty in respecting these principles is at the origin of Sraffa's errors in the treatment of joint production. Sraffa notices paradoxes (e.g. the real wage may increase with the rate of profit) but 'solves' them by transposing the results obtained for single-product systems. He arbitrarily assumes that negative prices do not appear. Filippini (1977) and Filippini and Filippini (1982) associate the occurrence of negative prices with the possibility of increasing the *r*-production per worker. There is no economic reason, however, to associate it with a notion of inefficiency (Duménil and Lévy 1984; Hosoda 1993; Lévy 1984): in the absence of free disposal, to produce less (e.g. less nuclear waste) is not being inefficient. Steedman (1975), the master of the counter-example – and an independent mind – has shown that positive profits may coexist with negative surplus values (because labour values may be negative, even for *g*-all-engaging systems), a result which undermines the Marxist explanation of the origin of profits.

Schefold's thesis (1971) is the starting point of the positive studies on joint production. The golden rule case was first examined by Steedman (1976), who established the squareness property. As for the existence result and its properties, Schefold (1978a) starts from a linear programming problem, in which the apparent objective is to minimize the wage ('not really in the spirit of Sraffa'!). He dubs it a 'von Neumann program', because of linear inequalities written in the wrong sense from a Sraffian point of view (a rate of interest is not a rate of profit). The positive counterpart is that he is pushed to clarify his interpretation of the classical approach in a stimulating methodological paper (1980). As the reader guesses, the road is sinuous from wage minimization to the golden rule properties. Salvadori (1982) solves the same problem directly, but fails to recognize its connection with Schefold's result.

Lippi's model (1979) can be thought of as a special case of Morishima's model, which distinguishes the capitalists' and workers' demands. Following Lippi, Schefold (1988) abandons the unrealistic golden rule assumption. Even if the existence of some difficulties is recognized, his conclusions are much too optimistic. For instance, uniqueness is restored because, by convention, Schefold selects the wage-maximizing technique *within* the subset of solutions. His opinion that 'the laws of value and distribution derived by Sraffa for single-product systems hold for joint production as well' is untenable: numerical examples of paradoxes within that framework are easily built by using the independence of the *g*-space and the *r*-space (Bidard 1997b) and more dramatic aspects will be developed in chapter 22. The distinction between white and black equilibria was introduced by Erreygers (1990, 1995a). The colour theorem is owed to Bidard and Erreygers (1998a) with an interpretation of the colour in terms of local dynamics. The formal conclusion is close to some general equilibrium results (Debreu 1970; Dierker 1972) and linear complementarity results: Lippi's model is indeed a linear complementarity problem (LCP) (Salvadori 1986) and the LCP literature reports some conclusions on oddity (Quint and Shubik 1997). Curiously enough, no orientation on the solutions seems to have been introduced in the LCPs (Cottle, Pang and Stone 1992). The colour theorem can be read as a contribution to this field.

8 Proof

The Lippi Theorem and the Colour Theorem can be proved by means of the geometrical arguments sketched in the chapter (Bidard and Erreygers 1998a). An alternative combinatorial proof is given in the Mathematical appendix, section 4. The following approach, based on a generalized Gale–Nikaido–Debreu (GND) lemma, will be used repetitively for existence problems:

Generalized GND Lemma. Let K be a convex compact set in R^n and z: $p \in K \rightarrow z(p)$ an upper-hemi-continuous correspondence with compact convex values into a bounded set $L \subset R^n$. If z satisfies the Walras inequality

$$\forall p \in K \quad \forall z \in z(p) \quad zp \leq 0 \tag{W}$$

then

$$\exists p^* \in K \quad \exists z^* \in z(p^*) \quad \forall p \in K \quad z^* p \leq 0.$$

The standard GND lemma is obtained when K is the unit simplex S and, then, the conclusion is written $z^* \leq 0$. When the standard lemma does not apply, the same result can be obtained by means of the following strategy of proof, which is often efficient for existence results concerning systems of inequations with complementarity relationships: (*i*) if necessary, set restrictions on the data (example: positive input and output matrices, positive labour vector), (*ii*) introduce a Walras equality by force, (*iii*) apply the generalized GND lemma to a subset S_ε of the unit simplex (avoid the boundary) and thus find a point $(p_\varepsilon^*, z_\varepsilon^*)$, (*iv*) show that this point remains in a compact set when S_ε comes close to S, (*v*) show that a cluster point of the $(p_\varepsilon^*, z_\varepsilon^*)$s is a solution to the problem, finally (*vi*) use a continuity argument to withdraw the temporary restrictions. The strategy is illustrated by the proof of a generalized Lippi Theorem that is useful in rent theory (chapter 17, section 4, Theorem 3). We introduce a subset (which is void in the standard Lippi Theorem) of goods labelled 1. In the economic interpretation these goods are endowments, whose net production is negative.

Theorem 6 (Generalized Lippi Theorem). Let $A = (A_0, A_1)$ and $B = (B_0, B_1)$ be two $m \times (n_0 + n_1)$ matrices, A being non-negative, l a $m \times 1$ semi-positive vector, $d = (d_0, d_1)$ a $1 \times (n_0 + n_1)$ vector with $d_0 > 0$ and $d_1 \ll 0$, $0 \leq g \leq r$ non-negative scalars. Assume that:

$$(A_1) \exists \bar{y} > 0 \;\; \bar{y}(B_0 - (1+r)A_0) \gg d_0 \quad \text{and} \quad \bar{y}(B_1 - (1+r)A_1) \geq d_1,$$
$$(A_2) \{y > 0, y(B_0 - (1+g)A_0) \geq 0\} \Rightarrow yl > 0.$$

Then there exists a solution $(y > 0, p_0 > 0, p_1 \geq 0)$ to the system (L'):

$$\begin{cases} (B - (1+r)A)p \leq l & [y] \\ y(B - (1+g)A) \geq d & [p]. \end{cases} \qquad (L')$$

Proof. For ε small, let S_ε be the subset of the unit simplex of R_+^{m+n+1} made of points (y, p, w) such that $w \geq \varepsilon$. The function z from S_ε to R^{m+n+1} defined as

$$z(y, p, w) = [Bp - (1+r)Ap - wl, -y(B - (1+g)A + wd,$$
$$yl - dp + w^{-1}(r - g)yAp]$$

satisfies the Walras identity. According to the generalized GND lemma:

$$\forall \varepsilon \;\; \exists (y_\varepsilon, p_\varepsilon, w_\varepsilon) \in S_\varepsilon \;\; \forall (y, p, w) \in S_\varepsilon$$
$$y[Bp_\varepsilon - (1+r)Ap_\varepsilon - w_\varepsilon l] + [-y_\varepsilon(B - (1+g)A) + w_\varepsilon d]p$$
$$+ w[y_\varepsilon l - dp_\varepsilon] + ww_\varepsilon^{-1}(r - g)y_\varepsilon Ap_\varepsilon \leq 0. \qquad (3)$$

Let us call (3′) the new inequality obtained when the last (non-negative) term on the left-hand side of (3) is dropped. When ε tends to zero, there exists a cluster point $(y^*, p^*, w^*) \in S$ which satisfies the same inequality (3′) for any $(y, p, w) \in S$. Therefore:

$$Bp^* - (1+r)Ap^* - w^*l \leq 0$$
$$-y^*(B - (1+g)A) + w^*d \leq 0$$
$$y^*l - dp^* \leq 0.$$

These inequalities and assumptions (A_1) and (A_2) exclude $y^* = 0$, $w^* = 0$ or $p^* = 0$. Therefore, $w^{*-1}(y^*, p^*)$ is a solution to (L').

12 Engaging systems

1 A desirable property

We consider a square system and a feasible growth rate g. The adjustment property means that the activity levels can be adapted to any given final demand d ($d > 0$). In single production, the property holds because the Leontief inverse $(I - (1 + g)A)^{-1}$ is semi-positive and even positive for basic economies. This is not the case in general joint production. However, the activity levels solution to the adjustment equation $yB = (1 + g)yA + d$:

$$y = d(B - (1 + g)A)^{-1} \tag{1}$$

are economically acceptable if the generalized Leontief inverse $L = L(g) = (B - (1 + g)A)^{-1}$ is semi-positive. Such a system (A, B) is called *g-semi-engaging*. For the sake of simplicity, we first assume the positivity of the Leontief inverse: (A, B) is then called *g-all-engaging*. Similarly, the prices of production solution to $Bp = (1 + r)Ap + wl$:

$$p = w(B - (1 + r)A)^{-1}l \tag{2}$$

are positive if (A, B) is r-all-engaging. An all-engaging system (i.e. which is x-all-engaging for some x) retains many economic properties of basic single-product economies. We propose an exhaustive study of these properties. It will be shown that an all-engaging system is well behaved when the rates of growth and profit belong to some interval, and that there exist unique and positive left and right eigenvectors associated with some critical eigenvalue $\Lambda = (1 + R)^{-1}$. These results generalize the *PF* properties (section 2). More precisely, the domain of regularity is an interval $]r_0, R[$. The existence of a lower bound r_0 leads to complications which did not appear for single-product systems (section 3). A geometrical interpretation is given in section 4. The indecomposability hypothesis is dropped in sections 5 and 6. Beyond their technical aspects, the notions introduced in this chapter aim at simplifying economic reasoning, as will be exemplified later by the treatment of sectors and fixed capital.

2 Notion of an all-engaging system

Definition 1. Let A and B be square semi-positive matrices, B with at least one non-zero row or column. For $g > -1$, system (A, B) is *g-all-engaging* if properties (3) and (4) hold:

$$\exists y_0 > 0 \quad y_0(B - (1+g)A) > 0 \tag{3}$$

$$\{y > 0, \quad y(B - (1+g)A) > 0\} \Rightarrow y \gg 0. \tag{4}$$

Relationship (3) means that *some* semi-positive surplus is obtained, i.e. the system is g-viable. Relationship (4) means that any surplus requires that *all* processes are operated: this is why the system is called g-all-engaging. Definition 1 is convenient for economic reasoning. For instance, let (A, B) be both g_1 and g_2-all-engaging. For $g_1 < g < g_2$, the system is g-viable (because this is still the case at the higher level g_2) and production requires that all processes are operated (because this is already the case at the lower level g_1). Therefore, conditions (3) and (4) remain satisfied for any g between g_1 and g_2: the property is satisfied in an interval. This conclusion would not have been so clear if the initial characterization had been the positivity of the generalized Leontief inverse matrix:

Theorem 1. System (A, B) is g-all-engaging if and only if matrix $B - (1 + g)A$ admits a positive inverse:

$$L(g) = (B - (1+g)A)^{-1} \gg 0. \tag{5}$$

Then the system is g-all-engaging in an interval $S' =]g_{\min} = g_0, g_{\max} = G[$.

When, starting from level g, the rate of growth increases, the activity levels $y(g) = d(B - (1+g)A)^{-1}$ also increase. This means that the physical g-net product per worker decreases. Similarly, an r-all-engaging system admits positive prices at the rate of profit r and the Ricardian trade-off property holds. Many other properties are likewise extended from basic single-product systems to all-engaging systems. For instance, in single production, the upper bound G of the rates of growth is associated with unique and positive row and column eigenvectors. Theorems 2 and 3 characterize all-engaging systems as those having similar properties.

Theorem 2. (A, B) is all-engaging (i.e. g-all engaging for some g) if and only if there exist unique (up to a factor) and positive activity levels q sustaining a uniform rate of growth G, with no surplus at this level:

$$\exists! q \gg 0 \quad qB = (1+G)qA \tag{6}$$
$$\nexists y > 0 \quad y(B - (1+G)A) > 0. \tag{7}$$

Vector q, which represents the activity levels sustaining maximum growth (von Neumann activity levels), can also be viewed as a standard commodity in Sraffa's sense. A positive standard basket does not always exist in joint production, but all-engaging systems are not general joint production. An all-engaging system can alternatively be characterized by the existence and properties of a positive price vector π at the rate $R = G$, which is associated with a zero wage. In Theorem 3, the characterization relies on a joint study of activity levels and prices:

Theorem 3. (A, B) is all-engaging if and only if there exist unique (up to a factor) and positive activity levels q sustaining a uniform rate of growth G, and a positive price vector π such that all processes yield a uniform rate of profit R for a zero wage:

$$\exists! q \gg 0 \quad qB = (1+G)qA \tag{8}$$
$$\exists \pi \gg 0 \quad B\pi = (1+R)A\pi. \tag{9}$$

Relations (8) and (9) imply that $G = R$ and that the vector π is unique up to a factor. The remarkable feature of Theorem 3 is that it ensures all-engagingness on the sole basis of the spectral properties of (A, B).

These properties generalize those of basic single-product systems $(A, B = I)$. (In all generality, single production means that matrix B has exactly one positive element in every row and column: a reordering of the processes and/or the commodities and a change in the physical units of measure then permit us to come back to $B = I$.) A more formal point of view is adopted in table 12.1. The tableau is mainly concerned with the values of λ for which the inverse $M(\lambda)$ of $\lambda B - A$ is positive. A value λ such that $det(\lambda B - A) = 0$ is called a generalized eigenvalue of (A, B) or, simply, an eigenvalue. 'Uniqueness' and the mathematical symbol '$\exists!$' mean uniqueness up to a factor. In Property 7 'basic single production' means that the matrix B has exactly one positive element in every row and every column and that the matrix $\alpha B + A$ is semi-positive and indecomposable for α great enough (similarly for Property 7′ in table 12.2, p. 117, except for indecomposability).

Note that table 12.1, and therefore Theorems 1, 2 and 3 which derive from it, does not assume the semi-positivity of A nor that of λ. If A is not

Table 12.1 g-*all-engaging systems*

Assumption: $\forall i \;\; B_i > 0 \quad \mathit{or} \quad \forall j \;\; B^j > 0$
$S := \{\lambda;\, (\lambda B - A)^{-1} \gg 0\}$

1. $\lambda \in S \Leftrightarrow \begin{cases} \exists y_0 > 0 \quad y_0(\lambda B - A) > 0 \\ \{(y > 0,\, y(\lambda B - A) > 0\} \Rightarrow y \gg 0 \end{cases}$

S may be void, but $S \neq \emptyset$ is equivalent to 2 or 3:

2. $\exists \Lambda \; \exists!\, q \gg 0 \quad qA = \Lambda qB$
   $\nexists\, y > 0 \quad y(\Lambda B - A) > 0$
3. $\exists \Lambda \; \exists!\, q \gg 0 \quad qA = \Lambda qB$
   $\exists \pi \gg 0 \quad A\pi = \Lambda B\pi.$

Then properties 4–8 hold:

4. $S =]\Lambda, \lambda_0[$, Λ generalized eigenvalue of (A, B).
5. $q = \lim_{\lambda \to \Lambda^+} d(\lambda B - A)^{-1}/\|d(\lambda B - A)^{-1}\| \gg 0$ (any $d > 0$) is the unique row eigenvector attached to Λ.
6. Λ is a simple root of $\mathit{det}(\lambda B - A)$.
7. $\lambda_0 = (1 + r_0)^{-1}$ is finite except for 'basic single production'.
8. For any generalized eigenvalue λ_h of (A, B) $|\lambda_0 - \lambda_h| \geq \lambda_0 - \Lambda$ (circle rule).

semi-positive and $B = I$, these properties constitute a first extension of the *PF* properties. In input–output analysis, negative elements are sometimes introduced because the price vector (2) is also written $p = (1 + r)B^{-1}Ap + wB^{-1}l$: this equation resembles a price of production equality in which the surrogate input matrix $B^{-1}A$ is not necessarily semi-positive. For the economic interpretation of the properties, we will continue to refer to the generalized Leontief inverse matrix, with $1 + r = \lambda^{-1}$ or $1 + g = \lambda^{-1}$.

Other extensions are possible. The following two generalizations are useful for the theory of fixed capital. When fixed capital is taken into account, the operation called 'vertical integration' leads to the formal elimination of machines and all happens as if final goods were produced by means of final goods. But the growth rate matters for integration, so that the integrated matrices depend on g. Theorem 4 transfers the g-all-engagingness property from a given pair (A_{g_0}, B_{g_0}) and an initial level g_0 to another pair (A_g, B_g) and a higher level g.

Theorem 4. Let a family (A_g, B_g) of square matrices depend continuously on a real parameter g varying in interval $I = [g_0, \bar{g}]$ $(g_0 < \bar{g})$. Assume that:

(*i*) (A_{g_0}, B_{g_0}) is g_0-all-engaging,
(*ii*) $\forall g \in I \quad \{y > 0,\, y(B_g - (1 + g)A_g) \geq 0\} \Rightarrow y \gg 0,$
(*iii*) $\forall g \in I \quad \exists p' > 0 \quad (B_g - (1 + g)A_g)\, p' > 0.$

Then (A_g, B_g) is g-all-engaging for any $g \in I$.

Vertical integration can also be performed on the price side. Then the integrated matrices depend on the rate of profit. In order to establish that the prices of the final goods have the same properties as in single production, the tool is a generalization of Theorem 3:

Theorem 5. Let $C(r)$ be an $n \times n$ real matrix which depends on a real parameter r, such that $c_{ij} = c_{ij}(r)$ admits continuous derivatives up to order $k+1$ ($k \geq 1$). Let R be a root of order k of $detC(r) = 0$, associated with a unique (up to a factor) and positive row vector q such that $qC(R) = 0$ and a unique and positive column vector π such that $C(R)\pi = 0$. Then matrix $C(r)^{-1}$ has a constant sign on each half-neighbourhood of R.

3 Bounds to regularity

We return to the examination of an all-engaging system (A, B) and look at the properties of basic single-product economies that cannot be extended. For instance, we know that the *PF* eigenvalue of a semi-positive matrix is the maximum real eigenvalue. The property does not hold for all-engaging systems in general. Consider indeed an 'inverted-single-product system' $I \rightarrow A$, with A indecomposable: the pair (I, A) is all-engaging by Theorem 3 but, owing to the inversion, the maximum rate of profit is now the *last* root. There is no general rule for locating the critical eigenvalue of an arbitrary all-engaging system.

However, the main difference between all-engaging and single-product systems stems from the existence of a lower bound r_0 of S'. Let us start from a value for which the Leontief inverse matrix $L(r) = (B - (1+r)A)^{-1}$ is positive. When the rate of profit decreases progressively, the matrix $L(r)$ decreases, remains positive for a while but, finally, a certain coefficient $L_{ij}(r)$ vanishes at $r = r_0$, then becomes negative. The phenomenon is not visible in single production because it occurs at $r_0 = -1$. For *all* multiple-product systems, on the contrary, matrix $L(r)$ has strictly negative elements at $r = -1$ (because B and B^{-1} cannot be simultaneously semi-positive), therefore the lower bound r_0 is strictly greater than -1. The system has a good economic behaviour on the range $[r_0, R]$ but nothing is ensured for values smaller than r_0.

If r_0 is negative, no property is lost on the set $[0, R]$ of economically significant rates. If r_0 is positive, the economic behaviour on $[0, r_0]$ cannot be predicted. We would therefore like to have some *a priori* information on the value of r_0, and a simple criterion providing an upper bound of r_0 would be useful: it could be an inequality $r_0 < r(\lambda_1, \ldots, \lambda_n)$, where $r(.)$ is a simple expression of the eigenvalues λ_i of (A, B). The criterion exists . . . but the inequality is reversed and provides a lower bound. Its exact formulation is given by the circle rule: the disk with centre $\lambda_0 = (1 + r_0)^{-1}$ going through Λ contains no other eigenvalue of (A, B). This rule echoes the maximality property of the *PF* eigenvalue.

Similar implications are drawn if we look at the rates of growth instead of the rates of profit. The adjustment property means that the system adapts itself to any demand. The study invites us to introduce a distinction, which was superfluous in single production, between final and intermediate demand: a g-all-engaging system can adapt itself to any variation of final demand (because the Leontief inverse is positive) but a decrease in the rate of growth leads to the potential loss of the property. It is not a coincidence that Stiglitz (1970) discovered a similar asymmetry between final demand and intermediate demand for fixed-capital systems.

4 Geometrical interpretation

Most algebraic properties can be visualized by means of a geometrical representation. In figure 12.1, with $n = 2$ goods and a given rate of growth g, two processes are represented in the g-space by the points $C_1(g)$ and $C_2(g)$, with $C_i(g) = (b_i - (1 + g)a_i)/l_i$ $(i = 1, 2)$. When one unit of total labour is shared between the two methods, the corresponding g-net output is a positive barycentre of $C_1(g) = C_1$ and $C_2(g) = C_2$, i.e. it is a point of the segment C_1C_2. The two conditions stated in Definition 1 mean that the segment C_1C_2 cuts the positive orthant and that neither C_1 nor C_2 belongs to this orthant. These properties imply that C_1C_2 cuts the whole orthant (Theorem 1). Let us now increase the rate of growth. The representative points $C_1(g)$ and $C_2(g)$ slide down along the straight lines (D_1) and (D_2). The all-engagingness property is preserved for some time. The angle (OC_1, OC_2) is more and more open and the limit value G is reached when the angle is flat. The origin O then belongs to segment $[C_1(G)\ C_2(G)]$: we have $0 = q_1c_1(G) + q_2c_2(G)$, where $q = (q_1, q_2) \gg 0$ are the standard proportions. Let us repeat the experiment the other way round: we start from a high level of the rate of growth and let it decrease. The system ceases to be g-all-engaging at the level g_0 when either $C_1(g_0)$ or $C_2(g_0)$ belongs to an axis. Consider now the price space. For any rate of profit r, the price vector in terms of wage is orthogonal to $C_1(r)C_2(r)$. At the level $R = G$, the eigenvector π referred to in (9) is orthogonal to the straight line $C_1(G)C_2(G)$.

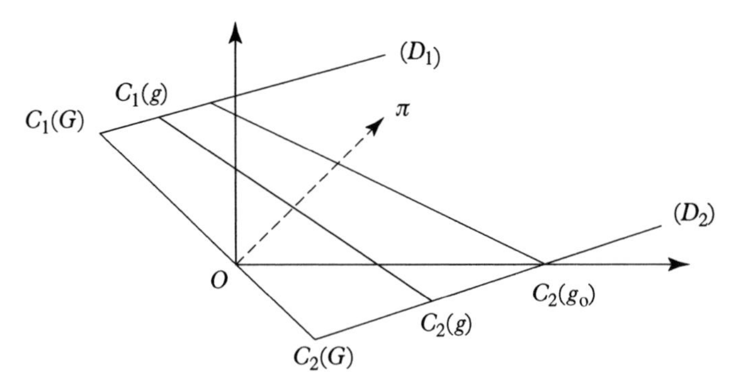

Figure 12.1 An all-engaging system

5 Semi-engaging systems

The difference between semi-engaging and all-engaging systems is the same as between decomposable and indecomposable semi-positive matrices.

Definition 2. For $g > -1$, (A, B) is *g-semi-engaging* if properties (10) and (11) hold:

$$\exists y_0 > 0 \quad y_0(B - (1+g)A) \gg 0 \tag{10}$$

$$\{y > 0, y(B - (1+g)A) \gg 0\} \Rightarrow y \gg 0. \tag{11}$$

These properties are equivalent to the existence and semi-positivity of matrix $L(g) = (B - (1+g)A)^{-1}$.

Definition 3. System (A, B) is physically decomposable if, after adequate permutations on their rows and columns, matrices A and B are written

$$A = \begin{bmatrix} A_{11} & 0 \\ A_{21} & A_{22} \end{bmatrix} \quad B = \begin{bmatrix} B_{11} & 0 \\ B_{21} & B_{22} \end{bmatrix} \tag{12}$$

where A_{ii} and B_{ii} are square matrices.

A physicaily decomposable system may be semi-engaging but cannot be all-engaging because of the presence of zeros in the Leontief inverse. The property generalizes the notion of decomposability encountered in single production, with two differences: first, in square single production, there exists a one-to-one correspondence between a process and the commodity it produces; therefore, when the commodities and processes

Table 12.2 g-*semi-engaging systems*

Assumption: $\forall i \quad B_i > 0 \quad or \quad \forall j \quad B^j > 0$ $T := \{\lambda; (\lambda B - A)^{-1} > 0\}$
1'. $\lambda \in T \Leftrightarrow \begin{cases} \exists y_0 > 0 \quad y_0(\lambda B - A) \gg 0 \\ \{y > 0, y(\lambda B - A) \gg 0\} \Rightarrow y \gg 0. \end{cases}$
If T is not void, then properties 2', 3', 7' and 8' hold:
2'. $\exists \Lambda \; \exists q > 0 \quad qA = \Lambda qB.$ $\exists y > 0 \quad y(\Lambda B - A) \gg 0.$
3'. $\exists \pi > 0 \quad A\pi = \Lambda B\pi.$
7'. $T =]\Lambda, \lambda_0]$, λ_0 finite except for 'single production'.
8'. Circle rule.

are renumbered in order to obtain the above canonical form, the same reordering applies to both sets. In joint production, the one-to-one link disappears and the permutations of rows and columns are independent. Second, a physically decomposable system may not be semi-engaging: Even in the most favourable case when (A_{11}, B_{11}) and (A_{22}, B_{22}) are both all-engaging, the partial Leontief inverse matrices may be positive on disjoint sets.

The mathematical properties of semi-engaging systems are given in table 12.2. Some are quite similar to those of all-engaging systems (existence of semi-positive eigenvectors) while others are poorer. In particular, the existence of semi-positive eigenvectors does not guarantee the semi-engagingness property.

Are all semi-engaging systems decomposable? The only exception occurs when (A, B) is all-engaging and the rate of growth coincides with the lower bound g_0:

Theorem 6. Let A and B be semi-positive with $(B - (1 + g)A)^{-1}$ semi-positive. Then (A, B) is either physically decomposable or r-all-engaging for r slightly greater than g.

6 Reducibilities versus decomposability

A distinction between basic and non-basic systems has been introduced in single production. In a non-basic economy there exists a square sub-economy which can work autonomously. This notion of physical decomposability has been generalized to multiple-product systems. Sraffa introduced a different concept: an agricultural economy is Sraffa-reducible though it is physically indecomposable. This shows that, in joint production, there is no all-encompassing definition of reducibility. Sraffa's proposal itself is only one of many alternatives, all of which are of interest to economists. Their common background is that, following some perturbation in some part of an 'X-reducible' economy, the ultimate influence of the modification remains local. The appropriate notion of X-reducibility depends upon the nature of the alteration.

This section opposes the concept of physical decomposability to all other notions of reducibility, this being reflected in the fact that the word 'decomposability' is now reserved to its physical meaning. Four notions of X-reducibility are examined. For a proposal to be acceptable, it must coincide with the standard notion when the multiple-product economy is reduced to single production. Our list of X-reducibilities is not, and cannot be, exhaustive. The risk is that of constituting an ill-assorted collection of definitions. In order to maintain a synthetic point of view, we shall prove Theorem 10 which applies to all notions we retain and, hopefully, to all potential definitions.

Definition 4 (Sraffa 1960). (A, B) is S-reducible (i.e. reducible in Sraffa's sense) if there exists a proper subset $\mathcal{J}$ of columns of A and B whose joint rank is at most equal to $card(\mathcal{J})$.

Theorem 7 (Manara 1968). (A, B) is S-reducible if and only if it is written $A = MA_1$, $B = MB_1$ where the system (A_1, B_1) is physically decomposable, matrix M being invertible.

As a consequence, (A, B) is S-reducible if and only if the matrices $B^{-1}A$, $A^{-1}B$, $(B - A)^{-1}A$, etc. are decomposable, provided that the inverse matrix exists. Let us examine the effect of a taxation on the S-non-basics. The price vector associated with the system $(A = MA_1, l, B = MB_l)$ is identical to the one associated with $(A_1, M^{-1}l, B_1)$ which is physically decomposable. Therefore, a taxation of the last goods has no incidence on the prices of the other commodities. Sraffa was mainly interested in the treatment of land. Consider an acre of land of a given grade. For an industrial process the input and output coefficients relative to land are zero; for an agricultural process, the quantity of 'produced' land is equal to the quantity 'used'. The corresponding columns of A and B being identical, their joint rank is equal to one and the system is S-reducible. Ricardo's statement that 'taxes on land fall wholly on landlords' is then justified.

The S-reducibility property is not preserved by a transposition of matrices. A dual notion is:

Definition 5. (Abraham-Frois and Berrebi 1980) (A, B) is AB-reducible if there exists a proper subset I of rows of A and B whose joint rank is at most equal to $card(I)$.

A system is AB-reducible if and only if A and B are written $A = A_1M$, $B = B_1M$ with (A_1, B_1) decomposable, or if AB^{-1}, etc., is decomposable. At a given growth rate, a change in the activity levels of the I processes modifies the surplus without requiring a change in the $\overline{I}$ processes. The payment of a tribute (chapter 5, section 5) affects only a part of the economy.

Another important concept for landowners is that of Bidard–Woods reducibility. Assume that the grade of land is modified by some intensive cultivation method, as represented by the data

$$A = \begin{bmatrix} + & 1 & 0 \\ + & 0 & 1 \\ + & 1 & 0 \end{bmatrix}, l \rightarrow B = \begin{bmatrix} + & 0 & 1 \\ + & 1 & 0 \\ + & 1 & 0 \end{bmatrix}.$$

The first column refers to corn, and the last two columns to grade-one and grade-two lands, respectively. The first method of cultivation modifies the soil, a grade-one land being transformed into a grade-two land. The second method restores the original quality, the third preserves the grade-one land. The total area of lands is preserved by any cultivation process, which is the meaning of equality $Au = Bu$ where $\tilde{u} = (0, 1, 1)$. Though system (A, B) is not S-reducible, Ricardo's proposition on the incidence of a tax still holds:

Definition 6 (Bidard and Woods 1989). System (A, B) is BW-reducible if it admits a semi-positive but non-positive generalized eigenvector:

$$\exists p_0 > 0, \ p_0 \not\gg 0 \quad Ap_0 = \tau \, Bp_0.$$

Theorem 8. If a tax p_0 is levied on commodities, the prices of commodities corresponding to the zero components of p_0 are unchanged.

A comparison of the pre- and post-tax prices shows that the post-tax prices fall by $p_0/((1 + r)\tau - 1)$. Therefore, the prices of the BW-basic goods (those corresponding to the zero components of p_0) are unchanged. For agricultural processes, lands are BW-non-basic with $\tau = 1$, therefore their prices decrease by the present value p_0/r of the perpetual tax.

Finally, and following Flaschel (1982), good i is said to enter directly into the production of good j if there exists some method k for which i is an input ($a_{ki} > 0$) and j an output ($b_{kj} > 0$). Then the sum $\sum_k a_{ki} b_{kj}$, in which we recognize the element (i, j) of matrix $\tilde{A}B$, is positive. Commodity

i can also enter indirectly into commodity j: for instance, the inputs which enter into the construction of a tractor enter indirectly into that of wheat. The condition that any commodity enters directly or indirectly into any commodity is that matrix $\widetilde{A}$B is indecomposable in the sense of single-product sytems:

Definition 7 (Flaschel 1982). (A, B) is F-reducible if matrix $\widetilde{A}B$ is decomposable.

Theorem 9. (A, B) is F-reducible if and only if $A_{I\bar{J}} = 0$ and $B_{\bar{I}\bar{J}} = 0$ for some proper subsets I and J.

For the activity levels $y = (y_I, y_{\bar{I}})$, the relationship $(y_{\bar{I}}A_{\bar{I}J}, yA_{\bullet\bar{J}}) \rightarrow (yB_{\bullet J}, y_I B_{I\bar{J}})$ shows that a change in the gross product $y_I B_{I\bar{J}}$ of goods $\bar{J}$ requires no change in the activity levels of the processes of type $\bar{I}$. The notion of F-irreducibility is useful for the study of pure fixed-capital systems.

We have distinguished four notions of reducibility, which all coincide with the usual concept if the economy is of the single-product type. In single production, a reducible system is semi-engaging, and this implies that many economic laws (positive prices, adjustment to demand, Ricardian trade-off) still hold. Can a reducible multiple-product system also be semi-engaging? The answer is negative, except for physically decomposable systems. The intuition is given by Theorem 6: if a multiple-product system were semi-engaging but physically indecomposable, it would be all-engaging; however, all-engagingness is too demanding for a X-reducible system which, therefore, cannot be semi-engaging either.

Theorem 10. No X-reducible ($X = S$, AB, BW or F) multiple-product system is semi-engaging, except perhaps a physically decomposable system.

Since the inverse matrix of a reducible system has some negative entries, the price vector $p(r) = w(B - (1 + r)A)^{-1}l$ may well have negative components. Even if it is positive, the wage and the rate of profit may vary in the same direction. Similar conclusions hold for the level of consumption and the rate of growth. Important economic properties are lost.

7 Conclusion

It is our hope that the properties listed in this chapter are exhaustive enough to cover every interesting aspect of the notion of an engaging system and leave economists with a useful tool box, with the technical work being done once and for all. The initial barrier in using the concept consists in modifying thought habits. In single production, a productive system is obtained by selecting one process for corn, one for iron, etc.: The flowers are picked up one after the other, making the approach analytical. The notion of an all-engaging system requires a change of standpoint. The system is considered as a bunch of methods and the questions addressed are: Is the system viable? Are all processes indispensable? The point of view becomes synthetic or global. Once mastered, the concept allows the use of natural language as a support for economic reasoning. An experiment on the theory of fixed capital, directly conceived in such terms, shows that more attention can then be devoted to the core of the problem. The fruitful concept of an all-engaging system is therefore expected to become increasingly popular among economists.

Another part of the study concerns the notion of reducibility. It has been shown that there is no all-encompassing concept. Several concepts are formally acceptable and economically relevant, but the consequences of reducibility(ies) are more dramatic than in single production, as the usual economic laws cannot hold.

8 References

The notion of an all-engaging system has been introduced by Schefold (1971), who showed that a 0-all-engaging system has a good economic behaviour on an interval $]0, R[$ and admits unique and positive left and right eigenvectors associated with eigenvalue $\Lambda = (1 + R)^{-1}$. Similarly for an r_0-all-engaging system on $]r_0, R[$. In his version of the converse statement (Theorem 3 above), Schefold (1978c; see Schefold 1989a, for the final state of the study) assumes only the semi-positivity of the eigenvectors and the irreducibility of the system in Sraffa's sense. The assumptions are not sufficient: it is easy to build a Sraffa-irreducible system with semi-positive but non-positive eigenvectors, so that the system is not all-engaging. The concept was independently rediscovered by Bidard (1978), the paper being finally published in 1996, alongside the properties stated in tables 12.1 and 12.2. We do not follow exactly Schefold's terminology: 'semi-engaging' has been substituted for 'all-productive'. A more significant departure is that Schefold uses 'all-engaging' to mean '0-all-engaging'. It seems preferable to use 'all-engaging' in the sense of 'g-all-engaging for some g' for two reasons: first, there is no reason to privilege values $g = 0$ or $r = 0$; second, Theorem 3 is crucial. Several mathematical extensions have been obtained (Bidard 1984d, for the notion of imprimitivity, Bidard and Zerner 1991, for Banach spaces).

9 Proofs

Let us prove the properties stated in table 12.1. The procedure goes from the general to the particular and the *PF* properties (chapter 4) are obtained here as a specification of table 12.1. The semi-positivity of A is not assumed, except when otherwise specified.

Proof of Property 1. If $\lambda \in S$, the two relationships

$$\exists y_0 > 0 \quad y_0(\lambda B - A) > 0 \tag{13}$$

$$\{y > 0, \quad y(\lambda B - A) > 0\} \Rightarrow y \gg 0 \tag{14}$$

are immediate. Conversely, let us admit (13) and (14). Let y be such that $y(\lambda B - A) \geq 0$. According to (14), any semi-positive vector on the half-line $y_0 + \alpha y$ (any non-negative scalar α) is in fact positive. Therefore y has no negative component:

$$y(\lambda B - A) \geq 0 \Rightarrow y \geq 0. \tag{15}$$

In particular $y(\lambda B - A) = 0$ implies that y and $-y$ are both non-negative, therefore $y = 0$ and matrix $\lambda B - A$ is bijective. Any semi-positive row vector z is then written $z = y(\lambda B - A)$ for some non-zero y. According to (15), y is semi-positive and, according to (14), it is in fact positive. Therefore, implication $\{z > 0 \Rightarrow z(\lambda B - A)^{-1} = y \gg 0\}$ holds, which shows that $(\lambda B - A)^{-1}$ is positive. ■

Note that (13) and (14) are equivalent to (13) and (16):

$$\{y > 0, y(\lambda B - A) \geq 0\} \Rightarrow y \gg 0. \tag{16}$$

(*Proof*: (16) implies (14); conversely, (13) and (14) imply $(\lambda B - A)^{-1} \gg 0$, hence (16)).

Proof of Property 4. Let (A, B) be λ_1-all-engaging and λ_2-all-engaging, with $\lambda_1 < \lambda_2$. Since any $\lambda > \lambda_1$ satisfies (13) and any $\lambda < \lambda_2$ satisfies (14), properties (13) and (14) hold for any λ between λ_1 and λ_2. Therefore S is an interval, which is open according to the characterization $(\lambda B - A)^{-1} \gg 0$. Let $S =]\Lambda, \lambda_0[$. Can we have $\Lambda = -\infty$? Assume that B has at least one positive element in every row (transpose otherwise). There exists $\alpha > 0$ such that the maximum component of $y_0 B$ is greater than $\alpha \|y_0\|$ for any $y_0 > 0$, therefore (13) cannot be satisfied when λ tends towards $-\infty$. Therefore, the set S is bounded from below. If $(\Lambda B - A)^{-1}$ existed, we would have $(\Lambda B - A)^{-1} = lim\ (\lambda B - A)^{-1}$ and, since matrix $(\lambda B - A)^{-1}$

is a decreasing function of λ for $\lambda \in S$, inequality $(\Lambda B - A)^{-1} \geq (\lambda B - A)^{-1} \gg 0$ would imply that Λ belongs to S. This is not the case because S is open, therefore the lower bound Λ is an eigenvalue of (A, B). ■

Proof of Property 5. Assume that there exists some $y \geq 0$ such that $y(\Lambda B - A) > 0$. For $\lambda = \Lambda + \varepsilon$, $\varepsilon > 0$ small, inequality $y(\lambda B - A) \geq y(\Lambda B - A) > 0$ with $\lambda \in S$ shows that y is positive. Consider $q \neq 0$ such that $q(\Lambda B - A) = 0$. For any scalar such that $y + \alpha q \geq 0$, the same property $y + \alpha q \gg 0$ holds. This being impossible, the partial conclusion is

$$y(\Lambda B - A) > 0 \Rightarrow y \not\geq 0. \tag{17}$$

Assume now that, for some $d > 0$, we have $\lim_{\lambda_t \to \Lambda^+} d(\lambda_t B - A)^{-1} = y$. Since y is a limit of positive vectors, we have $y \geq 0$; and since $y(\Lambda B - A) = \lim y(\lambda_t B - A) = d > 0$, (17) is violated. Therefore $\lim_{\lambda_t \to \Lambda^+} \|d(\lambda_t B - A)^{-1}\| = +\infty$ for any $d > 0$. Consider an accumulation point q of vectors $y(\lambda) = d(\lambda B - A)^{-1}/\|d(\lambda B - A)^{-1}\|$ when $\lambda \to \Lambda^+$ (therefore $\lambda \in S$, $y(\lambda) \gg 0$, $\|y(\lambda)\| = 1$). We have $q > 0$ and $q(\Lambda B - A) = \lim q(\lambda B - A) = \lim d/\|d(\lambda B - A)^{-1}\| = 0$, therefore q is a semi-positive eigenvector attached to the eigenvalue Λ. For $\lambda \in S$, (14) applied to $y = q$ shows that any semi-positive eigenvector is in fact positive. Finally, if there existed another non-proportional eigenvector, a semi-positive but non-positive eigenvector would be obtained by linear combination. Therefore q is also unique up to a factor. ■

Proof of Property 6. It has been shown that $E' = \{x;\ x(\Lambda B - A) = 0\}$ is spanned by a unique positive vector q. By transposition (the characterization by the positivity of the inverse matrix shows that the all-engagingness property is stable by transposition), the subspace $E = Ker(\Lambda B - A)$ has dimension one and is spanned by $\pi \gg 0$. $F = Im(\Lambda B - A)$ has dimension $n - 1$. Since any vector in F is orthogonal to $q \gg 0$, π does not belong to F. Therefore the vector π and a basis of F constitute a first basis of R^n. Vector $B\pi > 0$ and a basis of F constitute another basis. Let us take the vectors of the first basis and decompose their images by $\lambda B - A$ into the second basis. The corresponding matrix is written

$$D(\lambda) = \begin{bmatrix} \lambda - \Lambda & d_{12}(\lambda) \\ 0 & D_{22}(\lambda) \end{bmatrix},$$

with $d_{12}(\Lambda) = 0$ and $detD_{22}(\Lambda) \neq 0$ because the restriction of $\Lambda B - A$ to F is bijective. This shows that Λ is a simple root of the endomorphism represented by $\lambda B - A$. ■

Lemma 1 refers to single-product systems:

Lemma 1. Let M be a semi-positive indecomposable matrix. Then:

- the matrix $(\mu I - M)^{-1}$ is positive for any μ great enough;
- the eigenvalue Λ attached to a positive eigenvector has maximum modulus.

Proof. Let us consider the pair (M, I) of matrices and apply the two criteria referred to in Property 1. Inequality $\mu y_0 > y_0 M$ is satisfied for $y_0 \gg 0$ and μ great enough. The second criterion is also met, as a consequence of Theorem 1 in chapter 4 and the indecomposability hypothesis. Therefore $(\mu I - M)^{-1}$ is positive for μ great enough.

Let λ be any real or complex eigenvalue of M. By taking the moduli in the (possibly complex) equality $Mz = \lambda z$, inequality $Mx \geq |\lambda| x$ is obtained, x being the semi-positive vector whose ith component is the modulus of the ith component of z. Let us pre-multiply by the positive row eigenvector q associated with Λ. Inequality $\Lambda qx = qMx \geq |\lambda| qx$ implies $\Lambda \geq |\lambda|$. ■

Proof of Property 7. Assume first that B has exactly one positive element in every row and every column, its other elements being zero (hence $B^{-1} > 0$), and that $\alpha B + A$ is semi-positive and indecomposable for some $\alpha > 0$. Then, equality $(\lambda B - A)^{-1} = [(\lambda + \alpha)B - (\alpha B + A)]^{-1} = B^{-1}[(\lambda + \alpha)I - (\alpha B + A)B^{-1}]^{-1}$ holds, with B^{-1} semi-positive and $M = (\alpha B + A)B^{-1}$ semi-positive and indecomposable. By Lemma 1, the matrix $(\lambda B - A)^{-1}$ is positive for any λ great enough.

Conversely, assume $\lambda_0 = +\infty$, i.e. $(\lambda B - A)^{-1} \gg 0$ for any great enough λ, or $(B - \varepsilon A)^{-1} \gg 0$ for $\varepsilon \to 0^+$. If B were not regular, let $p > 0$ with $p \notin Im(B)$. We have $\lim \| (B - \varepsilon A)^{-1} p \| = +\infty$ (otherwise there would exist a vector x such that $x = \lim (B - \varepsilon_t A)^{-1} p$, hence $p = \lim (B - \varepsilon_t A)x = Bx \in Im(B)$. Let $x_0 > 0$ be a cluster point of the sequence $x_\varepsilon = (B - \varepsilon A)^{-1} p / \| (B - \varepsilon A)^{-1} p \|$. The equality $Bx_0 = \lim (B - \varepsilon A) x_0 = \lim p / \| (B - \varepsilon A)^{-1} p \| = 0$ implies that a certain column of B is zero. Similarly, by transposition, a certain row of B is also zero. This being excluded by the assumption on B, B is regular. We have $0 \ll (B - \varepsilon A)^{-1} = B^{-1} (I - \varepsilon AB^{-1})^{-1} = B^{-1}(I + \varepsilon AB^{-1} + o(\varepsilon))$, therefore $B^{-1} > 0$ and $B^{-1} + \varepsilon B^{-1}AB^{-1} \geq 0$ for ε small enough. Inequalities $B > 0$ and $B^{-1} > 0$ imply that B has exactly one positive element in every row and every column (because B is a bijection of R^n_+ into itself, the image of the ith axis is the jth axis, hence $j = \sigma(i)$ for some permutation σ of $\{1, \ldots, n\}$). After pre- and post-multiplication by $B > 0$, the inequality $B^{-1} + \varepsilon B^{-1}AB^{-1} \geq 0$ implies that the matrix $\alpha B + A$ is semi-positive for any

$\alpha > \varepsilon^{-1} > 0$. If $\alpha B + A$ was decomposable for α great enough, there would exist a proper subset I of indices such that $(\alpha B + A)_{I\bar{I}} = 0$, therefore $B_{I\bar{I}} = A_{I\bar{I}} = 0$ and the matrix $(\lambda B - A)^{-1}$ would not be positive. To sum up, the only case where λ_0 can be infinite is that of 'basic single production'. ■

Proof of Property 8. The equivalence

$$\forall \lambda \in S \qquad (\lambda B - A)^{-1} Bx = (\lambda - \lambda_h)^{-1} x \Leftrightarrow \lambda_h Bx = Ax \qquad (18)$$

establishes a one-to-one correspondence between the eigenvalues $(\lambda - \lambda_h)^{-1}$ of the matrix $(\lambda B - A)^{-1} B$ and the generalized eigenvalues λ_h of the pair (A, B). The *PF* eigenvalue of $(\lambda B - A)^{-1} B$ (this matrix is positive if B has no zero column; transpose otherwise) is associated with Λ in this correspondence, because in both cases the eigenvector is positive. Let λ_h be a generalized eigenvalue of (A, B) different from Λ. The equivalence (18) and the maximality property of the *PF* eigenvalue imply

$$\forall \lambda \in S \quad |\lambda - \lambda_h|^{-1} \leq (\lambda - \Lambda)^{-1},$$

or

$$\forall \lambda \in S \quad \lambda - \Lambda \leq |\lambda - \lambda_h|.$$

The inequality still holds for the limit value $\lambda = \lambda_0$. ■

Property 8 states that the circle centred at λ_0 and passing through Λ contains no generalized eigenvalue in its interior. Given the eigenvalues of (A, B) in the complex plane, the circle rule can be used to locate λ_0. Note, however, that if the critical eigenvalue Λ of (A, B) has maximum modulus, or even if its real part is maximum, the circle rule provides no useful information on the location of λ_0.

Proof of Property 2. Assume first that S is non-empty. We know by Property 5 that

$$\exists! q \gg 0 \quad q(\Lambda B - A) = 0. \qquad (19)$$

Moreover (20)

$$\nexists y > 0 \quad y(\Lambda B - A) > 0 \qquad (20)$$

is a consequence of (17). Conversely, we want to show that a system (A, B) for which (19) and (20) hold satisfies conditions (13) and (16). For any $\lambda > \Lambda$, the viability condition (13) is met by $y_0 = q$. If, for any $\lambda > \Lambda$, the set $Y(\lambda) = \{y; y > 0, \|y\| = 1, y(\lambda B - A) \geq 0\}$ contained a semi-positive but not positive vector $y(\lambda)$ then, by going to the limit when $\lambda \to \Lambda^+$, a vector y of the same type is obtained, which would be such that $y(\Lambda B - A) \geq 0$. But both the equality and the inequality are excluded by (19) and (20). Therefore, for some λ greater than Λ^+, the assumptions $y > 0$ and $y(\lambda B - A) \geq 0$ imply $y \gg 0$. For this λ, the conditions (13) and (16) are met, therefore λ belongs to S. This shows that S is non-empty. ■

Proof of Property 3. If $S \neq \emptyset$, a transposition of property (19) shows that

$$\exists \pi \gg 0 \quad (\Lambda B - A)\pi = 0. \tag{21}$$

Conversely (21) implies (20). Therefore conditions (19) and (21) imply (19) and (20) and, by Property 2, S is non-void. ■

Proof of Theorem 4. The subset $\mathcal{J} \subset I = [g_0, \bar{g}]$ defined by $\mathcal{J} = \{g; g_0 \leq g \leq \bar{g}, (A_g, B_g)$ is g-all-engaging$\}$ contains g_0 and is open in I. Assume that $[g_0, s[\subset \mathcal{J}$. For any g in $\mathcal{J}$, the system (A_g, B_g) is g-viable:

$$\exists z_g > 0 \quad \|z_g\| = 1 \quad z_g(B_g - (1+g)A_g) > 0.$$

By a compactness argument

$$\exists z > 0 \quad \|z\| = 1 \quad z(B_s - (1+s)A_s) \geq 0.$$

Assumption (*ii*) implies $z \gg 0$. If the above inequality were an equality, a contradiction would be obtained with assumption (*iii*). Therefore

$$\exists z > 0 \quad z(B_s - (1+s)A_s) > 0.$$

In conjunction with assumption (*ii*) for $g = s$, the two conditions set in Definition 1 are met. Therefore (A_s, B_s) is s-all-engaging, s belongs to $\mathcal{J}$ and $\mathcal{J} = I$. ■

Proof of Theorem 5. Let $tcof(r)$ be the transposed matrix of the cofactors of $C(r)$. We have $C(r)\ tcof(r) = a(r - R)^k I + o(r - R)^k$ with $a \neq 0$ and k integer, $k \geq 1$. The matrix $tcof(R)$ is non-zero, otherwise the order of R would be at least $k + 1$. The equality $C(r)\ tcof(R) = 0$ and the uniqueness assumption on π show that the columns of $tcof(R)$ are proportional to $\pi \gg 0$. Similarly, its rows are proportional to $q \gg 0$. Therefore all entries of $tcof(R)$ have the same sign. The equality $(r - R)^k C(r)^{-1} = a^{-1}\ tcof(R) + \varepsilon(r - R)$ shows that $C(r)^{-1}$ has a constant sign for r close to R^- or R^+. ■

Proof of Theorem 6. Let g_0 be such that $(B - (1 + g_0)A)^{-1} > 0$. The kth derivative of $(B - (1 + g)A)^{-1}$ at g_0 is written $(B - (1 + g_0)A)^{-1}D^k$ with

$D = A(B - (1 + g_0)A)^{-1} \geq 0$. If $\sum_{k=0}^{\infty} D^k$ is positive then, for any element (i, j), some derivative is strictly positive and the strictly increasing function $(B - (1 + g)A)^{-1}$ becomes positive at $g_0 + \varepsilon$: (A, B) is all-engaging. Or, if $\sum_0^{\infty} D^k$ is not positive, Theorem 1 in chapter 4, section 2 shows that D is decomposable and Theorem 3 in chapter 5, section 7 applied to $A(\lambda_0 B - A)^{-1}$ shows that the system (A, B) is physically decomposable. ■

Proof of Theorem 7. A matrix N which represents the decomposition of vectors $\{Ne_1, \ldots Ne_n\}$ in the natural basis $\{e_1, \ldots, e_n\}$ of R^n is also written $N = MN_1$, where N_1 represents the decomposition of $\{Ne_1, \ldots, Ne_n\}$ in a basis $\{f_1, \ldots, f_n\}$ and M the decomposition of $\{f_1, \ldots, f_n\}$ in the basis $\{e_1, \ldots, e_n\}$. Consider a S-reducible system and choose as vectors $\{f_j\}$ a basis of the subspace spanned by the columns (A_J, B_J), completed in order to obtain a basis of the whole space. By the very choice of the vectors $\{f_j\}$, we have $A = MA_1$ and $B = MB_1$ with $(A_1)_{J\bar{J}} = (B_1)_{J\bar{J}} = 0$. The converse is clear. ■

Proof of Theorem 8. Let p_0 be a tax vector such that

$$Ap_0 = \tau Bp_0. \tag{22}$$

In order that all processes yield the rate of profit r, the post-tax price vector π must satisfy

$$(1 + r)A\pi + wl = B(\pi - p_0). \tag{23}$$

Let us multiply both members of (22) by $-\alpha$ and add up to (23):

$$(1 + r)A(\pi - \alpha p_0/(1 + r)) + wl = B(\pi - (\alpha\tau + 1)p_0). \tag{24}$$

Choose α such that $\alpha/(1 + r) = \alpha\tau + 1$. One recognizes from (24) that the prices

$$p = \pi - \alpha p_0/(1 + r) \tag{25}$$

are the pre-tax prices. The difference between pre-tax prices p and post-tax prices π is given by (25), with $\alpha = (1 + r)/(1 - (1 + r)\tau)$. Hence, $p - \pi = p_0/((1 + r)\tau - 1)$. ■

Proof of Theorem 9. The characterization follows from Theorem 3 in chapter 5, section 7. ■

Proof of Theorem 10. According to Theorem 6, it suffices to show that an X-reducible system is not all-engaging.

(a) and (b). Let (A, B) be S-reducible. If some inverse matrix $(B - (1 + r)A)^{-1}$ were positive, matrix $(B - (1 + r)A)^{-1} B$ would be positive, therefore indecomposable, a contradiction with Theorem 7. A similar argument holds for an AB-reducible system.

(c) Let (A, B) be BW-reducible. Relation (22) implies that $(B - (1 + r)A)^{-1}Bp_0 = (1 - (1 + r)\tau)^{-1}p_0$, with p_0 semi-positive but not positive. Therefore the inverse matrix is not positive.

(d) Let (A, B) be F-reducible. Then, there exist some proper subsets I and J such that matrix $C = B - (1 + r)A$ satisfies $C_{IJ} \geq 0$ and $C_{\overline{I}\overline{J}} \leq 0$. Without loss of generality, I and J are proper subsets. Let us consider the matrices $C_{I\overline{J}}$ and $L = C^{-1}$:

- If there exists a row vector $y_I > 0$ with (card I) components such that $y_{\overline{I}}C_{I\overline{J}} \gg 0$, we have $y_IC_{I\bullet} = (y_IC_{IJ}, y_IC_{I\overline{J}}) > 0$. Then the equality $(y_IC_{I\bullet})L_{\bullet\overline{I}} = y_I(C_{I\bullet}\ L_{\overline{I}}) = 0$ excludes $L_{\overline{I}} \gg 0$, so that L is not positive.
- If there exists a column vector $x_{\overline{J}} > 0$ with (card $\overline{J}$) components such that $C_{I\overline{J}}\ x_{\overline{J}} \leq 0$, we have $C_{\bullet\overline{J}}\ x_{\overline{J}} = (C_{I\overline{J}}\ x_{\overline{J}}, C_{\overline{I}\overline{J}}\ x_{\overline{J}}) \leq 0$. Then the inequality $0 < x_{\overline{J}} = (L_{\overline{J}\bullet}\ C_{\bullet\overline{J}})x_{\overline{J}} = L_{\overline{J}\bullet}(C_{\bullet\overline{J}}x_{\overline{J}})$ excludes $L_{\overline{J}\bullet} > 0$, so that L is not positive.

As the Theorem of the Alternative applied to matrix $C_{I\overline{J}}$ asserts that if one of the above two cases occurs, (A, B) is not all-engaging. ■

13 From von Neumann to Sraffa

1 A universal property

There exist few universal properties of joint production, which hold for all systems, or all but a negligible subset. The duality between prices and quantities is one of them. This chapter establishes another universal law: in a neighbourhood of the maximum rates of growth and profit, almost all multiple-product systems behave like single-product systems. This statement seems to contradict two previous results: there are square systems without a positive standard basket, and all-engagingness is a specific property. The apparent contradiction can be solved if one turns to von Neumann's construction which introduces the choice of methods. It is not the initial system (A, B) which is all-engaging (this system is rectangular when the numbers of methods and commodities differ), it is its 'active part' which is extracted from it and made up of the effectively used methods and the non-overproduced goods. The result establishes a theoretical link between von Neumann's and Sraffa's models, defines the maximum rates of growth and profit without ambiguity and, finally, solves some paradoxes of Sraffa's model.

2 The von Neumann theory

We have already sketched the structure of the von Neumann theory in the simple frame of single production. The main strength of the construction is to deal with joint production and choice of technique. Its most significant restriction is the free disposal hypothesis, which was useless in single production because of the adjustment property. Let there be a multiple-product system $A \to B$ with m methods and n goods (with possibly $m \neq n$). The wage basket is given and incorporated into the input matrix, so that labour does not appear explicitly: the ith method is represented by $a_i \to b_i$. It is assumed that any commodity can be reproduced (B has no zero column) and any production requires some input (A has no zero row). The notions of rate of growth and rate of interest given in part I admit obvious extensions to multiple-product systems and, as explained in chapter 5, retaining the notion of strict rate of growth avoids a useless distinction between decomposable and indecomposable economies (for an alternative conception, see Kemeny, Morgenstern and Thompson 1956).

Definition 1. A rate of growth g is strictly feasible if there exist activity levels $y = (y_1, \ldots, y_m)$ such that the vector inequality

$$\exists y > 0 \quad (1+g)yA \ll yB \tag{1}$$

holds. The upper bound of the strict growth rates is denoted G.

Definition 2. The scalar r $(r > -1)$ is a rate of interest if inequality

$$\exists p > 0 \quad (1+r)Ap \geq Bp \tag{2}$$

holds. The minimum rate of interest, or equilibrium rate, is noted R_N.

The von Neumann problem concerns the choice of the methods sustaining the maximum rate of growth (the upper bound of the strict rates of growth satisfies a broad inequality instead of the strict inequality (1)). This rate depends on the family of selected methods, not on each method in isolation. The stress is on the distinction between the operated ($y_i > 0$) and the non-operated ($y_i = 0$) methods. Von Neumann's brilliant idea is to replace this coordination problem by an equivalent problem whose solution calls upon the entrepreneurs' selfish interest. The equivalence relies on a remarkable duality property. The mechanism considered by von Neumann calls for a price vector, which is publicly cried (by a grandson of Walras' auctioneer, we presume). Knowing the prices and the rate of interest, the entrepreneurs calculate the profitability of every available method. At equilibrium, competition among entrepreneurs leads to zero pure profits for the operated methods; similarly, competition among bankers leads to defining the equilibrium rate as the minimum rate of interest. These ideas are reflected in Definition 2. Von Neumann's hand leads the entrepreneurs to select the methods i for which equality $(1 + R_N)a_ip = b_ip$ holds. The fundamental result is that, for an adequate choice of the price vector, these methods coincide with those sustaining the maximum rate of growth:

Theorem 1. Let A and B be semi-positive, A with no zero row, B with no zero column. There exists a price vector $p > 0$ such that the most profitable methods are those sustaining maximum growth. Moreover the maximum rate of growth G is equal to the minimum rate of interest R_N, and the commodities overproduced at rate G have a zero price. Formally, the complementarity relationships (3) and (4) hold:

$$(1+G)yA \leq yB \quad [p] \tag{3}$$
$$(1+R_N)Ap \geq Bp \quad [y]. \tag{4}$$

3 Von Neumann and Sraffa

3.1 An all-engagingness property

A formal result can be used independently of the author's original intent. We use Theorem 1 as a tool to analyse Sraffa's model. Though Sraffa himself does not refer to the notion of regular growth, Definitions 1 and 2 are easily imported into his construction. The main conceptual difficulty is that the notion of rate of interest comes from neoclassical theory and cannot be identified *a priori* with a rate of profit. However, at von Neumann's equilibrium, inequality (2) is transformed into an equality for the operated methods, as shown by the complementarity relationships (4). In this particular configuration the rate of interest is a rate of profit. It is therefore a case of adopting opportunist behaviour, without worrying too much about the historical purity of the concepts dealt with.

At the maximum rate G, let us ignore the non-operated methods ($y_i = 0$), as well as the overproduced goods, whose price is zero. The operation amounts to truncating the corresponding rows and columns from matrices A and B. The matrices ($\overline{A}$, $\overline{B}$) extracted from the original system after these operations represent the *active part* of the system. Let q denote the truncated vector of activity levels, and π the truncated price vector relative to the non-overproduced commodities. With these notations, the complementarity relationships (3) and (4) are written

$$\exists q \gg 0 \quad (1+G)q\overline{A} = q\overline{B} \tag{5}$$
$$\exists \pi > 0 \quad (1+R_N)\overline{A}\pi = \overline{B}\pi, \tag{6}$$

with $G = R_N$. Flukes apart, the non-overproduced goods have a positive price, therefore vector π in (6) is normally positive. Let $\overline{m} \times \overline{n}$ be the common dimension of matrices $\overline{A}$ and $\overline{B}$. Equality (5) shows that the $\overline{m}$ rows of the matrix $C = \overline{B} - (1+G)\,\overline{A}$, which are vectors in $R^{\overline{n}}$, are linearly dependent; therefore, flukes apart, we have $\overline{m} \geq \overline{n}$. According to (6), the $\overline{n}$ columns of C, which are vectors in $R^{\overline{m}}$, are linearly dependent; therefore, flukes apart, we have $\overline{n} \geq \overline{m}$. Therefore the active part ($\overline{A}$, $\overline{B}$) is generically square ($\overline{m} = \overline{n}$) . Finally, the activity levels which sustain the maximum growth are generically unique. It follows from Theorem 3 in chapter 12, section 2 that:

Theorem 2. Generically, the active part $(\overline{A}, \overline{B})$ of a joint production system with free disposal is square and all-engaging.

3.2 *Quantities and prices*

Theorem 2 has important economic implications. Let us begin by the quantity side and the notion of a standard basket. Consider an example with three goods and three processes ($m = 3$, $n = 3$):

$$A = \begin{bmatrix} 1 & 1 & 1 \\ 2 & 3 & 2 \\ 3 & 1 & 5 \end{bmatrix} \rightarrow B = \begin{bmatrix} 3 & 4 & 1 \\ 5 & 4 & 5 \\ 1 & 10 & 2 \end{bmatrix}.$$

The system has no positive standard basket in Sraffa's sense, i.e. there is no positive row vector q_S such that $q_S A$ and $q_S B$ are proportional. We propose to treat the above data according to the von Neumann procedure. The maximum rate of growth is $G = 100$ per cent with $y = (1, 1, 0)$, the first commodity being overproduced. Therefore the active part is made of the first two processes and the last two commodities ($\overline{m} = \overline{n} = 2$). Equalities (5) and (6) hold for these 2×2 matrices $(\overline{A}, \overline{B})$ with $q = (1, 1)$, $\overline{\pi} = (1, 2)$ and $G = R_N = 1$. The 'standard activity levels' q are the positive part of the von Neumann activity levels y. This approach eliminates the difficulties encountered by Sraffa: a positive standard basket exists and, flukes apart, is unique up to a factor. The standard ratio is a root of $det(\overline{B} - (1 + G)\overline{A})$, usually not of $det(B - (1 + G)A)$. In this construction, the main innovation is that the standard proportions are only identified *after* an adequate treatment of the (square or rectangular) initial data. It implies a departure from Sraffa's methodology (separate treatment of a system before comparisons between systems) but eliminates a paradox.

Assume now that the rate of growth g is smaller than the maximum rate G. As long as g remains close to the maximum rate, the activity levels $\overline{y} = \overline{d}(\overline{B} - (1 + g)\overline{A})^{-1}$ are positive. The surplus produced in the active part is exactly equal to $\overline{d}$, the other goods being overproduced and disposed of freely: this is the adjustment property. The difference with single production is that the property holds only in a neighbourhood of the maximum rate and is lost for low rates of growth.

We now look at the price side. It has been noticed that the concepts of a rate of interest and a rate of profit have different historical and conceptual roots. However, von Neumann's result establishes a link between both notions: according to (6), the minimum rate R_N can be interpreted as a rate of profit associated with a zero wage. At the associated prices, the non-operated methods pay extra costs. We consider the scalar R_N as the maximum rate of profit in a Sraffian sense, even if this contradicts Sraffa's personal choice. Flukes apart, the maximum rate of profit is attached to a unique and positive price vector π, with a zero wage. The maximum rates of growth and profit are equal.

In von Neumann's analysis, labour is incorporated into the inputs as a wage basket. Let us reintroduce an explicit labour vector l. For a rate of profit slightly smaller than R (we now write R for R_N), the goods which are overproduced at rate G retain a zero price. The nominal wage w becomes positive and the prices of the non-overproduced commodities are $\overline{p}(r) = w(\overline{B} - (1 + r)\overline{A})^{-1}\overline{l}$. The operated methods maximize the real wage measured in terms of any commodity. The already mentioned adjustment property can be stated more precisely as a non-substitution property: the prices depend only on the rate of profit, not on demand for final goods or accumulation. However, at variance with single production, the property holds only on a left neighbourhood $[G - \alpha \leq g \leq r \leq G = R[$ of the maximum rates.

To sum up, it has been shown that almost all joint production systems behave like single-product systems for high rates of growth and profit, this being due to the emergence of an all-engagingness property. In order to let the property appear, one must go beyond a naive treatment of the data and first extract the active part of the system.

4 Geometrical illustration

Let us illustrate Theorem 2 for two goods. Geometry is a powerful heuristic tool, and it is by this means that the phenomena studied in this chapter have been discovered. Let us begin with two goods. In the g-space, a method i is represented by the vector $c_i(g) = (b_i - (1 + g)a_i)/l_i$ in R^2 or by its extremity $C_i(g)$. The division by l_i makes sense if labour is used in each process but has no incidence on the definition of the feasible rates of growth. Let $E(g)$ be the convex envelope of the points $C_i(g)$, prolonged westwards and southwards to take free disposal into account. g is a strict rate of growth if $E(g)$ cuts the interior of the positive orthant. When g increases, every point $C_i(g)$ slides in the southwest direction. So does the envelope $E(g)$, which is subjected to deformations. At the maximum rate G, $E(G)$ no longer cuts the interior of the positive orthant. Let us take a photograph at this very moment (figure 13.1).

Figures 13.1a and 13.1b show the normal exit configurations. In figure 13.1a, $E(g)$ goes out of the orthant through the origin 0, which is the barycentre of $C_1(G)$ and $C_2(G)$. The operated methods are the

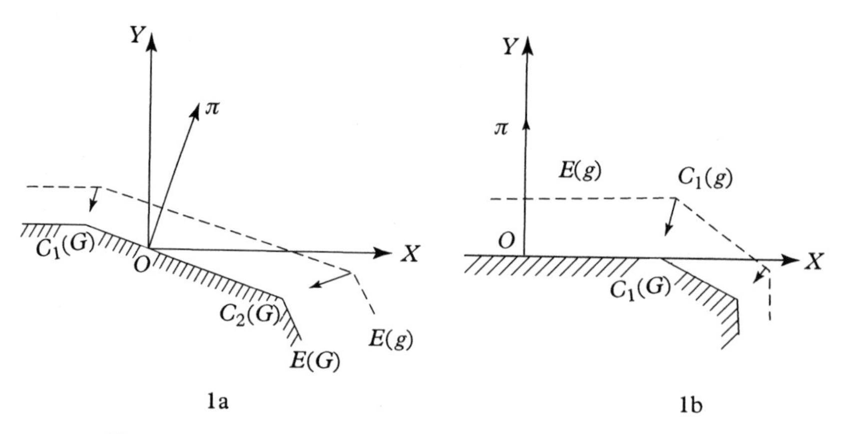

Figure 13.1 Normal exits

methods 1 and 2, and the standard basket $q = (q_1, q_2)$ is defined by $q_1c_1(G) + q_2c_2(G) = 0$. In figure 13.1b, the exit occurs through an axis: good X is overproduced. At the maximum rate, the active part of the system is made of the method 1 alone and the commodity Y, and the standard basket is reduced to good Y. Let us now look at these figures a moment before the exit, for $g = G - \varepsilon$. In figure 13.1a, the operated methods 1 and 2 are such that the segment $[C_1(g)\, C_2(g)]$ cuts the whole positive orthant: the active part of the economy has the adjustment property. In figure 13.1b, the good X remains overproduced and any quantity of Y can be produced by method 1 alone.

Figure 13.2 illustrates an exceptional configuration in which Theorem 2 does not hold. Here, the vectors a_1 and b_1 are proportional and method 1 alone suffices to produce X and Y at the maximum rate G: the active part is not square. The non-substitution property does not hold in a neighbourhood of G since, for $g = G - \varepsilon$, method 1 is combined with either method 2 or method 3 according to the composition of the basket d.

5 Conclusion

Von Neumann's approach constitutes a remarkable contribution to the analysis of multiple-product systems. Even if its starting point is distant from Sraffa's (rectangular systems, no explicit labour, free disposal, different concepts), the results can be connected to Sraffa's analysis. The chapter builds a bridge between both theories and let the first appear as a limit case of the second, when the rates of growth and profit are close

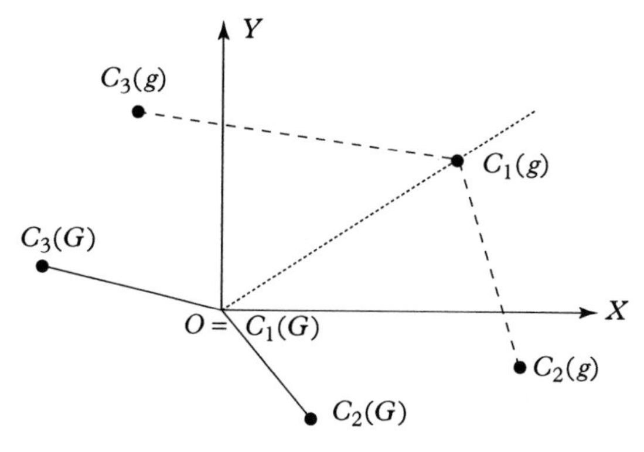

Figure 13.2 An exceptional case

to their common maximum value. By the same stroke, some paradoxes encountered by Sraffa are solved: flukes apart, the maximum rates of growth and profit are well defined and equal; the standard basket is positive and unique; in a vicinity of the maximum rates the all-engagingness property transfers the properties of single-product systems to general multiple-product systems. However these results require a transformation of Sraffa's approach: they renounce a purely formal treatment of the equations and replace it by economically meaningful operations. They also show that the methodology adopted in single production must be revised. In part I, we studied the behaviour of an isolated system, then compared alternative systems. In joint production, a selection of methods occurs inside a given system, even if it is initially square. The study of a system and the choice of technique are intimately connected and simultaneous.

6 Note on von Neumann

Von Neuman has only left an enigmatic hint on the origin of his reflection. What is known about his culture in economics (mainly, Kaldor's account (1989) on his reading Wicksell, whose influence is perceptible in a study devoted to the relationship between the rates of interest and growth), his intellectual environment (Menger's circle and its interest for general equilibrium) and, above all, the internal analysis of his work (the concept of a rate of interest and the normative approach) seem to leave little doubt on the sources of von Neumann's problem (Kurz and Salvadori 1993, defend an opposite opinion). However, von Neumann's theory gets close to classical theory because growth models are reproduction models.

The chapter follows Bidard (1986a). Schefold's study (1978a), already mentioned in chapter 11, section 7, is conceptually and technically intriguing. Schefold notes, without elaborating, that 'the "last" truncation [i.e. when the level of $g = r$ is high, C.B.] . . . behaves rather like a single-product system'. Bidard (1999b) studies the relationship between von Neumann's result and the fundamental theorem of linear programming.

14 The notion of a sector

1 From industries to sectors

In a single-product economy, an industry is the subset of methods which produce the same commodity. The classification fails in the presence of joint production. We examine how and when a concept of sector, generalizing that of industry, can be introduced in a multiple-product system framework.

The criterion retained is purely physical. It starts from the observation that, in single production, a productive system has two properties: in order to produce a positive basket, at least one method from every industry is operated (every industry is indispensable); and, as soon as a set of methods can produce a positive basket, it can meet any given demand vector by means of an adequate choice of its activity levels (adjustment property). More precisely, a single-product system with more methods than the number of commodities is 'super-adjustable' in the sense that any square and strictly viable system extracted from it has the adjustment property. We extend the property to several types of multiple-product systems, when a method is no longer characterized by the nature of its output (the identification of a sector by a dominant product would be only a disguise of single production). The notion of a sector makes a link between that of an all-engaging system and the choice of technique (section 2).

The concept of an engaging system assumes implicitly that all goods may be consumed. In the presence of pure capital goods, which are not consumed, the notions of adjustment and sector must be adapted (sections 3 and 4). The concept of vertical integration is especially useful for the study of fixed capital (section 5). Up to that point, only the adjustment to demand is examined. We distinguish the adjustment property from the non-substitution property. The former means that, under certain circumstances, a technique is independent of demand, the latter that the dominant competitive technique has the adjustment property and is determined by the rate of profit only. For sectoral models with pure capital goods, a weak form of the non-substitution theorem is established (section 6).

2 Sectors and final goods

Let (A, B) be a square $n \times n$ system and g a given and strictly feasible growth rate, say $g = 0$ (otherwise, replace the input matrix A by $(1 + g)A$: what matters is the inequality $g \leq r$). In this chapter, 'viable' is used for 'strictly viable', and 'engaging' for '0-semi-engaging'. In the presence of final goods only, the adjustment property means that equation $yB = yA + d$ admits a semi-positive solution for any semi-positive demand basket d and is equivalent to the semi-positivity of matrix $L = (B - A)^{-1}$. From an economic point of view, a more convenient form of the property has been elaborated in chapter 12: the system has the adjustment property (it is adjustable) if and only if it is viable and all its processes are indispensable. The indispensability condition can be reinterpreted as a minimality property:

Theorem 1. Let $(A, l) \rightarrow B$ be a viable system. If it has two of the three properties:
(*i*) it is minimum, i.e. no system extracted from it is viable
(*ii*) it is square
(*iii*) it is adjustable
it has the third one. It is then called *engaging*.

When the choice of method is introduced, the generalization of the adjustment property is:

Definition 1. A viable system has the super-adjustment property if any viable system extracted from it has the adjustment property.

In single production, the crucial facts that sustain the super-adjustment property are: (*i*) every viable set of processes admits at least one process in each industry, and (*ii*) the number of industries is equal to that of final goods. In joint production, a system with fewer methods than goods may be viable but, then, it cannot have the adjustment property. An extension of the property can be expected by substituting 'sector' for 'industry' in the above two statements. The processes are no longer classified according to the good they produce, but we retain a partition of the processes into indispensable groups.

Definition 2. A viable economy with n final goods and no pure capital goods is *sectoral* if there exists a partition of the set of processes into

n subsets, called sectors, such that any viable set of methods contains at least one process from each sector.

Theorem 2. A sectoral economy has the super-adjustment property.

The introduction of the notion of a sector implies a change in the point of view. Under the industry assumption, the type of a process is defined by the nature of its product: the industry is engraved in the process itself. On the contrary, the partition of a sectoral economy, which is characterized only by the indispensability property, has to be built by the observer on the basis of a comprehensive knowledge of the set of methods. Since the link between a sector and a specific commodity is broken, a sector can be associated with a 'colour' instead of a good and the indispensability property reinterpreted as a 'rainbow axiom'.

3 Adjustment with capital goods

Two kinds of commodities are now distinguished: f goods which are demanded for consumption but may also be used as inputs (final goods, such as wheat), and k goods which are used only for the production of other commodities (pure capital goods, such as fertilizers or fixed capital). Let the consumption goods be the first f commodities, and the pure capital goods be the last k ones ($f+k=n$). The columns of the matrices $A=[A', A'']$ and $B=[B', B'']$ are partitioned accordingly. The demand set, which is $D=R_+^n$ when there are final goods only, becomes $D=R_+^f\times\{0_k\}$ in the presence of capital goods.

Definition 3. Let there be f final goods and k pure capital goods. A set of processes is (strictly) *viable* if it can produce some vector in $R_{++}^f\times\{0_k\}$.

Definition 4. A set of processes has the *adjustment property* if it can meet any demand in $D=R_+^f\times\{0_k\}$ by means of a change in its activity levels. It is *minimum* if no proper subset of methods is viable.

In the presence of pure capital goods, Theorem 1 no longer holds:

Example 1. Let there be $f=1$ final good, $k=2$ capital goods and $m=2$ processes. The demand set is $D=R_+\times\{0_2\}=\{(+, 0, 0)\}$. The system

$$C=B-A=\begin{bmatrix} + & 2 & -1 \\ + & -2 & 1 \end{bmatrix}, \quad \text{i.e.} \quad C'=\begin{bmatrix} + \\ + \end{bmatrix}, \quad C''=\begin{bmatrix} 2 & -1 \\ -2 & 1 \end{bmatrix}$$

is viable (choose the same activity levels for both processes), minimum (an isolated process cannot produce a zero net product of capital goods) and has the adjustment property (any final demand of the type (+, 0, 0) is met). Yet it is not square.

A reflection on the nature and the role of the capital goods allows us to find adequate generalizations of Theorems 1 and 2. The result will be achieved in several steps. In this section, we concentrate on the adjustment property and point to the notion of independent capital goods. Section 4 introduces the notion of a sector in the presence of capital goods and returns to the super-adjustment property.

Even if squareness is lost when capital goods are introduced, the adjustment property lets us expect some relationship between the number of operated processes and that of produced commodities. Intuitively, the number m of processes represents the degrees of freedom in choosing the activity levels. Since the adjustment property deals with f different directions of final demand, one must have $m \geq f$. The $m - f$ remaining degrees of freedom are used to adjust the net product of pure capital goods to zero. Requiring them to be equal to the number k of pure capital goods would be too restrictive: in Example 1, the capital goods are linked in such a way that when one capital good disappears from the net product, so does the other. What matters is the number of *independent* capital goods, as measured by the rank of $C'' = B'' - A''$. This accounting is formalized in Definition 6 and justified by Theorem 3. A preliminary step eliminates the superfluous processes:

Definition 5. The process i is *superfluous* if it cannot be used for the production of any semi-positive net product:

$$\{y > 0, yC' > 0, yC'' = 0\} \Rightarrow y_i = 0.$$

A system has no superfluous process if

$$\exists y \gg 0 \quad yC' > 0 \quad yC'' = 0.$$

Example 2. Let the first two methods be those described in Example 1 and a third process be written $C' = [+]$, $C'' = [0, 1]$. The third process is superfluous.

The superfluous processes are economically irrelevant, but they interfere with the calculation of the number of independent capital goods: in Example 2, the presence of the third process makes the rank of C'' increase. This is why they are first dropped out.

Definition 6. A system with pure capital goods is *balanced* if it admits no superfluous process and if the number m of processes is equal to the number f of final goods plus the rank of matrix C''.

Theorem 3 below extends Theorem 1 to capital goods, 'square' being replaced by 'balanced'. Theorem 4 connects the engagingness property to a semi-positivity property of the inverse matrix (notation L stands either for 'left' or 'Leontief' inverse matrix).

Theorem 3. Consider a system with pure capital goods. If it has two of the three properties:
(*i*) it is minimum
(*ii*) it is balanced
(*iii*) it is adjustable
it has the third one. It is then called *engaging*.

Theorem 4. A system with capital goods $(A, l) \rightarrow B$, with $C = B - A$, is engaging if and only if it satisfies anyone of the equivalent properties:
(*i*) it can meet any given final demand $d = (d', 0)$ with $d' > 0$; for any final demand $d' \gg 0$ all processes are operated
(*ii*) any given final demand is obtained by means of a unique set of semi-positive activity levels, and no process is superfluous
(*iii*) there exists a unique matrix $L_{f,m}$ such that $LC = [I_f, 0_k]$, and L has semi-positive columns
(*iv*) C admits a right inverse matrix $R = [{}^{R'}_{R''}]$ such that $CR = I_m$, R' being unique with semi-positive columns (moreover, we have $L = R'$).

4 Sectors with capital goods

Some capital goods are specific to an industry or a sector. A more accurate criterion refers to the notion of proper capital goods. As in section 2, our intention is to restore the super-adjustment property (that is, any extracted viable system has the adjustment property), with the idea of checking it by means of a simple counting.

Production with fixed capital belongs to the genus of joint production: the tractor which enters into the annual cycle produces corn (the final good) and, simultaneously, a tractor that is one year older. However, if the tractor is not used elsewhere, the net product over its lifetime is reduced to corn only, as in single production. Traditionally, the fixed-capital theory retains four assumptions: (*i*) the fixed-capital goods are not consumed, (*ii*) every process produces one final good at most (the 'industry' assumption), (*iii*) every fixed-capital good is 'specific' or 'internal' to an industry (non-transferability) and, (*iv*) the fixed-capital goods can be disposed of freely. Our treatment weakens the last three hypotheses but, for clarity, we momentarily retain the industry assumption: a process is classified according to the unique final good it produces. When a machine intervenes in a final good industry, the non-transferability hypothesis means that it remains within that industry (the 'internal' machine). If, on the contrary, a machine were used to produce different goods according to its age, this intertemporal joint production would hinder a reduction to single production. The notion of a *proper* capital good is more precise: a capital good is called 'proper' if its zero net production in the economy implies its zero net production in every industry. Internal capital goods are proper, but the converse is not true:

Example 3. Let there be two machines M and N, whose age is denoted by index t. The data refer only to the inputs and outputs of the capital goods in the four yearly methods:

Industry α:		Industry β:	
	$0 \to 1M_0$		$0 \to 1N_0$
	$1M_0 \to 1M_1$		$1N_0 \to 1M_0 + 1N_1$
	$1M_1 \to 1M_2$		$1M_0 + 1N_1 \to 1M_1 + 1N_2$
	$1M_2 \to 0$		$1M_1 + 1N_2 \to 0$

Machine N (formally, three different capital goods N_0, N_1, N_2) is internal to industry β. When its net production vanishes, the four processes in this industry have the same activity levels; simultaneously, the net production of M in industry β vanishes. Therefore, a zero net production of all capital goods in the economy implies their zero net production in both industries: machine M is proper, though not internal to an industry.

When a capital good, e.g. a machine or a fertilizer, is utilized only in an industry, the most adequate theoretical treatment is to consider its production and its use as a part of that industry. Then the presence of internal (more generally, proper) capital goods does not modify the number of industries, but the industry now shelters processes which produce a capital good. An extension to the joint production of final goods is:

Definition 7. Let there be a viable economy with f final goods and p capital goods, and $D = R_+^f \times \{0_p\}$. It is a *sectoral economy with proper capital goods* if there exists a partition $S_\alpha, S_\beta, \ldots, S_\sigma$ of the set of processes into $\sigma = f$ subsets such that:

(*i*) (*Rainbow axiom*) At least one process from every sector must be operated in order to produce some $d = (d', 0) > 0$

(*ii*) (*Proper capital goods*) A zero net production of the capital goods at the global level implies their zero net production in every sector:

$$\{y > 0, y(B'' - A'') = 0\} \Rightarrow \forall\iota = \alpha, \ldots, \sigma \quad y_\iota(B''_\iota - A''_\iota) = 0$$

where y_ι denotes the sub-vector of activity levels relative to sector ι.

The number of sectors is equal to that of final goods. Note that the notion of balanced system (Definition 6) concerns the number of operated methods whereas the rainbow axiom (Definition 7) refers to the operated sectors. Theorem 5 generalizes Theorem 2 to economies with proper capital goods:

Theorem 5. A sectoral economy with proper capital goods has the super-adjustment property.

As opposed to the internal or the proper capital goods, the general capital goods are those which, by nature, are built in order to be used in different final goods industries or sectors. A young machine can be 'general' during its period of construction and become 'internal' once it has begun to be used. Even if the super-adjustment property can be recovered under certain conditions (Bidard and Erreygers 1999), the simplicity of the rainbow axiom is lost and the economic interpretation of the notion of a sector is affected by the transformation.

5 Vertical integration

We now examine an alternative treatment of the capital goods. The principle is to eliminate them from the original system and construct a surrogate economy, the 'vertically integrated system', in which the final goods are produced by means of final goods. The adjustment property holds for the integrated economy and, under certain conditions, can be transferred back to the original economy with capital goods. The idea of vertical integration stems from the theory of fixed capital: if a tractor is internal to the corn industry, its construction and use are intermediate steps in the production of corn. Example 4 gives a flavour of the approach.

Example 4. Let there be two final goods, corn and iron, and five processes. The first four processes describe the production of corn (good 1), the fifth that of iron (good 2). The first process produces a pure capital good, called 'new tractor' (good 3), jointly with corn. The new tractor enters into the second process as an input and reappears as a 'one-year-old tractor' (good 4) on the output side. Similarly, the third process uses the one-year-old tractor as an input and produces corn and a two-year-old tractor (good 5). In the fourth process the tractor is worn out. Labour being ignored, the corresponding matrices are written:

$$A = \begin{bmatrix} a_{11} & a_{12} & 0 & 0 & 0 \\ a_{21} & a_{22} & 1 & 0 & 0 \\ a_{31} & a_{32} & 0 & 1 & 0 \\ a_{41} & a_{42} & 0 & 0 & 1 \\ a'_{21} & a'_{22} & 0 & 0 & 0 \end{bmatrix}, \quad B = \begin{bmatrix} b_{11} & 0 & 1 & 0 & 0 \\ b_{21} & 0 & 0 & 1 & 0 \\ b_{31} & 0 & 0 & 0 & 1 \\ b_{41} & 0 & 0 & 0 & 0 \\ 0 & b'_{22} & 0 & 0 & 0 \end{bmatrix}.$$

($b_{11} = 0$ if the first period is entirely devoted to the construction of a tractor.) The corn industry consists of processes 1–4. Over the lifetime of a tractor, its output is reduced to corn only, as in single production. Instead of considering four consecutive years, an alternative is to look at the economy in a steady state ($g = 0$), when the numbers of births and deaths of machines are equal. The corn industry with tractors is equivalent to the single-product process (1) without tractors and the economy itself is reduced to the 2×2 economy (1)–(2):

$$a'_{11} \text{ corn } + a'_{12} \text{ iron } \rightarrow b'_{11} \text{ corn} \quad (1)$$
$$a'_{21} \text{ corn } + a'_{22} \text{ iron } \rightarrow b'_{22} \text{ iron} \quad (2)$$

with $a'_{11} = a_{11} + a_{21} + a_{31} + a_{41}$, $a'_{12} = a_{12} + a_{22} + a_{32} + a_{42}$ and $b'_{11} = b_{11} + b_{21} + b_{31} + b_{41}$.

If the growth rate g is non-zero, the number of t-year-old tractors is $1 + g$ times that of $(t + 1)$-year-old tractors, therefore the coefficients a'_{11} and b'_{11} of vertical integration in a generalized version of relation (1) depend on g. (Similarly, the reduction of a four-year project to a yearly process is not neutral for prices if the rate of profit is non-zero.)

Some specific features of Example 4 do not necessarily show up in the general case (jointly involved machines or capital goods):

- The matrix $C'' = B'' - A''$ has maximum rank, equal to the number k of pure capital goods.
- In order to eliminate the tractors from the net product, the same activity levels are applied to the four processes of the corn industry. What matters is that the combination sustaining the elimination of the capital goods is positive.
- The integrated economy is of the single-production type. What matters is that it is engaging.

When these conditions are met, the calculations of Example 4 can be generalized. Its successive steps are: (*i*) identification of relevant pure capital goods; (*ii*) elimination of these goods by means of a positive linear combination; and, (*iii*) observation of the reduced economy with final goods only. Then, the adjustment property is expected to hold for the initial economy with capital goods. Details follow.

Let the economy be represented by $C = B - A$. The capital goods are referred to in the sub-matrix C''. We rearrange the columns of C'' as $C'' = (\overline{C}'', \hat{C}'')$, where the r columns of $\overline{C}''$ have maximum rank (r is the number of independent pure capital goods). Since any vector y such that $y\overline{C}'' = 0$ satisfies $yC'' = 0$, we disregard the last columns $\hat{C}''$ (dependent capital goods) and concentrate upon the matrix $\overline{C} = (C', \overline{C}'')$. Let us identify r independent rows in $\overline{C}''$ and renumber the corresponding processes accordingly (say, in the last r rows). We obtain the configuration

$$\overline{C} = \begin{bmatrix} C_1' & \overline{C}_1'' \\ C_2' & \overline{C}_2'' \end{bmatrix}$$

where $\overline{C}_2''$ a $r \times r$ matrix with $rk(\overline{C}_2'') = r$. Every row of $\overline{C}_1''$ is a linear combination of the rows of $\overline{C}_2''$. Since the $(m - r) \times r$ matrix $G = -\overline{C}_1''(\overline{C}_2'')^{-1}$ is such that $\overline{C}_1'' + G\overline{C}_2'' = 0$, we have $[I, G]\overline{C} = [C_1' + GC_2', 0]$. Every row of the right-hand-side matrix represents the net product of a fictitious 'integrated' process, and the presence of zeros in the last columns indicates that the capital goods have been eliminated. The information contained in the original matrix with pure capital goods has been transferred and 'integrated' into the final goods matrix $C_1' + GC_2'$.

Definition 8. The $(m - r) \times r$ matrix $G = -\overline{C}_1''(\overline{C}_2'')^{-1}$ is the *integration matrix*. The $m - r$ processes whose net products are represented by the rows of the $(m - r) \times (m - r)$ matrix $\Gamma = C_1' + GC_2'$ are the *integrated* processes.

An application of these formulas to Example 4 (with $m = 5$ and $r = 3$) leads to

$$G = \begin{bmatrix} 1 & 1 & 1 \\ 0 & 0 & 0 \end{bmatrix}, \quad \Gamma = \begin{bmatrix} b_{11}' - a_{11}' & -a_{12}' \\ -a_{21}' & b_{22}' - a_{22}' \end{bmatrix}.$$

The entries of these matrices are interpreted as follows. The coefficients in the first row of the integration matrix G come from the fact that the tractors disappear from the corn industry when all activity levels are equal. Those in the second row reflect the absence of pure capital goods in the iron industry. The integrated matrix Γ is the net product matrix of the reduced model (1)–(2). The integration procedure is general, but the adjustment property depends on the properties of G and Γ:

Theorem 6. Consider a system with pure capital goods and such that $m = f + rk(C'')$ (m = number of methods, f = number of final goods, C''= columns of $B - A$ relative to the pure capital goods). Let G and Γ be the matrices obtained as in Definition 8. The adjustment property holds if and only if the integrated matrix is regular with $\Gamma^{-1} > 0$ and $\Gamma^{-1}G > 0$. The system is then engaging if G has no zero column.

Theorem 6 provides a simple algebraic criterion that can be applied mechanically, for instance to Examples 1, 2 and 4. In Example 2, the zero column in $G = [1, 0]$ signals the presence of a superfluous process.

6 A non-substitution result

Up to now, we have only considered whether demand can be met, not how to select methods. In a market economy, competition determines the choice of methods. In a long-run equilibrium and for a given demand vector $d = (d', 0)$, the activity levels y and the prices p in terms of wage are solution to the system (3):

$$\begin{aligned} &yB = yA + d \\ &Bp \leq (1 + r)\, Ap + l \quad [y] \\ &y > 0,\, p > 0,\, w = 1. \end{aligned} \tag{3}$$

This is a Lippi-type model with a zero growth rate (if the growth rate is positive, modify the first equation accordingly). Note, however, that free disposal of the final goods is not assumed here: since the construction is an extension of the theory of engaging systems to choice of methods, the adjustment property results from the semi-positivity of some Leontief inverse matrix. Theorems 7 and 8 below state non-substitution results for models without and with capital goods, respectively. Theorem 7 specifies 'positive' final demand in order to avoid the complications linked to reducibility; as usual, uniqueness holds for the price vector, not for the technique itself in case of switching. Theorem 8 generalizes the results obtained in the fixed capital theory by Stiglitz (1970) and Salvadori (1988a).

Theorem 7. Let there be a multiple-product economy without capital goods, which is sectoral according to Definition 2. Assume that:

- the rate of profit r is given ($0 \leq r$) and the system is strictly r-viable;
- labour is necessary for the production of a surplus.

There then exists one (up to indifference) dominant technique solution to (3), associated with a positive price vector. This technique is independent of the positive final demand and the growth rate g ($0 \leq g \leq r$). The price of every commodity in terms of wage is minimum, i.e. the real wage is maximum.

Theorem 8. Let there be a multiple-product economy with proper capital goods, which is sectoral according to Definition 7. Under the same two assumptions as in Theorem 7 and, moreover, the free disposal hypothesis for capital goods, there exists at least one dominant technique. A dominant technique and its associated price-and-wage vector are independent of final demand. The prices of final goods are positive, those of capital goods non-negative.

Theorem 7 extends the non-substitution property from single-product models to sectoral models without pure capital goods. Theorem 8 states a weak version of the same property in the presence of proper capital goods: a dominant technique exists, which is independent of final demand. The differences between the two statements are: (*i*) the dominant technique may not be unique; (*ii*) it may depend on the growth rate; and (*iii*) the prices of final goods may not be minimum.

7 Conclusion

The notion of a sector stems from the attempt to extend the adjustment and super-adjustment properties to multiple-product systems, including those with fixed capital: can the economy adapt itself to a change in demand only by changing the activity levels of its operated methods? Our approach is based on a partition of the set of processes into 'indispensable' sectors (the rainbow axiom). Then the super-adjustment property holds in the presence of internal or, more generally, proper capital goods. The notions of a sector and a proper capital good generalize those of an industry and a non-transferable capital good. They are dual to each other: the production of a final demand basket requires a production in every sector; symmetrically, a zero net product of proper capital goods requires their zero net product in every sector.

The change of concepts goes hand in hand with that of a standpoint. The notion of a sector illustrates the global point of view already advocated in the definition of an all-engaging system and extends it to the choice of methods. When the methods are selected through competition, the consequences of the introduction of proper capital goods are illustrated by the strong and weak versions of the non-substitution property (Theorems 7 and 8). One of the aims of the following chapters 15 and 16 is to understand the reason for the gap between these results and to reduce it through a deeper study of fixed capital models.

8 References

Johansen (1972) noticed the difficulties of extending the definition of industry to multiple-product systems, but thought the notion useful:

> There are now many conceivable bases for the definition of sectors: Similarities in output structure, similarities in input structure (or at least some common main inputs), similarities in some technological processes, organizational and/or geographical distinctions and perhaps also other criteria. The following considerations are valid regardless of how the sectors are defined, but the nonsubstitution assertion is most likely to hold when there are similarities in output structure for possible activities within a sector whereas output structures are markedly different as between sectors. (Johansen 1972, 390)

Herrero and Villar (1988, 148) do not specify how sectors are defined. They assume from the outset that the number of sectors is equal to the number of commodities and that any viable set of processes admits at least one process in each sector. The basic idea of the chapter is to combine the notion of an engaging system with the choice of technique (Erreygers 1994a). It follows several joint works with Erreygers (1998b, 1998c, 1999). The references relative to section 6 are given in chapter 16.

9 Proofs

Proof of Theorems 1–3. See Bidard and Erreygers (1998b) for direct proofs. In order to avoid repeating the same types of arguments for economies without or with capital goods, one may alternatively define a general framework and consider Theorems 1–3 as particular cases of a result relative to a set of demand baskets $D \subset R^n$, where D is a pointed closed convex cone in R^n. 'Pointed' means that the cone contains no straight line. The specifications $D = R^n_+$ or $D = R^f_+ \times \{0_k\}$ correspond to the absence or the presence of pure capital goods. A system has the adjustment property (relative to D) if, for any $d \in D$, there exists a non-negative solution y to $y(B - A) = d$. The basic ideas are, first, that the system must have a solution, independently of the non-negativity constraint on y. This requires that the linear application $B - A$ is surjective on D. Since $B - A$ is injective for a minimum system, the property can be checked by counting dimensions, hence the reference to 'square' or 'balanced' systems. Second, these activity levels must be semi-positive. By the strict viability hypothesis, equality $y_0(B - A) = d_0$ holds with y_0

semi-positive and some d_0 in the relative interior of D. If the solution y to $y(B - A) = d$ had a negative component, the solution to $y'(B - A) = d'$, where d' is an adequately chosen convex combination of d_0 and d, would be semi-positive with a zero component, thus violating either the minimality hypothesis or the rainbow axiom. Therefore the solution to $y(B - A) = d$ exists and is positive for any $d \in D$, hence the adjustment or super-adjustment property. ■

Proof of Theorem 4.

- Statements (*i*) and (*ii*) follow from Theorem 3.
- For an adjustable system, the equation $yC = e_i$ admits a unique semi-positive solution $y_i \in R_+^m$, where e_i is any of the first f unit vectors of R_+^{f+k}. Let L be the matrix obtained by stacking the y_is. We have $LC = [I_f, 0_k]$. L is uniquely defined and all its columns are semi-positive as soon as no process is superfluous. Conversely, the unique solution to $yC = (d', 0)$ is then $y = d'L$. Therefore, conditions (*ii*) and (*iii*) are equivalent.
- If the system is engaging, the transposed matrix $\widetilde{C}$ is injective. Therefore, C admits a right inverse matrix: $CR = I_m$. Since $L = L(CR) = (LC)R = [I, 0]R = R'$, R' inherits the properties of L. Conversely, if $CR = I_m$ with R' unique, equation $C'x' + C''x'' = 0$ implies $x' = 0$, otherwise the vector x could be added to a column of R in equality $CR = I$ and change the value of R'. Implication

$$[C', C'']x = 0 \Rightarrow [I, 0]x = 0$$

holds and, therefore, there exists a matrix L such that $[I, 0] = LC$. Since L coincides with R', it is unique with semi-positive columns. Condition (*iii*) is met and the system is engaging. ■

Proof of Theorem 5. Let there be a minimum subset of methods such that $y(B - A) = (d_0', 0)$ for some $d_0' \gg 0_f$, where $y = (y_\alpha, \ldots, y_\sigma)$ are the activity levels within the $\sigma = f$ sectors. Consider the square system made of the f (fictitious) reduced processes that are written $y_\iota A_\iota' \rightarrow y_\iota B_\iota'$, with f final goods and no capital goods. Our intermediate goal is to show that the reduced system meets the assumptions (*i*) and (*ii*) of Theorem 1:

- These methods are viable because they produce d_0'.
- They are minimum: otherwise there would exist non-negative scalars $\lambda = (\lambda_\alpha, \ldots, \lambda_\sigma)$, not all positive, such that some $\overline{d}' \gg 0_f$ would be obtained in the reduced economy; then the net product $(\overline{d}', 0_k)$ would be obtained in the original economy for activity levels $\lambda * y = (\lambda_\alpha y_\alpha, \ldots, \lambda_\sigma y_\sigma)$ (the hypothesis concerning the proper capital goods

is used at this stage): a contradiction with the sectoral hypothesis is obtained.

- The system is square.

By Theorem 1 relative to economies with final goods only, any vector $d' > 0_f$ can be produced by the reduced processes, for adequately chosen activity levels λ'. Then, the net product $(d', 0_k)$ is obtained for the activity levels $\lambda' * y$ applied to the original economy with capital goods. Hence, the super-adjustment property. ■

Proof of Theorem 6. The system $yC = d = (d', 0)$ is written:

$$y_1 C_1' + y_2 C_2' = d' \tag{4}$$

$$y_1 \overline{C}_1'' + y_2 \overline{C}_2'' = 0 \tag{5}$$

$$y_1 \hat{C}_1'' + y_2 \hat{C}_2'' = 0. \tag{6}$$

Since, by construction, any solution (y_1, y_2) to (5) is a solution to (6), we disregard (6). From (5), we obtain $y_2 = -y_1 \overline{C}_1''(\overline{C}_2'')^{-1} = y_1 G$. The system (4) is then written as $y_1(C_1' + GC_2') = d'$, or $y_1 \Gamma = d'$. Since $m = f + rk(C'')$, matrix Γ is square. If Γ is singular, there is no solution for some positive vector d' and the adjustment property does not hold. If Γ is regular, the unique solution to (4)–(5) is $y_1 = d'\Gamma^{-1}$, $y_2 = d'\Gamma^{-1}G$. The semi-positivity of y for any $d' > 0$ requires that Γ^{-1} and $\Gamma^{-1}G$ are semi-positive. Moreover, the system is engaging if no process is superfluous, i.e. no component (y_1, y_2) is identically zero. This is equivalent to the fact that G has no zero column. ■

Theorem 8 coincides with Theorem 1 in chapter 16, where a complete and self-contained theory of fixed capital is elaborated. Theorem 7 also follows from the constructions in chapter 16, but a direct derivation of Theorem 7 from Theorem 8 is instructive. Let us admit Theorem 8 and assume that there are no capital goods.

Proof of Theorem 7. According to Theorem 8, there exists a solution to the system (3) for any semi-positive basket d, with operated methods independent of d. For a positive rate of accumulation g, equality $yB = (1+g)yA + d$ is also written $yB = yA + d'$, where $d' = d + gA$ is another final demand vector. Therefore the operated methods are also independent of g. Consider now an arbitrary square and viable technique $(\overline{A}, \overline{B})$ extracted from the sectoral economy and which is associated with positive prices $\overline{p}$ in terms of wage. According to Theorem 2, $(\overline{A}, \overline{B})$ has the adjustment property, therefore the matrix $(\overline{B} - (1+r)\overline{A})^{-1}$ is semi-positive for $r = 0$. It keeps the property for positive levels of r as long as the inequality $(\overline{B} - (1 + r)\overline{A})^{-1}\bar{l} \gg 0$ holds, and this is the case by assumption at the actual rate of profit. By definition of the competitive price system $(p, w = 1)$, inequality $\overline{B}p - (1 + r)\,\overline{A}p \leq \bar{l}$ holds. A pre-multiplication by the inverse matrix leads to $p \leq \overline{p}$: the competitive prices are minimal across all techniques associated with positive prices. Therefore, they are also uniquely defined. ■

15 Austrian and one-machine models

1 Two fixed-capital models

From a theoretical standpoint, production with fixed-capital is at the junction between the 'single' and the 'multiple' production type. This location explains why fixed-capital systems inherit disparate economic properties. An agricultural process uses seeds and a tractor for the production of wheat; but it also produces, simultaneously, a tractor which differs from the one that entered into production, since it is older. The fixed-capital theory oscillates between these two poles: on the one hand, when the project is decomposed into yearly processes, an older machine is produced jointly with the final good, except in the last period; on the other hand, over the lifetime of a tractor – from the beginning of its construction to its abandonment as scrap – the only net product consists of one final good. Because of the joint production aspects, the economic behaviour differs from that of single production. However, since the whole project produces wheat only, a reduction of the initial gap and a recovery of the properties of single-product systems is expected. This programme is implemented in the analysis of fixed-capital systems. We limit ourselves to the study of regular paths.

Since many economists of different schools of thought have contributed to the elaboration of the fixed-capital theory, the reference to a 'programme' suggests coordination among the participants. The different schools never collaborated, even if a common direction of research was perceived. Disagreements are underlined at the very outset of discussions: Hicks affirms that the Austrian model's superiority is due to its isolating of the intertemporal dimension ('vertical' relations) to the detriment of the interindustrial ones ('horizontal' relations). On the contrary, one of the aims of *PCMC* is that of demonstrating the fundamental flaw of the Austrian conception. Nevertheless, our retrospective presentation ignores these anathemas and establishes parallels among 'Austrian', 'orthodox' and 'post-Sraffian' contributions. The ultimate justification of this standpoint lies in its theoretical, rather then historical, logic and in the unity that is highlighted beyond the fragmentation of the models. It is that unity, and only that, which enables us to conceive a general problem. Its resolution makes the previous contributions appear as particular cases which have been treated with varying degrees of elegance (an unfortunate feature of the literature on the topic is the abundance of convoluted proofs and false assertions). We wish to convince the reader that the chief problem is of a conceptual nature: once the right standpoint is defined, the obstacles are swept aside.

Unlike chapter 14, we are not interested at this stage in defining the largest theoretical framework. The standard assumptions, e.g. the industry hypothesis and the non-transferability of machines between industries, are retained. Two crucial hypotheses allow us to focus on one objective:

- The *one-machine hypothesis*. Only one type of machine is produced and used in every industry: therefore, there are f types of machines (at most) if there are f final goods. There is no harm in simplifying the formalization by assuming a unique type of machine (tractor) used in the corn industry only. Its varieties $M_0, M_1, \ldots, M_{T-1}$ are identified by their age. The other industries are of the single-product type.
- The *truncation hypothesis*. The economic lifetime of a machine is determined endogenously and can be shorter than the physical life T. A 'project', when truncated at length t, stops with the production and the free disposition of machine M_t. Its 'tail' between t and T is abandoned.
- The objective is to show that the economic behaviour of such fixed capital systems is identical to that of single-product systems once the lifetime $\hat{t} = \hat{t}(r)$ of every machine is optimally adapted to the level of distribution. The choice of the optimal lifetime is similar to a choice of technique and is determined by the search for extra profits.

The chapter is organized in almost independent parts corresponding to the truncation (sections 2 and 3) and non-truncation (section 4) hypotheses. In each part, we begin with the neo-Austrian model where inputs and outputs represent quantities of corn. The model being standard in economic analysis when corn flows are replaced by money flows, the well-known investment criteria – namely the present value (PV) criterion and the internal rate of return (IRR) criterion – are used as starting points. It will be shown that the model has nice properties, for instance that the criteria coincide under the truncation hypothesis, contrary to conventional wisdom. As the neo-Austrian intertemporal model ignores interindustrial relationships, the robustness of the conclusion has to be guaranteed by its extension to multisector models. Hence, the study of fixed-capital models of the Sraffian type. The presentation avoids most calculations and underlines the identity of the results obtained in the Austrian and multisectoral models.

2 The Austrian project and truncation

2.1 *Investment criteria*

In a neo-Austrian model, an investment project is described by a flow-input/flow-output sequence $(a_0, \ldots, a_{T-1}) \rightarrow (b_1, \ldots, b_T)$. a_t represents the quantity of corn invested t periods after the beginning of the project, b_{t+1} the gross product one period later. We look at the Austrian model as an extension of the corn model to intertemporal economies. Labour has been replaced by a given real wage and incorporated in the inputs. Constant returns to scale prevail. Given a rate of interest r (interest, profit and discount rates are identified), the present value of the project is [1]

$$PV_T(r) = -a_0 + \sum_{i=1}^{T-1}(b_i - a_i)(1+r)^{-i} + b_T(1+r)^{-T}. \qquad (1)$$

The 'investment polynomial' $(1 + r)^T PV_T(r)$ is:

$$I_T(r) = -a_0(1+r)^T + \ldots + (b_t - a_t)(1+r)^{T-t} + \ldots + b_T. \quad (2)$$

The index T will be omitted when there is no ambiguity and we will loosely refer to $I(r)$ as the present value: what matters is its sign (moreover, it is a present value, but calculated at date T). By definition, an IRR makes the present value equal to zero, i.e. it is a root r_0 of the investment polynomial. The following factorization plays an important role in the construction:

$$\begin{aligned} I(r) = (r_0 - r)[a_0(1+r)^{T-1} + (a_1 + \pi_0)(1+r)^{T-2} + \ldots + \\ (a_t + \pi_{t-1})(1+r)^{T-t-1} + \ldots + (a_{T-1} + \pi_{T-2})]. \end{aligned} \qquad (3)$$

(The reason why, in the bracket, the generic coefficient of the polynomial is written down as $a_t + \pi_{t-1}$ is mysterious for the moment.) The identification of polynomials (2) and (3) leads to the formulas

$$(a_{T-1} + \pi_{T-2})(1 + r_0) = b_T, \qquad (4.1)$$

$$\forall t = 1, \ldots, T-2 \;\; (a_t + \pi_{t-1})(1 + r_0) = b_{t+1} + \pi_t \qquad (4.2)$$

which define the sequence π_t by induction, from $t = T - 2$ to $t = 0$.

[1] Martin Faustmann (1849) was the first economist to deal with present value. The idea comes from his ancestor, Dr Faust, a famed specialist of the value of time.

Two investment criteria are often referred to. The PV criterion states that the best project is the one whose present value, calculated for a given rate of interest, is non-negative and maximum. The IRR criterion contemplates the project which admits the greatest IRR. Since Fisher (1907), it has been known that difficulties appear in the use of the IRR criterion: multiple IRR may coexist and, even if the IRR is unique, the criteria may diverge. The recommendation found in textbooks is to stick to the PV criterion because the PV represents extra profits, so that the PV criterion is consistent with the standard analysis of competition whereas the IRR criterion is a proxy with no robust theoretical ground.

2.2 *The truncation hypothesis*

The truncation hypothesis is that an intertemporal project can be stopped at any date t ($t < T$). The 'truncated' project is written $(a_0, \ldots, a_{t-1}) \rightarrow (b_1, \ldots, b_t)$ with corresponding changes in the investment polynomial. The economic lifetime is then shortened with regard to the physical lifetime. The choice of the economic lifetime is similar to a choice between T different projects, corresponding to $t = 1, \ldots, T$, even if only one intertemporal project was contemplated at the beginning. The lifetime is decided at date 0.

Why should an entrepreneur truncate a project? The decision is consistent with the profit-maximization behaviour if the costs associated with the 'tail' of the project, between t and T, exceed the corresponding receipts: the maintenance costs or repairs are too high. Therefore, the first truncation criterion is that the PV of the tail is negative. It invites us to calculate the value of the tail(s). Let the T-year project be decomposed into a sequence of T one-year processes:

$$
\begin{array}{lcl}
a_0 & \rightarrow & b_1 + 1M_0 \\
a_1 + 1M_0 & \rightarrow & b_2 + 1M_1 \\
\ldots & & \\
a_t + 1M_{t-1} & \rightarrow & b_{t+1} + 1M_t \\
\ldots & & \\
a_{T-2} + 1M_{T-3} & \rightarrow & b_{T-1} + 1M_{T-2} \\
a_{T-1} + 1M_{T-2} & \rightarrow & b_T.
\end{array}
\tag{5}
$$

The first relationship makes a brand-new 'tractor' appear jointly with the first crop. The tractor is used in the following periods and is getting older, until the last period when it is transformed into scrap with no value. It must be understood that the tractor may have no physical reality: the decomposition means only that the second annual process cannot begin in the absence of investment during the previous year. But the farmer who started the project may sell it after a few years. The price of the transaction is called the price of the tractor, if the tractor really exists; if not, what is bought by the second farmer is the possibility of starting his own production process at date t instead of date 0. From an economic point of view, the physical tractor is nothing but the materialization of a right and the distinction between both interpretations of M_t is irrelevant. Hicks had a less abstract interpretation and assumed a period of construction of the tractor (during t_0 years), followed by a period of utilization. This simple profile amounts to setting $b_1 = \ldots = b_{t_0} = 0$ and considering M_{t_0} as the new machine, the previous outputs $M_0, \ldots, M_{t_0-1}$ being machines *in utero*. This conception is unduly restrictive and we retain the general formalization (5).

The price of the t-year-old tractor[2] M_t can be calculated backwards or forwards, the values being equal at equilibrium. The backward calculation (the seller's point of view) takes into account the past discounted costs, minus the past crops. In the forward calculation (the buyer's point of view), the value of M_t is the present value of the future crops, minus that of the future seeds. Therefore, the value of M_t is the value of the tail after date $t+1$:

First truncation criterion. A neo-Austrian project must be truncated if a machine has a negative value.

This result is consistent with decomposition (5): truncation at date $t+1$ amounts to abandoning a negatively valued tractor M_t in order to increase the profits of the corresponding yearly process. Let us start the calculation from the last annual process (5). In terms of corn and for a given discount rate r_0, the value $p(M_{T-2})$ of the last machine is determined by the relationship (6.1). More generally, the value $p(M_t)$ once known, the value of the machine M_{t-1} is defined by (6.2):

$$a_{T-1} + p(M_{T-2}) = b_T/(1+r_0), \tag{6.1}$$

$$a_t + p(M_{t-1}) = [b_{t+1} + p(M_t)]/(1+r_0). \tag{6.2}$$

The surprise is that the same recursive laws intervene in these Bellman-type (1957) formulas as in (4). Therefore $\pi_t = p(M_t)$ and another criterion is obtained:

[2] In the theory of fixed capital, minor complications appear in the notations: the tractor of age t is produced at date $t+1$ by the $(t+1)$th one-year process. Moreover, in a matricial representation, the inputs dated t and the outputs dated $t+1$ receive the same row index.

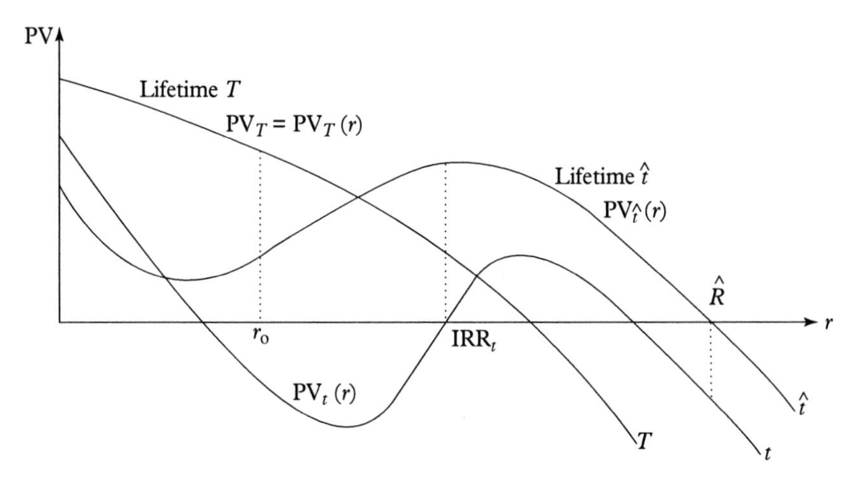

Figure 15.1 Investment polynomials and optimal truncation

Second truncation criterion: Let r_0 be a given IRR. A neo-Austrian project is worth truncating if and only if some negative value π_t appears in the factorization (3) of its investment polynomial.

Except if it has a simple profile, a project may have several IRRs. Here enters the truncation theory. The arguments are developed in three steps:

(*i*) Consider the factorization (3) of the investment polynomial. The presence of several IRRs requires that the second factor admits negative coefficients. Therefore, some π_t is negative and some truncation is profitable.

(*ii*) Consider the effect of a profitable truncation on the investment polynomial. Let R_m denote the maximum IRR of the non-truncated project. When truncation occurs, the PV, which was zero before truncation, becomes positive at R_m because the negative weight of the tail is eliminated. Since the present value is negative when the rate of interest tends to infinity, it turns out that the new truncated project has a root greater than R_m: an economically justified truncation increases the maximum IRR.

(*iii*) Let us plot in figure 15.1 the T polynomials associated with the T possible lifetimes $t = 1, \ldots, T$. Among the IRRs, which are the intersections of these curves with the horizontal axis, let us isolate the greatest one $\hat{R}$, which is an IRR of the project of length $\hat{t}$. If this $\hat{t}$-project had another IRR, it would follow from point (*i*) that a new truncation would occur, and from (*ii*) that an IRR greater than $\hat{R}$ would exist. This being excluded, the $\hat{t}$-project has a unique

IRR. Therefore, the investment polynomial is positive up to $\hat{R}$, in particular for any IRR of the other investment polynomials ($t \neq \hat{t}$). Since the present value of the $\hat{t}$-project is positive when the present value of a t-project is zero, it is advantageous to switch from the lifetime t to $\hat{t}$. Conversely, once the system has been truncated at length $\hat{t}$, the other investment polynomials are all negative at $\hat{R}$, and a switch to another lifetime would cause losses. The conclusion is:

Investment criteria: In a neo-Austrian model, the optimal truncation according to the PV criterion is the one associated with the maximum IRR, and this is the unique IRR of the optimal truncation. Therefore, the PV and the IRR criteria coincide.

The coincidence between the IRR and the PV criteria is an unexpected result. The basic reason is that, at equilibrium with constant returns, the extra profits as measured by the present value are zero. Therefore, the equilibrium rate of interest *must* be an IRR (it turns out that it is the maximum rate). The restrictive assumption in the construction is the equilibrium hypothesis itself. In practice, an investment is undertaken because it yields more than the current rate. Out of equilibrium, the two criteria continue to diverge (figure 15.1 for $r = r_0$).

The optimal truncation can be determined in several ways. The one considered above consists in writing down all investment polynomials and calculating all their positive roots, then picking up the *maximum maximorum*. It refers to the first factor in the right-hand side of (3). Another criterion contemplates the second factor which, for the optimal truncation, is the longest one with positive π_ts. A third procedure, in the spirit of the market algorithm, consists in truncating the initial process when a negatively priced machine appears; in the new system the prices of the machines change (they depend on the lifetime of the project); a new truncation may appear, etc. In this algorithm, the 'recuperation' must not be forgotten. Indeed, imagine a tractor which is physically efficient at age seven but inefficient after this age. In the initial system, the present value of the seven-year-old tractor may be negative, because it summarizes in one scalar the whole story from age seven to the life horizon; then, the first truncation eliminates the tractors of age seven even though they are efficient. The mistake will be corrected at the next step by recuperation, which is the possibility of dragging the seven-year-old tractor out of the ditch where it is lying, at a zero price. The operation lengthens the project and becomes effective because it yields extra profits. The algorithm converges towards the optimal truncation.

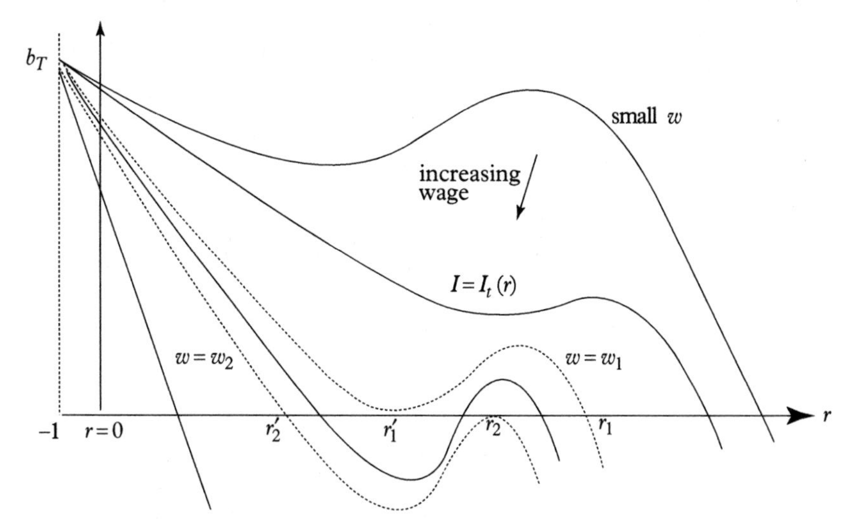

Figure 15.2 The investment polynomial for different wages

2.3 The Ricardian law

Let us examine the relationship between the real wage and the rate of profit (because of the Ricardian flavour of the problem, we refer to the rate of profit rather than the rate of interest). Up to now the real wage was not apparent in the model. But let every input coefficient be decomposed as $a_t = a_t' + wl_t$, where a_t' is a quantity of seeds, l_t the amount of labour and w the real wage. For a given length t of the project, the relationship between the real wage and the IRRs is written $I_t(r, w) = 0$ where

$$I_t(r, w) = -(a_0' + wl_0)(1+r)^t + \sum_{i=1}^{t-1}(b_i - a_i' - wl_i)(1+r)^{t-i} + b_t. \qquad (7)$$

For a given wage, several solutions in r may coexist (multiplicity of the IRRs). When the wage increases, all coefficients of the investment polynomial decrease, therefore the value of I_t $(t = 1, \ldots, T)$ decreases. Figure 15.2 shows a family of investment polynomials for a given lifetime and increasing wages.

Because of the downward movement of the investment polynomials, the greatest IRR $r = \bar{r}(w)$ is decreasing and, when the hump of an investment polynomial touches the horizontal axis (at $w = w_2$), it falls from r_2 to r_2' (note that the discontinuity is associated with the coexistence of two IRRs). Therefore the maximum IRR $\bar{r}(w)$ is a decreasing, though not necessarily continuous, function of w. Assume alternatively that the

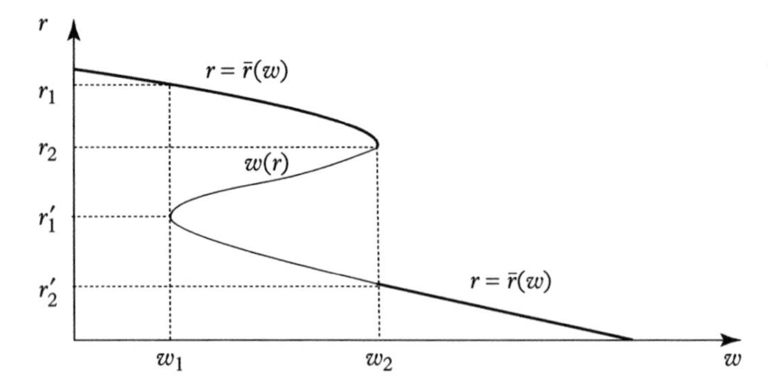

Figure 15.3 The w–r relationship for a given lifetime

rate of profit is the exogenous variable. Solving equation $I_t(r, w) = 0$ in w defines a unique wage $w = w(r)$ which is a continuous, though not necessarily monotonous, function of r. These results are visualized in figure 15.3 for a given lifetime: the Z-shaped curve represents the set $\{(w, r); I_t(r, w) = 0\}$ as it is deduced from relation (7) and figure 15.2. For a given w, the upper bold curve is the $\bar{r} = \bar{r}(w)$ curve; for a given r, $w = w(r)$ is unique.

Figure 15.3 shows the w–r relationship for an arbitrary lifetime, in the absence of truncation. In figure 15.4, T similar curves are drawn, corresponding to all possible lifetimes. When truncation is introduced, it is the maximum IRR for a given wage which matters, i.e. we are interested in the upper envelope in figure 15.4. We have noticed that the discontinuities in the $\bar{r}(w)$ curve are associated with the occurrence of multiple IRRs. Since the IRR is unique for the optimal truncation, this phenomenon cannot happen on the upper envelope corresponding to the sequence of optimal truncations. In conclusion, we have proved that, in a neo-Austrian model with truncation, the w–r relationship is well defined, continuous and decreasing for the sequence of optimally truncated projects.

3 The multisector one-machine model

3.1 Centre and prices

The neo-Austrian flow-input/flow-output model is poor because the interindustrial relationships are ignored. The specific structure of the input and output matrices of a multisector fixed-capital model reflects the production and the use of a machine within an industry. We assume that

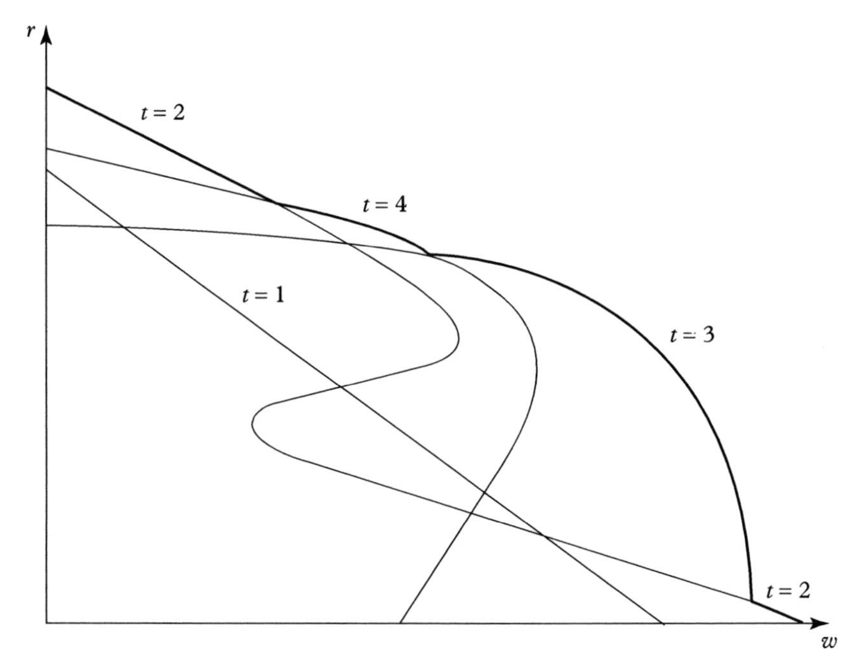

Figure 15.4 The w–r relationship for different lifetimes and optimal truncations

every process produces one final good at most and that the machines are not shiftable among industries. We retain the one-machine hypothesis: (i) at most one type of machine, with different varieties according to age, is produced and used in every industry, and (ii) the structure of production for the machines is an ageing process. With two final goods, wheat and iron, and a 'tractor' used in the wheat industry, which lasts for $T = 3$ years (no machine in metallurgy for simplicity), the structure is illustrated by data:

$$A = \begin{bmatrix} a_{11} & a_{12} & 0 & 0 & 0 \\ a_{21} & a_{22} & 1 & 0 & 0 \\ a_{31} & a_{32} & 0 & 1 & 0 \\ a_{41} & a_{42} & 0 & 0 & 1 \\ a'_{21} & a'_{22} & 0 & 0 & 0 \end{bmatrix}, \; l = \begin{pmatrix} l_0 \\ l_1 \\ l_2 \\ l_3 \\ l'_0 \end{pmatrix} \rightarrow B = \begin{bmatrix} b_{11} & 0 & 1 & 0 & 0 \\ b_{21} & 0 & 0 & 1 & 0 \\ b_{31} & 0 & 0 & 0 & 1 \\ b_{41} & 0 & 0 & 0 & 0 \\ 0 & b'_{22} & 0 & 0 & 0 \end{bmatrix}$$

An F-irreducibility hypothesis is introduced for simplicity. Let the prices be denoted p'_1, p'_2 for the final goods, p''_t for the t-year-old tractor (the previous notations were $p(M_t)$ and π_t). The lifetime of the tractor is temporarily given. The price equations are written:

$$(1+r)(a_{11}p'_1 + a_{12}p'_2) + wl_0 = b_{11}p'_1 + p''_0 \quad \vdots\ 1 \qquad (8)$$

$$(1+r)(a_{21}p'_1 + a_{22}p'_2 + p''_0) + wl_1 = b_{21}p'_1 + p''_1 \quad \vdots\ (1+r)^{-1} \qquad (9)$$

$$(1+r)(a_{31}p'_1 + a_{32}p'_2 + p''_1) + wl_2 = b_{31}p'_1 + p''_2 \quad \vdots\ (1+r)^{-2} \qquad (10)$$

$$(1+r)(a_{41}p'_1 + a_{42}p'_2 + p''_2) + wl_3 = b_{41}p'_1 \quad \vdots\ (1+r)^{-3} \qquad (11)$$

$$(1+r)(a'_{21}p'_1 + a'_{22}p'_2) + wl'_0 = b'_{22}p'_2 \qquad (12)$$

That system of five equations and five unknowns is solved in two steps. First, multiply (8)–(11) by the scalars $(1+r)^{-t}$ as indicated, and add them up in order to make the prices of the tractors disappear. After division by $b_{11} + b_{21}(1+r)^{-1} + b_{31}(1+r)^{-2} + b_{41}(1+r)^{-3}$, the prices p' of final goods turn out to be the solution to the reduced 2×2 system

$$(1+r)\hat{A}p' + w\hat{l} = p', \qquad (13)$$

where $\hat{A}$ is a 2×2 semi-positive matrix (two industries and two final goods). Relation (13) resembles a single-product equation, the difference being that the matrix $\hat{A}$ and the vector $\hat{l}$ both depend on the rate of profit: $\hat{A} = \hat{A}(r)$, $\hat{l} = \hat{l}(r)$. The economy $(\hat{A}, \hat{l}) \rightarrow I$, as opposed to its original extensive form (A, B), is called the 'centre' of the system, in Schefold's words. The reduction to the centre reflects the fact that, over the lifetime of the tractor, the product is reduced to wheat only, as in single production. After reduction, the prices are calculated successively: those p' of the final goods are first obtained by solving (13); those p'' of the tractors of various ages are then deduced from (8)–(11).

If the matrix $\hat{A}$ were independent of the rate of profit, the admissible rates would be defined by their upper bound and the prices of the final goods would be positive. Since $\hat{A}$ depends on r, the prices of the final goods are positive when inequality $(1+r)Frob[\hat{A}(r)] \leq 1$ holds, i.e. when the rate of profit belongs to the set of the type $\mathcal{J} = [-1, R_0] \cup \ldots \cup [R_{h-1}, R_h] \cup \ldots \cup [R_{m-1}, R_m]$ (figure 15.5).

In a comparison with the Austrian model, the values R_h are analogous to the IRRs and the 'holes' in $\mathcal{J}$ to the parts on which the investment polynomial is negative. The limit values R_h are such that

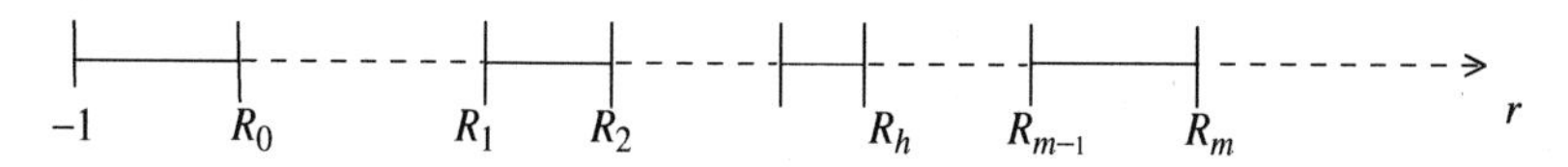

Figure 15.5 The set $\mathcal{J}$ of positive prices for final goods (given t)

$(1 + R_h)Frob[\hat{A}(R_h)] = 1$. They are associated with a zero wage and a positive standard basket $\hat{q}_h = (\hat{q}_{1h}\, \hat{q}_{2h})$ within the centre. These activity levels sustain a regular growth of the centre at rate $G_h = R_h$. Let the 2-vector $\hat{q}_h$ be developed as a positive 5-vector by replacing its component $\hat{q}_{1h}$ relative to the reduced agricultural industry by $(q_{1h}^{(0)}, \ldots, q_{1h}^{(3)})$ where $q_{1h}^{(t)} = \hat{q}_{1h}(1 + G_h)^{-t}$ is the activity level of the tth yearly agricultural process. In the absence of fixed capital in metallurgy (for simplicity), we have $q_{2h} = \hat{q}_{2h}$. A positive standard basket q_h of (A, B) is obtained, which sustains a regular growth of the whole economy at rate $G_h = R_h$. Though the notations become involved, the principle of the analysis is simple and consists in playing accordion between the original fixed-capital economy (the yearly processes) and its centre (the reduced industries). What has been done is, first, a reduction of the fixed-capital economy to a single-product economy, for which a standard commodity is identified; then, an expansion of these standard proportions leads to standard proportions for the original economy.

Let us now look at the prices p'' of machines. When both members of the price equation $(1 + r)Ap + wl = Bp$ are pre-multiplied by the positive standard row vector q_0 attached to R_0, condition $p > 0$ and the inequality

$$(1 + r)\, q_0 Ap \leq (1 + r)\, q_0 Ap + wq_0 l = q_0 Bp = (1 + R_0)\, q_0 Ap$$

imply $r \leq R_0$. Therefore, it is only on the *first* interval $]-1, R_0[$ that the prices of all goods may be positive.

3.2 *Effects of truncation*

We now drop the assumption that the economic lifetime is exogenous. The theory of truncation presumes that the ageing machines can be disposed of freely, and the truncation is effective if an ageing machine is negatively priced. What can be said about the truncated system? Let the t-year-old tractor be the first negatively priced machine ($p_t'' < 0$). When the positive price vector $(p', \overline{p}'', w)$ where $\overline{p}''$ is the price sub-vector relative to the first $t-1$ tractors, is applied to the truncated economy, the truncated system yields extra profits (elimination of a negatively priced output). Therefore the centre of the truncated system is more profitable than the centre of the non-truncated system, for the price vector (p', w). Since the centres of the truncated and non-truncated systems are both of the single-product type and differ only by the coefficients relative to the corn industry, the centre of the truncated system pays a higher wage for the given rate of profit. So does (accordion!) the truncated system, with regard to the non-truncated system.

We have described the effects of the first truncation. A new price vector is calculated in the new system and the initial truncation is followed by other truncations or recuperations until an optimal truncation is found. For a given rate of profit, the optimal truncation is wage-maximizing. When the rate increases, the wage in terms of the final goods decreases continuously. A transition between two truncations occurs when the price of a machine vanishes, and the transition is smooth (same prices at the switch point). Other properties of the optimal truncation, which generalize those obtained for the Austrian model, are:

- The maximum feasible rate of profit for the whole economy is the *maximum maximorum* rate among all truncations.
- For the optimal truncation $\hat{t}(r)$, the prices of the final goods are positive at any rate within the interval $]-1, r]$ (the reason is that it is only on the first interval of $\mathcal{J}$ that all goods may be positively priced; this being the case at r for the optimal truncation, any g smaller than r belongs to the first interval, hence to $\mathcal{J}$). Since the prices of the final goods at the rate of profit g are obtained as the product of the first n rows of the Leontief inverse $L(g)$ by the labour vector, which is semi-positive but arbitrary, these rows are positive for any $g \leq r$.

We have considered only the price side. A difference with the Austrian model is that the adjustment of the activity levels to demand becomes a question in multisector models. Up to now, the one-machine model has been characterized only by a specific distribution of its input–output coefficients. An additional feature is that the machines, being pure capital goods, are not demanded for final consumption. Let us look at quantities and activity levels. For any given growth rate g ($g \leq r$), the demand vector $d = (d', 0)$ is met by means of the activity levels $y = (d', 0)L(g)$, which are positive since the first n rows of the inverse matrix are positive. Therefore the fixed-capital system has the adjustment property. More precisely, since the optimal truncation is determined only by the rate of profit, independently of the demand for accumulation or consumption, with a unique associated price vector, the non-substitution property holds.

4 Fixed capital without truncation

4.1 The Austrian project without truncation

The truncation hypothesis sets that an intertemporal project of length T can be interrupted before its natural end without further implication. In a representation by a succession of one-period processes, the future after date t $(0 < t < T)$ is formally encapsulated into a 'machine' that appears on the output side of the tth one-year process and the input side of the next one. But the free disposal hypothesis is often irrelevant for non-material machines: it offers the opportunity to cut down a forest without enduring the subsequent soil erosion.

This section studies the neo-Austrian model without truncation. Once begun, a project must go to its end even if, at a certain date, the value of the tail is negative because of low productivity, important repairs or winding-up costs. In section 2, the contradiction between the investment criteria was encountered, then eliminated by means of the truncation hypothesis. The paradox now resurfaces and one must live with it. Similarly, the Z-shaped wage-profit curve represented in figure 15.3 cannot be 'improved' and transformed into the decreasing upper curve in figure 15.4 by further analysis. We concentrate our attention on three questions: (*i*) In the presence of several IRRs, is there any reason to give a priority to one of them, for instance the greatest rate? (*ii*) Is there a theoretical foundation to the IRR criterion? (*iii*) Free disposal of machines being no longer allowed, what happens to the Neumannian equality between the minimum rate of interest and the maximum rate of growth? These questions have been examined by Atsumi (1991). Atsumi's arguments are involved and not perfect in their details. If the logical flaws can be repaired, the complexity stems from the theoretical framework itself, which considers the economy over an infinite horizon. The main difference between the finite and the infinite horizon is that, in the first case, a final bill is presented to the entrepreneurs whereas, in the second case, the winding-up costs of the old projects can be permanently financed by the receipts of the younger ones. Therefore, a sequence of projects which is not profitable in the finite horizon may, if adequately managed through time, become profitable in the infinite horizon.

In order to have a flavour of these phenomena, consider a typical Austrian project with finite lifetime: $(a_0, \ldots, a_{T-1}) \to (b_1, \ldots, b_T)$. The project cannot be interrupted once started (the non-truncation hypothesis) and is more simply represented by the sequence $(c_0, \ldots, c_\tau, \ldots, c_T)$ of its net products, c_τ being the algebraic difference between the crop and the seeds at date τ: $c_\tau = b_\tau - a_\tau$, with $c_0 = -a_0$ and $c_T = b_T$.

It begins by an investment ($c_o < 0$) and admits constant returns. One may also represent it by its investment polynomial $I(X) = c_0 X^T + \ldots + c_\tau X^{T-\tau} + \ldots + c_T$. A positive root ρ of the investment polynomial is an internal factor of return (IFR) of the project (the reference to factor ρ rather than to the rate $\rho - 1$ is natural in the calculations).

Let us take a numerical example and consider the project $(-1, 6, -11, 6)$ with a modest zero net product over four periods. Its investment polynomial $I(X) = -X^3 + 6X^2 - 11X + 6 = -(X-1)(X-2)(X-3)$ admits three roots, which are the IFRs $\rho_1 = 1$, $\rho_2 = 2$ and $\rho_{\max} = 3$. The present value of the project is positive for a discount factor β in $]0, 1[$ or $]2, 3[$ and negative if β lies in $]1, 2[$ or if $\beta > 3$. For instance, if the discount factor is 1.5, the PV criterion leads to a rejection of the project. As for the IRR criterion, its application is unclear in the presence of several IRRs. (Needless to say, if truncation were allowed, the project would be reduced to the two-year sequence $(-1, 6)$ and all problems would disappear.) What can be done with this project and what is its optimal management? Let there be an economy in which, at every date t, a new project gets started at activity level $y_t \geq 0$. Since projects have been previously launched at dates $t-1, \ldots, t-T$, the surplus at date t amounts to $s_t = y_t c_0 + y_{t-1} c_1 + \ldots + y_{t-T} c_T$ if $t \geq T$, otherwise the values of y_t with negative indices are replaced by zero. Any finite sequence of activity levels applied to the original project generates a daughter project that has the same characteristics (zero overall net product, same IFRs, etc.). But consider an infinite chronicle, for instance a geometrical chronicle $y_t = \lambda^t$. The surplus at date t, $t \geq 3$, amounts to $s_t = -\lambda^t + 6\lambda^{t-1} - 11\lambda^{t-2} + 6\lambda^{t-3} = \lambda^{t-3} I(\lambda) = -\lambda^{t-3}(\lambda - 1)(\lambda - 2)(\lambda - 3)$. For any λ slightly smaller than $\rho_{\max} = 3$, the surplus is positive and grows at rate λ: the upper bound of the rates of growth is the maximum IRR.

In an infinite horizon economy, it would be a mistake to follow the PV criterion and not to invest when the discount factor is $\beta = 1.5$: an entrepreneur who manages the project in order to sustain a growth factor greater than 1.5 obtains pure profits. More generally if, following the neoclassical definition, a rate of interest is a discount factor such that no pure profit can be obtained, then any factor of interest must be at least equal to the maximum factor of growth $\rho_{\max}$. Conversely, it can be shown that any scalar greater than $\rho_{\max}$ is an interest factor. The role played by the maximum IFR is partly clarified by the following remark: the activity levels $y^t = 2^{t+1} - 1$ generate the sequence of surpluses $(-1, 3, 0, 0, \ldots)$, therefore the project $(-1, 3)$ is a daughter project of $(-1, 6, -11, 6)$, and the mother can do as well as the daughter in terms of growth and profitability.

The lessons of the example are general. We retain that, in an infinite horizon, the maximum rate of growth and the minimum rate of interest are equal (von Neumann equality), and both are equal to the maximum IRR of the project. It is right to refer to the IRR criterion in this framework whereas the use of the PV criterion might lead to erroneous decisions.

4.2 *One machine without truncation*

Despite Atsumi's statement that the neo-Austrian approach to the theory of capital offers a significant advantage for economic theory (1991), we do not consider a property as significant if it fails to pass the test of multisector models. The question is whether the previous results can be adequately extended to the one-machine model without truncation.

A neo-Austrian model can be viewed as an intertemporal corn model. When several final goods and interindustrial relationships are introduced, the one-machine model is obtained (one machine per industry). Let all machines have identical lifespans T (otherwise a project can be fictitiously lengthened by adding further periods with no input and no output). With f final goods and f industries, the input and output matrices (A, B) have dimensions $f(T+1) \times f(T+1)$. The generalized eigenvalues associated with a *positive* row-eigenvector are of special interest: let us call them the *PF* eigenvalues. Their distribution is the same as in figure 15.5, where the final goods are positively priced on the set $\mathcal{J}$. The only significant difference from the Austrian model is that other eigenvalues, not associated with positive activity levels, may exist. However, the gap is not visible in figure 15.5 because the superfluous roots are located in the 'holes' of $\mathcal{J}$. The concepts used for the study of the neo-Austrian model can be extended:

- An IFR ρ of a fixed-capital model is the inverse of a *PF* value. It is a regular growth factor of the economy. (The name IFR is consistent with the terminology adopted for the Austrian model, since ρ is a root of the investment polynomial when (A, B) is the matricial representation of an Austrian project.)
- Scalar $\alpha > 0$ is a strict growth factor if there exists a positive sequence $\{s\}$ of feasible surpluses such that $s_{t+1} \gg \alpha\, s_t \gg 0$ for any great enough t.
- Scalar $\beta > 0$ is a strict interest factor if:

$$\forall \{s\} \text{feasible}, \{s\} \neq 0 \quad \forall N \quad \exists t > N \quad \sum_{\tau=0}^{t} \beta^{-\tau} s_\tau \ll 0.$$

Theorem 1. Assume that:
(A_1) any process begins with an investment;
(A_2) any final good i enters directly or indirectly into the production of any final good j.

Let α^*, β^* and $\rho_{\max}$ be, respectively, the upper bound of the strict growth factors, the lower bound of the strict interest factors and the greatest IFR, if any (otherwise, set $\rho_{\max} = 0$). Then $\alpha^* = \beta^* = \rho_{\max}$. If $\rho_{\max} > 0$, a price vector exists, with a zero wage and positive components p^* for final goods, such that all processes yield the factor of profit $\rho_{\max}$ per period.

Once the prices p^* of final goods are known, those of the machines of different types and ages are calculated step by step, starting from the creation of the new machine to the end of its lifetime: the only unknown at each stage is the price of the aged machine. This price is the PV of its future incomes and may be negative if the project is inefficient at the end of its life.

According to Theorem 1, the economically significant value is the maximum IFR. Note that:

- Under the non-truncation hypothesis, only the minimum IFR can be associated with positive prices for all commodities. Therefore, only those fixed-capital systems with a unique IFR can admit positive prices for machines.
- By analogy with single production and the *PF* theorem, it might have been expected that, in the presence of several *PF* values, the economically significant value would correspond to the maximum root of $\lambda B - A$ and therefore, because of the inversion $\lambda = \rho^{-1}$, to the minimum IFR. This is Sraffa's suggestion (*PCMC*, § 64) but it is nonetheless the greatest root that matters.
- Choice of technique can be introduced in the model by adding further rows to A and B which describe alternative uses of a machine. When the additional rows describe the free disposal of the machine at every age, the theory of truncation turns out to be a particular case of the theory of non-truncation.

5 Conclusion

The truncation hypothesis leads to an endogenous determination of the lifetime of machines, which depends on distribution. The results obtained for the neo-Austrian model have been generalized to the multisector one-machine model and all properties of single-product systems have been recovered (positivity of prices, w–r trade-off, non-substitution, etc.).

The combination of the free disposal hypothesis and deeper economic analysis eliminates all paradoxes. The only snag is that the conclusion goes farther than expected: Theorem 8 of chapter 14 let us hope only for a weak form of the non-substitution theorem. It cannot be said that the theory of fixed capital has become transparent as long as the cause of the surprise, although pleasant, is not understood. The reason of this similarity is hidden and becomes an issue in chapter 16. The truncation theory will turn out to be a special case of a more general theory, but its autonomous presentation is useful.

The natural framework for the study of fixed capital without truncation and the IRR criterion is that of an economy with an infinite horizon. Though the analysis becomes complex, the notions of rate of growth and rate of interest are basically unchanged. The maximum rate of growth and the minimum rate of interest are both equal to the maximum IRR associated with positive activity levels. This result generalizes the von Neumann equality and provides a theoretical justification for the use of the IRR criterion in an infinite horizon. The comparative study of the behaviour of the fixed-capital model with or without free disposal clarifies the role of the free disposal hypothesis.

6 Historical notes

The logical reconstruction to which we have proceeded must be distinguished from the historical elaboration of the truncation theory. The Austrian economists considered the 'roundaboutness' of an investment as a measure of its 'quantity of capital'. It depends on the interest rate, which is the price of capital. The idea of a relationship between the duration of the investment and the rate of interest is then natural (Böhm-Bawerk, 1889; Hayek 1931). When applied to one project instead of the comparison between different projects, it leads to the endogenous determination of its lifetime. So did Wicksell (1923) in his study of Åkerman's (1923–4) model. Wicksell discovered that the rate of interest could not be identified with the marginal productivity of capital, but the lifetime is indeed a decreasing function of the rate of interest in his simple model. This 'Austrian' property is not general (Hagemann and Kurz 1976).

The possible occurrence of multiple IRRs was known to Fisher (1907). The rediscovery of the paradox by Pitchford and Hagger (1958) initiated discussions in the *Economic Journal*. The truncation hypothesis is due to Soper (1959) and Karmel (1959), immediately followed by Wright (1959). Soper showed that the IRR is unique for the truncation which maximizes the IRR. Karmel (1959) and Silcock (1959) noticed a flaw in Soper's proof. Karmel's proof is rigorous but with no clear economic content. The idea of truncating a machine with a negative price and, by so doing, of maximizing the PV, comes from Wright (1959). Unaware of Wright's work, Arrow and Levhari (1969) published the same results in the same journal ten years later (Arrow 1983). The argument for the uniqueness of the IRR is that the PV, *when* the lifetime is optimally adjusted to the interest rate, is a decreasing function of that rate. The same argument is used by Hicks (1970, 1973). Flemming and Wright (1971) have shown that, under the truncation hypothesis, the IRR remains unique for generalized discount formulas of the type $PV(r) = \sum_{i=0}^{t} \beta_i(r)(b_i - a_{i+1})$ if the relative weights $\beta_i(r)/\beta_{i-1}(r)$ attached to the successive periods decrease with r. (The standard formula corresponds to $\beta_i/\beta_{i-1} = (1 + r)^{-1}$.) The above reconstruction of the truncation theory in the Austrian framework is based on the factorization formula (3) and the identification of the π_t's with the prices of the machines (Bidard 1991).

Sraffa introduces the multisector one-machine model in chapter X of *PCMC*. He shows that the machines can be eliminated from the price equations and that the prices of final goods are then the solution of a single-product-like system. He also determines the depreciation profile for a machine of constant efficiency. There is no need for truncation if the efficiency is constant or increasing. If not, the idea of an endogenous determination of the lifetime was known in Cambridge: Joan Robinson quoted the case of cars, whose life is longer in India than in Britain because of the smaller cost of labour. In the multisector case, the first results were obtained by Schefold (1971) in his PhD thesis: it is shown that the prices of the final goods in wage units all increase or all decrease after an arbitrary truncation and that the w–r curve is decreasing as long as the machines are positively priced. The formalization hesitates between a one-machine and a several-machine model. The reference to the one-machine model and the role of the 'centre' are clarified in Schefold's later paper (1974), which establishes the main results of the truncation theory. His thesis being virtually finished, Schefold discovered the neo-Austrian works when Hicks gave a seminar in Switzerland. Baldone (1974) and Varri (1974) obtained similar results simultaneously: their common interest in the theory of fixed capital came from a seminar delivered by Morishima. After some work in common, they split for personal reasons but finally reached close 'truncation theorems'.

Twenty-five years later, the intensive use of matricial calculation in these studies looks awkward. The present chapter delineates a line of reasoning which reaches the conclusion with minimum calculations. We moreover retain three conceptual critiques to post-Sraffian works. First, following *PCMC*, the post-Sraffian economists substitute a distinction between 'finished' goods (i.e. final goods and new machines) and old machines for the usual one between final goods and machines. This partition is only a source of confusion and is inconsistent with the very idea of reduction, which aims at eliminating the prices of all machines (Bidard 1997b). Second, the adjustment of activity levels to a given demand is ignored or treated too rapidly. Third, a deeper critique is that the crucial operation is *not* the reduction to the centre in order to eliminate prices but the dual procedure on quantities, called vertical integration (see chapter 16). The starting point of the above presentation is a study of the maximum rate of profit in the multisector fixed-capital model (Bidard 1998b). Its conclusions, when applied to the Austrian model, lead to the identification of the two investment criteria. Then, the isomorphism between the basic features of neo-Austrian and post-Sraffian theories of truncation becomes clear.

Our reinterpretation of post-Sraffian studies as an extension of neo-Austrian results to multisector models does not aim at historical truth. We look at the neo-Austrian formalization as a heuristic tool and take advantage of its simplicity to guess general properties. Note that Burmeister (1974) denies the equivalence between truncation and the free disposal hypothesis and that Atsumi (1991) and McKenzie (1991) suggest that the neo-Austrian model cannot be converted into matricial form with semi-positive input and output matrices. In some sense, these opinions are close to the traditional post-Sraffian position which sets the interindustrial model against the intertemporal approach. For a post-Sraffian point of view on the neo-Austrian theory, see Hagemann (1987).

When truncation is not allowed, the idea of the double equality $\alpha^* = \beta^* = \rho^*$ is clearly expressed by Atsumi (1991) but the maximum rate of growth is not calculated and the formal arguments are dubious. Instead of introducing the notion of strict interest factor, Atsumi defines a factor of interest as a scalar β such that $\limsup_{t\to\infty} PV(t, \beta) \leq 0$ for any feasible sequence of surpluses. One should retain 'lim inf' instead of 'lim sup' in order that the factors of interest be $[\rho^*, +\infty[$. The fact that Atsumi's arguments cannot be directly extended to multisector models may explain his profession of faith in the Austrian model. In the multisector case, the proofs are technical: they deal with infinite horizon and rely on a combination of fixed-point and duality arguments (Bidard 1999a). Cantor and Lippman (1983, 1995) study a neo-Austrian model with an additional cash-in-advance constraint and find a theoretical justification to the *minimum* IRR. Sonin (1995) is concerned with the divergences between the conclusions relative to the minimum and the maximum IRR.

16 Fixed-capital theory

1 One theory

This chapter provides a general theory of fixed capital with truncation on a regular growth path. Its starting point is a series of questions on the results already obtained:

- Why does a one-machine model behave like an Austrian model (chapter 15)?
- Why do they both behave like a single-product systems (chapter 15)?
- Why, on the contrary, does there exist a gap with the results obtained for more general models (chapter 14)?

The method followed consists in starting afresh and rebuilding the whole theory. The reconstruction is far from being naive since we know the type of result we want to obtain, the enigmas we want to solve and the tools which have already proved their efficiency (mainly, the notion of vertical integration). We first consider the more general model with *machines used jointly* in the same industry or sector. The associated properties constitute the basic ground for all fixed capital models. Then we instil further specifications, drop by drop. Each drop enriches the properties until the behaviour of a single-product system is finally recovered. The procedure makes a precise parallel between a specification of the model and a property. Moreover, since the drops are all of the same nature, it turns out that the behaviour of a fixed-capital model is entirely governed by one of its features, namely the reproduction of the pure capital goods.

2 A general fixed-capital model

Some repetitions of already established results are justified by the desire to have a self-contained construction and organize its content in the most adequate way. Since we retain the regular growth assumption, let us first remind ourselves of Lippi's result (chapter 11, sub-section 5.1): Under

the assumptions
(A1) $-1 < g \leq r$,
(A2) $\exists y > 0 \quad y(B - (1 + r)A) \gg 0$,
(A3) $\{y > 0, y(B - (1 + g)A) \geq 0\} \Rightarrow yl > 0$.
and the free disposal hypothesis, there exists a solution ($y > 0, p > 0$) to system (L):

$$\begin{aligned} yB &= (1+g)yA + d \\ Bp &\leq (1+r)Ap + l \quad [y]. \end{aligned} \tag{L}$$

A fixed-capital model is a multiple-product system with a certain number of characteristics:
(FC_1) There are f goods identified as *final goods* and k goods identified as *pure capital goods or machines*. The machines are not consumed.
(FC_2) *Rainbow*. The processes are partitioned into f sectors. For the given rate of growth g, a semi-positive surplus in final goods requires at least one operated process in each sector.
(FC_3) *Truncation*. The machines can be freely disposed of.
(FC_4) *Non-shiftability*. A machine intervenes in one sector only.
(FC_5) *Technical assumptions*. Conditions (A) of the Lippi Theorem hold.
Assumption (FC_1) permits the joint production of both types of goods, and the final goods may be used for production. It leaves some degree of freedom in the distinction between final goods and pure capital goods: if a commodity is produced in order to be used in several sectors (an all-purpose machine), its classification as a final good, even if it is not consumed, avoids violating the non-shiftability assumption which does not apply to final goods. The names 'machine' or 'fixed capital' given for simplicity to all pure capital goods may suggest a classification according to age: this is not the case here. Consider, for instance, a brand-new truck T which, when used in some yearly process, produces a truck U, itself used in another yearly process producing the truck V. Let there be another process in which T appears on the input side and V on the output side (because the new truck T is used more intensively or under harsher conditions). Should V be considered as a one- or two-year-old truck? The problem is avoided when one refers to the trucks as different capital goods T, U, V. The dating of the capital goods, even when possible, is useless: the intertemporal aspect of production with fixed capital is inessential for the axiomatic approach, though it remains important for applications. Assumption (FC_2) has already been used to define the notion of a sector (chapter 14). There are as many final goods as sectors but, in general, a sector is not characterized by a dominant product. However, in order to concentrate on the core of the construction,

Table 16.1 *Properties of basic single production*

0a. Weak non-substitution:	For a given rate of growth, the competitive technique is independent of final demand
0b. Positivity of prices:	The prices of final goods are positive.
1. Squareness:	The competitive technique is square (number of operated methods = number of produced goods)
2. Non-influence of g:	It is also independent of the rate of growth
3a. Non-substitution:	The competitive price vector is unique up to the numéraire and depends only on the rate of profit
3b. Ricardian trade-off:	The prices in terms of wage increase with the rate of profit
4. Wage maximization:	Among all techniques, the competitive technique is wage-maximizing at the given rate of profit

the reader may adopt the simpler industry hypothesis (one final good at most per industry; if a process produces pure capital goods only, these are attached to a specific final-good industry by the non-shiftability assumption). In this case, the second condition in the rainbow axiom implies that the system is irreducible. Whatever the variant adopted, the rainbow axiom implies that, if there were final goods only and no choice of technique, the Leontief inverse $L(g) = (B - (1+g)A)^{-1}$ would be positive (of course, there are pure capital goods but the intention is to eliminate them from the integrated system). The statement of (FC_3) as a truncation hypothesis is reminiscent of the models studied in chapter 15 even if, in the absence of an age structure, the word 'truncation' is less natural. Note that the final goods are not disposed of freely: the adjustment property is defined in a strict sense for final goods. Assumption (FC_4) means that every machine is internal to a sector (the more general notion of a proper capital good is less intuitive): the 'type' of a machine is then defined by its sector.

Our aim being to build a bridge with the properties of basic single product-systems, let us summarize them in table 16.1. Their unusual order will be that of their recovery in the construction. The idea which sustains the whole theory is that production with fixed capital is a type of joint production close to single production: over the lifetime of a tractor, only corn is produced. In a steady state, an intertemporal analysis can be replaced by a cross-section analysis: at a given moment of time, some tractors appear while others disappear, so that the net product of the industry is reduced to corn. The operation that sustains this point of view is called *vertical integration*. More generally, on a regular growth path, all quantities increase at a constant rate. The notations are: the rows of (A, l, B) representing the processes in sector i are (A_i, l_i, B_i) and the columns are partitioned as $A_i = (A'_i, A''_i)$ and $B_i = (B'_i, B''_i)$ according to the distinction between final and capital goods; a vector y of activity levels is decomposed as $y = (y_1, \ldots, y_f)$ where y_i is the sub-vector of activity levels inside sector i ($i = 1, \ldots, f$).

Definition 1. Let g be given. The activity levels $y = (y_1, \ldots, y_i, \ldots, y_f)$ sustain vertical integration if there is no machine in the g-net product. Since every machine is internal to a sector, vertical integration is equivalently written as (1) or (1.i):

$$y(B'' - (1+g)A'') = 0 \tag{1}$$

$$y_i(B_i'' - (1+g)A_i'') = 0 \quad \text{for any } i = 1, \ldots, f. \tag{1.i}$$

A weak non-substitution result (chapter 14, section 6, Theorem 8) constitutes the only general property of fixed-capital models. Let us explain its logic in plain words. Let $g = 0$ for simplicity and consider a strictly 0-viable economy with fixed capital, i.e. the economy can produce some net product $d = (d', 0_k)$, where $d' \gg 0_f$ is the demand for final goods and 0_k the demand for pure capital goods. A vertically integrated sector i can be assimilated to one surrogate process $(y_iA_i', y_il_i) \rightarrow y_iB_i'$, as if the final goods were produced directly by means of final goods. Let us maintain the relative activity levels within every sector but change them between sectors (y_i is replaced by $\lambda_i y_i$, for $i = 1, \ldots, f$): The net product of all capital goods remains nil and the activity levels λ_i apply to the surrogate processes. The surrogate economy, with no capital goods, has two properties: it is viable and, by the rainbow axiom, all processes are indispensable. This implies the adjustment property: there exist activity levels $\bar{\lambda}_i$ which fit to a given final demand basket $\bar{d}'$. Then the activity levels $(\ldots, \bar{\lambda}_i y_i, \ldots)$ applied to the original economy lead to the desired net product $(\bar{d}', 0)$ and the associated prices are independent of the activity levels:

Theorem 1 (weak non-substitution). Consider a fixed-capital model with $g = g_0$. For any final demand $d = (d', 0) > 0$ there exists a solution ($y = y(d) > 0$, $p > 0$) to the Lippi model. In this solution, the prices and the operated processes are independent of the demand for final goods. The prices of final goods are positive, those of capital goods non-negative.

Theorem 1 introduces an implicit distinction between final demand, for which the adjustment property holds, and the demand for capital measured by the rate of accumulation. Changing g has no major incidence in single production. For fixed-capital systems, on the contrary, the operated processes and the prices, which are independent of final demand by Theorem 1, may depend on the growth rate. The phenomenon was discovered by Stiglitz (1970), whose argument is noteworthy for its simplicity: let corn be produced by means of new and old tractors working simultaneously. On a regular path at rate g, the proportion between new and old machines reflects the demographic trend. If the production function is differentiable, the relative amount of these inputs is also governed by their relative prices. Therefore the relative prices and the operated technique change with the growth rate. Another example with a finite technology is instructive:

Example 1 (dependence on the growth rate). Consider the data

$$A = \begin{bmatrix} 2 & \vdots & 2 \\ 2 & \vdots & 4 \\ 0 & \vdots & 1 \end{bmatrix}, \quad l = \begin{pmatrix} 1 \\ 1 \\ 0 \end{pmatrix}, \quad B = \begin{bmatrix} 6 & \vdots & 7 \\ 8 & \vdots & 6 \\ 0 & \vdots & 0 \end{bmatrix}, \quad r = 1.$$

The first commodity is the unique final good, the second commodity the unique capital good. (All our examples assume one final good and one industry: the phenomena we point out occur in *simple* models.) The third process is the disposal of the machine. Calculation shows that, at the competitive equilibrium, the first two processes are operated if $1/2 < g_0 < 1$ and the last two if $g_0 > 1/2$. The point $g_0 = 1/2$ is a Stiglitz point, when a change in technique is due to a change in the growth rate (the notion is dual to that of switch point, when the cause is a move in the rate of profit).

3 Smoothness of vertical integration

More assumptions are required to go further. The common characteristic of the following axioms (VI) (for Vertical Integration) is to pay attention to the production of machines by means of machines (without reference to their 'age'). The activity levels $y_i = y_i(g)$ which sustain vertical integration, i.e. a zero net supply of machines after accumulation, are polynomials in g, but their behaviour when g varies is more or less complex.

Consider first the squareness property. Production with fixed capital is rectangular when the number of operated methods falls short of that of commodities (the relevant notion is that of 'balanced' system, studied in chapter 14). This is the case in Example 1 at the Stiglitz point: then the second process is operated alone and produces one final good and one machine. The phenomenon occurring at $g_0 = ½$ is that, for the second process operating alone, the matrix $\overline{C} = b_2 - (1 + g_0)a_2 = [\overline{C'}, \overline{C''}]$ has the unusual property that its part $\overline{C''}$ relative to the machine (here, it is a 1×1 matrix) is reduced to [0]: the rank of $\overline{C''}$ is 'small'. *A contrario*, a sufficient condition to restore squareness is:

(VI$_1$) (saturation axiom). Let (A_i'', B_i'') be the sub-matrix which describes the use and production of the machines of type i. For any semi-positive row vector y_i sustaining vertical integration, the number of positive components in y_i is at least equal to that of machines of type i involved (i.e. used or produced) when the activity levels y_i apply, plus one.

Theorem 2. Let a fixed-capital model satisfy axiom (VI$_1$). Then the operated part is square (number of operated processes = number of produced commodities).

Assumption (VI$_1$) holds generically: if μ_i capital goods are involved, the corresponding rows in $C_i'' = B_i'' - (1+g)A_i''$ belong to a subspace of dimension μ_i and are expected to be of maximal rank. Therefore any non-zero vector y_i such that $y_i C_i'' = 0$ (zero g-net product of machines) is expected to have at least $\mu_i + 1$ non-zero components. (Note, however, the case of land considered as a capital good, with $g_0 = 0$: the case fits with our formalization, but the land component of the net product is automatically zero and this prevents axiom (VI$_1$) from holding.) Condition (VI$_1$) is violated at a Stiglitz point. The rupture with squareness is more dramatic for Stiglitz points than for switch points because of the lack, instead of the excess, of simultaneously operated methods.

Axiom (VI$_2$) is a continuous version of (VI$_1$) but loses its generic character. It assumes that the same methods can sustain vertical integration when the rate of growth changes. Then the distinction introduced in Theorem 1 between final demand and demand for accumulation disappears.

(VI$_2$) (continuous integration axiom). Let a fixed-capital model for which condition (VI$_1$) holds for a solution $(y(g_0); p)$ to the Lippi problem (L), and T be the set of the then operated processes: $y(g_0) = ((y_T(g_0), 0)$. When g varies in interval $I = [g_0, \overline{g}]$, $\overline{g} \leq r$, vertical integration is sustained by positive and continuous activity levels $y_T(g)$.

Theorem 3. For the solution to (L) referred to in (VI$_2$) the operated processes do not depend on the growth rate g, $g \in I$. The associated prices do not depend on final demand nor the growth rate.

As noticed by Salvadori (1988a) and contrary to Stiglitz's claim, a dominant technique is not necessarily unique:

Example 2 (Non-uniqueness). For the data (one final good, one industry, one capital good)

$$A = \begin{bmatrix} 2 & 4 \\ 2 & 1 \\ 6 & 6 \\ 0 & 1 \end{bmatrix}, \quad l = \begin{pmatrix} 1 \\ 1 \\ 1 \\ 0 \end{pmatrix}, \quad B = \begin{bmatrix} 4 & 9 \\ 6 & 1 \\ 15 & 9 \\ 0 & 0 \end{bmatrix}, \quad 0 \leq g_0 < 1/4, r = 1,$$

axiom (VI_2) holds over interval $I = [0, 1/2]$ but three dominant techniques coexist. They are: processes 1 and 2 with $p' = 1, p'' = 1, w = 1$; processes 2 and 3 with $p' = 2/3, p'' = 1/3, w = 1$; processes 3 and 4 with $p' = 1/3$, $p'' = 0, w = 1$.

How can uniqueness be restored? The idea explored in axiom (VI_3) is that, in general joint production, the competitive solution is unique under the golden rule hypothesis. In order to have a unique solution, it suffices to extend (if possible!) the interval I considered in (VI_2) until it contains the value $g = r$.

(VI_3) (extended integration axiom). Condition (VI_2) holds in interval $I = [g_0, r]$.

Theorem 4. Let a fixed-capital model satisfy axiom (VI_3). The prices of the effectively produced commodities are unique and depend only on the rate of profit. Moreover the w–r curve is decreasing, whatever the wage basket is.

Since the price vector and the operated processes are the same for $g = g_0$ and $g = r$, it is tempting to go further and conclude from the golden rule that the competitive wage is maximum. A counter-example to this intuitive assertion is:

Example 3. (No wage-maximization). Consider the data

$$A = \left[\begin{array}{c:cc} 1 & 2 & 3 \\ 2 & 0 & 0 \\ 0 & 3.5 & 3.5 \end{array}\right], \quad l = \begin{bmatrix} 1 \\ 1 \\ 1 \end{bmatrix}, \quad B = \left[\begin{array}{c:cc} 4 & 5 & 4 \\ 0 & 1 & 4 \\ 15 & 0 & 0 \end{array}\right], \quad g_0 = 0, r = 1.$$

The first commodity is the only final good, whereas columns 2 and 3 refer to two varieties of machines used for its production. The two machines can also be freely disposed of (these processes are not written down here). Axiom (VI_3) is met since the activity levels $y(g) = (21 + 21g, 7(1 + g)$

$(2+g)$, $22-10g)$ sustain extended integration at rate g. For $r=1$, the three processes are operated and the unique price vector in terms of wage is $p=(1;1,1)$. The competitive real wage then amounts to one unit of the final good. However, by operating the first process alone and eliminating the machines in excess, the real wage rises up to two units of the final good for the same rate of profit (this not being a competitive solution because process 3 yields extra profits when the machines have a zero price).

Axiom (VI_4) extends the integration requirement (VI_3) from any solution T to any set M of methods sustaining the growth rate g_0 and yielding at least the rate of profit r. Such a set is not necessarily competitive because more profitable processes may coexist. In Example 3, axiom (VI_4) is not satisfied: the set M reduced to process 1 alone sustains the rate of growth $g_0=0$, but not the rate $g=r=1$.

(VI_4) (super-integration axiom). Consider any g_0-viable and r-admissible subset M of methods (i.e. there exist positive activity levels $y_M(g_0)$ applied to the methods in M which sustain the g_0-net production of some basket $(d', 0)>0$ and a positive price vector for which all methods in M yield at least the rate of profit r). Then, for $g_0 \leq g \leq r$, vertical integration is sustained by positive and continuous activity levels $y_M(g)$.

Theorem 5. Let a fixed-capital model satisfy axiom (VI_4). For a given rate of profit, the competitive technique is wage-maximizing, whatever the wage basket is.

4 Applications

All the properties stated in table 16.1 have been recovered. What remains unclear is whether the axioms of vertical integration are easily manageable. Let us look at their application to the one-machine model. In this model, every industry j uses one machine at most, with different varieties corresponding to age. A process of type j produces a machine which is one year older than the one it uses, until the end of its life. Then:

- As long as machines only are considered, the structure of the part (A'', B'') of the input and output matrices relative to the machines are identical in the neo-Austrian and the one-machine models. Since this is the only fact that matters for axioms (VI), the Austrian model and the one-machine model share the same properties.
- Given the structure of (A_i'', B_i''), the activity levels sustaining the vertical integration of the ith industry at rate g are $y_i(g) = ((1+g)^t, (1+g)^{t-1}, \ldots, 1+g, 1, 0, \ldots, 0)$, t being the economic lifetime of the ith machine. Therefore all axioms (VI) hold, Theorems 1–5 apply and a one-machine model behaves like a single-product system.

A comparison with the specific proofs of chapter 15 illustrates the powerfulness of the vertical integration approach. Another application is: assume that the matrices (A'', B'') relative to the fixed-capital goods are written

$$A''_j = \begin{bmatrix} 0 & 0 & 0 \\ 1 & 0 & 0 \\ + & 1 & 0 \\ + & + & 1 \\ & I_T & \end{bmatrix} \rightarrow B''_j = \begin{bmatrix} 1 & 0 & 0 \\ 0 & 1 & 0 \\ 0 & 0 & 1 \\ 0 & 0 & 0 \\ & 0_T & \end{bmatrix}.$$

(The one-machine model is obtained when the signs '+' in A'' are replaced by zeros.) This hierarchical structure being also compatible with all axioms (VI), we conclude without further calculations that the properties of single-product systems still hold.

5 Conclusion

The questions at the origin of our reflection on fixed capital models with truncation can now be answered. The one-machine model and the Austrian model have the same behaviour because their structure relative to the production of machines by means of machines is identical; they behave like a single-product system because the structure is simple enough to have rich properties; this is not the case for all fixed-capital models, which therefore have poorer economic properties. The crux of the matter is to define the right approach. This done, fixed-capital theory is a ten-page construct centred on the concept of vertical integration. The economic properties of these models depend upon the production of machines by means of machines and the degree of smoothness of vertical integration.

6 References

Mirrlees' (1969) and Stiglitz's (1970) results do not seem compatible with ours. Mirrlees' non-substitution theorem states the uniqueness of the price vector. What Mirrlees indeed proves is that the equilibrium prices have a price-minimization property corresponding to our Theorem 5. However, his paper does not set any axiom analogous to (VI). The reason is that Mirrlees' conception of a fixed-capital model is based on the notion of project which, *ex hypothesis*, is vertically integrated by means of smooth activity levels (Mirrlees 1969, 75). Similarly, Stiglitz assumes that the total amount of the 'same' machine can be aggregated over its lifetime and works with an index H_m of the 'quantity' of the machine m. The authors do not give details about the micro-structure of production, whereas the passage from the disaggregated structure to the vertically integrated model is the core of the problem. A similar comment applies to the notion of 'plant' referred to in post-Sraffian literature, which aims at assimilating several machines to a unique machine.

Consider a fixed-capital model with industries. Instead of describing the internal organization of the industry j, let us look at it as a 'black box' whose aim is to produce the final good j. If the choice of specific methods and activity levels within the box does not minimize the price of the final good j, is it not obvious that this organization will be ousted when opened to competition, because a competitively produced final good will be cheaper? As stressed by Stiglitz (1970, 544): 'Minimizing steady state prices in terms of, say, labor numeraire, . . . is the important characteristic of competitive equilibria.' There is a general agreement among economists on this 'important characteristic'. Stiglitz concludes that the competitive technique is wage-maximizing and the equilibrium vector unique. The point of Example 3 is that the 'important characteristic' does not hold for production with fixed capital! The statement is a typical misuse of the normative properties attributed to competition.

Salvadori (1988a) formalizes the industrial variant of the fixed capital model and states the right version of the weak non-substitution theorem. But Salvadori (1988b) erroneously attributes a squareness property to fixed-capital systems: if this was true, the Stiglitz points would disappear and the growth rate would not matter. In Kurz and Salvadori (1995), the other results classified under the heading 'jointly utilized machines' concern either the golden rule or joint production with a dominant product (moreover there is no need for a specific theory of scraps when that of fixed capital is adequate). Our notion of vertical integration differs from the one used by Pasinetti (1973, 1988) which is close to Sraffa's notion of sub-system, but the common idea is to let some goods disappear from the net product. The construction itself is new.

7 Proofs

Proof of Theorem 1. Let us assume temporarily that the f final goods can also be freely disposed of. Then there exists a solution $(y_0 > 0, p > 0)$ to the Lippi system for any given vector $d_0 \in R_+^{f+k}$. Choose d_0 such that the final demand d_0' for consumption goods is positive and that for pure capital goods is zero. If, at equilibrium, some final goods are disposed of, increase d_0' by the corresponding amount. We have thus found *some* vector $\overline{d} = (\overline{d}_0', 0)$, with $\overline{d}_0' \gg 0_f$ and a solution (y, p) to the corresponding Lippi system for which, by construction, the final goods are no longer disposed of, so that the temporary hypothesis concerning free disposal can now be dropped. Let $y = (y_1, \ldots, y_f)$ be the activity levels within the f sectors and consider the square system made of the f (fictitious) reduced processes which are written $y_i A'_i \to y_i B'_i$, with f final goods and no capital goods. This system can produce $\bar{d}'_0 \gg 0_f$ and, by the rainbow axiom, all its methods are required to obtain a positive g-net product. These being the conditions defining semi-engagingness (chapter 12, section 5, Definition 2), the fictitious system has the adjustment property: there exist activity levels $\bar{\lambda}_i$ which adjust the g-net product of final goods to any given final demand basket $\bar{d}'$ ($\bar{d}' > 0$). The activity levels $(\ldots, \bar{\lambda}_i y_i, \ldots)$ applied to the original economy lead to the g-net product $(\bar{d}', 0)$ (the hypothesis that the machines are internal or proper is used here). The profitability inequalities and equalities still hold for the same price vector. Moreover, it follows from the indispensability of labour that, for any $d = (d', 0) > 0$, we have $dp = y(B - A)p \geq y[B - (1 + r)A]p = yl > 0$. By choosing d equal to one unit of final good j, it turns out that its price p_j is positive. ■

Proof of Theorem 2. Let μ_i be the number of capital goods of type i which are effectively produced. If $\mu_i = 0$, at least one process of type i is operated by the rainbow axiom. If $\mu_i \geq 1$, the activity levels y_i corresponding to processes of type i are such that $y_i(B''_i - (1 + g_0)A''_i) = 0$, once the free disposal of capital goods has been explicitly written down. By (VI_1) and after summation over i, the total number of operated processes is at least equal to that of operated machines plus that of final goods, i.e. to the number of produced commodities. It becomes exactly equal after reduction. A square solution is thus obtained. ■

Proof of Theorem 3. Consider a solution $(y(g_0), p)$ obtained for $g = g_0$ and, for $g \in I$, let us apply the activity levels $y_i(g)$ to the processes of type i. The reduced process $(a'_i(g), a''_i(g), l_i(g)) \to (b'_i(g), b''_i(g))$ is obtained, with $b''_i(g) = (1 + g)a''_i(g)$ by definition of $y_i(g)$. Let us restrict the attention to the pair of matrices $((A'(g), B'(g))$ whose ith row is $(a'_i(g), b'_i(g))$ and consider the assumptions of Theorem 4 in chapter 12, section 2: condition (i) holds; condition (ii) is a consequence of the rainbow axiom; condition (iii) holds for the price vector p' of final goods in $p = (p', p'')$, because

$$\begin{aligned}(B'(g) - (1 + g)A'(g))p' &\geq (B'(g) - (1 + r)A'(g))p' \\ &= l(g) - (B''(g) - (1 + r)A''(g))p'' \\ &= l(g) + (r - g)A''(g)p'' \\ &> 0.\end{aligned}$$

Therefore the pair $(A'(g), B'(g))$ is g-all-engaging. As a consequence, whatever the final demand $d > 0$ is, there exist relative activity levels λ such that $(\ldots, \lambda_j y_j(g), \ldots; p)$ is a solution to the corresponding Lippi problem. The associated prices $p = (p', p'')$ are independent of the growth rate. ■

Proof of Theorem 4. Consider a solution to (L) for the rate of profit r and the rate of growth g_0, with $g_0 \leq r$. By Theorem 3 and axiom (VI_3), the same operated methods and the price vector can be transferred up to the rate of growth $g = r$. When $g = r$, any semi-positive basket δ of final goods is obtained as an r-net product, because $(A'(r), B'(r))$ is r-all-engaging. Let us choose a basket $\delta = e_j$ made of the final good j only. For a given r, Theorem 2 in chapter 11, section 3 shows that vector p' is uniquely defined by $p'_j = \min\{\pi_j; \pi \text{ supports } e_j\}$ and does not depend on g or d. According to the second characterization of the price vector in the same Theorem, the scalar p'_j increases with the rate of profit. Therefore, the w–r curve is decreasing. ■

Proof of Theorem 5. Consider any g_0-feasible technique compatible with the rate of profit r. Let us restrict the set of available methods to those operated in this technique. A new fixed-capital model is obtained, for which (VI_3) holds. Therefore, any basket δ can be obtained as an r-net product. According to Theorem 2 in chapter 11, section 3, its value in terms of wage is equal to the minimum quantity of labour necessary to produce it as an r-net product, when the only methods inside the extracted technique are operated. For a solution to (L), the minimum is calculated over a larger set of processes, therefore the value of δ cannot be greater. In conclusion, the solution to (L) is wage-maximizing. ■

17 Rent theory

1 The difficulty of reproduction

Land reproduces itself in a one-to-one proportion and its available quantity is an absolute constraint. This scarcity is revealed when the demand for agricultural products is sufficiently high. It gives birth to a third category of income, distinct from wages and profits: landowners receive *rents*. After discussing the notions of extensive and intensive rents, we will show that the laws valid for extensive rent cannot be generalized and that the existence of a cost-minimizing system constitutes a problem. This question is treated in a general model. We will establish an indeterminacy theorem that states the existence of a continuum of solutions, as distribution among profits, wages and rents remains arbitrary. This result seems contradictory of Ricardo's reflections on the links between capitalist accumulation and the long-run evolution of distribution. After having analysed the reason for this gap, we will elaborate a 'Ricardian' model which permits us to state simple results (this is the least easy of all the tasks in this field).

2 Land and joint production

Agricultural production falls within the theory of joint production because it ensures the production of wheat and the simultaneous reproduction of land. An agricultural method is written

$$\text{current inputs} + \Lambda \text{ land} + l \text{ labour} \rightarrow \text{agricultural product} + \Lambda \text{ land}. \tag{1}$$

By denoting π the price of the acre of (homogeneous) land, the associated price equation is:

$$\begin{aligned}(1+r)\,(\text{value of inputs}) + (1+r)\Lambda\pi + wl \\ = \text{value of agricultural product} + \Lambda\pi.\end{aligned} \tag{2}$$

An alternative is to treat land in an implicit fashion. Land then disappears from (1), which looks like a single-product method. By denoting ρ the rent per acre, the price equation is written:

$$(1+r)\,(\text{value of inputs}) + \Lambda\rho + wl = \text{value of agricultural product.} \tag{3}$$

The comparison between (2) and (3) establishes the relation between the price of land and its annual rent: $\rho = r\pi$. Conversely, the price of land is obtained by capitalization of rent: $\pi = \rho/r$. The approaches relying on joint production or on rent are formally equivalent, but the second perspective makes explicit the distribution of the value added in three types of income: profits, rents and wages. The economic category of rent is thereby rendered autonomous and is no longer subsumed in that of profit: it reflects the social distinction between landlords and capitalists.

Lands are in demand because of their productive services. They are not specialized and can be used for a variety of cultures. The choice of the culture depends on the demand of various products as well as prices. Since the prices depend on distribution and specialization, these unknowns are codetermined. In the absence of technical progress in agriculture, the reproduction of each land limits to zero the regular growth of the economic system. The calculation of prices associated with a positive rate of profit leads us to abandon the rule that has been followed, until now, of a rate of profit not surpassing the von Neumann rate of growth. Finally, systems with lands are reducible in the Sraffa and Bidard–Woods sense. Therefore, 'the taxes on rent fall wholly on landlords' (Ricardo, *Principles*) and 'thus cannot affect the prices of the commodities' (*PCMC*, § 85), for a given rate of profit or real wage.

The emergence of rent theory can be related to the contributions of Turgot (1766), Smith (1776 [1976]) and Anderson (1777 [1968]). Its elaboration at the beginning of the nineteenth century was provoked by the discussions about the opening of the British market to foreign commodities. This decision would have provoked a fall in the corn price and rents while increasing profits. The debates of 1815 among West, Malthus, Torrens and Ricardo reflect the political struggles within the ruling classes as well as the level of theorization that Political Economy had reached. Two pure types of rent are identified. Their distinction remains useful even though it is relegated to a less significant status in the general formalization.

Extensive rent is born of the difference between the quality of lands: if lands of superior quality do not suffice to produce the required quantity of corn, the complementary supply is provided by the sowing of low-grade lands with higher production cost. The difference in the cost on lands of superior quality is pocketed by the owner of high-grade lands and constitutes the extensive rent. But, as Ricardo notes, 'It often and, indeed, commonly happens that before . . . the inferior lands are cultivated, capital can be employed more productively on those lands which are already in cultivation' (1817 [1951], ch. II). In these conditions, the farmers tend to privilege the 'intensive' cultivation method on a certain part of the land. The coexistence of two methods on the same land is rendered possible by the existence of an 'intensive rent' whose effect is that of equalizing the unit costs. The first method is less costly per unit of wheat (this is why it is initially used) but less productive per acre (this is why the second method is used when demand increases); a rent per acre weighs more heavily on each unit of wheat. An adequate level of intensive rent makes the total cost uniform and allows for simultaneous use of two methods on the homogeneous land. The preliminary study of these two pure varieties offers us an insight into the difficulties encountered in rent theory. An important rule is that a land with a given quality does not pay rent unless it is totally used. Otherwise, the competition with owners of unused lands leads to the reduction of rent to the point of cancelling it: in perfect competition, there is no 'absolute' rent and marginal land, which is only partially exploited, yields no rent.

The classical notion of rent is often related to the hypothesis of decreasing returns and the notion of pure profit in the neoclassical theory. Our formalization assumes constant returns with limitation of resources. It implies the decline of 'monetary returns': a farmer who invests three consecutive sums of E euros on different lands starts with the investment which produces the maximum amount of wheat, continues with the one providing an average return and terminates with the poorest of all (it is tempting yet misleading to identify this order with that of the land's intrinsic qualities). The decrease of returns is less clear on a homogeneous land where successive investments can be assimilated to 'layers of capital'. If the first layer increases production by ten quarters and the second by twenty quarters, then it might seem that the returns have increased. But our man will understand that it would be better to pass two layers of capital over half of the surface rather than just one layer over the entire terrain. Returns then decrease as a consequence of a rational choice and not as a result of an *ad hoc* hypothesis (Sraffa 1925).

3 Two pure types of rent

3.1 *Extensive rent*

Extensive rent arises from the necessity of cultivating lands of various qualities in order to satisfy demand. Let us assume only one method of cultivation per grade of land. The best grounds yield a rent that is equal to the differential cost with the marginal land. Formally, if the lower index 1 denotes wheat and the upper index $1, \ldots, k, \ldots, q$ the quality of the utilized land, the price equation associated with the land of quality k is written

$$(1+r)\left(\sum_j a_{1j}^{(k)} p_j\right) + wl_1^{(k)} + \rho^{(k)}\Lambda^{(k)} = p_1, \quad \rho^{(k)} \geq 0. \tag{4}$$

Let m designate the marginal land, which is partially cultivated. Then $\rho^{(m)} = 0$ and the price equation becomes

$$(1+r)\left(\sum_j a_{1j}^{(m)} p_j\right) + wl_1^{(m)} = p_1. \tag{5}$$

The prices of the n commodities are determined by the $n - 1$ equations linked to the industrial system and by (5), which reflects the conditions of marginal production in agriculture. At these prices, the $m - 1$ qualities of fully exploited lands are those for which rent $\rho^{(k)}$ defined by (4) is positive. Let us look at the order in which lands are used, for a given rate of profit, when the demand for wheat increases. It must be noted that condition (4) with $\rho^{(k)} \geq 0$ is also written as $(1+r)(\sum_j a_{1j}^{(k)} p_j + wl_1^{(k)}) \leq p_1$, and is analogous to that which expresses the existence of an extra profit in a single-product system with choice of method. Assume that the $n - 1$ industrial methods are given. Let us complete them successively by each of the q methods of agricultural production that corresponds to each of the q qualities of land. Figure 17.1 represents the q wage–profit curves associated with these q square techniques.

For the rate of profit r_0, let us start from such a low level of demand that any grade of land furnishes a sufficient quantity of wheat. In the absence of rent, the theory of technical choices in single production tells us that the operated method is wage-maximizing. Namely, it is method 1 in figure 17.1. Let us increase demand, and assume that the land marked 3 has become marginal. At the associated prices, methods 1 and 2 in figure 17.1 yield extra profits. That is to say, lands of quality 1 and 2 procure positive rents. On the contrary, the potential rent is negative on

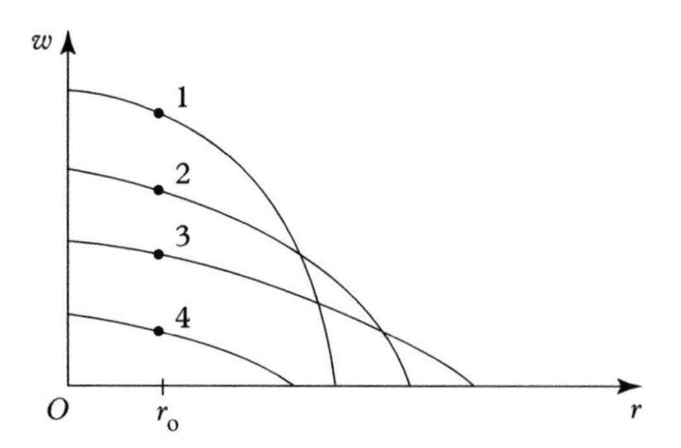

Figure 17.1 Lands with positive rents

land 4. This means that land 3 cannot be used without using lands 1 and 2. Hence:

Theorem 1. Let the rate of profit be given and rent be of the extensive type. When demand increases, lands are exploited in the order of real wages that they yield in the absence of rents (beginning with the highest wage).

The order of cultures is well defined. A land that is used for a certain level of demand remains cultivated for a higher level (this phenomenon will not be observed in the case of intensive rent). A regularity also holds in the variation of prices:

Corollary. Under the assumptions of Theorem 1, wheat is the produced commodity whose price increases the most when demand increases; but the rents and the prices of lands grow even more rapidly than the price of wheat.

The limits of these regularities are:

- The order of cultivation varies with the rate of profit. This result comes to light when we look at figure 17.1 for two levels of the rate of profit. Its lesson is that the 'quality' of a land is not an intrinsic datum since the land that seems to be of the best grade under certain conditions does not remain so when distribution changes.
- The order of rents may differ from that of cultivation. Let there be three lands with one method per land, wheat being the only produced good:

Land 1: $6/11$ wheat $+$ 1 labour $+$ 1 acre $L^{(1)} \rightarrow$ 1 wheat $+$ 1 acre $L^{(1)}$
Land 2: $5/11$ wheat $+$ 1.3 labour $+$ 1 acre $L^{(2)} \rightarrow$ 1 wheat $+$ 1 acre $L^{(2)}$
Land 3: $5/11$ wheat $+$ 2 labour $+$ 1 acre $L^{(3)} \rightarrow$ 1 wheat $+$ 1 acre $L^{(3)}$.

At the rate of profit $r = 10\%$, the order of cultivation of lands when demand increases is 1, 2, 3. When a high level of demand requires the cultivation of land 3, the prices are determined by the third method ($p^{(3)} = 1$, $w^{(3)} = 0.25$) and the rent on land 1 is inferior to that on land 2 ($\rho^{(1)} = 0.15$, $\rho^{(2)} = 0.175$).

3.2 *Intensive rent*

We now consider a simple model with pure intensive rent. Let there be one quality of land of total area $\overline{\Lambda} = 1$ and two methods of production of wheat:

method 1$'$: $(a'_{11}, \ldots, a'_{1n}) + l'_1$ labour $+ \Lambda'$ land $\rightarrow$ 1 wheat $+ \Lambda'$ land
method 1$''$: $(a''_{11}, \ldots, a''_{1n}) + l''_1$ labour $+ \Lambda''$ land $\rightarrow$ 1 wheat $+ \Lambda''$ land.

Moreover, $n - 1$ industrial goods are produced by means of these goods themselves, wheat and labour. The industrial methods are given and the economy is basic.

Three techniques can be envisaged. Two techniques (I') and (I'') correspond, respectively, to the utilization of method 1$'$ alone, resp. 1$''$ alone, on a part of the land; the rent is then zero. The third technique (II) uses the agricultural methods 1$'$ and 1$''$ simultaneously with the cultivation of the entire ground and intensive rent. In order to study the choice of technique, we plot the corresponding r–w curves in the same figure 17.2. For techniques (I') and (I''), land is free and the curves are of the single-product type. For a uniform rent ρ per acre the prices attached to technique (II) are solution to

$$(1+r)\left(\sum a'_{1j}p_j\right) + wl'_1 + \rho\Lambda' = p_1 \qquad (6.1')$$

$$(1+r)\left(\sum a''_{1j}p_j\right) + wl''_1 + \rho\Lambda'' = p_1 \qquad (6.1'')$$

$$(1+r)\left(\sum a_{ij}p_j\right) + wl_i = p_i \quad (2 \leq i \leq n) \qquad (6.i)$$

$$\rho \geq 0. \qquad (7)$$

After a normalization of prices, there remain $n + 1$ unknowns: the normalized prices $p(r)$, the wage $w(r)$ and the rent $\rho(r)$. We allow the rate of

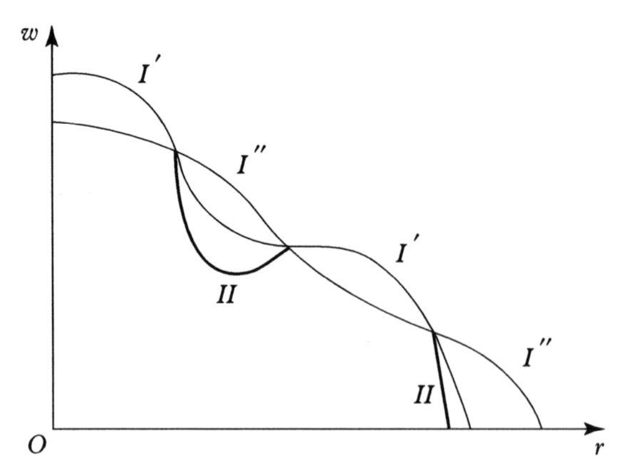

Figure 17.2 $r - w$ curves and land

profit to vary but assume that the linear system (6) with $n+1$ equations and $n+1$ unknowns admits a unique solution on the interval of the variations of r. Nothing, however, guarantees that the rent $\rho(r)$ thus obtained is non-negative. To specify the sign of $\rho(r)$, let us write the system (6) for $\rho = 0$: it turns out that a change in the sign of $\rho(r)$ corresponds to a point at which techniques (I') and (I'') are equally profitable, since their associated price equations are then compatible. Therefore, the points where the rent cancels itself out are the switch points between (I') and (I''). In between two switch points, the rent retains a constant sign that is alternatively positive and negative. In figure 17.2, the curve $w_{II}(r)$ associated with technique (II) has been drawn only over the intervals in which the rent is positive.

When the rent is positive, (6.1′) can also be written $(1+r)(\sum a'_{ij}\, p_j) + w l_1''' = p_1$ with $l_1''' > l_1'$. Thus, wage $w_{II}(r)$ is the one associated with a fictitious technique identical to (I'), except that it uses more labour. Therefore, the corresponding wage is lower: curve $w_{II}(r)$ is located under $w_{I'}(r)$ and, by a similar argument, under $w_{I''}(r)$. It is not certain that curve $w_{II}(r)$ is decreasing. Indeed, the rent does not vary in a monotonous way since it is zero at every switch point. If the rent decreases significantly, the profits and the wages may increase simultaneously. If the rent increases, the trade-off between wage and profit is re-encountered:

Theorem 2. Consider a technique with intensive rent and let the rate of profit increase. If the rent in terms of wage does not decrease, the real wage decreases whatever the numéraire is.

With homogeneous land, the dominant technique is not always wage-maximizing (see figure 17.2) and depends on demand. The very existence of a dominant technique, which meets demand and is cost-minimizing, is unclear. In order to illustrate the existence problem, let us set a level of demand that can be satisfied by technique (I'') utilized alone but not by the less productive technique (I'). This demand can also be satisfied by the mixed technique (II) which makes a partial use of the productive method $1''$. Two cases are distinguished:

- Let the rate of profit belong to an interval where the rent is negative. Method $1'$ cannot be operated alone since it does not meet demand. Method $1''$ cannot be used alone either, since method $1'$ is less costly. Finally, methods $1'$ and $1''$ cannot operate together since the rent would be negative. Therefore the requirements deriving from the demand and the cost-minimization conditions cannot be simultaneously fulfilled.
- If the rate of profit belongs to an interval on which the rent is positive, techniques (I'') and (II) are simultaneously dominant.

This example shows that the existence of an adequate set of prices, rents and activity levels is not always assured.

4 Technical choice with rent

4.1 Existence results

We present here a general model of technical choice with rent. The m available methods of production are represented by a matrix $A_{m,n}$ with n inputs (other than lands), a matrix $\Lambda_{m,q}$ of lands (q qualities of lands), a labour vector $l_{m,1}$ and a matrix $B_{m,n}$ of n produced goods (other than lands): $(A, \Lambda, l) \rightarrow B$. The ith row of the matrix Λ represents the quantities $\Lambda_i^{(1)}, \ldots, \Lambda_i^{(q)}$ of q varieties of lands utilized in the ith process. Let $y > 0$ be the $1 \times m$ row vector of activity levels, $\overline{\Lambda} \gg 0$ the $q \times 1$ column vector of the areas of the q varieties of lands, $p > 0$ the $n \times 1$ column vector of goods (other than lands), $\rho \geq 0$ the $q \times 1$ column vector of rents, and $w > 0$ the wage. A first block of inequations with complementarity relationships is written

$$Bp \leq (1 + r)Ap + \Lambda\rho + wl \qquad [y] \qquad (8.1)$$

$$y\Lambda \leq \overline{\Lambda} \qquad [\rho]. \qquad (8.2)$$

Relation (8.1) means that, at current prices, rents and wage, the operated methods yield the normal rate of profit whereas the non-operated methods pay extra costs. Relation (8.2) means that the cultivated lands do not exceed the available areas, with a zero rent on partially cultivated lands. A second block takes account of demand. Salvadori's hypothesis (1986, 1987) is that the net product $d > 0$ is given. Under the free disposal hypothesis the system is written as (9.1)

$$y(B - A) \geq d \qquad [p] \tag{9.1}$$

$$y > 0,\ p > 0,\ w > 0,\ \rho \geq 0. \tag{9.2}$$

The assumptions are:

(A_1) The rate of profit is given and positive.

(A_2) Labour is indispensable to the production of commodities:

$$\{y > 0, y(B - A) \geq 0\} \Rightarrow yl > 0.$$

(A_3) The r-product $d > 0$ is strictly feasible:

$$\exists \bar{y} > 0 \quad \bar{y}(B - (1 + r)A) \gg d \quad \text{and} \quad \bar{y}\Lambda \leq \bar{\Lambda}.$$

Theorem 3. Under assumptions (A), there exists a solution (y, p, w, ρ) to the system (8)–(9).

Theorem 3 is reassuring because the previous analyses cast into doubt the very existence of a solution. Its weak point is that final demand is considered as exogenous and is defined before employment, prices and incomes, which are endogenously determined variables. In order to avoid this critique, we modify the expression of final demand and let it depend on prices, incomes and consumption habits specific to each class. Let us introduce the demand functions for the final goods $f_c(p, R_c)$, $f_w(p, R_w)$ and $f_l(p, R_l)$ of the capitalists, the workers and the landowners, respectively. The relations (10) below express that the global demand is met, with free disposal of overproduced goods:

$$y(B - A) \geq f_c(p, ryAp) + f_w(p, wyl) + f_l(p, \bar{\Lambda}\rho) \quad [p] \tag{10.1}$$

$$y > 0,\ p > 0,\ w > 0,\ \rho > 0. \tag{10.2}$$

The assumptions become:

(B_1) The demand functions $f_i(p, R_i)$ ($i = c$, w or l) are defined for $p > 0$, $R_i \geq 0$. They are semi-positive, continuous and satisfy the identity $f_i(p, R_i)p = R_i$.

(B_2) Any net product requires some land, directly or indirectly:

$$\{y > 0, y(B - A) \geq 0\} \Rightarrow y\Lambda > 0;$$

(B_3) The rate of profit r is smaller than the von Neumann rate of (A, B), lands excluded:

$$\exists\, \overline{y} > 0 \quad \overline{y}(B - (1 + r)A) \gg 0.$$

Theorem 4. Under assumptions (B), there exists a set of activity levels, prices, wage and rents solution to the system (8)–(10) and for which the vector of rents is semi-positive.

The non-nullity of rents implies that at least one quality of land is totally cultivated. Such is not the case in Theorem 3 when the exogenous demand for final goods is low.

4.2 *Indeterminacy of distribution*

In the theory of prices of production it is customary to set *one* distribution variable exogenously. The intuition is that the same applies to Theorem 4: for a given wage, the rate of profit is determined on the marginal land and rents are then obtained as differential costs. We shall call an indeterminacy theorem the existence of *two* degrees of freedom in distribution. An illustration is provided by the corn model (which reveals itself to be more realistic with the introduction of land). Let there be a unique quality of land and a unique method of production: a wheat + Λ land + l labour $\rightarrow$ 1 wheat + Λ land. When land is completely cultivated and each class consumes all of its income, the equality $(1 + r)a + \overline{\Lambda}\rho + wl = 1$ is the *only* link among the three distribution variables (r, w, ρ).

Theorem 5 (Indeterminacy Theorem). Under the hypotheses of Theorem 4 and for a given rate of profit, there exists a solution to (8)–(10) for which the total amount of rents represents the wage of L workers, $L > 0$ arbitrarily given.

5 A Ricardian model

According to Ricardo, the chief purpose of Political Economy is 'to determine the laws governing distribution' (Preface to *Principles*). This ambition is incompatible with the Indeterminacy Theorem. This discrepancy obliges us to question the model which Ricardo had in mind. It must initially be remarked that the model (8)–(10) describes a situation of simple reproduction: a permanent expansion of the economy is incompatible with the intrinsic scarcity of lands, hence the hypothesis (B_1) on the absence of savings. This does not correspond to the situation theorized by Ricardo where there is accumulation and progressive distortion of activity levels (the relative expansion of the industrial sector with regard to the agricultural sector); consequently, the structure of prices is deformed whereas rents increase. We propose to construct a simple model of Ricardian inspiration and see how it differs from the one retained above.

Let there be three sectors of activity: agriculture, industry (metallurgy) and domestic services (the domestics being in the service of the landowners). The agricultural sector provides wheat, produced by means of wheat and labour. We consider a simple model of extensive rent, with differences of land qualities but only one method per land. The total area of the land of quality i is one acre (the assumption is but a normalization); if it is wholly cultivated, it uses one unit of labour and produces one unit of wheat from $a(i)$ seeds. The lands are therefore exploited in the order $a(0) < a(1) < \ldots$:

$$a(i) \text{ corn} + 1 \text{ labour} + 1 \text{ acre } L^{(i)} \rightarrow 1 \text{ corn} + 1 \text{ acre } L^{(i)}. \quad (11)$$

Under these hypotheses, a unique symbol x_t designates the total area of cultivated land at date t, agricultural employment and the gross production of wheat; finally, x_t also indicates the quality of marginal land. The real wage consists of wheat and is historically fixed at a level w. The rate of profit r_t is obtained on marginal land and results from (12):

$$(1 + r)\, a(x) = 1 - w \quad (12)$$

(the time index t is omitted). The rent on the land of quality $i = 1, \ldots,$ x results from the differential cost of production with the marginal land, hence $\rho_i = (1 + r)(a(x) - a(i))$. By denoting $A(x) = \sum_{i=1}^{x} a(i)$ the total amount of seeds, the total rents amount to $(1 + r)(xa(x) - A(x))$. The landowners spend their entire income on the employment of domestics, whose number is z:

$$(1 + r)(xa(x) - A(x)) = wz. \quad (13)$$

Let us consider the industrial sector. Each unit of iron (iron is the industrial good and a commodity consumed by the capitalists) is produced by means of b units of iron and one unit of labour. The same variable y designates the industrial employment and the gross production of iron. The equation

$$(1 + r)bp + w = p \quad (14)$$

determines the price p of the industrial good. The total profits drawn from agriculture and industry amount to $\pi = rA(x) + bryp$. Let us assume for the moment that the capitalists do not save and designate by $f_{c1}(p, \pi)$ their consumption in wheat, the remainder being devoted to the consumption of iron. The workers consume only wheat and the landowners employ domestic servants. In a stationary state, the equation

$$w(x + y + z) + f_{c1}(p, rA(x) + bryp) = x - A(x) \tag{15}$$

expresses the equality between the final demand for wheat (by the workers and the capitalists) and its net supply. The iron market is then automatically balanced. For a given real wage, the system of four equations (12)–(15) has five unknowns: three unknown activity levels x, y, z, the rate of profit r and the price p of the industrial good. The indeterminacy result holds, since there remains one degree of freedom for fixing the rate of profit. In this approach, no law of distribution is conceivable. In what way is Ricardo's logic different? The chief difference pertains to Ricardo's very problem – the study of the impact of the development of capitalism on reproduction. Ricardo fixes the attained level of accumulation or compares the situations corresponding to different levels of accumulation.

In order to translate this hypothesis in the (12)–(15) model, we represent the given development level of capitalism by the activity level y of the industrial sector. A degree of freedom disappears and, thus, the profits and the rents are determined by the real wage. To push this exercise further, let us imagine that capitalists consume iron only ($f_{c1} = 0$). Then, on the one hand, the three components of the wheat demand are industrial wages, agricultural wages and rents (these being entirely transferred to the domestics, who consume wheat). On the other, the value of the net supply of wheat is divided among agricultural profits, agricultural wages and rents. One sees that the equilibrium on the wheat market is reduced to the equality of industrial wages and agricultural profits: (15) is replaced by

$$wy = rA(x). \tag{16}$$

Let the real wage be definitively fixed. For a given level y of development, the agricultural employment x and the rate of profit r are determined by (12) and (16), whose solution is written $r = r(y)$, $x = x(y)$. Thereafter, the level z of domestic employment and the price p of iron result from (13) and (14).

As an exercise in comparative statics, let us see how these magnitudes evolve with the level of development. The left-hand side of (12) is an increasing function of x and r. For a given wage, there is therefore a trade-off between the level of the rate of profit $r = r(y)$ and the agricultural employment $x = x(y)$. Therefore, the rate of profit and the rents evolve in opposite directions. Ricardo regards as realistic the case in which

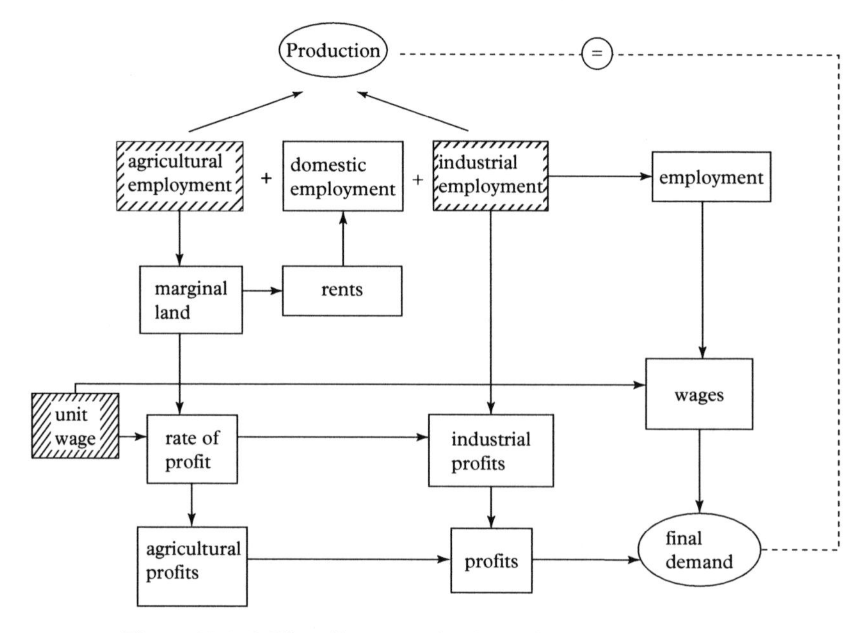

Figure 17.3 A Ricardian reproduction scheme

capitalist accumulation requires the mobilization of a greater number of workers. More lands must be cultivated, the rent increases and the rate of profit diminishes. This conclusion justifies Ricardo's fears as well as his recommendations: accumulation would risk being hindered by the level of the rents, unless one were to import cheap foreign grains.

Figure 17.3 proposes a graphical presentation of the interdependencies expressed in the model (12)–(15). The three entries of this Ricardian labyrinth are the real wage w, the agricultural employment x and the industrial employment y. The other magnitudes are endogenous. Moreover, the agricultural employment x is not an independent variable: it is determined by the balance, on the wheat market, between demand and supply. Therefore, for a given real wage, all relevant magnitudes (rate of profit, rents, etc.) are functions of the level of industrial development, represented by variable y.

6 References

The brief chapter XI of *PCMC* has inspired the writings of Quadrio-Curzio (1966, on extensive rent), Montani (1972, 1975), Kurz (1978), Guichard (1979), Abraham-Frois and Berrebi (1980), Saucier (1981) and Klimovsky (1985). D'Agata (1983) has built examples of non-existence and non-uniqueness. Papers have been edited by Arena *et al.*

(1982), Bidard (1987) and Steedman (1988). Salvadori (1986) introduced demand explicitly and proved the first general existence result. Erreygers (1990) obtained a uniqueness result by considering 'colours'. Section 3 has been the core of discussions with Woods, whose alternative echo is found in Woods (1990). Sections 4 and 5 follow Bidard (1991).

7 Proofs

Sraffa showed a poor grasp of technical points but a potential talent in mathematics. The following two proofs are inspired by his ways of reasoning.

Proof of Corollary to Theorem 1. For a given rate of profit and an increasing demand the evolution of the price of corn obeys Theorem 2 in chapter 9, section 3, the direction of change being from a dominant towards a dominated technique. Therefore, the real wage decreases and corn is the good whose relative price increases the most. Let corn be chosen as numéraire. The production cost (rent excluded) $(1+r)\ (\sum a_{1j}^{(k)} p_j) + wl_1^{(k)}$ on the land of grade k decreases when the marginal land changes from m to $m+1$. Therefore the rent on land k must increase in order that the total costs remain equal to one. Similarly for the price of each acre of land k. ■

Proof of Theorem 2. Let us choose as numéraire the good i whose relative price decreases the most between r_1 and r_2 $(r_1 < r_2)$ and compare the price equations for that good at r_1 and r_2. The value $(1 + r)\ (\sum a_{ij}\, p_j)$ of its physical inputs increases. As the total costs remain equal to one, the real wage w/p_i or the rent $\rho = (\rho/w)\ (w/p_i)$ must decrease. Since ρ/w does not decrease by assumption, the wage w/p_i in terms of good i decreases. *A fortiori*, this is also the case for any other commodity. ■

Salvadori (1986) established Theorem 3 as a consequence of a linear complementarity property (Dantzig and Manne 1974). The reader will notice that, in the following short proof, land does not appear explicitly in the pseudo-input matrix A' and appears negatively in the pseudo-output matrix B' (but the argument is formally sound). This treatment parallels Sraffa's statement: '[The lands are] employed in production, but not themselves produced' (*PCMC*, § 85).

Proof of Theorem 3. Apply the generalized Lippi Theorem (chapter 11, section 8, Theorem 6) to the extended matrices and vectors $A' = (A, 0)$, $B' = (B, -\Lambda)$, $p' = (p, \rho)$, $d' = (d, -\overline{\Lambda})$, and $g = 0$. ■

Proof of Theorem 4. The proof exemplifies the strategy defined in chapter 11, section 8. For $t > 1$ let $w = 1$ and $(y, \rho, p) \in Y_t \times S \times P_t$, with $Y_t = \{y; \forall j\ t^{-1} \leq y_j \leq t\}$, S unit simplex in R^m, $P_t = \{p; \forall i\ t^{-1} \leq p_i \leq t\}$. The continuous function $z(y, \rho, p) = (Bp - (1+r)Ap - \Lambda\rho - l, y\Lambda - \overline{\Lambda}, f_c(p, ryAp) + f_w(p, yl) + f_1(p, \overline{\Lambda}\rho), -y(B - A))$ satisfies the Walras identity. According to the GND lemma

$$\begin{aligned} &\forall t \quad \exists(y_t, \rho_t, p_t) \in Y_t \times S \times P_t \quad \forall(y, \rho, p) \in Y_t \times S \times P_t \\ &y[Bp_t - (1+r)Ap_t - \Lambda\rho_t - l] + [y_t\Lambda - \overline{\Lambda}]\rho \\ &+[d(p_t, ry_tAp_t, y_tl, \overline{\Lambda}\rho_t) - y_t(B - A)]p_t \leq 0. \end{aligned} \tag{17}$$

Let us momentarily assume that matrix Λ is positive. When t tends towards infinity, it is left to the reader to check that, under assumptions (B_1) and (B_3), we have $\|y_t\| \nrightarrow \infty$, $\|p_t\| \nrightarrow 0$ and $\|p_t\| \nrightarrow \infty$. An accumulation point $(y_0 \geq 0, \rho_0 > 0, p_0 > 0, w_0 = 1)$ of the sequence is a solution to system (8)–(10). The general result is then obtained by a continuity argument: the semi-positive matrix Λ satisfying (B_2) is approximated by a sequence of positive matrices Λ_t. The reader will check that the sequence of solutions remains bounded. A cluster point exists and is a solution to (8)–(10). ■

In this proof, the vector of rents belongs to the unit simplex by construction and, therefore, the solution is such that $w = \sum_k \rho_k$.

Proof of Theorem 5. For a given scalar $L > 0$, let S' be the subset of R^m_+ defined by $S' = \{\rho; \rho > 0, \sum_{k=1}^m \overline{\Lambda}_k\rho_k = L\}$. The proof of Theorem 4 is unchanged when S' is substituted for the unit simplex S. The solution then obtained satisfies equality $\sum_k \overline{\Lambda}_k\rho_k = wL$. ■

Part III

Questions of method

18 An agenda

Prelude to a Critique of Economic Theory: how should it be interpreted?

Before judging, one must identify. As a starting point, restore the specificity of Sraffa's programme. His theory of choice of technique constitutes grounds for reflection, although it cannot be defended. The challenge is to reconstitute its originality by relying on the methodological hints provided in the text. One can then examine the significance of the construction and its applicability.

Is a critique of Marshall or Böhm-Bawerk equivalent to that of economic theory? Like Walras, Sraffa is conscious of the complexity of the interactions. The crucial question concerns the relationship with intertemporal equilibrium. Read Arrow, Debreu, Malinvaud and Morishima. Exploring separately Sraffa's approach and the general equilibrium theory is the means of avoiding their *a priori* identification. If, after scrutiny, one must resign oneself to that identification, it will be a conscious one. Can one oppose two conceptions of production? Or think reproduction without equilibrium? Or dissociate production and distribution? This is an element of the classical approach. Marginal equalities, certainly. Wicksell is a profound author.

Advance slowly. The methodology does not constitute a straightjacket but rather a guideline that we can choose to accept or reject according to its efficiency.

Always give primacy to economic analysis.

19 A Sraffian theory of choice of technique

1 A theoretical divide

The title of this chapter and its content are contradictory in an obvious way: the differences with the last sections of *PCMC* are more striking than the similarities. The brief § 96 of *PCMC* devoted to choice of technique in joint production proceeds by means of analogies with single production and its assertions are false. Once this is acknowledged, one has a choice between rejecting the approach or returning to its foundations. We have chosen the second option: What constitutes the specificity of the approach, and how should it be developed? Therefore, one can speak of the reconstructed theory as Sraffian, even if it is not from Sraffa himself.

The invalidity of the conclusions of *PCMC* creates an interesting problem. Sraffa reaches a point where, not knowing how to choose among neighbouring techniques, he incorrectly appeals to considerations regarding the maximization of wages. His statement is not acceptable, but the problem is formulated in those terms only because Sraffa has chosen a particular path whose difficulties he himself has acknowledged, even if he fails to overcome them. We will follow the same path up to the point where the problem arises and, at this very juncture, proceed to elaborate a more reliable answer. Our effort consists in identifying specific methodological traits and respecting their explicit presuppositions. The reconstruction undertaken here is deemed to be distinct from that of the general equilibrium theory. It resolutely situates itself in what may be termed a 'fundamentalist' perspective: the thesis is that Sraffa has laid the basis of an *original* theory of choices of technique characterized by methodological choices of which we duly present a complete formalization.

After a brief presentation of the methodology (section 2), we compare two arbitrary neighbouring n-sets in terms of profitability and show that a consistency property, which was automatically met for single-product systems, must hold for a local working of the market algorithm (section 3). Then we identify the candidates, that is, the family $\boldsymbol{C}$ of dominant n-sets (section 4); the notions of requirements and techniques are useless at this stage. Next, we examine the techniques, that is, the family $\boldsymbol{T}$ of n-sets which satisfy the requirements for use. Two constructions are presented. The first draws exclusively upon the insertion axiom and permits us to rediscover and situate Lippi's result in a general framework (section 5). The second, that relies on the insertion and consistency axioms, is closer to Sraffa's own approach (section 6). In both cases, the objective is to demonstrate the existence of a dominant technique by proving that the family of candidates and the family of techniques have a non-empty intersection. Variations in the definitions of these families are introduced in order to study other properties (uniqueness, convergence). Section 7 provides two illustrations, section 8 draws some conclusions. Section 9 scrutinizes Sraffa's own analysis.

2 An original methodology

Sraffa's conceptual and methodological originality can be attributed to the following elements:

- The *algorithmic approach*: the construction is based on an algorithm whose principle has been discussed in chapter 9. The starting point is the n-set of the currently operated methods. At the ruling rate of profit, the associated prices are used for calculating the profitability of any alternative method. A new method that yields extra profits is substituted for an old one. New prices are established. The procedure is followed up to the point where a technique for which no available method yields extra profits is found. These stylized dynamics of technical change are linked to the classical tradition (Schefold 1980).
- The concept of *requirements for use*. This concept is introduced in a note to § 50 of *PCMC*:

> Incidentally, considering that the proportions in which the two commodities are produced by any one method will in general be different from those in which they are required for use, the existence of two methods of producing them in different proportions will be necessary for obtaining the required proportion of the two products through an appropriate combination of the two methods.

It may be the case that no combination of methods fulfils the requirements for use and, then, the corresponding n-set is not acceptable in the economy:

Definition 1. Let there be n commodities. An n-set is called a technique if it fulfils the requirements for use.

Post-Sraffian researchers have identified the notion of requirement for use with that of demand. Then, the requirements for use are met when there is equality of supply and demand. This interpretation raises the question of its compatibility with Sraffa's approach, without prejudging the latter from the very outset. Textual study of Sraffa's writings unambiguously demonstrates that the introduction of the term 'requirements for use' is not innocent: his project is one of isolating, if not altogether banishing, demand in the construction of prices of production. We interpret his indications as follows: the requirements for use imply the existence of constraints on the actual productive system. In a general theory, such constraints need not be described explicitly and are taken into account through the restrictions they impose to the productive system. In this respect, Sraffa's study of rent theory is typical: he avoids mentioning demand (which is explicitly referred to by the classical economists) and looks only at the consequences of the fact that more agricultural products must be produced. Similarly, the central question in our construction is: which productive systems can meet the constraints? These n-sets, called the techniques, are acceptable while others are not, and that is all that matters for a general theory of *prices of production*, not the origin of the constraint. When this selection is undertaken without the nature of requirements being specified, the starting point of the analysis is a given list of techniques. The procedure does not exclude, however, an analytical expression of requirements. In such a case, the reader can her/himself construct the list of techniques. Nevertheless, by basing itself solely on a list, the general theory conserves a qualitative character and the retained properties are of a combinatorial nature. (A parallel can be drawn with the mathematical theory of topology: in metric spaces, the open sets are built by means of a distance, but the general theory considers only the stability of the open sets for some operations and not their construction.)

Unwilling to specify the requirements, Sraffa succumbs to the temptation of ignoring them after making a single reference. He does not specify the content of the new concept and, worse, forgets it after its introduction. This is his main error and the source of all his others. In our construction, the requirements are present in the form of restrictions imposed on the admissible combinations of methods. Several variants of this idea will be presented. The restrictions imposed on the techniques have five common characteristics: (*i*) they do not describe the nature of the requirements; (*ii*) they concern the stability of the family of techniques; (*iii*) they deal with the functioning of the market algorithm: they compare neighbouring techniques (i.e. which differ by only one method) and possess a local character; (*iv*) they present themselves as answers to problems identified by Sraffa; and (*v*) they are posited as axioms: they are variants of insertion and consistency properties already discussed, but one must keep in mind that the properties established in single production are not necessarily valid in joint production; hence, their status as axioms.

A technique is dominant if, at the associated prices, no available method yields extra profits. The aim of the theory is to study the dominant techniques at a given rate of profit. The difficulty with this approach is that of transition from local and qualitative axioms to global and quantitative results.

3 Market algorithm and consistency

In the presence of choice of technique, the market algorithm (chapter 9) describes how a method is replaced by another on the basis of a profitability criterion. The principle of the algorithm is unchanged in joint production, but it makes a significant difference to consider multiple-product systems instead of single-product systems. In the geometrical approach already used in chapter 11, section 3, every method i is characterized by its r-net product per worker $c_i = c_i(r) = (b_i - (1 + r)a_i)/l_i$ or the extremity C_i of this vector. For two commodities, consider three methods, named 1, 1′ and 2, and compare the neighbouring 2-sets (1, 2) and (1′, 2). We wonder which of the alternative methods 1 or 1′ is selected by the market on the basis of its cheapness.

The three configurations are represented in figure 19.1. In figure 19.1a, the point $C_1' = C_1'(r)$ is above the straight line C_1C_2, which means that the method 1′ yields extra profits at the prices p_{12} associated with (1, 2); after the method 1′ has been substituted for the method 1, the new 2-set (1′, 2) is obtained. But C_1 is also above the straight line $C_1'C_2$, i.e. the method 1 just excluded yields extra profits at the prices $p_{1'2}$! We therefore return to (1, 2), etc. In other terms, the consistency property seen in (chapter 9, section 3) is violated here. Figure 19.1b exhibits the opposite paradox: process 1′ is not profitable at prices associated with (1, 2), and process 1 is not profitable either at prices associated with (1′, 2). Figure 19.1c is the only one where the strong consistency property holds: process 1′ yields extra profits at the prices p_{12} and, after its insertion, process 1 is not profitable at the new price vector $p_{1'2}$. The nature of the distinction between figures 19.1a and 19.1b on the one hand, and 19.1c on the other, is described by Theorem 1.

Definition 2. Let there be two neighbouring n-sets $\mathcal{J}$ and $\mathcal{J}'$, which differ by one method ($j \in \mathcal{J}, j' \in \mathcal{J}'$). For a given rate of profit, let $p_{\mathcal{J}}$ (resp. $p'_{\mathcal{J}}$) the prices associated with $\mathcal{J}$, resp. $\mathcal{J}'$). The two n-sets can be compared unambiguously if either method j' yields extra profits at prices $p_{\mathcal{J}}$ and

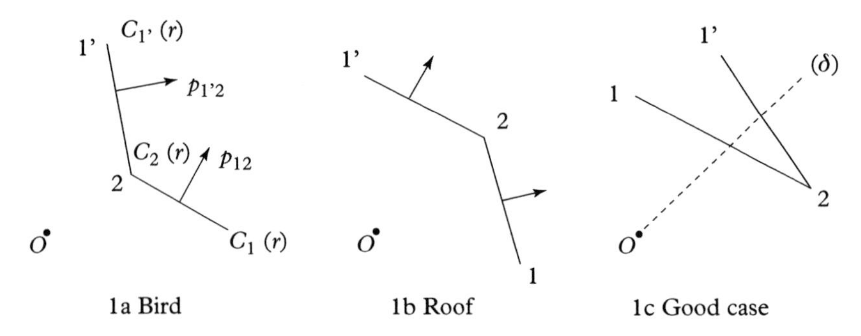

Figure 19.1 Comparison of neighbouring n-sets (r-space)

method j pays extra costs at prices $p_{\mathcal{J}'}$ ($\mathcal{J}'$ is preferred to $\mathcal{J}$), or j yields extra profits at prices $p_{\mathcal{J}'}$ and j' pays extra costs at prices $p_{\mathcal{J}}$ ($\mathcal{J}$ is preferred to $\mathcal{J}'$).

Theorem 1 (strong consistency criteria). Let $\mathcal{J}$ and $\mathcal{J}'$ be two neighbouring n-sets. They can be compared unambiguously if and only if one of the two equivalent properties holds:

- $det(c_1, \ldots, c_j, \ldots, c_n)$ and $det(c_1, \ldots, c_{j'}, \ldots, c_n)$ have the same sign, where $c_i = c_i(r)$ is the r-net product of the ith method;
- the two n-sets have an interior r-net product δ in common.

Then the preferred n-set is the one which maximizes the scalar $w/\delta p$.

In general, the common r-net basket δ cannot be interpreted as a wage basket (it may well have negative components). The existence and uniqueness of a dominant technique requires that the configurations 1a and 1b are eliminated. The market algorithm works locally in case 1c, when only two neighbouring n-sets are compared. If all techniques have a common r-net basket δ, the algorithm converges towards the dominant technique, which maximizes $w/\delta p$; if not, the existence of a dominant technique is unclear and constitutes the main object of the chapter. We first study the dominant n-sets, then the techniques, and finally try to show that the two families have a common element.

4 Candidates

The dominant n-sets, which are called the candidates, are independent of the specification of the techniques.

Definition 3. An n-set I of methods is a candidate if there exists a price vector (p, $w = 1$) for which all methods in I yield the ruling rate of profit, whereas no alternative method yields extra profits.

The structure of the candidates is studied first, by exploiting the geometrical tool introduced in chapter 9, section 3. For a given rate of profit, let the vectors $c_i = c_i(r) = (b_i - (1 + r)a_i)/l_i$ be in the general position. Consider the convex hull of $\{0, C_1, \ldots, C_m\}$. The candidates are represented by the facets of this convex hull not containing the origin. If the restriction concerning the origin is momentarily ignored, the candidates look like the facets of a diamond and, therefore, have a noteworthy property:

Theorem 2 (replacement property). If the 'extreme' methods are ignored, the family $\boldsymbol{C}$ of candidates has the property: any $(n - 1)$-set of a candidate belongs to exactly one neighbouring candidate. An equivalent statement is: given a candidate and a method in it, there is one and only one way to replace this method in order to obtain another candidate.

In the r-space, the $n - 1$ vectors common to two neighbouring candidates span a vectoral hyperplane and the vectors by which the candidates differ are located in different half-spaces. The algebraic formulation of the property is:

Theorem 3 (orientation). Given two neighbouring candidates $(1, \ldots, j, \ldots, n)$ and $(1, \ldots, j', \ldots, n)$, the determinants $det(c_1(r), \ldots, c_{j'}(r), \ldots, c_n(r))$ and $det(c_1(r), \ldots, c_j(r), \ldots, c_n(r))$ have opposite signs.

The replacement property can be given a purely combinatorial interpretation: let a candidate $(i_1 i_2, \ldots, i_n)$ be written as a 'number' $i_1, i_2 \ldots i_n$ when considered as a member of a family (the order of the 'figures' in a 'number' does not matter, except when an orientation is introduced). The replacement property can be checked directly from the list of numbers, without need for a description of the methods or a geometric representation. For instance, for $n = 3$, family $\{123, 134, 142, 523, 534, 524\}$ has the replacement property. Theorem 3 assigns a value $+1$ or -1 to any ordered number, with opposite signs for neighbouring numbers.

5 Pre-technologies

5.1 *The insertion axiom*

We now consider the notion of *technique*, independently of that of candidate, but keep in mind the market algorithm. A technique is an n-set which satisfies the requirements for use. In joint production, a difficulty appears:

With single-product industries, each process can be identified by the commodity which it produces, so that when an additional method is introduced there is no doubt as to which of the pre-existing methods it is an alternative to. When, however, each process produces several commodities, and each commodity is produced by several methods, this criterion fails. And the problem arises of how to identify among the pre-existing methods the one to which the new method is an alternative. (*PCMC*, § 96)

The problem is one of insertion. Because of the restrictions induced by the necessity to meet the requirements for use, it is not guaranteed that the new method can be substituted for a previous one. Hence the axiom:

Definition 4 (Strong insertion axiom). A *pre-technology* is a non-void family $\boldsymbol{T}$ of n-sets, called techniques, that satisfies the strong insertion axiom: given a technique ('old' methods) and a 'new' method, there exists exactly one way to substitute the new method for an old one in order to obtain a new technique.

The axiom is purely combinatorial. For instance, for $n = 3$, the family of 3-sets $\{123, 234, 345, 451, 512\}$ satisfies the strong insertion axiom and is a pre-technology. The nature of the requirements is not defined and the starting point is the list of techniques. There exist two simple ways to build pre-technologies:

- The *Jim techniques*. Let $I_1, I_2, \ldots, I_n$ be a partition of the methods into n non-empty subsets. The collection $I_1 \times I_2 \times \ldots \times I_n$ satisfies the strong insertion axiom. It is dubbed a Jim family.
- The *Julius techniques*. Let every method i be associated with a non-zero vector d_i in R^n and (d) be a given direction (d and the d_is are in general position). The collection of n-sets $(i_1, \ldots, i_n)$ such that direction (d), i.e. either vector d or $-d$, is positively generated by vectors $(d_{i_1}, \ldots, d_{i_n})$, is dubbed a Julius family. As the geometrical representation suggests (Mathematical appendix, figure A.2), if direction (d) is positively generated by n vectors ('old' vectors), there exists exactly one way to substitute a new vector for an old one in order that (d) is positively generated by the new n-set of vectors. In compact terms, a Julius family is a pre-technology. In the Lippi problem examined in chapter 11, section 5, the techniques are such that the final demand basket d is positively generated by the g-net vectors $(c_{i_1}(g), \ldots, c_{i_n}(g))$. They are 'almost' a Julius family and become exactly of this type when the collection is completed by the n-sets generating $-d$.

5.2 *Existence and oddity*

A dominant technique is an n-set that is simultaneously a candidate and a technique. We now have all the elements to state a first general existence result. Assume that the commodities can be freely disposed of. Then a dominant technique, if any, is associated with non-negative prices. From an economic point of view, the 'freak' n-set made of the n free disposal methods must be discarded, because it is associated with a zero price vector and is not productive.

Theorem 4. Let there be a number of methods, including the free disposal methods, and a pre-technology. The system is assumed to be strictly r-viable and labour is required to obtain a semi-positive net product. Then, if the n-set made of the n free disposal methods is a technique, there exists generically an odd number of dominant techniques associated with semi-positive prices.

The result is noteworthy for its simplicity. Its weak point is the assumption, which seems to have little economic relevance, that the freak n-set is indeed a technique. Let us illustrate Theorem 4 and explain why it admits the Lippi Theorem as a corollary. Let us associate its g-net product with every method and, for a given final demand vector $d > 0$, consider all the n-sets which can positively generate either d or $-d$. This is a family of Julius techniques. Since the g-net product of a free disposal process is a negative amount of the disposed commodity, the freak n-set generates $-d$ and is a technique. Theorem 4 applies. The dominant techniques associated with semi-positive prices in terms of wage are those which generate the basket d and are the solutions to the Lippi problem. Therefore, flukes apart, the Lippi problem admits an odd number of solutions.

Theorem 4 is closely related to a 'naked', i.e. combinatorial and not geometrical, variant of the Sperner lemma that is stated in the Mathematical appendix. Under additional conditions which hold for the Lippi problem, the oriented version of the naked lemma (Mathematical appendix, section 3) states that the number of 'white' dominant techniques exceeds by one that of 'black' solutions. Therefore the Colour Theorem (chapter 11, section 5) is also a corollary of the construction.

The proof of Theorem 4 is algorithmic. The algorithm, however, is not our usual tool: the market algorithm proceeds from a technique from a neighbouring one, by insertion of a profitable method, and stops when a candidate is found. Figure 11.5 in chapter 11, section 5 shows that the procedure may fail to converge for the Lippi problem because a bird configuration is met. Theorem 4 is based on a dual algorithm: It proceeds from a candidate to a neighbouring candidate and stops on a technique. Its economic content is less clear.

6 Technologies

6.1 Quasi-technology and convergence

This section is closer to Sraffa's ideas. An additional condition is required for the working of the algorithm: the bird configuration must be discarded. The consistency property is ensured in single production:

> While the *extent* of the cheapness of one method of production relatively to the other will vary according as the comparison is carried out in system I or in system II, the *order* of the two methods as to cheapness must be the same in the two systems. (*PCMC*, § 93, emphases in the original)

But a new axiom must be introduced to guarantee a similar property in joint production.

Definition 5. A *quasi-technology* is a non-void family $\boldsymbol{T}$ of techniques satisfying the two axioms:

- *Insertion axiom* (variant 2). If a method 2 yields extra profits at the prices associated with technique $T_1 \in \boldsymbol{T}$, there exists at least one way to substitute it for some method 1 belonging to T_1 in such a way that the new n-set is a technique $T_2 \in \boldsymbol{T}$.
- *Consistency axiom* (variant 2). At the prices associated with the new technique T_2, the just excluded method 1 pays extra costs.

Theorem 5. For any technique T_1 in a quasi-technology, there exists a sequence $T_1 \rightarrow T_2 \rightarrow \cdots \rightarrow T_r$ of neighbouring techniques which are successively preferred and such that T_r is a dominant technique.

In Definition 5, contrary to Definition 4, the insertion axiom does not require the uniqueness of the insertion. Similarly, the consistency axiom applies to at least one of the feasible insertions and is compatible with the roof case as well as the good case in figure 19.1. Theorem 5 is an existence and convergence result. Let us stress its precise statement concerning convergence. If, at a certain step, a method can be inserted in several ways or if several methods are simultaneously profitable (only one of them being inserted), the market algorithm can progress in different directions. In single production, the choice has no incidence and the algorithm converges ultimately towards the unique dominant technique. Two phenomena can occur in joint production:

- The final technique T_r may depend on the path.
- Since there are finitely many techniques, a path converges as soon at it admits no cycle. Theorem 5 ensures the existence of a convergent path but does not exclude the coexistence of a 'long' cycle of the type $T_1 \to T_2 \to \cdots \to T_6 \to T_1$ (the consistency axiom excludes the short cycle $T_1 \to T_2 \to T_1$). An example will be given in section 7.

6.2 *Robustness, softness and uniqueness*

We now examine whether the dominant technique is unique. The precise question concerns the uniqueness of the dominant price vector since, at a switch point, two dominant techniques are associated with the same price vector (itself defined up to a factor). Definition 4 is compatible with a roof configuration and, therefore, with the coexistence of two dominant techniques. Another condition must be introduced to guarantee uniqueness. The strong consistency axiom retains the 'good case' illustrated by figure 19.1c and described in Theorem 1.

Definition 6. A *technology* is a non-void family of n-sets, called techniques, that satisfies the two axioms:

(*i*) *Insertion axiom* (variant 3). Given a technique T_1 and a method c_2, there exists a technique T_2 obtained by inserting c_2 in T_1 in place of some old method c_1.

(*ii*) *Strong consistency axiom*. Given two neighbouring techniques T_1 and T_2, one of them is preferred over the other on the basis of both prices p_1 associated with T_1 and prices p_2 associated with T_2.

The insertion axiom does not require the uniqueness of the insertion, but the property holds:

Theorem 6. In a technology there is one and only one way to insert a method into a technique.

By eliminating the roof configuration we can anticipate the uniqueness of the dominant technique. Figure A.7 in (Mathematical appendix, section 5) provides a counter-example with $n = 3$ goods and $m = 5$ methods. An additional axiom is required to ensure uniqueness:

Definition 7. A technology is *robust* if any two techniques T_i, $i \in I$, and T_j, $j \in \mathcal{J}$, have a common interior r-net product.

Definition 8. A technology is *soft* if, for any given method i inside technique $T = (c_1, \ldots, c_i, \ldots, c_n)$ and any given technique $T' = (c'_1, \ldots, c'_j, \ldots, c'_n)$, method i can be replaced by some method j in T', in such a way that T and the neighbouring n-set $(c_1, \ldots c'_j, \ldots, c_n)$ satisfy the strong consistency condition.

The robustness axiom ensures uniqueness immediately (because two candidates have no common interior r-net product) but compares any two techniques, contrary to the spirit of the algorithmic approach. The softness axiom is local but its economic content is less clear. It turns out that the softness axiom is the local version of the robustness axiom:

Theorem 7. In a technology, the robustness and the softness axioms are equivalent properties. They guarantee the uniqueness (up to indifference) of the dominant technique.

This result is difficult to establish. The first step consists in showing that robustness implies uniqueness, the equivalence of the axioms being obtained in a second step. Details are given in the Mathematical appendix, section 5, where a refinement of the axioms also allows us to separate the question of uniqueness from that of existence.

7 Two applications

The two examples examined in this section are intended to add some flesh to the abstract construction of section 6. In the first example, the requirements for use are defined explicitly and a Julius technology is obtained. In the second, the list of techniques is given (a Jim technology), the procedure being closer to the general idea of the approach.

We first return to the golden rule problem examined in chapter 11, section 5. With $g = r$, let the vector $d_i = c_i(g) = c_i(r)$ be associated with method i. The n-sets generating the given basket $d = \delta$ constitute a technology (Definition 6) which moreover is robust (Definition 7). The existence, convergence and uniqueness results follow from Theorems 5 and 7. However, the direct treatment seen in chapter 11 is simpler because its arguments are identical to those used in single production. The second application is more instructive:

Theorem 8. Let there be n commodities and m methods which are partitioned into n 'colours' $I_1, \ldots, I_n$, such that $det(c_{i_1}(r), \ldots, c_{i_n}(r)) > 0$ for any $i_1 \in I_1, \ldots, i_n \in I_n$, and let the techniques be the n-sets made of one method of every colour. Their collection is a Jim technology. There exists a unique dominant technique. Starting from any technique, the dominant technique can be reached by the market algorithm in n steps at most.

Since, according to Theorem 1, the positivity of the determinants ensures the strong consistency condition, the family of techniques considered above is a technology (Definition 6), which moreover is soft (Definition 8). Therefore Theorem 8 is a corollary of Theorems 5 and 7 (a direct proof is given in section 10). A numerical example is: let there be $n = 3$ commodities and $m = 6$ methods, which are partitioned into three colours

$$c_1(r) = \begin{pmatrix} 6 \\ -3 \\ 2 \end{pmatrix}, \quad c_2(r) = \begin{pmatrix} 6 \\ 1 \\ -4 \end{pmatrix};$$

two blue methods

$$c_3(r) = \begin{pmatrix} 2 \\ 6 \\ -3 \end{pmatrix}, \quad c_4(r) = \begin{pmatrix} -4 \\ 6 \\ 1 \end{pmatrix};$$

two white methods

$$c_5(r) = \begin{pmatrix} -3 \\ 2 \\ 6 \end{pmatrix}; \quad c_6(r) = \begin{pmatrix} 1 \\ -4 \\ 6 \end{pmatrix}$$

two red methods

All determinants $(c_{blue}, c_{white}, c_{red})$ are positive because they have a dominant diagonal. The relationships between the eight Jim techniques are visualized in the diagram

$$\begin{array}{ccccccccccccc}
246 & & & & 246 & & & & 246 & & & & \\
\downarrow & & & & \downarrow & & & & \downarrow & & & & \\
146 & \rightarrow & 145 & \rightarrow & 245 & \rightarrow & 235 & \rightarrow & 236 & \rightarrow & 136 & \rightarrow & 146 \rightarrow \ldots \\
& & \downarrow & & & & \downarrow & & & & \downarrow & & \\
& & 135 & & & & 135 & & & & 135 & &
\end{array}$$

where an arrow between two neighbouring techniques $T_1 \rightarrow T_2$ indicates that T_2 is preferred to T_1 for both price systems. The dominant technique is 135. The remarkable feature of the example is the existence of a loop $146 \rightarrow 145 \rightarrow 245 \rightarrow 235 \rightarrow 236 \rightarrow 136 \rightarrow 146 \rightarrow \cdots$ This phenomenon shows that the strong consistency axiom does not prevent the existence of cycles, and that the convergence of the algorithm must be understood as explained in the comments on Theorem 5. Its important lesson concerns the nature of the problem of choice of technique in joint production. A general description of an algorithm is: given a family of 'things', an algorithm defines a way to jump from one thing to another. The usual argument to establish convergence consists in attaching a 'Lyapunov (1907) value' to every thing and showing that the value increases from one step to the next. Then the algorithm admits no cycle and a final position is reached (a 'dominant thing'). This is the argument used in single production and the golden rule case: the 'things' are the techniques, the wage rate acts as the Lyapunov function and the wage-maximizing technique is dominant. The general problem is of a different nature: the existence of loops shows that the sequence of techniques cannot be L-monotone towards an L-maximizing dominant technique, whatever the function L is. The convergence arguments are subtle. Two noteworthy characteristics of the proof of Theorem 8 are: (*i*) the existence result is based on a fixed-point argument, not a maximization property; and (*ii*) convergence is established *after* existence and as a consequence of it, not the other way round. The general arguments relative to technologies, which are developed in the Mathematical appendix, section 5, are based on combinatorial geometry and have similar features.

8 Conclusion

The main difficulty of this chapter is of a conceptual nature: economists are so accustomed to thinking in terms of supply and demand that, in spite of Sraffa's explicit rejection of the approach, they reinterpret his writings in this framework. As a consequence, all post-Sraffian studies on choice of techniques can be viewed as particular cases of either the Lippi model or the Morishima model. This interpretation has been facilitated by the inconsistencies of Sraffa's own analysis. Sraffa introduces the concept of requirements for use, but his desire not to describe the requirements explicitly leads him to ignore them. Consequently his construction relies only on a formal analogy with single production and becomes unacceptable. The approach followed avoids this trap. It is its faithfulness to the general methodology of *PCMC* that allows us to interpret this construction as an implementation of Sraffa's ambition. No constancy of returns is required; the requirements for use are not identified to demand but are thought of, more abstractly, as a constraint imposed on the operated methods. Then the search for a dominant technique is that of the compatibility between this constraint and the cost-minimization condition. It is important to carry through this programme and to stress its originality. The first question is not whether Sraffa is right or wrong in rejecting the supply and demand approach, but whether or not an alternative approach is conceivable.

9 Switches and fakes

The main methodological and analytical characteristics of Sraffa's approach to choice of technique in single production have been delineated in chapter 9, section 6: for a great enough rate of profit, only one technique is admissible. When the rate of profit decreases progressively, the (w, r) point follows the corresponding wage–profit curve, until the first switch point at which a deviation occurs. Because of the deviation, the (w, r) point follows the upper envelope of the wage–profit curves. Therefore, at any rate of profit, the selected technique is wage-maximizing.

Can the construction be adapted to joint production? Let three methods 1, 2 and 3 produce two commodities jointly. In the extension of the reasoning to joint production, the significant gap is that three square systems (12), (13) and (23), instead of two, can be built, hence *three* wage curves $w_{12}(r)$, $w_{13}(r)$ and $w_{23}(r)$. At a switch point, the three methods are equally profitable, the price and wage vector is common to the three systems and the three wage curves have a common intersection. Let us start from the maximum level of the rate of profit, say R_{12}, and the corresponding system (12). When the rate of profit decreases and reaches the first switch point, the previously excluded method 3 becomes profitable, but it is unclear whether it will replace method 1 or 2 and, therefore, whether the (w, r) point will continue along the $w_{13}(r)$ or the $w_{23}(r)$ curve. Sraffa identifies this insertion problem explicitly. His proposal, which is to select the system (13) or (23) that maximizes the wage, is justified only by analogy with single production. Our contention is that even a stronger argument in favour of that rule would not suffice, because the approach itself suffers from an internal weakness that Sraffa overlooked (Bidard and Klimovsky 2004).

Imagine that, in a representation in the w–r space for *some* numéraire, two of the three wage–profit curves intersect but their intersection does not belong to the third curve. Then:

- Since switches generate intersections of the three curves, the intersection of two curves only is a 'fake' switch.
- If a fake switch is located on the upper envelope, the maximization property would imply a change of method at a point where no switch occurs.

Therefore the notion of a fake switch is both methodologically consistent with Sraffa's dynamic approach and destructive for its analytical conclusions. But do fakes exist? For two goods and *given the numéraire basket*, consider a rate r_0 such that the surplus generated by one method alone after accumulation at rate r_0 coincides with the direction of the numéraire. In formal terms, let a_1 and b_1 be the input and output vectors per worker of method 1, and r_0 be such that vector $b_1 - (1 + r_0)a_1$ is equal to w_0 units of the numéraire. Such a value r_0 exists as soon as the vector representing the numéraire basket is located in the angle defined by vectors $b_1 - a_1$ and $b_1 - (1 + R)a_1$. We claim that r_0 is a fake switch point. The argument is: after accumulation at rate r_0, method 1 alone, and therefore any square system which contains method 1, can produce w_0 units of the numéraire. Under the golden rule hypothesis, the wage in terms of that numéraire is therefore equal to w_0. Since the wage does not depend on whether the economy follows a golden rule path, w_0 is also the wage associated with any system using method 1. Therefore, at the rate of profit r_0, both systems (12) and (13) admit that level of the wage. The other method 2 or 3 inside the system plays a role in the determination of the price vector p_{12} or p_{13} but has no influence on wage. As opposed to (12) and (13), the third system (23) has no relationship with method 1 and its specific wage. This means that, at the rate r_0, the wage is equal to w_0 for systems (12) and (13), but not for (23). The point (r_0, w_0), which belongs to both wage–profit curves $w_{12}(r)$ and $w_{13}(r)$ but not to the third curve $w_{23}(r)$, is a fake switch point. The generalization to an n-commodity economy ($n \geq 2$) is:

Definition 9. Let there be an n-commodity economy with a given numéraire basket. r_0 is a fake switch point if the numéraire is obtained as a positive combination of $n - 1$ baskets $b_i - (1 + r_0)a_i$ generated by $n - 1$ methods.

Theorem 9. Let there be $n + 1$ methods of production. At the rate of profit r_0, the two square systems which contain the $n - 1$ methods mentioned in Definition 9 yield the same wage in terms of the numéraire, whereas any other square system normally yields a different rate. Therefore a fake corresponds to the intersection of two wage–profit curves only.

A numerical example with two commodities and three methods illustrates the notion:

$$\begin{array}{llll} \text{Method 1:} & 20X + 20Y + & 1L \rightarrow & 21X + 27Y \\ \text{Method 2:} & 20X + 20Y + & 1L \rightarrow & 23X + 25Y \\ \text{Method 3:} & 30X + 30Y + & 1L \rightarrow & 36X + 34Y \end{array}$$

According to the commodity chosen as numéraire, the three wage–profit curves are:

X as standard:	Y as standard:
$w_{12}(r) = 8 - 40r$	$w_{12}(r) = 8 - 40r$
$w_{13}(r) = (38 - 220r)/(3 + 10r)$	$w_{13}(r) = (38 - 220r)/(5 - 10r)$
$w_{23}(r) = (18 - 100r)/(1 + 10r)$	$w_{23}(r) = (18 - 100r)/(3 - 10r)$.

The observations are:

- Whatever the standard is, the three wage–profit curves intersect at $r^* = 0.1$, which is a switch point.
- When Y is the standard, point F_1 ($r = 0.05$; $w = 6$) belongs to both curves $w_{12}(r)$ and $w_{13}(r)$, but not to the third curve $w_{23}(r)$. It is a fake switch point, which disappears with the change of standard. As a matter of fact, method 1 alone produces 6 units of commodity Y when the rate of accumulation is 0.05. Since F_1 is located on the upper envelope of the wage curves, its presence modifies the shape of the upper envelope, as if a switch were possible at $r = 5$ per cent.
- Similarly, F_2 ($r = 0.15$; $w = 2$) with Y as standard, and F_3 ($r = 4/30$; $w = 2$) with X as standard, are fake switches.
- An economist who has a complete knowledge of the wage curves can identify a switch point and three fakes, but is unable to decide which system is operated at a given rate of profit: in joint production, the transfer of the choice of technique from the price space to the distribution space is impossible.

Post-Sraffian literature often recognizes that the identification of cost-minimizing and wage-maximizing systems cannot be sustained, if only on the grounds that the first notion is independent of the composition of the wage basket, not the second. But it spares itself the trouble of scrutinizing Sraffa's own reasoning and proceeds by substitution. This reinforces our contention that the post-Sraffian readings and reconstructions should not be immediately identified with an implementation of Sraffa's intent.

10 Proof

The chief statements of the chapter (Theorems 4, 5 and 7) concern the study of a structure, called technology, which is typically a source of reflection for a mathematical research. The general proofs are provided in the Mathematical appendix. A direct proof of Theorem 8 (Bidard 1984b) constitutes training on the topic.

Proof of Theorem 8.

(*i*) *Robustness and uniqueness*. The insertion property is immediate. According to Theorem 1, the positivity of neighbouring determinants implies the strong consistency property. Therefore the family of the Jim techniques is a technology. Consider any two Jim techniques $T = (c_i, i \in I)$ and $T' = (c'_i, i \in I')$ and the matrix M obtained by decomposing the n vectors $(c'_i, i \in I')$ into basis $(c_i, i \in I)$. Since the determinant of any principal $L \times L$ minor extracted from M is the determinant of the Jim technique $(c'_i, i \in L; c_i, i \notin L)$, it is positive: M is a P-matrix (Gale and Nikaido 1965), and this implies the existence of vectors $\delta \gg 0$ and $x \gg 0$ such that $\delta = Mx$. Therefore δ is simultaneously a positive combination of vectors $(c_i, i \in I)$ and of the columns of M, i.e. of vectors $(c'_i, i \in I')$. This shows that any two techniques have some interior common vector (robustness property). Since two dominant n-sets have no interior common r-net basket, the dominant technique, if any, is unique.

(*ii*) *Existence of a dominant technique*. Let all methods be normalized by setting $l_i = 1$ and let K_j, $1 \leq j \leq n$, be the compact convex hull of all vectors $c_j(r)$ of colour j. With each $x = (x_1, \ldots, x_n) \in \Pi_j K_j$, let us associate the price vector $p = f(x) \in R^n$ such that $x_1 p = \cdots = x_n p = 1$ (its existence and uniqueness follow from $det(x_1, \ldots, x_n) > 0$). The vector p belongs to a compact convex set P in R^n. With each vector $p \in P$ and any j, let us associate the set $\gamma_j(p) = \{x_j \in K_j; x_j p = \max K_j p\} \subset K_j$. The correspondence

$$f \times \prod_j \gamma_j : \prod_j K_j \times P \to P \times \prod_j K_j$$

satisfies the assumptions of the Kakutani Theorem. Therefore it admits a fixed point $(\ldots, x^*_j, \ldots; p^*)$. For such a point we have

$$\forall j = 1, \ldots, n \quad \forall x_j \in K_j \quad x^*_j p^* = 1 \geq x_j p^*.$$

If x^*_j is a barycentre of two points in K_j, the same inequality holds for these points. One can therefore assume that x^*_j is a vertex c^*_j of K_j, i.e. it represents a method of colour j. The inequalities mean that the corresponding Jim technique $T^* = (\ldots, c^*_j, \ldots)$ is dominant.

(*iii*) *Convergence*. Consider the dominant technique T^* and an arbitrary technique $T = (c^*_1, \ldots, c^*_k, c_{k+1}, \ldots, c_n)$ which has its first k methods in common with T^*. T^* is also dominant for the reduced Jim technology made of methods $\{c^*_1, \ldots, c^*_k, c^*_{k+1} \text{ or } c_{k+1}, \ldots, c^*_n \text{ or } c_n\}$. At T's prices some method, c^*_l, $l > k$, is profitable, otherwise both techniques T and T^* would be dominant for the reduced technology and the uniqueness property would be violated. After insertion of c_l^* in T, a new technique T^+ is obtained (with $T \rightarrow T^+$), which has one more method in common with T^*. Therefore T^* can be reached in n steps at most, this being compatible with the coexistence of loops. ■

20 The structure of general equilibrium

1 Walras first

In this chapter, we abandon the theory of prices of production and turn to that of the general equilibrium. The logical foundations of Walras' (1874 [1988]) grandiose project have been confirmed by Arrow and Debreu (1954) and have made the updated Walrasian theory into a reference in the study of perfect competition. All alternative theories must necessarily measure up to it. Neither the interest in a simplification of the model nor the operational value of economic calculation should conceal the fact that the constructions of Jevons, Menger, Marshall, Böhm-Bawerk or Clark are different and their ambitions less far-reaching than that of Walras. Therefore, let us deal with Walras first.

The difference with classical theory is visible in the very structure of the *Eléments*: the core of the theory of prices is already present in the reflection on exchange, before the introduction of production and reproduction. Since the reader is familiar with this theory (Debreu 1959), our project is to provide a presentation that sheds light on it in a particular fashion with a view to the examination of possible articulations with the classical theory of prices. The exercise requires simplifying certain aspects and underscoring others. We grant ourselves the right to take up the existing fragments and arrange them in a manner that is most adequate to our research.

Section 2 presents a simplified version of the general equilibrium theory in the static case, which is extended to a finite horizon in section 3. Sections 4 and 5 are devoted to a discussion of the relationship between efficiency and competition in finite and infinite horizon. Finally, Walras' theory of capitalization is discussed.

2 Static equilibrium

2.1 *Utility, never*

The neoclassical theory substitutes the distinction between consumers and entrepreneurs for that of workers and capitalists, which was central for classical economists. The consumers draw their incomes from 'initial endowments'. These may be of any nature but, in economies with production that are of interest to us, they are chiefly identified with labour and capital goods. The value of a consumer's income is that of his endowment (plus a possible part of total profits). It is assumed that the supply is entirely sold at the announced prices. Traditionally, theory assigns a preorder of preferences to each consumer, then derives a demand function by maximizing utility under a budget constraint. This detour has little to do with the existence of an equilibrium and is mainly of significance for the normative properties relative to consumption. It is therefore not a drawback, for our concern, to set aside the notion of utility and choose the demand function as our starting point. (The continuity of the demand function requires a survival condition: such details do not affect the argument.) Consumer i is then characterized by a demand function $d_i(p, R_i)$ which depends on prices and income (more precisely, wealth) and is assumed to satisfy three properties: (*i*) it is continuous; (*ii*) the budget constraint is saturated; (*iii*) there is no monetary illusion.

The firms are price-takers and profit-maximizers. Increasing returns to scale being incompatible with competition, we assume that the returns are decreasing or constant. The case of decreasing returns is comparable with the rent theory and can be reduced to the case of constant returns with a hidden factor: for instance, the production function $Q = f(K)$, f concave, is also written $Q = F(K, H) = Hf(K/H)$, where F is homogeneous and H is a hidden factor available in quantity $\overline{H} = 1$ (McKenzie 1959). The rent then coincides with the payment for the hidden factor. In the presence of decreasing returns, the pure profits are added to the incomes resulting from the endowments.

The case of constant returns is our main concern. According to Walras' dictum, there is neither profit nor loss in the equilibrium position: if the maximum profit were positive (resp. negative), it could be increased by doubling (resp. halving) the activity levels. The nullity of pure profits has two consequences:

- If the equilibrium is reached for quantities (y^-, y^+) of inputs and outputs, the same profit, which is both zero and maximum, is obtained on the ray $(\lambda y^-, \lambda y^+)$, for any $\lambda > 0$. The effective level of production is determined by demand.

- The fact that the profit is simultaneously zero and maximum implies the existence of a specific relation between the prices of inputs and outputs. In single production, the price of the product is equal to its cost of production.

In the absence of externalities, it is equivalent to maximize profits for every firm or at the industry level, or to maximize them for the whole country considered as a giant production box (decentralization principle). The existence of a finite number m of methods avoids discussing marginal equalities. The technology is then described by a pair (A, B) of input and output matrices. Since the Walrasian construction treats labour on the same footing as any other input, one of the columns of the input matrix concerns labour (assumed to be homogeneous, for simplicity). This matrix is therefore expanded with regard to the formalization retained up to now. If, among the N goods, one distinguishes N_1 resources (labour, raw materials, . . .) and N_2 final goods, the matrices A and B have dimensions $m \times N_1$ and $m \times N_2$, respectively; after stacking columns with zeros, we may consider them as matrices of dimension $m \times N$, with $N = N_1 + N_2$. The free disposal hypothesis ensures the non-negativity of prices.

2.2 *General equilibrium*

Let $p_1 \in R_+^{N_1}$ be the prices of the N_1 factors, $p_2 \in R_+^{N_2}$ that of the N_2 products and $y \in R_+^m$ the activity levels. If the supply of endowments is inelastic, it is defined by a row vector ω; if not, let us note $g(p_1, p_2) \in R_+^{N_1}$ the total supply of factors. We consider a system of inequalities with complementarity relationships (Bidard and Franke 1987b):

$$yA \leq g(p_1, p_2) \quad [p_1] \tag{1}$$

$$Bp_2 \leq Ap_1 \quad [y] \tag{2}$$

$$h(p_1, p_2) \leq yB \quad [p_2] \tag{3}$$

Inequality (1) means that the demand for factors is met and that the factors in excess supply have a zero price (free disposal hypothesis). Inequality (2) means that no activity yields pure profits and that the operated methods have a zero profit. Inequality (3) expresses that the household's demand in final goods is met and that the goods in excess supply have a zero price. In order to approach Walras' own conception of equilibrium, one can assume that the demand for a good tends to infinity when its price tends to zero. Inequality (3) is then replaced by equality

$$h(p_1, p_2) = yB. \tag{3'}$$

The problem of general equilibrium is that of the existence of a price vector (p_1, p_2) and activity levels y which are solution to the system (1)–(3) or (1)–(3′). The Walras identity is the key argument. This law states that, whatever the price vector is, the values of the notional supply and the notional demand are identical. Or, alternatively, the value of the excess demand function $z = z(p)$ is zero. The Gale (1955) – Debreu (1956) – Nikaido (1956) Lemma lets the identity play a central role in the very existence of the equilibrium:

GND Lemma. Let z: $S \rightarrow R^N$ be a continuous function defined on the unit simplex S of R^N_+, with values in R^N, that satisfies the Walras identity $\forall p \;\; z(p)p = 0$. Then:

$$\exists p^* \in S \quad z(p^*) \leq 0 \quad [p^*].$$

The conclusion means that p^* is an equilibrium price vector. We refer to the GND lemma every time we want to stress that the presence of a Walras identity implies the existence result. Our concern is to underline not so much the technical unity of apparently diverse problems as their theoretical unity. The GND lemma can be applied to Walras' problem itself:

Theorem 1. Assume that:

(A_1) The input matrix $A > 0$ has no zero row and the output matrix $B > 0$ no zero column.

(A_2) the supply of resources $g(.)$ and the demand for final goods $h(.)$ are defined on the set $D = \{(p_1, p_2) \in R^{N_1} \times R^{N_2}; p_1 > 0, p_2 \gg 0\}$. They are both continuous and semi-positive.

(A_3) if $p_1 > 0$ and if the sequence $\{p_2^k\}_{k \in N}$ converges to some p_2 with a zero component j, then $h_j(p_1, p_2^k) \rightarrow \infty$ as $k \rightarrow \infty$.

(A_4) the factor supply function $g(.)$ is bounded.

(W) the Walras law holds:

$$\forall (p_1, p_2) \in D \quad g(p_1, p_2)p_1 = h(p_1, p_2)p_2. \qquad (W_1)$$

Then there exists a general equilibrium, i.e. a solution $p_1^* > 0$, $p_2^* \gg 0$, $y^* > 0$ to the system (1) – (3′).

The left-hand side of equality (W_1) represents the value of final demand, whereas the right-hand side is the consumers' total income: (W_1) is a variant of the Walras identity. The existence of finitely many methods is an inessential hypothesis which shows that the general equilibrium theory is not intimately linked to a differentiability hypothesis. Aside from existence, uniqueness, stability and convergence are expected. Sufficient conditions are known (Arrow and Hahn 1971) but none of them is general. Walras thought that the equilibrium is reached spontaneously if no obstacle hinders the working of the 'market forces' and it has long been expected that the dynamics of the Walrasian tâtonnement would indeed lead to an equilibrium. Scarf's (1960) counter-example pointed at the limits of this programme. In this book, we do not study the dynamics of either Walrasian or Sraffian disequilibrium models. These questions are important but a clear distinction between the study of equilibrium and that of stability or convergence is desirable, especially in order not to confuse an intertemporal equilibrium with a disequilibrium path: there is enough to discuss about equilibrium itself.

3 Intertemporal economies

To introduce time and reproduction within the general equilibrium theory is a necessary step before comparison with classical theory. The production function as Walras conceived it describes the instantaneous transformation of pumpkins into coaches: 'Production, however, requires a certain lapse of time. We shall resolve the . . . difficulty purely and simply by ignoring the time element at this point' (Walras, 1874 [1988], § 207). This convention is an obstacle for studying reproduction, be it that of final goods (§ 207) or new capital goods (§ 251). In modern equilibrium theory, time is taken into account by means of a simple reinterpretation of the atemporal model. Up to now, the commodities have been distinguished according to their nature: wheat, iron, labour, etc. Let us introduce $T+1$ dates ($t = 0, \ldots, T$).[1] Period t elapses between dates t and $t+1$. The date at which a commodity is available, or labour is employed, matters for the agents. Hence the fruitful idea to distinguish the commodities according to their nature *and* their date of availability. This once done, the goods become dated goods: there are $N(T+1)$ dated commodities. Production is an operation which, once it is decomposed into a sequence of one-period processes, admits inputs dated $t-1$ and produces outputs dated t. Flukes apart, the prices of two dated goods differ. An intertemporal price vector is written $p = (p_0, \ldots, p_T)$ where $p_t = (p_{1t}, \ldots, p_{it}, \ldots, p_{Nt})$ is interpreted as a present price: p_{it} is the price to be paid *today* for a delivery of a unit of commodity i at date t. The notion of present price is the first concept in that construction (on the contrary, usual economic calculations start from the value at date t, then find its discounted equivalent).

[1] Theorists disagree on whether 'today' corresponds to date $t = 0$ or $t = 1$.

The notion of a dated good is a remarkable device and the only question is whether it is remarkable for its strength or its weakness. There are many reasons for rejecting a conception of time in which all constraints are perceived today and all decisions taken today. But these reasons hold only if another approach that takes uncertainty and expectations into account is substituted for this one. This not being the case in the present study, we adopt the poor and rudimentary conception of time conveyed by the intertemporal equilibrium theory. An intertemporal equilibrium is defined as an intertemporal price vector and its associated optimal productions and demands, which are such that, for any dated good, demand is met by supply (the price of an overproduced good is zero by the free disposal hypothesis). With constant returns, the intertemporal no-profit condition is written

$$Bp_{t+1} \leq Ap_t \quad [y_t] \tag{4}$$

where y_t are the activity levels during period t, p_t the price of the inputs for date t and p_{t+1} that of the outputs for date $t+1$. If there are finitely many dates, the existence theorem holds under the same assumptions as Theorem 1 interpreted in an intertemporal framework. Its crucial hypothesis is the intertemporal Walras identity: in an intertemporal framework, the identity is equivalent to that between savings and investment.

By definition, the rate of interest of good i between dates t and $t+1$ is the scalar $r_{i,t}$ defined as $1 + r_{i,t} = p_{i,t}/p_{i,t+1}$. The theory of the rates of interest turns out to be a part of that of the relative prices. In general, the rates differ according to the commodity and the period. As long as one considers the relative prices at a given date, any commodity can be selected as numéraire. A common practice is to specify a commodity '*m*' whose value is set equal to one for every period. Let us call it 'money'. The list of intertemporal prices is then split into a sequence of monetary rates of interest, plus the list of monetary prices for every period. Changing the commodity called money results in a change in the monetary rates and the monetary prices. An exception occurs when the relative prices are independent of the period. When vectors p_t and p_{t+1} are proportional all commodities have the same own rate of interest. Let p be the constant relative prices. Inequality (4) is written

$$Bp \leq (1 + r_t)Ap \quad [y] \tag{5}$$

which looks like a price of production relationship. The comparison of general equilibrium prices and classical prices is based on (5) and will be pursued in chapter 22.

4 Efficiency and competition

4.1 The concept of efficiency

This section examines the equivalence, or near-equivalence, between efficiency and profit-maximization. Since the welfare results rely on the notion of utility which is kept out of the classical theory, we retain only the notion of productive efficiency. The data of 'the planner's problem' are a given stock of endowments and a given set of methods. The objective is to organize production in order to maximize the physical net product. By definition, production is organized efficiently if it is not possible to increase the net product of all goods simultaneously.

In a first step, let production be conceived as an instantaneous transformation of endowments into final goods. The efficiency problem is a *difficult* problem. Two levels of difficulty are distinguished:

- *Coordination within an industry.* Let there be three methods to produce A, with constant returns:

$$1X + 4Y \to 1A, \quad 4X + 1Y \to 1A, \quad 3X + 3Y \to 1A.$$

None of these methods is inefficient, when compared each with another. But the third method is dominated by a convex combination of the other two methods and should not be used.

- *Coordination between industries.* Consider two methods of production for A and two for B:

$$\text{industry } A \begin{cases} 1X + 5Y \to 1A \\ 3X + 3Y \to 1A \end{cases} \quad \text{industry } B \begin{cases} 5X + 2Y \to 1B \\ 2X + 3Y \to 1B. \end{cases}$$

Instead of producing $1A + 1B$ by means of a joint use of the first methods, the planner would better use the last two methods: this saves $1X + 1Y$ on inputs, which can be used to increase the net product. The property at stake is that the switch from the first to the last two methods results in substitutions among the inputs of A and those of B which, on the whole, are both X-saving and Y-saving. The statement of the same idea is simpler in the presence of a continuum of methods: if the marginal rates of substitution (MRS) between inputs differ among industries, adequate transfers save inputs at the economy level: therefore a coordination between industries requires the equality of their MRS.

4.2 Where prices appear

The planner can help her/himself by choosing a price vector and following the cost-minimization rule. Let p_X and p_Y be two *arbitrary* positive prices attributed to the inputs. Consider the cost-minimizing method for the production of one unit of A. Relative to it, another method is described by a variation ΔX and ΔY of its inputs. The inequality $p_X \Delta X + p_Y \Delta Y \geq 0$ means that the alternative method is more costly. If there exists a method 1 which is less X-intensive and more Y-intensive and another method 2 with the opposite characteristics, the inequalities

$$-(\Delta X/\Delta Y)_1 \leq p_Y/p_X \leq -(\Delta X/(\Delta Y)_2 \qquad (6)$$

hold. They show that the prices and the rates of substitution between inputs are closely connected. In the presence of a continuum of methods, (6) is transformed into an equality between the relative input prices and the marginal rate of substitution. Therefore, the marginal rates are the same across industries, which is a necessary condition for efficiency.

Up until now, the focus has been on the input side. The planner finds symmetric difficulties on the output side. The relevant analytical concept is that of substitution between outputs, which is referred to as a rate of transformation. Again, the planner can help her/himself with a price vector: arbitrary positive prices being attributed to the produced commodities, the planner chooses the value-maximizing technique. In order to solve the input-side and the output-side problems simultaneously the planner can take a price vector for inputs, another for outputs, then maximize the profit. The methods selected by these means are efficient. Moreover, the use of shadow prices is a 'universal' device: any efficient production can be reached by means of an adequate choice of positive prices. The equivalence between efficiency and profit-maximization admits only one exception: if a commodity is free, there is no incentive for a profit-maximizing agent to optimize its use or production, so that production may be inefficient. This case apart, profit-maximization leads to an efficient state (Koopmans 1957).

Let us introduce time into the efficiency problem. As the concept of a dated good draws an analogy between an intertemporal economy and a static economy, the results can be transferred to intertemporal economies with finite horizon. Let us be more specific and consider a planner who organizes production over the time horizon T. For $t = 0, \ldots, T$, let ω_t be the endowments at date t (they are exogenous data), y_t the gross product obtained from the investment of the previous period (if $t \geq 1$) and x_t the inputs for the next period (if $t \leq T - 1$). The organization of intertemporal production consists in selecting inputs x_t at date t and feasible outputs y_{t+1} at date $t + 1$. They lead to a specific chronicle $d_t = \omega_t + y_t - x_t$ of net products. Dynamic efficiency requires efficiency within every period. An additional condition is relative to coordination between consecutive periods: at any date t, the rate of transformation between two outputs in period t must be equal to the rate of substitution between the same goods considered as inputs in period $t+1$. Profit maximization for given intertemporal shadow prices ensures both properties. The discussion is summarized below. Y_t denotes the production set during period t, i.e. notation $(x_t, y_{t+1}) \in Y_t$ means that input vector x_t can be transformed into output vector y_{t+1}. Convexity and free disposal are assumed.

Definition 1. Consider an intertemporal economy with a finite horizon. The endowments ω_t and the technology Y_t are given at any date t. A non-negative chronicle of net products $d = (d_0, \ldots, d_T)$ is *feasible* if there exists an intertemporal sequence $(x_t, y_{t+1}) \in Y_t$ such that:

$$\begin{array}{ll} t = 0 & x_0 + d_0 \leq \omega_0 \\ \forall t = 1, \ldots, T-1 & x_t + d_t \leq \omega_t + y_t \\ t = T & d_T \leq \omega_T + y_T. \end{array} \tag{7}$$

A feasible chronicle is *maximal* if there is no alternative feasible chronicle d' such that $d'_t \geq d_t$ for any t with $d'_t > d_t$ for some t. Then the organization of production is efficient. A feasible chronicle is *competitive* if there exists a semi-positive sequence of price vectors $p = (p_0, \ldots, p_T)$ such that:

(*i*) Inequalities (7) hold with complementarity relationships with prices.
(*ii*) The sequence (x_t, y_{t+1}) is profit maximizing.

Theorem 2. In an intertemporal economy with a finite horizon:

(*i*) Any competitive chronicle associated with a positive price vector is maximal.
(*ii*) Any maximal chronicle is obtained as a competitive chronicle for some adequately chosen semi-positive price vectors.

5 Efficiency in an infinite horizon

5.1 *The lost equivalence*

In an infinite horizon, the number of dated goods becomes infinite and the Walras identity no longer guarantees the existence of an equilibrium. We restrict our attention to the loss of the equivalence between efficiency and competitiveness. This is shown by two examples. Consider first the intertemporal corn model in an infinite horizon, and let $d = (d_0, \ldots, d_t, \ldots)$ be an infinite feasible chronicle of net products. Since the product obtained at date $t+1$ amounts to $y_{t+1} = ax_t$ if there is no waste of corn, the no-profit condition holds for the price vector $p_t = a^t$. Therefore *any* feasible chronicle, be it non-maximal, is sustained by competitive prices. A second example considers stationary states. Let there be the gross production function $Q_{t+1} = F(K_t, L_t)$ where K_t and Q_{t+1} represent quantities of corn. The endowments consist of ω_0 units of corn at date 0 and $L_t = (1+g)^t$ units of labour at dates $t = 0, 1, \ldots$ The production function is also written $q_{t+1} = f(k_t)$, where $f(k_t) = (1+g)^t F(K_t/(1+g)^t, 1)$, with f concave, $f'(0) = \infty$, $f'(\infty) = 0$ ('the canonical neoclassical model'). If the present price of corn decreases at the constant rate r, the quantity per head $\hat{k}$ invested at date t is constant and defined by the marginal equality $f'(\hat{k}) = 1 + r$. Let ω_0 be great enough ($\omega_0 > \hat{k}$). The dynamics of the competitive path are: at date 0, quantity $d_0 = \omega_0 - \hat{k}$ is consumed and $\hat{k}$ is invested; at any other date, quantity $f(\hat{k}) - \hat{k}$ is consumed and $\hat{k}$ is invested: the competitive path is stationary up from $t = 1$. Compare this with another path on which the constant quantity of capital is $\hat{k} - \varepsilon$, $\varepsilon > 0$. The consumption per head at date 0 increases by ε, and that at the other dates changes by $[f(\hat{k}) - (1+g)\hat{k}] - [f(\hat{k} - \varepsilon) - (1+g)(\hat{k} - \varepsilon)] = \varepsilon\,(g - r)$. The conclusion is that the competitive path is inefficient if the rate of interest is smaller than the rate of growth, generating an overaccumulation of capital. On the contrary, a quasi-stationary path is efficient if $g > r$ (Malinvaud 1953; Starrett 1970).

As a third example, let there be a differentiable model with one or several factors and, in a stationary state, consider a marginal perturbation which, for simplicity, is designed to modify the surplus of a unique commodity during a finite time: Its effects are described by the variation $\varepsilon a = \varepsilon(a_0, \ldots, a_T)$ of the surpluses between dates t to $t + T$. Inefficiency is established if the operation leads to an increase of the surplus at every date, i.e. if the vector a is positive (or negative: in this case, modify the sign of ε). But assume, for instance, that the intertemporal changes in the surpluses are represented by the vector $a = (1, -1.5, 4)$ at the successive dates t, $t+1$ and $t+2$. Though the operation is not conclusive at first sight, consider the transform which repeats the same basic operation one period later after doubling its activity level. The overall result is the positive change (1, 0.5, 1, 8): intertemporal inefficiency is revealed in a finite time. It is also possible that a perturbation leading to the sequence of surpluses εa cannot reveal inefficiency in a finite time, but it does so in an infinite time by repeating the perturbation for all dates, as it is the case for $a = (1, 1, -1)$. The proof of the following criteria (Bidard, 2003) for steady states relies on the same mathematical techniques as those used for the study of fixed capital without truncation:

Theorem 3. A marginal change leading to the sequence of surpluses $\varepsilon(a_0, \ldots, a_T)$ reveals inefficiency in a finite time if and only if the polynomial $A(x) = \Sigma_{t=0}^{T} a_\tau x^t$ has no positive root. It reveals inefficiency in an infinite time if and only if it has no root in [0, 1].

5.2 *Three efficiency criteria*

For the neoclassical model $Q_t = f(C_{t-1})$ in a steady state, the net product is maximum for the level C^* of capital defined by the golden rule $f'(C^*) = 1$, f being the gross production function. Consider a non-steady chronicle supported by the sequence $(C_1, \ldots, C_t, \ldots)$ of capital stocks. Intuitively, a competitive economy accumulates too much capital if C_t often exceeds C^*, i.e. if the marginal productivity of capital is often smaller than one. As the marginal productivity is equal to the ratio between consecutive prices, we have $p_0/p_t = \Pi_{s=0}^{t-1} f'(C_s)$. If the stock of capital is 'too high', $1/p_t$ is 'too small' and the competitive path is inefficient. Cass' (1972a) criterion relates inefficiency with the convergence of the series $1/p_t$. The result can be extended to multisector models with a unique consumption good (Cass 1972b).

Theorem 4. Let $Q_t = f(C_{t-1})$ with f smooth (f of class C^2 such that $f(0) = 0$, $0 \leq f'(\infty) < 1 < f'(0) < \infty$, $\beta < f'' < \alpha < 0$). A feasible path is inefficient if and only if the series $\sum_t 1/p_t$ converges.

The second criterion is geometrical (Bidard 1999c). Efficiency over an infinite horizon normally requires checking either an infinity of conditions or one condition in an infinite dimensional space. The idea here explored is to characterize efficiency as a geometrical property in the finite dimensional commodity space R_+^N. Let us retain a description of the technology at date t by the production set $Y_t = \{(x_t, y_{t+1})\}$ of inputs and outputs (the inputs are counted positively). Taking into account the endowments ω_{t+1} at date $t+1$ and the free disposal hypothesis, the inputs for the production of z_{t+1} must belong to the set

$$\varphi_t(z_{t+1}) = \{x_t; (x_t, z_{t+1} - \omega_{t+1}) \in Y_t\} \subset R_+^N. \tag{8}$$

The isoquant correspondence φ_t is a set-valued mapping from R_+^N into R_+^N. Given a feasible chronicle $d = (d_0, \ldots, d_{t+1})$, the 'advances' at date 0 necessary to generate d belong to

$$W_t = d_0 + \varphi_0(d_1 + \varphi_1(d_1 + \varphi_2(\ldots + \varphi_t(d_{t+1})))). \tag{9}$$

Theorem 5. The feasible chronicle d is maximal if and only if ω_0 is a minimal element of $W = \cap_{t=0}^{\infty} W_t$ for the partial order $\leq$ in R_+^N.

Assume that the exogenous endowments are available at date $t = 0$ only ($0 = \omega_1 = \omega_2 = \ldots$) and that all processes are of the single-production type. A technique is then represented by a square matrix of inputs A_t with activity levels y_{t+1} (the index $t + 1$ attached to the activity levels of period t reminds us that y_{t+1} is the output at date $t + 1$). Then the correspondence φ_t is simply written $\varphi_t(y_{t+1}) = \{y_t; y_t \geq y_{t+1} A_t\}$ for some $A_t \in Y_t$ and Theorem 5 becomes:

Theorem 6. Consider a single-product system with constant returns and endowments at date 1 only. The feasible chronicle d is maximal if and only if ω_0 is a minimal element of the set W:

$$W = \left\{ \sum_{t=0}^{\infty} d_t A_{t-1} \ldots A_1 A_0;\ A_i \text{ available technique in period } i \right\}. \qquad (10)$$

The next step transfers the characterization in terms of prices. An additional 'primitivity' hypothesis (P) is introduced:

Theorem 7. Let there be a single-product system with constant returns and endowments ω at date 0 only, and let condition (P) be satisfied: there exists an integer T such that any good dated t enters indirectly as an input into the production of any good dated $t + T$. For any maximal chronicle, there exists a sequence $(p_0, \ldots, p_t, \ldots)$ of semi-positive competitive price vectors sustaining the chronicle and such that $\omega p_0 = \sum_{t=0}^{\infty} d_t p_t$. Conversely, a feasible chronicle which is sustained by positive price vectors and satisfies this equality is maximal.

The last characterization returns to Malinvaud's (1953) seminal study. Malinvaud strengthens the concept of competitive prices. The idea is that the stock of capital goods invested at date t must be large enough to sustain the tail $(d_{t+1}, d_{t+2}, \ldots)$ of the chronicle, but not too large in order to avoid inefficiency (Definition 2). Definition 3 guarantees that the produced inputs are productive and, therefore, positively priced. In this definition, 'technically possible' means that we refer only to the production set, irrespectively of the available inputs.

Definition 2. Given a feasible chronicle of net products $d = (d_0, \ldots, d_t, \ldots)$, Malinvaud prices are competitive prices sustaining d and which moreover satisfy the terminal cost-minimization condition (M): for any t, the total value of the inputs x_t at date t is minimal among all inputs x_t' which make the production of $(d_{t+1}, d_{t+2}, \ldots)$ feasible after date t. (For

(M) to be satisfied, a sufficient condition is the transversality condition $\lim_{t\infty} x_t p_t = 0$.)

Definition 3. Let the commodities be partitioned into non-produced inputs (which appear only in the endowments, such as labour) and produced commodities. The technology is non-tight if, in any period, it would be technically possible to increase (strictly) the output vector and reduce (strictly) the non-produced but effectively used inputs, thanks to a more intensive use of the produced inputs.

Theorem 8. Any competitive chronicle associated with positive Malinvaud prices is maximal. Conversely, if the technique is non-tight, any maximal chronicle is obtained as a competitive chronicle associated with semi-positive Malinvaud prices.

Malinvaud's and Cass' results have initiated many researches of the characterization of efficiency (Radner 1967; Majumbar 1974; Benveniste and Gale 1975; Benveniste 1976, etc.).

5.3 Competition and inefficiency

What can be said about competitive chronicles over an infinite horizon when condition (M) is not satisfied? How can the competitive chronicles be characterized within the family of feasible chronicles? Theorem 9 (Bidard 1999c) states that the competitive chronicles have no specific property at all: we mean that any feasible chronicle of net products is sustained by *some* profit-maximizing sequence of inputs and outputs. The flexibility hypothesis introduced in Definition 4 assumes that the accumulated capital can be used efficiently in the future, therefore the inefficiency of a chronicle cannot be detected in a finite time.

Definition 4. The economy is *flexible* if two conditions hold:

(*i*) The technology is non-tight;

(*ii*) For any feasible chronicle d of net products and any t, there exists a maximal chronicle $d' = (d_0, \ldots, d_t, d'_{t+1}, \ldots)$ with the same first t terms.

Theorem 9. In a flexible economy with infinite horizon, any feasible chronicle of net products can be generated competitively.

To sum up, the notion of efficiency refers to the chronicle of net products, independently of the way it has been obtained. The statement 'the net product results from competition' has a rich economic content in finite horizon. In an infinite horizon, it gives information on the internal mechanics (equality of the rates of substitution and transformation) but its value in terms of net product drops to zero.

6 The programme

Our objective is to compare the theory of general equilibrium and that of prices of production. The initial step consists in examining each theory separately. Once both structures have been analysed, the conditions for a comparative study come to light. It is only in an intertemporal framework that a common thread in the constructs is found. Intertemporal economies describe the production of commodities dated $t + 1$ by means of commodities dated t. The inputs themselves can either be taken from the endowments or produced. It is clear that if huge stocks of oil are known to be available in the year 2010, neither before nor after, the price of energy and the whole price system will change considerably over time. Regular prices require regularities in the intertemporal distribution of the endowments and the agents' behaviour. Three simple cases are propitious for the elucidation of the relationships between general equilibrium prices and prices of production:

- A non-produced resource is available at every date in a fixed quantity (land).
- The endowments are available at the initial date only and permit us to start the production process. After this date, all inputs must have been produced.
- An intermediate case occurs when a resource is available for greater or fewer periods, according to demand. This is the case for exhaustible resources.

7 Walras' theory of capitalization

7.1 Formalization

The *Eléments d'Economie Politique Pure* studies the theory of exchange (sections II and III), production (section IV), then accumulation and credit (section V). In section V the agents save and buy a bond which ensures future incomes. The real counterpart of the bond is an investment in capital goods. A simplified version of the model distinguishes c pure consumption goods (C), k capital goods (K) which can be produced and live indefinitely, and f non-reproducible factors like labour or land. The technology is represented by

$$\begin{array}{c} \\ (C) \\ (K) \end{array} \begin{array}{c} \begin{array}{ccc} (C) & (K) & (F) \end{array} \\ \begin{pmatrix} 0 & A_1 & L_1 \\ 0 & A_2 & L_2 \end{pmatrix} \end{array} \rightarrow \begin{array}{c} \begin{array}{cc} (C) & (K) \end{array} \\ \begin{pmatrix} I & 0 \\ 0 & I \end{pmatrix} \end{array}.$$

Let (y_1, y_2) be the activity levels. The stocks $\bar{k}$ and $\bar{f}$ of capital goods and factors being given at the beginning of the period, the feasibility constraints are written

$$y_1 A_1 + y_2 A_2 \leq \bar{k} \quad [v] \tag{11}$$

$$y_1 L_1 + y_2 L_2 \leq \bar{f} \quad [w] \tag{12}$$

Let $v \in R_+^k$ be the price vector for the *use* of capital goods during one period (prices of the services of capital goods) and $w \in R_+^f$ the price vector of factors. Total income amounts to $R = \bar{k}v + \bar{f}w$. Its distribution between consumption and savings depends on the prices π of the consumption goods and that of the 'saving-good' S: the owner of one unit of S anticipates a perpetual income equal to one monetary unit. At the rate of interest i, the price of S is $\sum_{t=1}^{\infty}(1+i)^{-t} = i^{-1}$. The saving is materialized into one or the other of the produced capital goods: saving is not a demand for a specific capital good, as the agents are indifferent to the physical investment and interested only in its value. With investment goods assumed to be resistant to wear, the relationship between the purchase price p_j of a unit of capital good j and its rent v_j per period is $v_j = ip_j$. The relationships

$$\pi \leq A_1 v + L_1 w \qquad [y_1] \tag{13}$$

$$p = i^{-1} v \leq A_2 v + L_2 w \quad [y_2] \tag{14}$$

express the no-profit condition for the production of commodities. Let $x = x(\pi, p, R) \in R_+^c$ be the demand function for consumption goods and $s = s(\pi, p, R)$ the amount of savings. The inequalities with complementarity relationships

$$x \leq y_1 \qquad [\pi] \tag{15}$$

and $s \leq y_2\, p$, or

$$si \leq y_2 v \quad [i^{-1}] \tag{16}$$

mean that the demands for the consumption goods and the saving good are met. The budget constraint implies the identity

$$x(\pi, q, R)\pi + s(\pi, q, R) = R = \bar{k}v + \bar{f}w. \tag{17}$$

The t unknowns of the system (11)–(16) are the dual variables written into brackets. Because of the relationship (17), the function which associates to a t-uple of variables the difference between the two members of inequalities (11)–(16) (now re-written as ≤ 0) satisfies a Walras identity. After an adequate analytical treatment, the GND lemma applies and, therefore, a solution to the system (11)–(16) exists.

7.2 *Discussion*

This formalization of Walras' theory of capitalization is due to Morishima (1960, 1977). (The suggested proof, based on the GND lemma, is simpler.) Eatwell (1987) claims that the result is not economically significant. Eatwell's argument considers the vectors v and $x = A_2v + L_2w$ on both sides of (14). Given two positive vectors v and x, there exists a unique scalar i^{-1} such that the inequality $i^{-1}v \leq x$ holds with equality for at least one component and, flukes apart, the equality holds for a unique component. Therefore, the vector y_2 of complementary variables in (14) has normally one positive component. In economic terms, there is an investment in a *unique* capital good. Eatwell relates this property to the neo-Ricardian critique of capital theory and concludes:

> Walras' analysis of capital formation and credit, far from being the triumphant confirmation of his theory of pure economics, is a failure which brings his whole system into question. He is unable to overcome the contradiction between saving in general as a homogeneous fluid magnitude and the heterogeneity of capital goods. This contradiction could be overcome by expressing the endowment of capital goods as a single magnitude – their value. But the value of the endowment cannot be part of the data of the problem without engendering circular reasoning. Walras, in avoiding this circularity, constructed a system in which whilst the method of specifying the data is logically sound, the equations are inconsistent. (Eatwell 1987, 872)

The argument would be correct if vectors v and x were exogenous data: then all ratios x_j/v_j are normally different. It is of no value when v and x are *endogenous* variables: Eatwell's analysis is not a triumphant confirmation of his views.

The consistency of Walras' construction can be criticized from a different point of view. Since the rate of interest is an endogenous variable which depends, *inter alia*, upon the present amount of capital goods, its level changes between two consecutive periods, contrary to an implicit assumption of the calculations (see the estimate of the present value of a permanent income). New capital goods are added to the stock at the end of the period and a new system of inequations holds for the next period. Moreover, prices at date $t + 1$ are overdetermined, according as date $t + 1$ is considered as the end of period t (first system) or the beginning of period $t + 1$ (second system). The conclusion is that Walras' theory of capitalization cannot be read in terms of intertemporal equilibrium. But it can be re-interpreted as a 'temporary equilibrium' (Hicks 1939; Grandmont 1982): spot markets are open, but the only forward market is that of the saving good for the next period. Then the agents save, i.e. buy the saving good according to their price expectations. In Walras' equations, the agents do not incorporate price changes in their profitability calculations: a rationalization of the hypothesis is that they have static expectations (d'Autume 1982). At the temporary equilibrium all markets clear but the agents' expectations for the next period will not be realized. The economy follows a path of mistakes, jolting between windfall profits and disappointments, and may even collapse. The formalization requires too much from the price system: with arbitrary endowments, the prices should balance supply and demand on all markets and ensure the equiprofitability of all activities. In spite of this failure, it is noteworthy that Walras was deeply interested in the question of long-term prices and intended to show that, when capital is accumulated, there exists a tendency towards uniform profitability in all industries. This 'classical' part of his message (Duménil and Lévy, 1991) has often been forgotten by his successors, but finds its way in the modern developments of the turnpike theory.

21 The marginal equalities

1 The dispute over marginal equalities

Marginal equalities are a mathematical expression of the agents' optimization behaviour. Since the same maximization hypothesis is adhered to by all the competition theorists, it is curious that discord concerning their validity lingers. This is because these equalities are put into relation with the theory of capital. The concept of the marginal production of capital creates a problem since, aside from the corn model, capital is a set of disparate goods. Measuring capital presupposes a prior homogenization by means of the price vector, so that capital becomes a value. The marginal productivity of capital is then a ratio between the variation of the product and the initial variation of capital, both measured in value terms. The question is whether, in accordance with Clark's (1899) views, the ratio is equal to the rate of interest, as this is usually taken up by economic calculation when capital is an argument in an aggregate production function $Q = F(K, L)$. Such a production function can be built for a corn model and the rate of interest is indeed equal to the marginal productivity of capital. In the more complex frame considered in Åkerman's problem, Wicksell concluded, on the contrary, that a difference exists between marginal productivity and the rate of interest and showed that the phenomenon is due to variations in relative prices. The impossibility of constructing an aggregate production function manifests itself through other paradoxes, the most famous of these being the one pertaining to the reswitching of techniques.

Contrary to Clark's assertions and Böhm-Bawerk's attempts, the concept of the 'real quantity of capital' is theoretically unfounded. The post-Sraffian theorists have fed this debate and furnished a varied set of paradoxes (Harcourt 1972; Kurz 1987). The question first crystallized on the reswitching phenomenon (Symposium of the *Quarterly Journal of Economics*, 1966) which was originally denied by neoclassicals (Levhari 1965). These insights are valuable and must be recalled. But the debates about marginal equalities and capital theory have an ideological emphasis which, on the whole, has been detrimental to the post-Sraffian stream of thought. A typical unfortunate argument is: 'A comparison between the Euler identity $Q = F(K, L) = F'_K K + F'_L L$ and the accounting equality $Q = rK + wL$ shows the logical equivalence between the two relations $F'_K = r$ and $F'_L = w$. Since the theory of capital proves that the first equality is wrong, the real wage is not equal to the marginal productivity of labour.' We stress, on the contrary, that under a differentiability hypothesis, the Sraffa-type models imply the equality between the wage and the marginal productivity of labour. Though we do not claim that this is Sraffa's own position, we consider that it would be inconsistent to study the model and not to mention one of its necessary consequences (Bellino 1993 is an exception).

Sections 2–6 are devoted to the discussion of marginalist laws within a Sraffian framework, even if this requires the consideration of infinitely many methods. It becomes possible to examine the validity of such statements as:

- The marginal rate of substitution between inputs is equal to the ratio of their prices.
- The real wage is equal to (*not*: is determined by) the marginal productivity of labour.
- Is there a trade-off between the wage and the demand for labour?

These questions are examined in sections 2 and 3, before the debates on capital theory. This choice avoids letting the confusions about capital theory spoil the whole field of marginal equalities. In sections 4, 5 and 6 we examine the more complex notion of 'marginal productivity of capital', then wonder if it is equal to the rate of interest. Section 7 proposes a toast to the profession. The rejection of some superficial critiques is also a contribution to the post-Sraffian theory in its endeavour to build a solid alternative, inasmuch as it is an invitation not to make vain efforts in applying them in a wrong direction.

2 The marginal productivity of labour

Let there be constant returns. In a multisector economy with choice of technique, let (A, l) be the operated technique at the rate of profit r, $(A + \Delta A, l + \Delta l)$ at the rate of profit r', with (p, w) and (p', w') as associated prices. At rate r, (1) defines the prices of production, whereas (2) means that the alternative technique is more costly. Inequality (3) is obtained by subtraction:

$$(1 + r)Ap + wl = p \tag{1}$$

$$(1 + r)(A + \Delta A)p + w(l + \Delta l) \geq p. \tag{2}$$

$$(1 + r)(\Delta A)p + w\Delta l \geq 0. \tag{3}$$

Conversely, let $r' = r + \Delta r$ and its associated technique be considered as the reference. A similar calculation leads to

$$(1 + r')(-\Delta A)p' + w'(-\Delta l) \geq 0. \quad (4)$$

These inequalities hold for any finite variation. For infinitesimal changes (dA, dl) associated with a variation $dr = r' - r$ of the rate of profit, the basic equality

$$(1 + r)(dA)p + wdl = 0. \quad (5)$$

follows from (3) and (4). All subsequent calculations are based on a similar principle.

Consider first a reproduction model with two goods X and Y. For simplicity, the technical coefficients in industry Y are fixed. Assume that inputs X and Y can be substituted for each other on an isoquant of X $(\Delta q = \Delta l_x = 0)$. Equality (5) is reduced to $(da_{11})\, p_x + (da_{12})\, p_y = 0$, or $-da_{12}/da_{11} = p_x/p_y$. Therefore, the marginal rate of substitution between inputs is equal to their price ratio. Similarly, the notion of labour productivity assumes that the material inputs are constant $(\Delta a_{1j} = 0)$ while the quantity of labour used in industry X varies. The level q of production varies with the amount of labour. Inequality $w\,\Delta l_1 \geq p_x\,\Delta q$ means that any alternative method is more costly than the present method. For infinitesimal changes, equality $dq/dl_1 = w/p_x$ is obtained.

Theorem 1. Under the differentiability hypothesis, the real wage in a Sraffa-type model is equal to the marginal productivity of labour.

Now it is written down! Some remarks are in order:

- The name 'marginal productivity of labour' suggests that this magnitude is a quality of labour alone. In fact, it depends on labour *and* the technique.
- Theorem 1 has nothing to do with the notion of aggregate capital.
- Theorem 1 expresses that, given the wage, which may well be exogenous and determined by social forces, the entrepreneurs maximize their profits by choosing the optimal quantity of labour. In a somewhat provocative interpretation, it is a Marxist law: the workers are free (they are separated from the means of production) and the entrepreneurs are free (not to employ them).

A consequence of the law is that, *under the differentiability hypothesis*, reswitching is excluded. The reswitching phenomenon is the theoretical possibility that a technique may be used for a low level of the rate of profit (= high level of the real wage), becomes more expensive than another for an intermediate level and, again, is cost-minimizing for a higher level.

This phenomenon does not occur in the corn model and is paradoxical if one admits the neoclassical parable, i.e. the representation of production as a function of a quantity of labour and a quantity of a homogeneous magnitude called capital. The reswitching phenomenon, established by Champernowne (1953–4), Robinson (1953–4) and Sraffa (1960), has been at the centre of the Cambridge debates, because it clearly undermines the logical foundations of the neoclassical aggregate production function. It may occur in the presence of finitely many methods or a continuum of methods. Why not under the differentiability hypothesis (note that differentiability requires a high enough dimension of the space of methods, in order to allow a marginal change of one input without changing the other inputs)? A simple economic argument is: given a technique within the family of available techniques, the marginal productivity of labour is well defined by local comparisons. So is the associated wage, according to Theorem 1. The use of the same technique at two levels of the rate of profit would imply that the wage would be the same, which contradicts the w–r trade-off. The originality of the reasoning is to combine a 'marginalist' and a 'classical' law: it is a 'WS' argument (W for Walras or Wicksell, S for Sraffa).

3 The demand for labour curve

Given the wage, the equality between the real wage and the marginal productivity of labour can be read as a demand for labour (we mean a quantity of labour per unit of product). When the wage varies, a curve is obtained. Is it decreasing? An apparent argument in favour of the property relies on the convexity of the isoquant. Next, we study the long-run demand for labour curve at the industry level and at the global level, in a fully adjusted economy.

3.1 Full-price adjustments

Assume that any two methods can work side by side and be combined at any activity levels, without external effect. Then the production function $q = F(a_{11}, a_{12}, l_1)$ is homogeneous and concave. The standard reasoning concerning the shape of the demand for labour curve is: since wage and labour are linked by the marginal equality $w = \partial F/\partial l_1$, the concavity property implies that $\partial w/\partial l_1 = \partial^2 F/\partial l_1^2$ is negative. Therefore, the demand for labour curve is decreasing.

The above argument assumes an autonomous variation of the wage: it describes the short-term effect of a wage shock. In the long run, a variation of distribution affects all relative prices and the overall perturbation is complex. Let us sketch the complete calculation in a two-good model. For simplicity, the coefficients in industry *Y* are fixed. The level of distribution is identified by the rate of profit *r*. In a long-term equilibrium, the six unknowns are the three technical coefficients (a_{11}, a_{12}, l_1) in industry *X* and the three prices (p_x, p_y, w) which are defined up to a factor λ. The six WS equations are those of the unit isoquant (6), the price of production equations (7) and (8) and the marginal equalities (9) which derive from cost-minimization under constraint (6):

$$F(a_{11}, a_{12}, l_1) = 1 \tag{6}$$

$$p_x = (1 + r)(a_{11} p_x + a_{12} p_y) + wl_1 \tag{7}$$

$$p_y = (1 + r)(a_{21} p_x + a_{22} p_y) + wl_2 \tag{8}$$

$$\lambda \partial F/\partial a_{11} = (1 + r) p_x, \lambda \partial F/\partial a_{12} = (1 + r) p_y,$$

$$\lambda \partial F/\partial l_1 = w. \tag{9}$$

(Theorem 1 applied to the third equality (9) implies $\lambda = p_x$. Note also that the marginal productivity of input *X* in industry *X* is equal to $1 + r$, which is consistent with the intertemporal equilibrium theory.) Solving the system of equations (6)–(9) for a given distribution *r* defines one point (l_1, r) on the demand for labour curve. The slope of the curve is obtained by comparing it with another point; or, closer to the spirit of calculus, one can differentiate the initial equations, obtain a 6×6 linear system in the variables $(da_{11}, da_{12}, dl_1, dp_x, dp_y, dw)$ and, finally, solve it as a function of dr. The slope of the demand for labour curve is then defined by the sign of dl_1/dw or $- dl_1/dr$. These calculations are lengthy. Suffice it to say that a numerical example can be built in which an increase of the real wage modifies the technical coefficients in such a way that the 'fully adjusted' demand for labour increases.

3.2 *Quantity adjustments*

Such complex substitutions between several physical inputs and labour do not occur in a two-good economy in which both industries use labour and only one material input. Then every industry becomes less labour-intensive when the wage increases. Can it be concluded that a higher wage leads to a lesser employment per unit of product? The answer is still negative, but the argument now relies on inter-industrial adjustments: after a change in distribution, a switch in the operated methods requires an adjustment in the activity levels in order to maintain the net product. As a consequence, even if every industry becomes less labour-intensive, the economy on the whole may be more labour-intensive if the adjustment gives more weight to the more labour-intensive industry.

Let there be two industries (called sectors), one pure consumption good A and one pure capital good C:

$$c_c\, C + l_c L \rightarrow 1C \quad \text{(sector } I\text{)} \tag{10}$$

$$c_a\, C + l_a L \rightarrow 1A \quad \text{(sector } II\text{)}. \tag{11}$$

For simplicity, the technical coefficients (c_c, l_c) in sector I are fixed, at least temporarily. Commodity C is used to produce the consumption good A, with substitution between capital and labour in sector II, as described by the smooth isoquant $f(c_a, l_a) = 1$. The net product consists of one unit of the consumption good A. When the wage increases, sector II employs less labour and more capital, because of the substitution effect. But the higher permanent level of capital in sector II requires a higher activity level in sector I, which tends to increase employment in that sector. The global effect on employment superimposes a substitution effect that is detrimental to employment and a level effect that favours it. The calculations are simple: let $c_a(w)$ and $l_a(w)$ be the amount of capital and labour per unit of product in sector II, for the real wage w ($p_a = 1$). The activity levels sustaining the net (or 'integrated') production of one unit of A are $y_I = c_a/(1 - c_c)$ and $y_{II} = 1$, because the capital then produced matches exactly the amount used. The direct and indirect employment per unit of A amounts to

$$l(w) = y_I l_c + y_{II} l_a = \frac{l_c}{1 - c_c} c_a(w) + l_a(w). \tag{12}$$

Expression (12) is a positive combination of a decreasing function $l_a(w)$ and an increasing function $c_a(w)$. One can easily find hypotheses under which the labour curve is increasing, contrary to a usual neoclassical claim.

In summary, two different reasons for the demand for labour curve to be locally increasing have been found: either complex price effects within an industry, or quantity effects at the economy level. This result is not connected with the identification of capital to a homogeneous magnitude and is extraneous to the debates on capital theory *sensu stricto*.

4 The marginal productivity of capital

The question of the marginal productivity of capital is natural, once that of labour has been examined. Since the marginal equalities are linked to the neoclassical theory, we refer to the rate of interest rather than profit. The corn model is our starting point. In the presence of a continuum of methods, the production function is written $Q = F(K, L)$, in which the capital K is a quantity of corn input and Q a quantity of corn output. A direct calculation, parallel to that relative to labour, shows that the rate of interest is equal to the marginal productivity of capital. One may alternatively use the identities $Q = F'_K K + F'_L L$ and $Q = rK + wL$ to deduce the marginal equality relative to capital from that relative to labour (but the reasoning holds for that model only).

In contradistinction with the corn model, the 'capital' in multisector models is a heterogeneous amount of capital goods. To speak of capital in general requires a homogenization procedure. The natural method consists in aggregating the capital goods by means of the price vector: capital is the value of the invested capital goods. The ratio between the increase ΔQ of the value of the net product and that ΔK of capital is a pure number (for a given time period). The question is whether this ratio is equal to the rate of interest or not. We first examine under which circumstances the marginal productivity of capital is indeed equal to the rate of interest. The opposite assertion follows from Wicksell's (1923 [1934]) analysis. Wicksell's deep insights permit us to understand the coexistence of apparently contradictory positions and, therefore, it is in Wicksell's name that we maintain the existence of a procedure ensuring the expected marginal equality.

Let y be the vector of activity levels, which represents also the gross product. When the input matrix is modified by dA after a change in distribution, let us change the activity levels in such a way that the total quantity of labour employed remains constant: $d(yl) = 0$. The marginal productivity of capital can then be estimated. Let (p_0, w_0) be the prices and wage associated with the rate of profit r_0. Taking into account (1) and (5), one obtains

$$\begin{aligned}(1 + r_0)d(yAp_0) &= (1 + r_0)(dy)Ap_0 + (1 + r_0)y(dA)p_0 \\ &= (dy)(p_0 - w_0 l) - w_0 y(dl) \\ &= (dy)p_0 - w_0 d(yl)\end{aligned}$$

hence, since $d(yl) = 0$, $1 + r_0 = d(yp_0)/d(yAp_0)$. As $d(yp_0)$ is the variation of the value of the gross product and $d(yA)p_0$ that of capital, we have, in terms of net product:

Theorem 2. When adequately measured, the marginal productivity of capital is equal to the rate of interest.

5 A numerical example

5.1 A WS calculation

It is a conviction of many post-Sraffian scholars that the debates on capital theory have established that the marginal laws must be abandoned, as shown by Garegnani's (1970) statement: 'No definition of "capital" allows us to say that its marginal productivity is equal to the rate of interest.' The choice of commenting on Garegnani's assertion is dictated by a merit of his paper: the general reasons against the marginalist theory are illustrated by a numerical example that tries to fit the marginalist assumptions. Our numerical example retains the same structure (the differences will be discussed later). Garegnani presumes that the marginal equality relative to wage requires determining an amount of aggregate capital, which is maintained constant for the remaining operations. In his logic, since the marginal productivity of capital is not equal to the rate of interest, the real wage is not equal to the marginal productivity of labour and, therefore, the notion of demand for labour curve has no theoretical ground. The approach below illustrates the exactly opposite strategy. We retain the productive structure defined by the relationships (10)–(11), with choice of method in both sectors. The price equations, with wage paid *post factum* and good A chosen as numéraire, are

$$(1+r)c_c p_c + w l_c = p_c \tag{13}$$

$$(1+r)c_a p_c + w l_a = 1. \tag{14}$$

For a given rate of profit, the real wage $w = w(r)$ amounts to

$$w = [1-(1+r)c_c]/[l_a + (l_c c_a - l_a c_c)(1+r)]. \tag{15}$$

The integrated industry, whose net output consists of one unit of the consumption good, is obtained by operating methods (10) and (11) at the respective activity levels $y_c = c_a/(1-c_c)$ and $y_a = 1$. The integrated system is written

$$yC + lL \rightarrow yC + 1A \quad \text{with } y = c_a/(1-c_c), l = l_a + y l_c. \tag{16}$$

Assume that infinitely many methods are available: the methods producing one unit of the consumption good are parametrized by the input coefficients $(c_a = c_a(u), l_a = l_a(u))$ and those producing one unit of capital good by $(c_c = c_c(v), l_c = l_c(v))$. The numerical data are

$$c_a(u) = 0.5u^{-2}, l_a(u) = 0.5u^2$$

$$c_c(v) = 0.75v^{-1}, l_c(v) = 0.25v^3. \tag{17}$$

Assumption $v > 1$ guarantees the viability of the system. We now proceed to a neo-Ricardian, then a marginalist calculation.

Let us be a faithful neo-Ricardian. For a given rate of profit, the dominant methods $u = u(r)$ and $v = v(r)$ are those which maximize the real wage $w(u, v)$ given by (15). Calculation gives:

$$u(r) = v(r) = 1 + r \tag{18}$$

$$p_a = 1,\ p_c = 1 + r,\ w = (1 + r)^{-2} \tag{19}$$

$$y = c_a/(1 - c_c) = 2/(1 + r)(1 + 4r) \tag{20}$$

$$l = l_a + yl_c = (1 + r)^2(1 + 2r)/(1 + 4r). \tag{21}$$

Let us alternatively be a marginalist. The marginal rate of substitution between labour and capital being the same within both industries, we have $l'_a/c'_a = l'_c/c'_c$, and equality $u = v$ follows. According to data in (17), the production function in sector *I* is written $q_c = 0.75^{-3/4}0.25^{-1/4}c_c^{3/4}l_c^{1/4}$, therefore the marginal productivity of capital is $3^{1/4}c_c^{-1/4}l_c^{1/4} = v$. As the marginal productivity is equal to the interest factor, we obtain $u = v = 1 + r$, as in (18). In the consumption good industry, the production function is $q = 2\ c_a^{0.5}\ l_a^{0.5}$. The real wage, when calculated as the marginal productivity of labour in sector *II*, amounts to $(1 + r)^{-2}$, as in (19), etc. The demand for labour curve $l = l(w)$ is obtained by eliminating the parameter r between the expressions (19) of wage and (21) of labour. The example confirms the validity of the marginalist laws within a neo-Ricardian framework: the 'neo-Ricardian' wage-maximization and the 'neoclassical' equalities are one and the same WS rule.

5.2 *Rule or fog*

Let us now consider the marginal productivity of capital. Marginal productivity, when defined in physical terms as a ratio between an increase in the product and an increase in the capital good, is measured in units of *A* per unit of *C* and, therefore, is not a pure number like r. What is called 'marginal productivity of capital' is a ratio between a small variation in the *value* z of the product and the corresponding variation in the *value* k of capital. There are two diverging ways to measure this magnitude. Their common physical root, based on formulas (18)–(21), is represented in table 21.1.

They differ by the price vector used for estimating the values. When vector $(p_a(r_0), p_c(r_0))$ is used, the choice of the numéraire does not matter. Let us set $p_a(r_0) = 1$, hence $p_c(r_0) = 1 + r_0$ according to (19). The alternative relies on an evaluation by means of vector $(p_a(r) = 1, p_c(r) = 1 + r)$. The respective calculations are summarized in tables 21.2 and 21.3.

Table 21.1 *Real magnitudes*

Rate of interest r	System in use u, v	Integrated net physical product q	Integrated physical capital y	Number of workers l	Real wage w	Net physical product per worker q/l	Physical capital per worker y/l
r	$u = v = 1 + r$	1	$\frac{2}{(1+r)(1+4r)}$	$\frac{(1+r)^2(1+2r)}{1+4r}$	$\frac{1}{(1+r)^2}$	$\frac{1+4r}{(1+r)^2(1+2r)}$	$\frac{2}{(1+r)^3(1+2r)}$

Table 21.2 *Marginal calculation*

Rate of interest r	Price of A p_a	Value of product per worker $z = qp_a/l$	Price of C $p_c(r_0)$	Value of capital per worker $k = yp_c/l$	Marginal productivity of capital dz/dk
r_0	1	$z_0(r) = \frac{1+4r}{(1+r)^2(1+2r)}$	$1 + r_0$	$k_0(r) = \frac{2(1+r_0)}{(1+r)^3(1+2r)}$	
$r_0 + dr$	1	$z_0 + dz$ with	$1 + r_0$	$k_0 + dk$ with	
		$dz = \frac{-2r_0(5+8r_0)dr}{(1+r_0)^3(1+2r_0)^2}$		$dk = \frac{-2(5+8r_0)dr}{(1+r_0)^3(1+2r_0)^2}$	$dz/dk = r_0$

Table 21.3 *The Clark-Garegnani procedure*

Rate of interest r	Price of A p_a	Value of product per worker $z = qpa/l$	Price of C $p_c(r)$	Value of capital per worker $k = yp_c/l$	'Marg. prod. of capital' dz/dk
r_0	1	z_0	$1 + r_0$	$k_0(r) = \frac{2}{(1+r)^2(1+2r)}$	
$r_0 + dr$	1	$z_0 + dz$ with $dz = \frac{-2r_0(5+8r_0)dr}{(1+r_0)^3(1+2r_0)^2}$	$1 + r$	$k_0 + dk$ with $dk = \frac{-4(2+3r_0)dr}{(1+r_0)^3(1+2r_0)^2}$	$dz/dk = \frac{r_0(5+8r_0)dr}{4+6r_0}$

In table 21.2, the equality between the rate of interest and the marginal productivity of capital is obtained: $r_0 = dz/dk$. In table 21.3, the so-called 'marginal productivity of capital' dz/dk differs from r_0.

Intrepid explorers can look at Garegnani's (1970) terrific painting of the 'traditional theory'. But they should be aware that, first, Garegnani is not a faithful Sraffian: in his numerical example, the methods used in both industries depend on one parameter only ($u = v$ by *definition*), therefore the choices of methods are not independent and there is no basis for the wage-maximization property. Nor is he a faithful Walrasian, for the same reason: the differentiability hypothesis presumes a sufficient number of degrees of freedom on the isoquant, not only a 'derivative'; this is why an apparent reswitching is found in his calculations.

Cautious readers are invited to stop at the crossroads for a while. The two calculations of the marginal productivity of capital differ by the price vector retained to evaluate capital: table 21.2 makes use of a unique price vector $p(r_0)$, table 21.3 of two price vectors $p(r_0)$ and $p(r_0 + dr)$. An instant of reflection shows that the second procedure is self-contradictory. When the variations in the values $z(r)$ of the product and $k(r)$ of capital are calculated according to table 21.3, a change of numéraire, say good C instead of A, amounts to multiplying all the values by $\lambda(r) = p_a(r)/p_c(r)$. The 'same' marginal productivity becomes $d(\lambda(r)z(r))/d(\lambda(r)k(r))$ and is *not* equal to the previous value because the price ratio $\lambda(r)$ is not constant. If the so-called 'marginal productivity of capital' depends on the numéraire, it is pointless to enter into a discussion on whether it is equal or not to the rate of interest. The only conclusion that can be drawn from table 21.3 is that the procedure must be rejected.

An apparent objection to the procedure described in table 21.2 is that prices $p(r_0)$, instead of $p(r_0 + dr)$, are used to calculate the value of capital in the state associated with the new rate of profit $r_0 + dr$: calculations are based on 'false prices'. This, however, is not uncommon. The rule is followed by Sraffa himself for the choice of technique: a method is preferred to the present one if it yields extra profits at the *actual* prices, though the prices will change when the new method is operated. More generally, in a competitive economy, the entrepreneurs calculate as price takers, assuming that their microeconomic decisions have no influence on prices. Thanks to their myopia, they behave according to table 21.2, the pains issued from table 21.3 being reserved to theorists.

To sum up, a non-self-contradictory notion of marginal productivity is required before assessing the validity of the marginalist laws. As a result, the procedure described in table 21.3 is unfounded. If, on the contrary, the rules to calculate the marginal magnitudes are respected, the marginal equalities do hold in a Sraffa-type model. In particular, the equality of the marginal productivity of capital and the rate of interest is maintained for multisector models.

6 An Austrian forest

The theoretical statements established in section 5 do not mean that the right protocol is followed in standard calculations. Wicksell's model shows how great the temptation is to adopt an incorrect measure. The model is of the Austrian type. Assume that one unit of labour is required to plant a shrub. Then the forest grows as time passes. At some date t, a quantity $q = g(t)$ of wood is obtained by felling the forest, no labour being required for the operation. The choice of the length of production t is a simple case of the truncation theory. With continuous time, let ρ denote the instantaneous rate of interest. In a steady state, the quantities are expressed in terms of wood and reduced to quantities per head. Wicksell's equations are:

$$q = g(t) \tag{22}$$

$$w = g(t)e^{-\rho t} \tag{23}$$

$$k = g(t)(1 - e^{-\rho t})/\rho \tag{24}$$

$$\rho = g'(t)/g(t). \tag{25}$$

Equation (23) expresses that the real cost per worker is exactly covered by the present value of the product (Walras' no-profit condition). Equation (24) results from (22), (23) and identity $q = \rho k + w$; or, directly, capital per head is equal to the present value of the successive investments (which are reduced to the payment of wages): $k = \int_{-t}^{0} we^{-\rho u} du$. Equation (25) emerges from the no-arbitrage condition between marginal waiting and marginal borrowing: $g(t + dt) - g(t) = \rho g(t)dt$. In a neo-Ricardian spirit that Wicksell did not possess, (25) also flows from the wage-maximization property. Equation (25) determines the length of production $t = t(\rho)$ as a function of the rate of interest. Then the characteristics of production $q = q(\rho)$, $w = w(\rho)$ and $k = k(\rho)$ derive from (22), (23) and (24). If we adopt the Austrian production function $q = g(t) = t^{\gamma}$, the values are

$$\rho = \gamma t^{-1} \tag{26}$$
$$q = \gamma^{\gamma} \rho^{-\gamma} \tag{27}$$
$$w = \gamma^{\gamma} e^{-\gamma} \rho^{-\gamma} \tag{28}$$
$$k = \gamma^{\gamma}(1 - e^{-\gamma})\rho^{-\gamma-1}. \tag{29}$$

Ouch! The apparent marginal productivity of capital differs from the rate of interest:

$$dq/dk = (dq/d\rho) : (dk/d\rho) = \lambda\rho$$
$$\text{with } \lambda = \gamma/(1 - e^{-\gamma})(1 + \gamma) \neq 1. \tag{30}$$

The capital theory makes a distinction between models with one or several commodities. Though wood seems to be the only good involved in Wicksell's forest, the model is intertemporal and the concept of dated good matters. Let us therefore look at Wicksell's forest as a multicommodity economy, the specific price of the wood dated t being $e^{-\rho_0 t}$. Consider a change from ρ_0 to $\rho = \rho_0 + d\rho$. The hidden mistake in the above calculation consists in changing the price of the dated good and adopting value $e^{-\rho t}$. By so doing, the calculation follows the procedure of table 21.3. The reader is invited to check that, when the initial value $e^{-\rho_0 t}$ is maintained after a change in the rate of interest, the result fits with Theorem 2. The exercise shows that the 'right' marginal productivity of capital cannot be deduced from the relationship $q = f(k)$ between the present value of the product and that of capital. The reason advanced in section 5 can be adapted to the intertemporal framework: Let the origin of time be translated from $t = 0$ to $t = -1$; the present values of $q(\rho)$ and $k(\rho)$ are both multiplied by $\lambda(\rho) = e^{-\rho}$, so that the ratio $dq/dk = (dq : d\rho)/(dk : d\rho)$ is changed. If the magnitudes retained to define marginal productivity are sensitive to the choice of the numéraire or the origin of time, it is the concept itself that has to be fixed. Otherwise, the fuss about marginal equalities is a dispute over the colour of a logarithm.

7 Capital theory

An investor is indifferent to the nature of the capital goods that are the physical support of his investment. Only their value matters. The capital theory wonders if a homogenization of the capital goods (in terms of value or by any alternative means) can be a strong base for economic theory. This will be the case if a 'macroeconomic' production function of the type $Q = F(K, L)$ – or $q = f(k)$, after reduction to the magnitudes per worker – can be built (Samuelson 1962). The construction is ambitious: local analyses are sufficient to deal with marginal equalities, but the aim is to integrate them into a global representation. Is the operation possible? The theoretical solution, which is negative (Garegnani 1966), as shown by the reswitching phenomenon, is ignored in most textbooks and papers: the main value of this practical answer is that the irresistible progress of economic science is not hindered by doubts concerning its foundations.

7.1 *Time as capital*

Sections 7.1 and 7.2 discuss the construction and the properties of an aggregate production function $q = f(k)$ for an Austrian (or Wicksell-type) model, considered as the simplest model which is not directly expressed in terms of physical capital. A brief historical record helps to understand the parallels and differences between the two approaches. To speak about 'capital' in general is a tradition as old as capitalism, but the more precise idea to build an aggregate measure of capital can be traced back to marginalist scholars at the end of the nineteenth century. Böhm-Bawerk and the Austrian school argued that some adequately defined 'average period of production' could be considered as a measure of the roundaboutness of production, which itself means that more or less capital is invested. The more time Robinson spends in building tools, the more he invests in production, the more he delays present consumption in favour of a higher future consumption. The optimal delay is determined by the equality of the marginal productivity of waiting and the rate of interest. A low level of the rate of interest leads to the selection of more capitalistic, i.e. more roundabout, methods. Wicksell's model fits with this conception.

Unlike the Austrians, Clark does not identify time and capital and makes use of a production function of the $q = f(k)$ type. The Austrian and the American formalizations both consider capital as a measurable homogeneous magnitude but rely on different mental representations. Our purpose is to show that both constructs can be seen as isomorphic. Their equivalence is established by translating a Wicksell-type model into a Clark-type model, by means of a 'dictionary' φ which associates a quantity k of capital to a period of production t. The properties required are:

(*i*) When $k = \varphi(t)$, the quantities $q = g(t)$ and $q = f(k)$, respectively produced, are identical.
(*ii*) For any rate of interest, the optimal delay of production $\hat{t}(r)$ and the optimal quantity of capital $\hat{k}(r)$ are associated: $\hat{k} = \varphi(\hat{t})$.

Theorem 3. The index of capital $k = \varphi(t)$ and the production function $q = f(k)$ defined by the formulas

$$\forall t \quad k = \varphi(t) = \int_0^t g(u)du \tag{31}$$

$$f = g \circ \varphi^{-1} \tag{32}$$

ensure the equivalence between the Austrian intertemporal model and the corn model, as far as the choice of technique is considered.

Let us apply formulas (31) and (32) to the Austrian model with the production function $g(t) = t^{\gamma}$. Theorem 3 states that this model is equivalent to a Clark-type model where the production function per worker is $f(k) = (\gamma + 1)^{\gamma/(\gamma+1)} k^{\gamma/(\gamma+1)}$ and the correspondence between a lifetime t (Austrian representation) and a capital k (American representation) is given by $k = \varphi(t) = t^{\gamma+1}/(\gamma + 1)$. For a given rate of interest, an observer cannot distinguish between the two models. It seems that the only difference consists in choosing a specific representation of the world and a specific language. Had Austria been the dominant economic power, we economists would publish in the *Zeitschrift für Wirtschaftslehre* and consider the $q = f(k)$ representation as a convoluted variant of the standard Austrian model.

7.2 *A miracle*

With no real difference at all? Imagine that the *effective* production process in both countries is of the Austrian type, with $g(t) = t^{\gamma}$. Consider an observer who has to estimate the value of coefficient γ, knowing that the part of profits in national income is independent of the rate of interest and equal to 1/3. If the observer thinks in terms of an Austrian model (and it does so correctly, as the model is the perfect reflection of reality), he writes down equality $w/\rho k = 2$ and draws from relations (28)–(29) the conclusion that $e^{-\gamma} = 2/3$, hence the exact value $\gamma = 0.4$. His cousin, educated in America, thinks about the same productive system in terms of a neoclassical production function. He therefore estimates a production function of the Cobb–Douglas type $q = \alpha k^{\delta}$. Since the exponent $\delta = \gamma/(1 + \gamma)$ represents the part of profits, his own estimate is $\delta = 1/3$, hence $\hat{\gamma} = 0.5$. The reason for the discrepancy between the two results is that the $q = f(k)$ model behaves in a similar way to the Austrian economy as far as truncation is concerned, but cannot account for all aspects. For distribution, to think about an Austrian-type economy in terms of an American model is then misleading.

The reader is invited to ponder over one fact. When one thinks about the simplest Austrian model in terms of a corn model, the *theoretical* error of fit is, roughly, 20 per cent. The economists work on real economies which are much more complex and, therefore, whose representation in terms of a $q = f(k)$ model is even less satisfactory. However, when the econometricians give estimates of a complex reality in terms of an aggregate model, the *empirical* errors of fit are usually much smaller. Is the result not admirable? We economists work miracles or believe in mirages.

8 Conclusion

The Cambridge debates have produced heat and light. The critique of capital theory undermines the logical bases of any notion of capital conceived as a homogeneous magnitude or an argument of an aggregate production function. Nevertheless, we do not follow the post-Sraffian literature to its radical conclusions:

- The aggregate production function is not required for either the models or the marginal equalities.
- The equality between the marginal productivity of labour and the wage is a logical consequence of the profit-maximization behaviour. It permits us to build a demand for labour curve, which is not necessarily decreasing.
- It is only under an adequate measurement procedure which neutralizes the Wicksell-price effects that the very notion of marginal productivity of capital, where 'capital' is considered as the value of the capital goods, is meaningful. Once this preliminary condition is fulfilled (but that is not usual in intertemporal models) the marginal productivity of capital is indeed equal to the rate of interest.

The rejection of the notion of aggregate production function is compatible with the working of a WS calculus that is both marginalist and Sraffian. Its only difficulty consists in the simultaneous control of the concepts stemming from both constructs.

22 Intertemporal models and prices of production

1 A comparative study

This chapter studies the conditions under which the equilibrium intertemporal prices are compatible with a uniform rate of profit. We start from a simple production scheme within a Walrasian framework, which we enlarge later from one to several periods. There is no general reason why the intertemporal relative prices should be invariable, but this is the case if the economy is stationary or follows a regular growth path. Then the rate of interest in the sense of intertemporal equilibrium can be identified with the rate of profit in the classical sense. We will examine different models of regular growth in the light of this result. However, the uniformity of the rates of profit does not suffice to make prices of production appear unless there are as many operated processes as commodities. A scrutiny of the question leads to a critique of the Lippi model and the squareness postulate.

2 Reproduction in a Walrasian model

2.1 One-period model

The following system (W) is a simplified version of a one-period Walrasian model with constant returns:

$$\begin{aligned} yA &\leq \omega_0 & [p_0] \\ D_1(p_1, \omega p_0) &\leq yB & [p_1] \\ Bp_1 &\leq Ap_0 & [y]. \end{aligned} \qquad (W)$$

The first inequality means that the inputs do not exceed the endowments ω_0. These endowments, which are primary goods dated 0, are transformed into final goods dated 1. Function $D_1(.)$ is the demand for final goods, which depends on their price p_1 and the income ωp_0. The second inequality means that the final demand is met, free disposal being assumed. The third inequality is Walras' no-profit condition. The unknowns are the activity levels y and the prices p_0 and p_1 of inputs and outputs. Model (W) differs from the original Walrasian model in two respects: the treatment of demand is simplified and labour does not appear explicitly. Labour is considered here as a component of the endowments or, in a less Walrasian interpretation, every unit of labour has been replaced by a given wage basket incorporated into the input matrix A. The crucial hypothesis is that the whole income I is spent: $D_1(p_1, I)p_1 \equiv I$. Then the generalized Walras identity holds, in the sense that the equivalent system

$$\begin{aligned} z_0 &= yA - \omega_0 \leq 0 & [p_0] \\ z_1 &= D_1(p_1, \omega_0 p_0) - yB \leq 0 & [p_1] \\ z_2 &= Bp_1 - Ap_0 \leq 0 & [y] \end{aligned}$$

satisfies the identity $z_0 p_0 + z_1 p_1 + y z_2 = 0$. Under standard assumptions, the GND lemma applies and a general equilibrium exists.

The productive system represented by (W) can be described, in Sraffa's words, as 'a one-way avenue that leads from factors of production to consumption goods'. But, first, no concept of aggregate capital is referred to in the formalization; second, the reproduction of commodities can be introduced, provided that the horizon of the economy exceeds one period. The *Eléments d'Economie Politique Pure* proceed by successive deepenings and, far from contrasting two views of production, Walras considered the circular conception as an extension of the 'one-way' approach. Walras' theory of accumulation assumes the production of the capital goods. From an analytical point of view, the transformation requires only changing the meaning of function D_1 in the above model. In a multiperiod framework, D_1 is reinterpreted as total demand at date 1, i.e. the sum of final demand and investment. The crucial assumption becomes that the whole income is spent on either final goods or capital goods. In other words, savings equal investments.

In a two-period model (dates 0, 1 and 2), can the investment at date 1 be arbitrary? Period 0 and period 1 could then be treated separately, but this would lead to the coexistence of two price systems for the capital goods dated 1, depending on whether they are considered as outputs of period 0 or endowments for period 1. In order to eliminate this overdetermination, the invested quantities must be determined endogenously. This preliminary examination shows that the splitting of a T-period model into T one-period models requires a specific sequence of investments. Even when this condition is met, there is no general reason for the relative prices to be independent of time.

2.2 *Invariant relative prices*

In the theory of prices of production, the prices are independent of the date. Examining the conditions under which, in the theory of intertemporal equilibrium, the vector of relative prices has the same property constitutes the key to the relationships between both constructs. According to the logic of intertemporal equilibrium, there are as many differences between the same good at two dates as there are between two goods at the same date. To set the invariance of the relative prices seems as unrealistic as assuming that the exchange ratio between iron and wheat is identical to that between a table and a jacket. However, the argument omits the fact that the conditions of supply and demand of the same good at two dates are rather stable in the course of time.

In order that demand be constant or vary smoothly, one assumes that the final demand basket is proportional to expenses and that the part of wealth spent per period is constant. The supply depends on the endowments and the production function (and prices, but these are endogenous variables). Erratic fluctuations in the endowments or productivity would destroy the constancy of relative prices. Hence the hypothesis, adapted to our aim, that the technology and the endowments are constant or vary regularly. For simplicity, let the production functions be differentiable. On a regular growth path, the input vector increases homothetically, so that the marginal productivities are constant. Therefore the intertemporal relative prices, which are proportional to marginal productivities, are also constant:

$$p_t = (1 + r_t)p_{t+1}. \tag{1}$$

On a regular growth path, the state at date $t + 1$ is the same relative to that at t as the state at t relative to that at $t - 1$. Therefore the proportionality coefficient $1 + r_t$ is independent of the date and denoted $1 + r$. When labour is reintroduced explicitly, the input matrix is split as $A = (A', l)$ and Walras' no-profit condition is written

$$Bp_{t+1} \leq A'p_t + w_t l \quad [y_t]. \tag{2}$$

By setting $p_t = (1 + r)^{-t} p$ and $w_t = (1 + r)^{-t} w$, where p are the constant relative prices, the inequation (2) becomes

$$Bp \leq (1 + r)(A'p + wl) \quad [y]. \tag{3}$$

The price (in)equations (3) are formally similar to price of production (in)equations but have been obtained in an intertemporal equilibrium framework. In the neoclassical formulation, the factor $1 + r$ is a factor of interest (ratio between consecutive prices). In the classical formulation, it is a factor of profit. The concepts of interest and profit rates have many meanings in the economic literature, which must be analysed separately before being compared.

2.3 A general result

A balanced growth path is an infinite path which can be summarized in a one-period model. For given scalars r and g, its characteristics are caught into the generic model (B):

$$\begin{aligned} Bp &\leq (1+r)Ap + wl \qquad [y] \\ yB &\geq (1+g)yA + d(y,p) \qquad [p]. \end{aligned} \tag{B}$$

The unknowns are the activity levels y and the prices p $(w = 1)$. The final demand function $d(.)$ should rather be expressed as a function of incomes (or wealth) and prices. As it is, the interpretation of the model in an intertemporal framework requires that $d(.)$ is homogeneous in the activity levels. The hypotheses retained to establish the existence of a solution are basically those required for all Walrasian models:

- (A_1) The function $d = d(y, p)$ is defined, semi-positive and continuous on the set $\{(y, p); y > 0, p \gg 0\}$; when some components of p are zero, any basket obtained as $\lim d(y_t, p_t)$ for some sequence (y_t, p_t) which tends towards (y, p) is itself a demand basket for (y, p); when all components of p_t tend to zero, $\|d(y_t, p_t)\|$ tends to infinity.
- (A_2) $d(.,.)$ satisfies the identity

$$r\, yAp + yl = g\, yAp + d(y,p)p \tag{4}$$

which is economically interpreted as the equality of savings and investments.

- (A_3) A positive r-net product can be obtained:

$$\exists \bar{y} > 0 \quad \bar{y}(B - (1+r)A) \gg 0. \tag{5}$$

Theorem 1. Under assumptions (A_1)–(A_3), there exists a solution to the system (B).

Two further assumptions are often referred to:

- (A_4) Labour is required for the production of a g-net surplus:

$$\{y > 0, y(B - (1+g)A) \geq 0\} \Rightarrow yl > 0. \tag{6}$$

- (A_5) The rate of growth does not exceed that of profit:

$$-1 < g \leq r. \tag{7}$$

A consequence of (A_4) is that the value produced is positive (since $yBp \geq yl > 0$). A consequence of (A_4) and (A_5) is that the value of final demand is positive (since $d(y, p)p = yBp - (1 + g)\, yAp \geq yBp - (1 + r)\, yAp = yl > 0$). (A_5) also guarantees the efficiency of the balanced growth path. Lippi's Theorem, which assumes that demand is rigid, is a corollary of Theorem 1. The existence theorems relative to land (chapter 17, Theorems 3 and 4) are close to it.

3 The Morishima model

3.1 *Distribution and growth in a corn model*

Let there be two classes, the capitalists and the workers, whose consumption and saving behaviours differ. The capitalists' income is made up of profits. They save and invest a share s_c of profits ($0 \leq s_c \leq 1$). In a first version of the model, the workers receive wages only and spend them all: their propensity to save is zero. In the corn model, which is described by a unique method (a wheat + l labour $\rightarrow$ b wheat), the capitalists' income in terms of wheat amounts to ar, the savings and investment to ars_c, therefore the rate g of accumulation is $g = rs_c$. In the neoclassical tradition, this 'Cambridge formula' is interpreted as a determination of the rate of growth by distribution, with savings commanding investment. Kaldor (1955–6) and the post-Keynesians read it as a determination of distribution by investment: $r = g/s_c$. According to the direction retained for causality, the exogenous variable is r^* or g^*, the other variable being determined by the Cambridge relationship. Here, the rate of growth is considered as the exogenous variable.

If the workers save ($0 \leq s_w \leq s_c \leq 1$), a modification of the Cambridge formula is expected. Let us assume, following Pasinetti (1962), that the workers' savings are paid at a rate equal to the rate of profit. All happens as if the workers had a share θ ($0 < \theta < 1$) of total capital. The capital owned by the capitalists amounts to $(1 - \theta)a$, their income to $r(1 - \theta)a$, their savings to $rs_c(1 - \theta)a$. The capitalists' rate of investment remains therefore equal to rs_c. Since, in a long-run equilibrium, every class invests at the same rhythm, the Cambridge formula

$$r_P = g/s_c \tag{8}$$

still holds (index P is for Pasinetti). The reason is that the workers' savings on their whole income (wages W plus a part θ of total profits Π) compensate exactly the decrease in the capitalists' savings whose part of profits is now reduced by $\theta\Pi$. We thus have $s_w(W + \theta\Pi) = s_c\theta\Pi$, hence the distribution of profits between workers and capitalists: $\theta\Pi = s_w W/(s_c - s_w)$ and $\Pi_c = \Pi - s_w W/(s_c - s_w)$. Samuelson and Modigliani (1966) mention a limit to this reasoning: the capitalists' profits Π_c must be non-negative, which is written $s_w/(s_c - s_w) \leq \Pi/W$. The opposite case occurs when the propensities to save of the two classes are close but the other parameters matter especially if, as we now assume, there are several alternative methods to produce corn. When the potential profits accruing to the capitalists become negative, the pure capitalists disappear from the stage and the workers receive the whole national income ('the anti-Pasinetti regime'). The rate of profit is denoted r_{AP}. We have $W_t = (1+g)W_{t-1} = y_{t-1}(1+g)wl$ and $\Pi_t = y_{t-1} r_{AP}(ap + wl)$. The equality of savings and investment $s_w(W_t + \Pi_t) = y_{t-1}\, g(ap + wl)$ leads to the relationship between the rates of growth and profit which, in this one-class regime, depends on the organic composition of capital $\rho = ap/wl$, an endogenous variable:

$$r_{AP} = g/s_w - (1+g)/(1+\rho). \tag{9}$$

The complete model is made complex by the possibility of two types of equilibrium. But both regimes can be integrated within a unique formalization: the basic remark is that the limit case $\Pi_c = 0$ is a common frontier to the Pasinetti and the anti-Pasinetti regimes and that $r_P = r_{AP}$ in this case. This suggests that the sign of Π_c commands the relative levels of r_P and r_{AP}. The synthetic formula which defines the rate of profit in all cases is written $r = \min(r_P, r_{AP})$. These observations permit us to write down a unique model. The nature of its solution is determined endogenously.

3.2 *A multisector model*

The Morishima model (1964, 1969) is a disaggregated version of the previous corn model. It is a multisector model with joint production and choice of technique. In a version with advanced wages and a non-predetermined regime, it is written:

$$\begin{aligned} & Bp \leq (1+r)(Ap + wl) && [y] \\ & yB \geq (1+g)yA + d(p, w, y, r, g) && [p] \\ & yBp > 0, r > -1, w > 0, y > 0, p > 0 \end{aligned} \tag{M}$$

The function $d(.)$ is the sum of the two types of final demand. The final demand of the class i ($i = c, w$) depends on its income, its propensity to save s_i and the structure $f_i = f_i(p) \in R^n_+$ of its demand per unit of income. For an exogenous rate of growth g^*, the unknowns are the rate of profit r, the prices p, the wage w and the activity levels y. The hypotheses are standard:

- (H_1): strict r-viability $\exists y > 0, \bar{y}[B - (1 + g/s_c)A] \gg 0$.
- (H_2): Indispensability of labour $\{y > 0, y(B - A) \geq 0\} \Rightarrow yl > 0$.
- (H_3): The functions $f_i(p)$ are defined at least for any $p \gg 0$, with values in R^n_+, and their graphs are closed in $R^n_+ \times R^n_+$. They satisfy the identity $f_i(p)p = 1 - s_i$ $(i = c, w)$.

These hypotheses are a variant of the previous assumptions (A). The model improves upon Morishima's original model on two points: on the one hand, Morishima excluded the pure capital goods; on the other, our formalization considers the two regimes and determines the nature of the equilibrium endogenously. The results obtained for the corn model are generalized (Bidard and Hosoda 1987; Bidard and Franke 1987a):

Theorem 2. Under the hypotheses (H) and for a given rate of growth $g = g^*$, there exists a solution $(r, y, p, w = 1)$ to the system (M). According to whether the equilibrium admits two classes or one class of agents, the rate of profit r is defined either by the Cambridge formula (8) or by the anti-Pasinetti formula (9), with $r = \min(r_P, r_{AP})$.

An alternative characterization is that the organic composition of capital is high enough in a Pasinetti regime and low enough in an anti-Pasinetti regime. If the rate of profit r^* is the exogenous variable, the rate of growth being unknown, the conclusions are analogous: there exists a long-run equilibrium whose rate of growth amounts to either $g_P = r^* s_c$ or $g_{AP} = s_w(1 + r^*(1 + \rho))/(1 + \rho - s_w)$, the upper rate being significant: $g = \max(g_P, g_{AP})$. But a surprise occurs if the rate of profit is given and the wage paid *post factum*: an equilibrium may fail to exist.

4 The squareness question

4.1 A critique of Lippi's model

Post-Sraffian literature does not refer to the general model (B), only to its variants: mainly Lippi's model, more rarely Morishima's model. Lippi's model assumes that the final demand vector d is given. Our point is that the classical roots of Lippi's model are questionable because the model relies on a hidden hypothesis about the consumption structures (Bidard 1997b). Its data are the rate of profit r, the rate of accumulation g (say, $g = 0$) and a *given* net output (say, $3X + 1Y$). The endogenous variables (prices, wage and activity levels) determine the incomes. Only global demand is apparent in the model, not a demand function for every class. In order to fill the lacuna, let us adopt an hypothesis retained by the classical economists and assume that the respective compositions of the wage basket and the capitalists' consumption basket differ. For simplicity they are rigid, say, $2X{:}1Y$ for the capitalists' demand and $1X{:}0Y$ for the workers' demand (the amount effectively consumed by each class depends on its income). Then, solving a Lippi-type model leads to a contradiction, which stems from the fact that the real incomes can be determined in two independent ways: (*i*) On the one hand, only a distribution of the net product $3X + 1Y$ as $(2X + 1Y) + (1X + 0Y)$ is compatible with the consumption structures (this decomposition depends on the representative consumption baskets, not on (A, B, l, r)); (*ii*) on the other hand, the solution of the Lippi model defines activity levels, prices and incomes which depend on (A, B, l, r), not on the consumption baskets. The two answers are not consistent with each other and, therefore, the specification of differentiated demand functions leads to an overdetermination. The only possibility to escape overdetermination consists in *assuming* that the representative consumption baskets are identical, i.e. $3X{:}1Y$ for both classes. Then, when the national cake is shared among the agents, each class is more or less pleased with the size of its slice but none complains about its composition.

The conclusion is that Lippi's model relies on the implicit hypothesis that both classes have identical consumption baskets. The classical economists, on the contrary, always consider that the workers and the capitalists have different consumption habits (this is the way non-basics were first introduced, as luxuries consumed only by capitalists). The rigidity of the representative basket in Lippi's model also plays a role in the squareness of its solution. Let us set out this problem in detail, then return to the models.

4.2 *The squareness problem*

Let the rate of profit be given. The precise statement of the squareness problem is: are the number $\overline{m}$ of *operated* processes and the number $\overline{n}$ of *non-overproduced* commodities *generically* equal? Let us briefly comment on the italicized words:

- The question belongs to the theory of choice of technique. With m available processes and n commodities, choice of technique leads to the selection of $\overline{m}$ operated processes such that: (*i*) the technique made up of these $\overline{m}$ processes satisfies the requirements for use; (*ii*) every operated process yields the given rate of profit r.
- If some commodities are overproduced, they are partly disposed of and receive a zero price. We are interested in the number $\overline{n}$ of

non-overproduced commodities. Since free disposal has little to do with the debate on squareness, we assume that the requirements are satisfied exactly. We therefore set $\overline{n} = n$ and ignore the inessential distinction between exactly produced and overproduced commodities.

• Degeneracies and exceptional configurations are not considered here.

What can be said about the relationship between the number, $\overline{m}$, of operated processes and that, n, of commodities and prices? Since a price equation is associated with every operated process, the n prices in terms of wage are solutions to $\overline{m}$ independent equations, therefore the inequality $\overline{m} \leq n$ holds. The squareness problem is to investigate if $\overline{m} = n$. Why is it an important theoretical question? If the system is square ($\overline{m} = n$), the relative prices are the unique solution to the price equations

$$(1+r)Ap + wl = Bp \tag{10}$$

where A and B are the $n \times n$ matrices representing the operated methods. These prices are 'prices of production', because they are deduced from the observation of the productive system. Since, in joint production, the requirements for use matter for the selection of the operated methods, the theoretical scheme for the determination of prices is

$$\left.\begin{array}{l}\text{requirements for use}\\ \text{available processes}\end{array}\right\} \Rightarrow n \text{ operated processes} \Rightarrow n \text{ prices.}$$

On the contrary, if the number of operated processes falls short of that of commodities, the operated system is rectangular ($\overline{m} < n$), the matrices A and B have dimension $\overline{m} \times n$ and the price equations (10) leave $n - \overline{m}$ degrees of freedom on prices. Does this mean that every price vector solution to (10) is acceptable? No. The price vector is well defined but the $n - \overline{m}$ 'missing' relationships stem from the requirements for use. The scheme becomes

$$\left.\begin{array}{l}\text{requirements for use}\\ \text{available processes}\end{array}\right\} \Rightarrow \left\{\begin{array}{l}\text{requirements for use}\\ \overline{m} \text{ operated processes, } \overline{m} < n\end{array}\right\} \Rightarrow n \text{ prices.}$$

The difference is that the requirements now act *directly* on prices, as does demand in a neoclassical world: when a system is rectangular, the knowledge of distribution and the operated methods is not sufficient to determine prices. The point constitutes one of Jevons' (1871 [1965], ch. 5) objections against the classical theory of prices. Let us examine the arguments pro (this section) and con (section 5) the squareness property.

4.3 General argument for squareness

The introductory section to the study of joint production (*PCMC*, § 50) shows Sraffa's awareness of the fact that squareness is necessary to interpret prices as prices of production:

> We shall now suppose two of the commodities to be jointly produced by a single [process]. The conditions would no longer be sufficient to determine the prices. There would be more prices to be ascertained than there are processes, and therefore equations, to determine them. In these circumstances there will be room for a second, parallel process which will produce the two commodities by a different method and, as we shall suppose at first, in different proportions. Such a parallel process will not only be possible – it will be necessary if the number of processes is to be brought to equality with the number of commodities so that the prices may be determined. We shall therefore go a step further and assume that in such cases a second process . . . does in fact exist.

Sraffa does not explain why the number of processes *should* be 'brought to equality with the number of commodities'. Salvadori (1985) argues that 'if the number of processes is allowed to be less than the number of commodities involved, then requirements for use can be satisfied only by a fluke'. Schefold (1989a) notices that a price (or substitution) effect can explain the possible emergence of non-square systems, but he associates the effect with a neoclassical demand resulting from utility maximization. Kurz (1986) mentions an income effect. Finally, Salvadori and Steedman (1988; see also Franke 1986) claim that 'in the general case there is no way to justify the assumption of a number of processes equal to the number of commodities'. The references show that post-Sraffian literature has been late to recognize the existence of rectangular systems and remains silent on the consequences of this theoretical tremour. The ensuing analysis scrutinizes the economic reasons for the emergence of rectangular systems and studies the behaviour of such systems.

5 Rectangular system: why, when, how?

5.1 Substitution and income effects

A substitution effect or an income effect are two independent reasons which let rectangular systems appear. They are examined independently and successively. Consider first one process which produces two pure consumption goods W and M in a fixed proportion, and this is the only method to produce them. There exists a social demand for both products. Once this process is operated, squareness is lost. Rectangularity is compatible with uniformity of the rates of profit: loosely speaking, the relative prices p_W/p_M are first determined in order that the relative demands for the two goods be in the proportion of their supply; then some absolute level of p_W and p_M ensures that the profitability of the unique process which produces W and M is at the normal level. Any change in the tastes of the consumers between W and M leads to a change in relative prices. This argument is well known when W and M are identified as wool and mutton. The phenomenon at stake for adjusting demand and supply is the *price elasticity of demand.* Though these substitution effects can hardly be denied, their association with the idea of a utility-maximization behaviour explains the neo-Ricardian reservations on this topic.

Let us exclude the substitution effects by assuming that the individual demands are insensitive to prices: the demand of each class, capitalists and workers, has a given direction $d_c > 0$, resp. $d_w > 0$. We reject Lippi's implicit hypothesis and follow the classical tradition: the typical consumption baskets $d_c = 2X + 1Y$ and $d_w = 1X$ differ. A simple Morishima model is used to formalize the problem. Let the rate of profit be $r = 1$ and the rate of accumulation $g = 0$: all profits Π are spent on d_c and all wages W on d_w, hence the total demand $d(y, p) = (\Pi/d_c p)d_c + (W/d_w p)d_w$. (Note that the incomes are linear in the activity levels.) For two commodities X and Y, take an arbitrary 2-set of methods such that no other method yields extra profits at its associated prices. Is this candidate a solution to the model? The supply and the demand of each commodity are both linear in the activity levels. However, nothing ensures that the linear system has a positive solution, and this suggests that a square solution may fail to exist.

Alternatively, is it conceivable that method $\{1\}$ operating alone, say

$$1X + 2Y + 1l \rightarrow 4X + 3Y \text{ (activity level } y_1 = 1) \tag{11}$$

with

$$d_c = (2, 1), d_w = (1, 0), g = 0, r = 1, \tag{12}$$

is a solution? With regard to square systems, a degree of freedom is apparently missing, because one cannot play on the relative activity levels in order to adjust the net product to social demand: it seems implausible that the social demand has the same composition as the physical net product $3X + 1Y$. Let us try, however. For the coincidence to happen, and since $3X + 1Y = 1d_c + 1d_w$, capitalists and workers should consume the same amount of their respective consumption baskets: one must have $\Pi/d_c p = W/d_w p$. With $y_1 = 1$, we have $\Pi = p_X + 2p_Y$, $d_c p = 2p_X + p_Y$, $W = w$, $d_w p = p_X$ and the condition is rewritten:

$$(p_X + 2p_Y)/(2p_X + p_Y) = w/p_X. \tag{13}$$

Can (13) be met? In a square system, the answer would be negative because the price vector is already determined. In a one-method system, a degree of freedom exists: it stems from the fact that a *unique* price equation

$$2p_X + 4p_Y + w = 4p_X + 3p_Y \tag{14}$$

is associated with the unique operated method (11) and, therefore, it is possible to play on the relative prices p_X and p_Y in order to modify the distribution between wages and profits. If (13) and (14) are satisfied simultaneously by some positive price vector, method $\{1\}$ alone is a solution. This is indeed the case for $p_X = p_Y = w = 1$. If the other methods are not profitable at these prices, method $\{1\}$ alone is a rectangular solution.

On the whole, Morishima's result guarantees the existence of a solution but remains silent on its nature. The $\overline{m}$ operated methods and the n produced goods are such that $\overline{m} \leq n$, with $\overline{m}$ relations among prices. If $\overline{m} = n$, the solution is square: this is a 'price of production' solution, as the prices are defined by the operated methods and the rate of profit. But a square solution may fail to exist. For a rectangular solution ($\overline{m} < n$), the adjustment is obtained by means of the $\overline{m}$ activity levels plus the $n - \overline{m}$ degrees of freedom on prices. Rectangularity is not a degeneracy and is as probable as squareness (this type of solution becomes more probable when the number of commodities increases). For a rectangular solution, an observer who knows the rate of profit and the operated methods cannot guess the price vector without a direct knowledge of the demand schemes: the prices are not prices of production. What is peculiar in Lippi's model is that the implicit assumption $d_c = d_w$ allows us to know the direction of social demand *ex ante*: flukes apart, at least n methods are required to generate a given direction d in R^n, hence the squareness property. On the contrary, the common feature of the examples studied in this section is that social demand is not predetermined. But the underlying economic causes differ: the wool-and-mutton example relies on a substitution effect (price elasticity of demand) and the existence of one representative consumer. The second example is based on a pure distribution effect, when social demand varies *because* the consumers are different. Both causes interact in general models.

5.2 *Economic behaviour of rectangular systems*

The study of the w–r curve illustrates the striking differences between the economic behaviours of square and non-square systems. We use the data (11)–(12) as a numerical support for a general reasoning. Let the rate of profit vary. If the variation is drastic, the nature of the solution is modified. When r remains close to its initial value $r = 1$, technique $\{1\}$ remains dominant. How does the real wage vary? The answer is unexpected: the real wage is insensitive to the rate of profit! The reason is: when method 1 is used alone, the surplus per worker amounts to $3X + 1Y$. A solution corresponds to a decomposition of the net product into two components, the capitalists' demand (real profits) and the workers' demand (real wages). Since the directions d_c and d_w are different and fixed, the decomposition of the physical surplus is unique. Therefore, the real incomes do not vary when the rate of profit and the prices change. The $w = w(r)$ curve is horizontal, a phenomenon excluded for any square system and surely not a usual law of distribution in Ricardian economics: value and distribution are a veil! The economy is well defined in physical terms (inputs, outputs, consumption and even real profits) but the rate of profit remains undetermined. The difference of behaviour between square and rectangular systems is general: for a given rate of profit, square systems react to small changes by adapting the activity levels, not the prices; rectangular systems respond by changes in the activity levels and prices.

5.3 *Squareness and beyond*

Since the squareness property depends on the rigidity of final demand, one can worry about the degree of generality of the theorems established in part II by means of the Lippi model, when specific structures were given to the input and output matrices (A, B). For instance, do the results of the fixed-capital theory hold if final demand is not rigid? The answer is positive, because fortune and fixed-point theorems favour the brave. But if no assumption is set on (A, B), there exist only two cases when the squareness of the dominant technique is guaranteed *ex ante*. The first one is when the economy moves in a neighbourhood of the von Neumann growth path (chapter 13). A second case occurs when the social final demand is rigid. Otherwise, it may happen that the dominant technique is square but this possibility is only one of the possible outcomes, not more probable than any other configuration. Economic theory must be able to take into account the existence of rectangular systems.

Is there a reason for social demand to be rigid? *Ex post*, once the economic system is on the rails of a regular path, social demand repeats itself identically or proportionally from period to period, so that it might appear as being given. It would, however, be a methodological mistake to confuse exogenous data and endogenous magnitudes. Following Sraffa's – and, more explicitly, Garegnani's – interpretation, a feature often attributed to classical theory is to assume a given social product. But we have noticed that all agents must then have the same consumption structure, an assumption rejected by classical economists. An alternative is to start from the Morishima model. Then the social product is not given and results from a system of equations in which quantities and prices are determined endogenously and simultaneously. The methodological question at stake concerns the very possibility of treating quantities and prices *successively*. In the description of what he calls the 'surplus approach', Garegnani (1987) considers that the real wage, the social product and the technical conditions of production belong to the data of the problem ('it was natural to suppose the product to be known prior to its division among the classes'). The logical objection developed here is that the physical decomposition of the product between workers' demand and capitalists' demand leads to a physical determination of distribution which may be contradictory with the calculation of the price vector. Even if Garegnani admits that the above-mentioned data may not be totally independent (their interactions being studied 'outside the core'), the truth is that we are faced with a system of simultaneous equations with no way to treat them successively. In spite of Garegnani's opinion that 'any simultaneously quantitative treatment would [be] of little or no content', what else can we do when we are faced to the analytical necessity of rejecting the squareness axiom? Should the analysis itself be rejected?

The necessity of defining the status of each magnitude and setting consistent hypotheses is dramatically revealed by the study of pure joint production but exists for single-product systems as well: the social product after accumulation d, the relative composition of the consumption baskets d_w and d_c and one distribution variable cannot be simultaneous data. Though the starting point of the reflection seems rather specialized and technical, the discussion has led us to basic questions concerning the structure of the construction.

6 Conclusion

This chapter has explored the consequences of a basic property of intertemporal models: on a balanced growth path, the intertemporal prices admit a constant rate of interest. In a classical interpretation, the rate of profit is uniform. This parallel sets a number of methodological and analytical problems. Our claim is that no theory of long-term prices can dispense with a reflection on the following points:

(*i*) What are the relationships between intertemporal equilibrium prices and prices of production?

(*ii*) Is the balanced growth hypothesis crucial for the emergence of a uniform rate of profit?

(*iii*) Is the identity between savings and investments assumed?

(*iv*) Is the hypothesis of a given net product a part of the classical approach? If the answer is positive (Lippi's model), can the hypothesis be reconciled with a differentiation of the consumption baskets? Alternatively, if the consumption baskets differ, can the product be exogenously given? What are the exogenous data required for economic analysis and to what extent are they compatible with the characteristics attributed to the classical approach?

(*v*) Can methodological principles hold for single production only? To what extent do they also apply to multiple-product systems? Can the number of operated processes fall short of that of commodities? Are the prices sensitive to demand? Are their economic properties similar to those of prices of production? Can quantities and prices be treated successively?

7 Discussion

The assertion that a pure joint production model should necessarily be square is wrong. In a reply to my comments, Schefold (1985; 1997, chs. 13, 14, 15) misinterprets the argument when he associates it with a utility maximization behaviour that I have never invoked, then shifts the emphasis to a criticism of the neoclassical demand theory. His alternative proposals result in flexible and differentiated final demands which are additional sources for rectangularity. Moreover, the squareness property has no relationship with the free disposal hypothesis, rectangularity has no relationship with either dynamics or imperfect competition or a divergence between market prices and long-term prices. Rectangularity creates no incentive to bring the number of operated processes and produced commodities into equality. A second point is that the behaviour of a square Lippi model when the rate of growth is smaller than the rate of profit differs radically from that of a single-product system. A third point is that the relevance of the Lippi model itself is questionable under the hypotheses retained by the classical economists. But the ultimate objection to Schefold's (1989a, 43) striking formula

> The basic task is humble: to show that the laws of value and distribution derived by Sraffa for single-product systems hold for joint production as well . . . The partisan of Sraffian economics who . . . does not wish to enter the complications may be content and leave joint production at rest.

is that Schefold uses his intellectual authority to flatter human nature, which leads a number of economists to be already at rest.

8 Proofs

The proofs of Theorems 1 and 2 illustrate the strategy defined in chapter 11, section 8.

Proof of Theorem 1. By (A_2), the Walras identity holds

$$\forall y > 0 \quad \forall p \gg 0 \quad y[Bp - (1+r)Ap - l] + [(1+g)yA + d(y,p) - yB]\,p = 0. \tag{15}$$

Let y belong to the unit simplex S in R_+^m and p to the cube $K_t = \{p; \forall i = 1, \ldots, n \quad t^{-1} \leq p_t \leq t\} \subset R_+^n$ for $t > 1$. The application of the generalized GND lemma defines a pair $(y_t{}^* \in S, p_t{}^* \in K_t)$. When t tend to infinity, the assumptions are used to show successively that $\|p_t{}^*\|$ and $\|d(y_t{}^*, p_t{}^*)\|$ are bounded from above and $\|p_t{}^*\| \nrightarrow 0$. A cluster point (y^*, p^*) exists, with $y^* \in S$ and $p^* > 0$, which is a solution to the model (B). ■

Note that, the Walras identity (15) once established, it would have been more natural to apply the usual GND lemma to the function $(y, p) \rightarrow (Bp - (1+r)Ap - l, (1+g)yA + d(y,p) - yB)$, where (y, p) belongs to the unit simplex of R_+^{m+n}. But the solution $y = 0$ would then appear. The proof avoids this degeneracy. The Lippi theorem is, once again, a corollary of Theorem 1 (*Hint*: Assume that d is positive. Theorem 1 applies to the demand function $d(y,p) = \delta(y,p)\,d$ with $\delta(y,p) = [(r-g)yAp + yl]/dp$. If d is semi-positive, use a continuity argument.)

Proof of Theorem 2. Let us first delineate the conditions relative to the type of a solution. Let $w = 1$. Depending on whether the equilibrium is with one or two classes, the equality between savings and investment is written either

$$s_w((1+g)yl + r(yAp + yl)) = g(yAp + yl) \quad \text{with } r = r_{AP} \tag{16}$$

or

$$rs_c(yAp + yl) = g(yAp + yl) \quad \text{with } r = r_P. \tag{17}$$

Up to a positive factor, the difference between the first two members of (17) and (16) is

$$\Pi_c(y, p, r) = r(yAp + yl) - s_w(1+g)yl/(s_c - s_w). \tag{18}$$

Since the function Π_c is monotone in r, its values can be used to compare the solutions r_{AP} of (16) and r_P of (17): we have

$$r_P \leq r_{AP}(y, p) \Leftrightarrow \Pi_c(y, p, r_P) \geq 0 \Leftrightarrow \Pi_c(y, p, r_{AP}(y, p)) \leq 0. \tag{19}$$

A direct calculation shows that Π_c represents the capitalists' potential profits, whose sign determines the type of the equilibrium. Therefore the equivalences (19) imply

$$\text{Pasinetti-type equilibrium} \Leftrightarrow \Pi_c(y, p, r_P) \geq 0 \Leftrightarrow r_p \leq r_{AP}$$
$$\text{Anti-Pasinetti-type equilibrium} \Leftrightarrow \Pi_c(y, p, r_P) \leq 0 \Leftrightarrow r_{AP} \leq r_P$$

and we have $r = min\,(r_P, r_{AP})$ in any case. Let us now examine the existence question. The functions

$$\bar{z}_1(y, p, r) = Bp - (1 + r)(Ap + l)$$
$$\bar{z}_2(y, p, r) = (1 + g)yA + d(y, p, r) - yB$$

satisfy the identity

$$y\bar{z}_1 + \bar{z}_2 p = \begin{cases} (r_P - r)s_c\,(yAp + yl) & \text{if } \Pi_c\,(y, p, r) \geq 0 \\ (r_{AP}\,(y, p) - r)s_w\,(yAp + yl) & \text{if } \Pi_c\,(y, p, r) \leq 0. \end{cases} \tag{20}$$

Let us set $r(y, p) = min(r_P, r_{AP})$, $z_1 = \bar{z}_1(y, p, r(y, p))$ and $z_2 = \bar{z}_2(y, p, r(y, p))$. It follows from (20) that $yz_1(y, p) + z_2(y, p)p = 0$. A Walras identity is found and the remaining of the proof is purely technical. ■

The principle of the proof is unchanged if the rate of profit is given. An equilibrium exists, whether the wage is advanced or paid *post factum*. The exception concerns the case of a given rate of growth and a wage paid *post factum*. Consider for instance a corn model with $0 < s_w < s_c < 1$. In the anti-Pasinetti case we have $g = Gs_w$ and, in the Pasinetti case, $g \geq Gs_w$. No equilibrium exists if $0 < g < Gs_w$. In this counter-example, the non-existence result comes from an excessive rate of savings. Another example (Bidard and Franke 1987a) shows that the problem is more profound.

Morishima's (1964, 1969) initial proof is based on a fixed-point theorem of the Eilenberg–Montgomery (1946) type. Bidard and Hosoda (1987) made use of the GND lemma and extended the result to pure capital goods. Bidard and Franke (1987a) have integrated the endogenous determination of the type of equilibrium.

23 Long-term prices and exhaustible resources

1 A methodological challenge

The main argument of chapter 22 is that marginal productivities and, therefore, relative prices, are constant on a regular growth path. The condition of the nullity of pure profits is then analogous to a price of production equation wherein the rate of profit coincides with the rate of interest common to all goods. This property constitutes an anchoring junction between classical and neoclassical theories. The problem is to determine whether it can be extended beyond the limits in which it was stated initially. It can be approached by starting from post-Sraffian or post-Walrasian theories.

In classical authors' writings, the idea of constant prices is linked to the hypotheses of a constant difficulty of production and a stable demand. In order to adapt the reflection to the framework of classical thought, we privilege the idea of reproduction over that of scarcity as well as long-term over short-term issues. We will first examine the turnpike theory, then the case of single production (section 2). In the favourable cases, the existence of a tendency towards uniformization of long-term rates of profit is established. This classical idea was passed through Walras' work in his capitalization theory before being taken up in modern versions of long-term equilibrium.

Oddly enough, and in contradiction with the confessed ambition of studying reproduction, the few existing post-Sraffian studies dedicated to a general treatment of intertemporal economies are disappointing. In the absence of a deep knowledge of the general equilibrium theory (but the remark does not apply to Schefold, for instance), many post-Sraffian theorists misinterpret the theory and lack the guidelines that could situate their own contribution. The relationships between classical and neoclassical theories and the status of post-Sraffian theory are at stake. The case of intertemporal economy we have privileged is one of exhaustible resources, because it is the simplest in which regular growth is excluded. The topic was initially studied by Hotelling (1931). The corn–guano model constitutes the extension of the corn model to the theory of exhaustible resources (sections 3 and 4). We subsequently examine its generalization to multisector models (section 5). Finally, we review a few alternative post-Sraffian propositions which, by contrast, highlight the specificity of the approach upheld here (section 6).

2 Convergence towards long-term prices

2.1 Turnpike results

On a regular growth path, the intertemporal relative prices are prices of production. But a regular path requires permanent and specific proportions in the stock of capital goods at every date. Consider a square single-product economy with a demand proportional to a vector d. For a given growth rate, the stock of goods required at every date is proportional to $d(I - (1 + g)A)^{-1}$. A contradiction appears between these proportions and the exogenous endowments. A turnpike theorem concerns the long-run behaviour of an economy in which the endowments are not in the 'right' proportions and states that, under adequate hypotheses, the intertemporal competitive path converges towards a regular growth path. Without such results, a uniform rate of profit would occur only by fluke. The turnpike theorems transform a specific feature into a quite general property.

Ramsey (1928) and Solow (1956) proved the convergence towards a regular path. However, they considered capital as an aggregate magnitude and did not deal with the core of the problem, which is the initial wrong composition of the stock of capital goods. In this more specific sense, the aim is to show that capital goods available at a large enough date t, which result partly from the initial endowments and mainly from the saving and investment decisions up to that date, are almost in the right proportions. The first genuine turnpike theorem is owed to Dorfman, Samuelson and Solow (1958). The authors consider an initial endowment of capital goods and study the trajectory which maximizes the product at horizon T, with a required relative composition. As in the von Neumann problem, there is no explicit consumption. The turnpike theory (Radner 1961; McKenzie 1987) is also concerned with final demand. Its standard formulation consists in maximizing the intertemporal utility of a representative consumer. In order to avoid humps in intertemporal demand, the utility function is supposed to be smooth: it is described as a sum of partial utilities at every date, with a coefficient of psychological discount for time. Since a myopic behaviour might hamper the tendency towards a regular path, it is often assumed that the psychological preference for the present is not too high. The recent developments aim at the integration of these results into a general equilibrium framework (Bewley 1982). If the data are smooth, it is expected that the economy will evolve towards a regular growth path in the long run. The movement of the prices towards prices of production is only a tendency and the theoretical prices do not coincide exactly with prices of production.

2.2 *Single production*

Let us assume single production with constant returns and a given real wage, incorporated into the input matrix. The available methods are the same for all periods but the effectively operated methods depend on prices and, normally, vary with the period. With regard to joint production, single-product systems have two simple properties. First, the adaptation of the activity levels to the physical requirements is easy. Second, the no-profit condition

$$\overline{A}p_t = p_{t+1} \tag{1}$$

implies that the present prices for date $t + 1$ are determined by those for date t. By induction, all intertemporal prices are determined by today's prices and, in the absence of choice of technique, we have $p_t = \overline{A}^t p_0$. The initial price vector p_0 is determined endogenously but, under a primitivity hypothesis, its successive transforms by matrix $\overline{A}$ tend towards the Frobenius vector. In the long run, vector p_t is approximately equal to the Frobenius vector $\overline{p}$ of $\overline{A}$, and p_{t+1} to $\overline{p}/(1 + R)$. Equation (1) is then read $(1 + R)A\overline{p} = \overline{p}$, therefore the prices tend towards prices of production (Duménil and Lévy, 1985). In the presence of several methods, the cost-minimizing methods at date t determine the prices at date $t + 1$ and the convergence result can be generalized (see Dana *et al.*, 1989a,1989b, for a more elaborated version).

Theorem 1. Let T_i be the finite set, independent of the period, of the available methods of production for the ith commodity ($i = 1, \ldots, n$). The input vectors a_i are assumed to be positive. The relative prices tend towards the Frobenius vector $\hat{p}$ of the square matrix $\hat{A}$ associated with the maximum rate of profit.

3 The corn–guano model

3.1 *Why?*

Sections 3 and 4 investigate the behaviour of a model with one exhaustible resource, guano, used as a fertilizer in the production of one commodity, corn. Guano is considered here as a non-renewable resource with a zero extraction cost, whose stock is progressively depleted. The existence of a backstop method for the production of corn – that is, an agricultural method which does not use guano – guarantees the survival of the economy after exhaustion. Our objective is to determine the competitive path.

The theory of exhaustible resources is of great interest from a methodological standpoint. The challenge for post-Sraffian theory is whether it can adapt its long-term framework to deal with non-regular paths. In order of analytical complexity, the question of exhaustible resources follows that of single production, joint production and land and, therefore, constitutes the best starting point for further extensions. The royalty paid for an exhaustible resource is in some way similar to rent: a fertilizer upgrades land temporarily, so that a farmer is ready to pay for guano up to the level of the differential rent between the two qualities of land. The price of guano, or royalty, is indeed equal to the differential rent if the stock of guano is exhausted during the period. However, taking into account exhaustible resources introduces a qualitative gap in the analysis: the current price of an exhaustible resource increases at the interest rate in order to compensate its owner for waiting (Hotelling's rule). The intertemporal evolution of prices implies that a time index t is now attached to them. The question at stake is whether the 'classical method of long-period equilibrium' (according to the title of Parrinello's paper (1983) which introduced the topic in post-Sraffian debates) can be adapted to this framework.

Given this methodological aim, two objections are discarded from the very beginning. The first is that exhaustible resources, because of the extreme slowness of their depletion, can be treated on the same footing as land. The second maintains that the competitive solution, which presumes a perfect expectation of events that will happen in a distant future, is so unrealistic as to be of no relevance. These arguments carry weight for applications. The question we are interested in concerns the analytical treatment of the problem on the blackboard. An economist who is disturbed by the labour theory of value and imposes upon himself the intellectual requirement of working with a consistent theory of prices cannot be satisfied with the 'approximation' of royalty by rent. A consistent theory of exhaustible resources is as needed as a consistent theory of prices. The methodological issue explains the choice of the corn–guano model as a starting point. It constitutes an adaptation of the corn model to the case of exhaustible resources. Thanks to the simplicity of the model, the concepts remain transparent and the analytical treatment is straightforward, so much that the methodological issues are brought to the forefront.

3.2 *The model*

Let there be an exhaustible resource, guano, used as a fertilizer in the production of corn. The one-period production relationships are written:

$$a_1 C + l_1 L + 1G \rightarrow 1C \quad \text{(guano method)}$$
$$1G \rightarrow 1G \quad \text{(preservation of guano)}$$
$$a_2 C + l_2 L \rightarrow 1C \quad \text{(backstop method)}$$

Constant returns prevail. At date 0, production starts with the endowments. The input coefficient 1 in the guano method is a choice of the unit of measure for guano. The guano which has not been used up to a certain date is transferred to the next period and progressively depleted. Let T be the last date at which guano is available. From date $T+1$ onwards, the backstop technique is the only feasible method. Up to date T, the choice between the methods is dictated by cost minimization, therefore by the price system. In order to remain close to the post-Sraffian approach, let the intertemporal consumption of corn be given. The challenge is to find a number of economic laws.

The dynamics of royalties and prices are determined by the following considerations:

- At the moment of exhaustion ($t = T$) we expect the backstop method to be used alongside the guano method. Only by fluke would the then remaining supply of guano be sufficient to satisfy the whole demand for corn by means of the guano process: normally the remaining quantity is too low and the backstop process must be operated to fill the gap. This implies that at time T both processes are equally costly and that the royalty is then equal to the differential cost between the two methods. The corresponding equations determine the royalty z_T and either the real wage w_T (if the rate of profit is exogenously given) or the rate of profit r_T (if the real wage is given).
- After exhaustion ($t > T$), the price equation associated with the backstop method determines the missing distribution variable.
- Until exhaustion, the preservation process is effectively used and, therefore, must yield the ruling rate of profit ('Hotelling rule'). Since z_T is already known, the Hotelling rule determines the level z_t of the royalty at any date before exhaustion.
- Before exhaustion, the royalty is smaller than at date T (Hotelling rule, for a positive rate of profit), therefore the guano method is cheaper than the backstop method and is used continuously until the exhaustion of the resource ('guano first'). The evolution of the prices is governed

by the equation associated with the guano method, in which the only remaining unknown is the endogenous distribution variable.

If the rate of profit r is exogenously given (Bidard and Erreygers 2001a), the equations are written (with corn as the numéraire):

$$t = T \qquad (1 + r)(a_1 + w_T l_1 + z_T) = 1 \tag{2}$$

$$t = T \qquad (1 + r)(a_2 + w_T l_2) = 1 \tag{3}$$

$$t > T \qquad (1 + r)(a_2 + w_t l_2) = 1 \tag{4}$$

$$t \leq T \qquad z_t = (1 + r)^{t-T} z_T \tag{5}$$

$$t \leq T \qquad (1 + r)(a_1 + w_t l_1 + z_t) = 1. \tag{6}$$

w_T and z_T are first determined by solving (2) and (3); then the sequence of royalties and wages is obtained from (5) and (6). Alternatively, if the real wage is the exogenous variable, its corn equivalent is integrated into the corn input and the model becomes

$$bC + 1G \rightarrow 1C \tag{7}$$

$$1G \rightarrow 1G \tag{8}$$

$$aC \rightarrow 1C \tag{9}$$

with $0 < b < a < 1$. The following calculation has a strong post-Walrasian flavour. Let today's corn be chosen as the numéraire ($p_0 = 1$). The prices $p = (p_0, \ldots, p_t, \ldots)$ referred to are present prices and $\overline{p}_t$ is the present royalty per unit of guano for date t. As long as guano is not exhausted, the preservation process (8) is operated and the no-profit condition implies $\overline{p}_t = \overline{p}_{t+1}$, i.e. the present price $\overline{p}$ of guano is independent of the date (Hotelling's rule). The price dynamics are such that

$$p_t = bp_{t-1} + \overline{p} \qquad (t \leq T) \tag{10.1}$$

$$bp_T + \overline{p} = ap_T \qquad (t = T) \tag{10.2}$$

$$p_t = ap_{t-1} \qquad (t \geq T). \tag{10.3}$$

The level $\overline{p}$ of the royalty is defined by the condition: the sequence p_t starting from $p_0 = 1$ and obeying the induction formula (10.1) reaches value $\overline{p}/(a - b)$ at $t = T$. Calculation leads to the royalty formula (11). The price of guano once known, the intertemporal prices of corn are easily obtained:

Theorem 2 (Royalty formula). The present value of the royalty per unit of guano is constant through time. For a given wage and an exhaustion date T, it amounts to

$$\overline{p} : p_0 = \underset{(+)(-)(-)}{\overline{p}(a, b, T)} = \frac{b^T}{\dfrac{1}{a-b} - \dfrac{1-b^T}{1-b}}. \tag{11}$$

The present price of corn p_t decreases through time: for $t \leq T$

$$p_t / p_0 = f(T-t)/f(T), \text{ where } f(t) = 1 + \frac{1-a}{a-b} b^{-t}. \tag{12}$$

Let the date T of exhaustion be considered as a parameter. Note first a consequence of the identity between savings and investment. If consumption is high during the first periods, investment is low, so that guano is exhausted slowly: the more the agents consume corn, the slower the guano exhaustion! Next, the differential rent z_T and the endogenous distribution variable at the exhaustion date do not depend on T. Starting from these values, the royalties and the distribution variables at any date are defined in a unique way by backward or forward induction. Therefore, a change which leads to a quicker exhaustion ($T' < T$) does not alter the sequence of prices but only truncates it of its first $T - T'$ terms (translation principle).

In the technology examined up to now, guano and corn are used in fixed proportions. Let us introduce one or several other methods using guano. For a given real wage incorporated into the corn input, each method is characterized by a corn input c and a guano input γ. An investigation of the economic behaviour of the model leads to the following rules:

(*i*) The potential order of use of the methods as time passes goes from the more to the less guano-intensive method (this chronology is also necessary for intertemporal efficiency). For an effective use of all methods, the isoquant must be convex, neither too hollow nor too flat.

(*ii*) The introduction of a more (resp. less) guano-intensive method accelerates (resp. slackens) the resource depletion.

(*iii*) When guano is being exhausted, and flukes apart, the marginal method using guano and the backstop method are operated simultaneously. Two methods using guano do not usually overlap.

(*iv*) Let $\Delta p_t = p_{t+1} - p_t$. The sequence of corn prices satisfies inequalities

$$\Delta p_t < 0, \Delta^2 p_t > 0, \Delta^3 p_t \cdot \Delta p_t \leq [\Delta^2 p_t]^2. \tag{13}$$

(v) Consider the influence of the exhaustion date. The level of the royalty at the exhaustion date results from the equal-cost condition. For $t \leq T$, the forward induction formula

$$p_{t+1} = min\{cp_t + \gamma \overline{p}; (c, \gamma) \text{ available method}\} \quad (14)$$

is rewritten backwards as

$$p_t = max\{c^{-1}(p_{t+1} - \gamma \overline{p})); (c, \gamma) \text{ available method}\}. \quad (15)$$

Therefore, the prices before exhaustion are uniquely defined. So are the cost-minimizing methods. Suppose that, for $T = 40$, the guano-intensive and the guano-extensive methods are successively used for fifteen and twenty-five periods, and let a change in intertemporal consumption reduce T to 30. The translation principle, extended to choice of technique, implies that the same methods are now used for five and twenty-five periods, respectively, with unchanged prices:

Theorem 3 (Translation principle). Consider a change in demand or the initial stocks which leads to a quicker exhaustion. Let the origin of time be translated at the exhaustion date. The new dynamic path (operated methods, intertemporal prices and royalties) is obtained by eliminating the first steps of the previous path.

3.3 *Intertemporal distribution*

With regard to the traditional Ricardian laws of distribution, the important new feature is that the operated processes and a given distribution variable do not completely determine the other distribution variable. An observer who knows the rate of profit cannot guess the real wage: with the same operated method, the wage changes every period. More precisely, the wage decreases progressively and reaches its permanent level at the exhaustion date. A symmetrical phenomenon occurs when the real wage is given and the rate of profit is endogenous. But how is the rate of profit measured? In a pure corn model, it is defined in physical terms as the ratio between the physical net product and investment. After the exhaustion date, the factor of profit amounts to $1 + r = a^{-1}$. Consider the model with only one guano method. Before exhaustion, the guano input is a substitute for more seeds and costs as much as $\overline{p}/p_t$ units of seeds. Production with guano being equivalent to the fictitious method $(b + \overline{p}/p_t)\ C \rightarrow 1C$, the factor of profit during the tth period ($t \leq T$) is $1 + r_t = (b + \overline{p}/p_t)^{-1}$. According to equality $(b + \overline{p}/p_t)^{-1} = p_t/(bp_t + \overline{p}) = p_t/p_{t+1}$, the rate of profit is nothing but the own interest rate of corn. The rate of profit changes with t and, instead of a unique relationship $r = r(w)$, the wage-rate of profit relationship is now written $(r_1 = r_1(w), \ldots, r_t = r_t(w), \ldots)$. This phenomenon lets appear that the standard assumptions previously retained for the study of distribution (constant wage or constant rate of profit) are arbitrary in the presence of exhaustible resources.

4 Rates of profit and numéraires

4.1 *A mixed numéraire*

A change in the numéraire means a change in the standard by which the real profitability of activities is measured. When relative prices vary with time, so does the relative value of two standards. Therefore the profitability depends on the numéraire. The intertemporal path itself is affected through the choice of technique and the conceptual framework itself has to be adapted (Bidard and Erreygers 2001b). Let us replace our previous corn numéraire by a corn-and-labour numéraire made of d units of corn and one unit of labour. The prices and wages then obey equality

$$\forall t \quad dp_t + w_t = 1. \tag{16}$$

We first examine the implications for the simple corn model which is the future of the corn–guano model when guano is exhausted. An important difference with the traditional approach is that the following calculations do not assume (but do not exclude either, at this stage) that the prices 'at the beginning' (i.e. at the exhaustion date T in the full model) coincide with the long-term prices: the initial price p_T is treated as a parameter. From date T onwards, the sequence of prices is determined by its initial value p_T, (16) and the recursive equation

$$p_{t+1} = (1 + r)(a_2 p_t + w_t l_2). \tag{17}$$

After elimination of w_t, the dynamical equation of the corn price is written

$$p_{t+1} = (1 + r)\alpha_2 p_t + (1 + r)l_2 \tag{18}$$

with $\alpha_2 = a_2 - l_2 d$ (α_2 may be positive or negative). The long-term price p^{**} associated with the backstop process is such that

$$p^{**} = (1 + r)\alpha_2 p^{**} + (1 + r)l_2. \tag{19}$$

If $p_T = p^{**}$, the price remains at this level; if not, it converges towards p^{**} provided we have $|\alpha_2| < 1/(1+r)$. We assume that the conditions ensuring the positivity and the convergence of prices and wages are met.

4.2 *The natural path*

The discussion on the dynamics before exhaustion is organized in three steps: the natural path, the guano paths and the actual paths. The date T at which guano is exhausted is considered as exogenous. Let us first assume that the guano process is operated from $t = 0$ to $t = T$. The sequence of prices, wages and royalties follows the rules

$$p_{t+1} = (1+r)(a_1 p_t + w_t l_1 + z_t) \qquad (t = 0, \ldots, T-1) \qquad (20)$$

$$z_t = (1+r)^t z_0 \qquad (t = 1, \ldots, T) \qquad (21)$$

$$dp_t + w_t = 1 \qquad (t = 0, \ldots, T) \qquad (22)$$

$$a_1 p_T + w_T l_1 + z_T = a_2 p_T + w_T l_2. \qquad (23)$$

This dynamical system admits $(3T + 2)$ equations and $(3T + 3)$ unknowns ($T+1$ prices, $T+1$ wages and $T+1$ royalties). The system has one degree of freedom: we can, for instance, take the initial corn price p_0 as given; but we may alternatively choose the initial royalty z_0, or the final price p_T, or the final royalty z_T, etc. But once a value p_θ (or z_θ) is given, the future *and* the past of the price trajectory are uniquely defined: the forward equation (20), when rewritten backwards, defines p_t as a function of p_{t+1}. The backward and the forward points of view are equivalent and the choice between them is only a matter of convenience.

In the present case, the backward approach brings to light the main analytical difficulty. Assume that the price p_T is given arbitrarily; the values w_T and z_T result from the numéraire equation and the equal-cost condition (23). Then, the royalty at date $T-1$ is known and p_{T-1} follows from (20) and the numéraire equation. Step by step, the whole sequence of prices before T is uniquely defined. But since, in the forward equation (20), p_{t+1} is a positive combination of the values at date t, a backward reading of the same equality shows that p_t is a non-positive combination of the values at date $t+1$. Therefore, it is likely that the unique price sequence, reconstituted backwards, leads to negative prices in a finite time, which can be smaller than T.

This remark applies, in particular, when p_T is the long-term price p^{**} of the backstop method, whose value has no relationship with the characteristics of the guano method. Therefore, flukes apart, the hypothesis that the long-term prices prevail at the exhaustion date is inconsistent with a long enough use of guano. This justifies the calculation made in sub-section 4.1, which did not presume that equality. With a mixed numéraire, the corrosive effect of negative coefficients leads us to wonder whether a solution can even be conceived: does there exist at least one adequate choice of the corn price or the royalty at the exhaustion date such that the prices, wages and royalties remain positive for an arbitrarily long path before exhaustion? From (20), (21) and (22), the dynamics of prices are defined by the recursive formula (with $\alpha_1 = a_1 - l_1 d$)

$$p_{t+1} = (1+r)l_1 + (1+r)\alpha_1 p_t + (1+r)^{t-T+1} z_T \tag{24}$$

in which the royalty z_T is chosen as the exogenous parameter. The price p_T results from the numéraire equation and the equal-cost condition:

$$p_T = (\alpha_2 - \alpha_1)^{-1}[z_T - (l_2 - l_1)]. \tag{25}$$

Relationships (24) and (25) define the sequence of prices $p_{T-\tau}$ before date T, as a function of z_T. Let p^* be the 'long-term' price of corn *if* guano were free (unlike p^{**}, p^* is only a potential price):

$$p^* = (1+r)l_1 + (1+r)\alpha_1 p^*. \tag{26}$$

It is assumed that p^* is positive, smaller than p^{**} and

$$|\alpha_1| < 1/(1+r). \tag{27}$$

Theorem 4 gives the explicit value of the prices (24) before exhaustion, as a function of an exogenous royalty at the exhaustion date.

Theorem 4. For a given royalty z_T at the exhaustion date, the prices before exhaustion are

$$p_{T-\tau} = p^* + (1+r)^{-\tau}(1-\alpha_1)^{-1} z_T + [(1+r)\alpha_1]^{-\tau} C \tag{28}$$

in which the constant C is defined by

$$(\alpha_2 - \alpha_1)^{-1}[z_T - (l_2 - l_1)] = p^* + (1-\alpha_1)^{-1} z_T + C. \tag{29}$$

(The value of C defined by (29) ensures consistency between formulas (25) and (28) for $\tau = 0$.) By (27), the coefficient of C in (28) is greater than one in absolute value. In order to avoid an explosive behaviour of prices when τ tends to infinity, we assume that C is equal to zero. Value $C = 0$ defines the 'natural' path that we study first. On this specific path, $\bar{z} = z_T$ has a well-defined level and the value p^* becomes an effective limit price on the natural path . . . after a reverse of time: $p^* = \lim_{\tau\to\infty} p_{T-\tau}$. The characteristics $(\bar{z}, \bar{p}, \bar{w}) = (\bar{z}_T, \bar{p}_T, \bar{w}_T)$ of the natural path at the exhaustion date derive from (29) with $C = 0$. Some noteworthy formulas are:

$$\overline{z} = (1 - \alpha_1)(1 - \alpha_2)^{-1}[1 - (1 + r)\alpha_2](p^{**} - p^*) \quad (30)$$

$$\overline{p} = r(1 + r)^{-1}(1 - \alpha_2)^{-1} p^* + [1 - r(1 + r)^{-1}(1 - \alpha_2)^{-1}] p^{**} \quad (31)$$

$$\overline{p}_t - p^* = (1 + r)^{t-T}(\overline{p} - p^*) \quad (32)$$

$$\overline{e}_{T-\tau} - \overline{e} = -(1 + r)^{-\tau}\overline{e}. \quad (33)$$

In these equalities, the bars refer to magnitudes defined on the natural path. Formula (30) defines the natural royalty at the exhaustion date as a function of $p^{**} - p^*$. Formula (31) defines the natural price at the exhaustion date as a barycentre of p^* and p^{**}. Formula (32) is a second 'Hotelling rule' relative to the evolution of the natural price of corn. In formula (33), $\overline{e}_{T-\tau}$ represents the extra costs that would be implied by the use of the backstop method on the natural path, and $\overline{e}$ is the limit when τ tends to infinity (guano is then free). Formula (33), a third 'Hotelling rule', shows that $\overline{e}_{T-\tau}$ is positive: the hypothesis, implicit in the previous calculations, that the guano method is cost-minimizing on the natural path is now justified.

4.3 *Guano paths and actual paths*

The natural path is only one among many possible paths. We first examine whether it is possible for the guano process to be used continuously between times $t = 0$ and $t = T$ when prices differ from their natural values. This is what we call a guano path. Then we will consider the more general trajectories.

For simplicity, we assume that α_1 is positive. On a non-natural guano path, the coefficient of C in (28) is greater than one to the power τ, therefore the price or the wage become negative for a sufficiently large value of τ. But, for a given T, there exist guano paths such that the price, wage and royalty are positive during T periods: it suffices to take the characteristics close enough to those of the natural path. Then the price, wage and royalty deviate from their natural levels, but have not time enough in T periods to become negative. The deviation between a guano path and the natural path is described by studying $\Delta p_t = p_t - \overline{p}_t$:

Theorem 5. Let $\alpha_1 > 0$. The guano paths converge monotonically towards the natural path up to the exhaustion date T.

Before applying mechanically the formulas relative to the guano paths, two questions have to be answered: (*i*) are the price, wage and royalty positive on a guano path?, and (*ii*) is the guano process cheaper than the backstop process? Normally we would have to check these properties for every date between $t = 0$ and $t = T$, but it suffices to check them at $t = 0$:

Theorem 6. Let $\alpha_1 > 0$. On a guano path, the price and the wage are positive and the guano method is always cheaper than the backstop process if these properties hold at date $t = 0$.

The guano paths assume an uninterrupted use of the guano method before exhaustion. Other types of trajectories exist, which are called the actual paths. We assume the positivity of α_1 and α_2 (if not, the backward dynamics would not be univocal). Theorem 6 asserts that a trajectory which makes use of the guano process at some date uses it until exhaustion. Therefore, besides the guano paths, the actual paths are of the type: backstop method, then guano method until exhaustion, and finally backstop method again (a dynamic 'reswitching' phenomenon in the theory of exhaustible resources). For a given exhaustion date, an actual path is characterized by one parameter. Theorem 7 summarizes some results concerning existence, uniqueness and comparative statics:

Theorem 7. For $\alpha_1 \neq \alpha_2$ ($\alpha_i > 0$), the forward and the backward dynamics are characterized by either the level of p_0, or p_T, or z_T. Until exhaustion, the actual paths are of the type backstop method, then guano method (or, directly, guano method). The number of periods during which the backstop method is initially used is negatively correlated with the level of the royalty. For $\alpha_1 < \alpha_2$ (resp. $\alpha_1 > \alpha_2$), a high price path (resp. low price path) is associated with a high royalty.

5 Multisector models with exhaustible resources

5.1 *The measures of profit*

The properties of multisector economies with infinite horizon hold for models with exhaustible resources. For instance, there exist Malinvaud prices which sustain a maximum chronicle of net products. Since the theory of exhaustible resources is not intrinsically linked to joint production, assume that every process produces one commodity. Starting from an endogenously determined initial price vector, the sequence of prices is uniquely determined by the cost-minimization and the no-profit rules. Before exhaustion, the Hotelling rule holds. After exhaustion, the only significant difference with the single-product economies as they were studied in part I is that the stock of the then available commodities is an endogenous magnitude. The long-term prices tend towards the prices of production associated with the cost-minimizing backstop technique.

Let the real wage be incorporated into the input matrix. As shown by the parallel 'post-Sraffian' and 'post-Walrasian' calculations made in section 3, we do not oppose these approaches and propose to read the characteristics of a competitive Walrasian path according to the classical notions. The translation takes into account the idiosyncracies of both languages. In particular, the adaptation of intertemporal analysis to a classical interpretation must pay attention to two differences: first, the primary tool of post-Walrasian analysis is the notion of present price whereas the classical economists considered current prices (the distinction between 'market' and 'normal' prices is another matter); second, the word 'profit' has different meanings which must not be confused. The Walrasian profits are the entrepreneurs' income after the payment of wages *and* the remuneration of capital, whereas the profits in the classical sense correspond to the remuneration of capital. It has already been noticed that, when the Walrasian prices π_t and π_{t+1} are proportional, the no-profit equality (here, 'no profits' is understood as no pure profits in the neoclassical sense) $A\pi_t = B\pi_{t+1}$ with $\pi_t = (1 + R)\pi_{t+1}$ means that the rate of profit is R (here, 'profit' is understood in the classical sense). In general intertemporal models, the short-term competitive prices do not vary proportionally to themselves and the question of measuring profits in the classical sense arises. Walras' no-profit equation is a 'preservation of value' condition. If prices decrease, the same nominal value represents a greater real value. In any case, the real rate depends on the standard of measure δ. The general formula is

$$\text{real rate of profit } r_t = (B\pi_{t+1}/\delta\pi_{t+1}) : (A\pi_t/\delta\pi_t) - 1. \tag{34}$$

The simplification introduced by the no-profit equality leads to

$$r_t = \delta\pi_t/\delta\pi_{t-1} - 1. \tag{35}$$

Formula (35) shows that the (short-term) real rate of profit is the own rate of interest of the standard basket. There are some degrees of freedom in the choice of the standard of measure, though the choice must be economically sensible. Considering that consumption is the ultimate aim of economic activity, Fisher (1930 [1986]) advocated the choice of the representative consumption basket as standard.

An alternative proposal is found in Torrens' (1821) works: the real profits during period t are zero when, with the proceeds at date $t + 1$, the entrepreneur can buy the same amount of inputs as those invested at date t. More generally, the rate of profit is equal to the potential expansion rate if all proceeds were devoted to a proportional reinvestment in the same industry. Torrens' definition amounts to choose the input basket of industry i as its standard basket: there are as many standards as industries. In order to explore the properties of such a measure, we consider a two-industry economy

$$\begin{array}{l} aX + bY \rightarrow 1X \\ cX + dY \rightarrow 1Y \end{array} \quad \text{with} \quad A = \begin{bmatrix} a & b \\ c & d \end{bmatrix}$$

with prices σ_1 and τ_1 for the outputs X and Y at $t = 1$. We assume $c/a \neq d/b$, otherwise, the standard of measure is unique. The Torrens' factors of profit are $1 + r_X = \sigma_1/(a\sigma_1 + b\tau_1)$ and $1 + r_Y = \tau_1/(c\sigma_1 + d\tau_1)$. These short-term rates are equal if and only if $\pi_1 = (\sigma_1, \tau_1)$ is the Frobenius vector of A, i.e. the prices π_1 are the long-term prices. Therefore, when the short-term rates of profit are measured *à la* Torrens, they are necessarily distinct except if the long-term prices prevail. On the contrary, the choice of a unique standard δ affects the measure of the short-term rate of profit, but not the uniformity property itself.

For a given standard, the choice of the real wage as the independent exogenous variable is a simplification: the difficulties linked to the measure of profits are confined to the interpretation of the results. The choice of the rate of profit as the independent variable sets a problem of measurement from the very beginning: the standard basket matters for the determination of the intertemporal path itself.[1]

5.2 *A generalization*

Let the rate of profit be given. Can the results of section 4 be generalized to a multisector economy? We retain a number of simplifications: a unique exhaustible resource (guano), which can only be used for the production of corn; in the corn industry there is a choice between a guano method and a backstop method. In the other industries there is no choice of method. The numéraire is either corn or a basket of commodities, or a mixed goods-and-labour basket. The dynamics after exhaustion are governed by the equations relative to the economy without guano. Before exhaustion, the evolution of prices and royalties can be written in a compact way as

$$(1 + r)A_1' p_t' + w_t l_t' = p_{t+1}' \tag{36}$$

[1] The non-neutrality of the standard of measure is unexpected in non-monetary models. Let us however notice a similar phenomenon for the monopoly theory in a general equilibrium framework.

where A_1' is the extended matrix obtained from A_1 by introducing one more column (the guano inputs) and one more row (the preservation of guano), and the last component of the extended price vector p_t' is the royalty at date t. At the exhaustion date, the royalty is defined as a differential rent. According to (36), the price vector at t is obtained as the product of a non-positive matrix $(1+r)^{-1}A_1'^{-1}$ by a combination of the labour vector and the price vector at $t+1$. In order that all the prices before exhaustion be positive, the prices at the exhaustion date must be specific and differ from the long-term prices associated with the backstop technique, flukes apart.

The reason why we have introduced a mixed numéraire in the corn–guano model becomes clear: this is a simple trick to anticipate the results of multisector models while retaining the structure of a one-commodity model. It turns out that the hypotheses, notations and results of section 4 can be reinterpreted and extended: a_1 becomes matrix A_1, p_t, l and C are column vectors, d a row vector, the maximum modulus of the eigenvalues of matrices $(1+r)(a_1 - l_1 d)$ and $(1+r)(a_2 - l_2 d)$ is smaller than one, etc. Then all formulas of section 4 remain valid. For instance, the trajectory used as landmark is the natural path corresponding to the choice $C = 0$, (32) shows that the natural prices move in the plane $(\overline{p}, p^*)$, etc.

6 Theoretical appraisals

6.1 *History and analysis in post-Sraffian literature*

Post-Sraffian theory is not unified: Roncaglia (1978) does not interpret Sraffa's equations as long-term price equations, the qualification 'neo-Ricardian' is sometimes attached to economists who are openly non-Marxians, Garegnani's and Pasinetti's positions are notoriously distinct, etc. Therefore, any reference to 'the' post-Sraffian school is necessarily fuzzy. We understand it as reflecting a prevailing opinion among scholars interested in the development of classical ideas, as inspired by Sraffa's interpretation. The search for a majority in the diversity leads us to underline the influence of Garegnani's ideas. His somewhat dogmatic interpretation has favoured a certain fossilization of the post-Sraffian school, even if the primary responsibility falls to the scholars themselves.[2]

The development of economic analysis is an ordeal. Innovators take risks, including that of being wrong, which constitute the best antidote

[2] The scholars interested in a presentation more sympathetic to Garegnani's views must read Petri's mimeo (2000). This work proposes a global interpretation of the nature of Sraffa's critique and constitutes also a noteworthy attempt at communication between Sraffians and neoclassicals.

against scholastic views. We will refer here to Schefold and Kurz and Salvadori (hereafter, K and S), whose works have contributed to the development of post-Sraffian theory and encompass a general vision of the classical approach in both its historical and analytical aspects. We are here concerned by their interpretations of the classical and marginalist theories. As an application, we will examine their treatment of the question of exhaustible resources.

The historical views on the development of economic theories are part of their identification. They matter for the very definition of the classical and neoclassical theories and the conception of their relationships (see also Duménil and Lévy 1987b, 1991, 1993). Most post-Sraffians adopt a periodization marked by a *methodological* rupture which does not coincide with the emergence of marginalist theory itself. According to Garegnani (1976), the change of framework between the old and the new approaches (from 'long-period positions' to 'steady states') occurred with Hicks' (1939) *Value and Capital*; since Hicks has been influenced by Keynes' (1936) *General Theory*, it has become usual to date the switch from the late 1920s or the 1930s. What is the nature of the rupture? Garegnani claims that the long-period method was adopted by the classical *and* the first neoclassical authors (J.B. Clark, Böhm-Bawerk, Marshall, Wicksell), but was then abandoned in favour of short-term views. Expectations, not long-term tendencies, play a major role in Keynes' and Hicks' constructions: the long-run trajectory is conceived as a sequence of short-run, or temporary, equilibria. Garegnani attributes the move to the difficulties met with the notion of capital (this is a most disputable point).

Post-Sraffians reject the American, Austrian, Swedish and British versions of the marginalist theory and its modern versions (Arrow–Debreu) as well. But the periodization adopted by Garegnani is compatible with a large variety of opinions concerning Walras' theory itself, depending on whether the elements of discontinuity with the classical school (endowments, utility, one-way avenue from factors of production to consumption goods) or continuity (long-term views in the fifth section of the *Eléments*) are stressed. Garegnani himself insists on Walras' failure to build a consistent theory of capital formation and tries to connect it with the impossibility of aggregating capital, i.e. he attempts to demonstrate the intimate unity of Walras' theory with the 'Austrian' and 'American' versions. The point has been examined in chapter 20 in the discussion of Eatwell's (1987) contribution (chapter 20, section 7). At the opposite pole, K and S (1995) are so favourable to Walras' analysis that it becomes a question of grasping the reason for this astonishing similarity:

> If there is only one service . . ., if land services are not in short supply . . ., and if 'fixed' capital is actually circulating capital . . ., then the set of [Walrasian] equations is nothing else than the set of [price of production] equations investigated in Chapter 4 of the present book. Moreover, in Chapters 7 and 9 fixed capital will be introduced in a set of equations which are analogous to [the Walrasian] equations. (Kurz and Salvadori 1995, 25–6)

K and S respond (1995, 25) that 'It is beyond the scope of this book to discuss in details the merits and demerits of Walras's general equilibrium analysis' but some hints are found in chapter 14. There, K and S make a number of negative comments on the *modern* general equilibrium theory (Arrow–Debreu) and conclude that

> The modern versions of the demand and supply approach are beset with several methodological and conceptual difficulties which raise serious doubt about their usefulness. (1995, 467)

In which sense are Walras' theory and the Arrow–Debreu analysis so different as to justify this historical and conceptual partition? K and S sustain their views by a bold reinterpretation of the tâtonnement process:

> A total break with the traditional method of analysis and its concern with long-period positions of the economic system characterized by a uniform rate of interest (profit) was finally effectuated in the so-called Arrow–Debreu model . . . In the Arrow–Debreu analysis, as opposed to that presented by Walras with its long-period orientation, general equilibrium cannot be thought of as a 'center of gravitation'. (1995, 460–1, 463–4)

> Walras calls . . . tâtonnement [a process according to which] the system is said to converge or gravitate toward an equilibrium characterized by a uniform rate of net income. (1995, 441; also 483)

Their report on the modern theory ignores Malinvaud's contribution (1953) and the turnpike theory (is it a coincidence that one of the inventors of the Arrow–Debreu–McKenzie model is a specialist of the turnpike theory?). Hence the claim 'The study of intertemporal models with an infinite time horizon was begun by Bewley in 1972' (1995, 462).

On the contrary, Schefold's interpretation, which also retains Garegnani's thesis of the methodological rupture, introduces no significant distinction between Walras and the modern general equilibrium theory. Schefold (1997) studies the turnpike theory, arguing that the construction meets difficulties with the concept of capital: 'The long-term equilibrium can be demonstrated to exist only if the paradoxes of capital theory can be excluded' (1997, 426; analytical details in Schefold 2000, 363–91).

Schefold's main point is that the classical notion of long-period equilibrium and the neoclassical notion of intertemporal equilibria with own rates of interest converging eventually must not be identified:

> It should be recalled that Ricardo does not seem to have thought of uniform rates of growth. (1997, 454)

> Sraffa's book is in part a reaction to the emergence of intertemporal equilibrium. (1997, 441)

> In neoclassical textbooks, long-period equilibria are discussed as stationary equilibria or equilibria of balanced growth . . . . The interest in the classical theory of the long period derives in part from the hypothesis that a uniform rate of profit is compatible with different rates of growth in different industries. (1997, 441)

No room is even left for gravitation models: 'The peculiar status of the assumption of the uniform rate of profit [is to be] an axiom' (1997, 450–1).

Compare with K and S's position on the emergence of constant prices:

> It has been indicated repeatedly, though, commencing with Chapter 1, that in order to exhibit this property [prices do not change through time, C. B.] an economic system has to fulfil certain requirements. For instance . . . in the presence of nonconstant returns to scale the system must be stationary. Otherwise, relative prices would have to change. (1995, 339)

It is noteworthy that, in their comparisons between the classical and neoclassical theories, neither K and S nor Schefold discuss the marginal equalities. Their common convictions as well as their divergent views are reflected in their respective studies on exhaustible resources.

6.2 *A conceptual mismatch*

In order to study intertemporal problems, K and S (1995, chapter 12) write down equation

$$(1+r)Ap_t + w_{t+1}l = p_{t+1}. \tag{37}$$

Since the comments on the economic meaning of the equation are the same as in previous chapters, the reader is inclined to think that the concept of rate of profit is not affected by the fact that the prices are time-dependent. For simplicity, let the real wage be given and incorporated into the input matrix. Equation (37) becomes

$$(1+r)\overline{A}p_t = p_{t+1}. \tag{38}$$

We refer to r as the 'KS rate'. Notice that:

- A variation of the KS rate has no influence on the relative prices at a given date.
- The KS rate and the real wage are independent variables.
- Equation (38) defines a positive sequence of price vectors, whatever the level of the KS rate is: the KS rate has no upper bound.

These unexpected properties have led K and S to an unobtrusive but significant change of their position: they now reinterpret the KS rate as a 'nominal' rate of profit (K and S 1997, 2000, 2001) and claim that, long-period positions apart, the concept of real rate of profit is 'merely a name' and 'see no reason to employ it'. A simple reconstruction of K and S' formalization sheds light on its nature. Our starting point is Walras' no-profit condition (as time is explicitly taken into account, it is in fact Arrow's and Debreu's rewriting of Walras' condition)

$$A\pi_t + \omega_t l = \pi_{t+1} \tag{39}$$

or

$$\overline{A}\pi_t = \pi_{t+1}. \tag{40}$$

It is immediately seen that (37) and (38) can be formally derived from (39) and (40) by the transform

$$p_t = \pi_t(1+r)^t \qquad w_t = \omega_t(1+r)^{t+1} \tag{41}$$

for an arbitrary scalar r. (A crucial difference with the operation performed in section 5 is the lack of a standard of value.) The failure of the transform to recover classical prices is apparent when the KS rate in (37)–(38) is zero. Then the Walrasian equations (39)–(40) and the KS equations (37)–(38) coincide formally. But equations (39)–(40) mean that the pure profits in the neoclassical sense (*after* remuneration of capital) are zero, not that the profits in the classical sense (*before* remuneration of capital) are zero. By extension, the general KS equations (37)–(38) cannot mean that the rate of profit in the classical sense is equal to r. This conceptual mismatch introduces a bias in K and S' constructs and appraisals. Two examples are:

- The similarity observed between Walras' equations and a set of prices of production is misplaced: in Walras' theory, the prices of inputs and outputs are identical because production is instantaneous, a weak assumption which leads to a superficial similarity with the properties of a long-term position. This does not mean that, even with instantaneous production, the neoclassicals ignore profits, viewed as the remuneration of capital: otherwise, the Walrasian equations would be a refinement of the labour theory of value.

- K and S' interpretation justifies surreptitious imports within post-Sraffian theory. Take a post-Walrasian result, like the characterization of finite efficient chronicles by Walrasian competitive prices. Apply the transform (41) to the prices: in which sense can it be claimed that a pale xerox of established statements is either new or has 'classical features'? K and S' paper (2000) is an algebraic transcript of Malinvaud's geometric proof, adapted to exhaustible resources. Moreover, the authors fail to understand the nature of the problem in an infinite horizon and only 'prove' that an infinite efficient chronicle is sustained by competitive prices (compare with Theorems 8 and 9 in chapter 20, section 5). How is the whole procedure compatible with their criticisms of post-Walrasian theory? The recantation of the notion of profit and that conception of the relations between classical and neoclassical theories are hardly defensible, on either historical or conceptual grounds.

6.3 *Alternative formalizations*

Following Parrinello's (1983) appeal, several attempts have been made to deal with exhaustible resources in a classical framework. Piccioni and Ravagnani (2002) have made a parallel between the theory of royalties and the Marxian theory of absolute rent, but their analysis excludes Hotelling's rule and lacks explicit formalization. Parrinello (2001) himself writes down a simple model with one exhaustible resource, oil. In an attempt to draw a parallel, suggested by Sraffa himself ('Natural resources . . . such as land and mineral deposits', *PCMC*, §85) with the theory of intensive rent, he assumes that an 'observer' notices that corn is produced by two methods simultaneously during several consecutive periods. Parrinello writes down the corresponding price equations and, in order to avoid overdetermination, must assume that the technical coefficients fulfil an improbable 'rank condition'. The identification of this condition with Sraffa's 'given quantity' hypothesis and the role attributed to the observer in the construction are both problematic.

Schefold (1989b, 2001) introduces a distinction between the resource *in situ* ('in ground') and the extracted resource ('above ground'). The idea is that the price of the resource *in situ* increases every year according to the Hotelling rule, whereas the prices of the extracted resource and the other produced commodities change only spasmodically, in between the end of a 'decade' (the long period) and the beginning of the next. Inside a decade, the inputs of the reproducible commodities and the outputs are evaluated at constant prices. Schefold (1989a, 222) notices that some economists 'might prefer to define . . . the prices of commodities with reference to the beginning and the end of the period'. If the outputs were calculated at the prices prevailing at date $t + 1$, system (37) would be obtained. Schefold rejects this possibility 'because it blurs the classical notion of the rate of profit': the economists referred to in the above quotation are 'those who are familiar with the neoclassical theory of exhaustible resources, which is more directly oriented towards an explanation of market prices.' (In the classical tradition, 'market prices' are associated with transitory shocks of supply or demand and temporary adjustment failures, but no phenomenon of this type is taken into account here.) The best interpretation we can give is that Schefold's system constitutes an attempt to adopt a measure of profit *à la* Torrens. But the notion of decade and the asymmetrical treatment of the resource *in situ* and the reproducible commodities lead to contradictions: the formalization does not fit with Schefold's comments and leaves open the possibility of arbitrage between the end of a decade and the beginning of the next.

The construction presented in sections 3–5 stems from Erreygers' (1996a) idea of the corn–guano model. Many discussions have led to a progressive unification of initially divergent analyses. The reader will find outspoken discussions of the corn–guano model in the *Metroeconomica* symposium (2001). In spite of their divergences, the researchers share the conviction that progress should come from a reflection on new challenges. The main value of the theory of exhaustible resources does not concern guano or oil: it is to reveal the possible interpretations of classical theory and, hence, to help define a research programme.

7 Conclusion

The study of intertemporal models outside regular paths is illustrated by the theory of exhaustible resources. The best starting point is the corn–guano model. For a given distribution variable (real wage or rate of profit), the novelty with regard to the traditional post-Sraffian approach is that the price and the other distribution variable (rate of profit or real wage) move as time passes, even when the same technique is operated. When the numéraire includes labour, the dynamics of the corn–guano model become more involved. There exists a unique 'natural' path allowing for positive prices, wages and royalties whatever the number of periods before exhaustion is. For a given exhaustion time T, all paths close to the natural path sustain positive prices during T periods. Flukes apart, the prices at exhaustion are not the long-term prices of the backstop method and, therefore, they continue to fluctuate after exhaustion. This preliminary study of the corn–guano model is a methodological device to delineate the main issues for multisector models with exhaustible resources, while preserving the simplicity of a one-commodity model.

Our ultimate objective is to compare the post-Walrasian and post-Sraffian theories. Given this aim, the unrealistic hypotheses introduced (pure competition, perfect foresight), which are common to the theories we compare, are harmless. The methodological innovation of the study consists in stressing the unity of the economic theory of competition. This principle allows us to make use of Walras' no-profit condition, then translate the results in post-Sraffian terms. The translation pays attention to the concept of rate of profit, whose definition is not immediate and is partly a matter of convention.

24 An overview

1 Method

We have been guided by two methodological principles in writing this study:

- First, the link with economic analysis is never broken. The history of economic thought is a guide, but economic analysis is both the iron and the fire.
- Secondly, the logic of a construction is explored and respected as such, before embarking on comparisons or critiques.

From this standpoint, the most significant contribution concerns the choice of technique in joint production. Its origin lies in the untenability of Sraffa's position and the question is that of re-establishing a rigorous analysis while remaining faithful to his ideas, which discard an approach based on supply and demand. This exercise aims at testing and validating the retained principles. It is within this perspective that one must understand the construction elaborated in chapter 19. One may challenge this interpretation of Sraffa, but one should notice its consistency: its critique presupposes the elaboration of an alternative interpretation that has similar qualities. Elsewhere, such as in chapter 13, it is the abandonment of a presupposition of Sraffa's – the study of each isolated system before their mutual comparison – that has enabled us to elucidate relations with von Neumann's theory.

The critique of the notion of aggregate capital is taken for granted. However, one risks devaluing the classical theory if one compares it with the American or the Austrian versions of the neoclassical theory. The only theory worthy of comparison is that of general equilibrium. Hence, we have paid attention to the Walrasian as well as post-Walrasian versions of the theory. Its structure is clarified in a particular fashion, namely, we have on the one hand eliminated the notion of utility and on the other developed those aspects of it which concern reproduction. This presentation can be inscribed within the horizon of a certain Walrasian heritage and is justified by the nature of the pursued objective.

Respecting intellectual rules does not preclude making choices. From time to time, the retained principles seem or indeed are contradictory. In order to avoid an analytical paralysis, we have retained the constant returns hypothesis that Sraffa explicitly rejected. By underscoring this divergence, we have avoided the prospects of making Sraffa's convictions appear dull or replacing them with lukewarm or hazy notions. Nevertheless, one must confront the contradiction itself: although the developments contained in this study are inspired by Sraffa's initial project, they diverge from it significantly. The ultimate stake is that of highlighting the specificity of classical analysis with regard to the dominant theory and its relationship with contemporary economic thought.

2 The results

The study of single production has uncovered the economic laws which govern these systems. The domain of the variation of the growth and profit rates is well defined and the maximum rates are equal ($G = R$). In particular, the viability property (existence of a physical surplus) and the profitability property (existence of a positive profit) are equivalent. The prices are positive for all rates of profit lower than the maximum rate and depend on distribution. The adjustment property ensures the possibility of producing the exact desired surplus. Faced with a multiplicity of methods, the criterion for choice is the search for short-term extra profits. The dominant technique thus selected depends only on the rate of profit and is wage-maximizing. When the rate of profit increases, all prices in terms of wage increase (the real wage decreases) with a complex movement of relative prices. Finally, in a study more oriented towards the history of economic thought, we have endeavoured to measure the evolution of the difficulty of production consecutive to a technical change and define an adapted concept of standard.

The aim of the study of joint production is not simply that of relativizing the laws of single production. It also enables us to specify their domain of application and to classify them. In single production, these laws are inextricably entwined whereas they can be isolated in joint production. We can therefore identify the systems for which some laws are valid, study the relations among different properties and order them hierarchically. Two main categories of productive systems have drawn our attention: the all-engaging systems and those with fixed capital.

The all-engaging systems are those whose generalized inverse Leontief matrix is positive. This property holds as long as the rates of growth and profit remain within a certain interval whose upper limit defines the maximum rates G and R. A unique positive standard and a unique vector of positive prices are associated with the maximum rates $G = R$. Conversely, the uniqueness and the positivity of the vectors attached to the maximum rate characterize all-engaging systems. When the growth and profit rates vary, the economic behaviour of the system is globally similar to single production as long as the inverse matrix remains positive: the adjustment property, the positivity of prices, the trade-off between wage and the profit rate, etc. remain valid. This is the case for sufficiently high rates. The properties are lost for low growth and profit rates.

While all-engaging systems seem very specific, it is remarkable that almost all joint production systems possess this property when approaching the maximum growth rate. In order to establish this result, we have turned to von Neumann's construction which retains the free disposal hypothesis while immediately raising the question of choice of technique. This theory defines a maximum growth rate and a minimum interest rate (in the neoclassical sense) that are equal. If one isolates the operated methods and the non-overproduced commodities, the active part of the system is square and all-engaging. This property bridges the gap between Sraffa's and von Neumann's analyses. The maximum rate of profit is defined, in all generality, as the equilibrium rate of the von Neuman model. This, in turn, confers a universal character on the equality $G = R$. The von Neumann path corresponds to the limit case of standard proportions (regular and maximum accumulation without surplus) and its associated prices are prices of production for a zero wage. When approaching the maximum rates, multiple-product systems behave like single ones. For low rates of accumulation or profit, these properties are again lost.

The notion of a sector is located at the junction of the concept of an all-engaging system and the theory of technical choices. It is based on a partition of the set of methods which extends the applicability of the notion of an industry to certain types of joint production. The criterion retained for the sake of this partition is that of the indispensability of each sector. This approach proceeds from a global vision of the functioning of the economy. The sectoral economies possess properties that are analogous to those of single production, such as the non-substitution property. By isolating the core of the problem, the concept of a sector proves to be a powerful analytic tool, as illustrated by the theory of fixed capital.

Economies with fixed capital constitute another important category of multiple-product systems. Their analytical treatment aims at eliminating the fixed capital goods through formal manipulations. This operation, which is called vertical integration, is relevant since it reflects the economic nature of fixed capital as an intermediary good. Since the vertically integrated system is simple (it is reduced to a single-product or an all-engaging system), its properties are rich. The strategy consists in tracing back certain properties of the integrated economy to the initial one with fixed capital. The truncation theory assumes the free disposal of the machines whose economic lifespan is endogenously determined. A chain of elementary reasonings has enabled us to specify the economic properties, which are similar to those of single production. This result has been established first for the neo-Austrian model, considered here as an extension of the corn model to the intertemporal framework. It clarifies the theoretical relations between the traditional investment criteria (value added and internal rate of return, IRR). It has then been extended to multisector economies as long as there is only one machine per industry or sector.

With the simultaneous use of several machines, only a weak form of the non-substitution property remains: the dominant technique adjusts itself to the final demand but the technique itself depends on the rate of accumulation. The central question involves explaining this difference of behaviour. The strategy we have adopted sheds light on this mystery: the integrated system is always simple and its economic properties are rich. Nevertheless, depending on the degree of the complexity of vertical integration, these properties cannot be transferred to the initial system. Thus, the economic behaviour of a fixed-capital model depends on the regularity of its vertical integration. That diagnosis justifies our approach: it consists in starting from a general model, then specifying one by one some significant properties of vertical integration. The expected economic properties are then progressively recovered. *A posteriori*, the results obtained by the truncation theory stem from the extreme smoothness of integration when there is one machine per industry. More generally, the analysis explains the differences in the economic behaviour of various fixed-capital models and enables us to identify their respective properties. Two aspects of this study illustrate the link between the methodological principles and our permanent objectives:

- The effort purports to find the adequate standpoint as well as the relevant concepts. A minimum of calculation suffices once the problem is well formulated.
- The economic properties are ranked according to the order in which they are recovered when stronger and stronger regularity constraints are imposed.

The study of fixed capital without truncation enables us to measure the impact of the free disposal hypothesis. Negatively priced machines, which would be discarded if truncation were possible, must be used until the end of their physical lives. Despite the absence of free disposal, the von Neuman equality is maintained and the critical value $G = R$ is the highest

IRR or, for multisector models, its adequate generalization. This construction provides a theoretical foundation for the IRR criterion.

The study of systems with land(s) explicitly takes demand into account and determines the lands to be cultivated. The existence result is completed by a curious indeterminacy property governing relations among wages, profits and rents. Several examples demonstrate the difficulty of establishing general laws. Moreover, the fact that systems with land are reducible (several distinct meanings can be given to this notion in joint production) implies that certain properties are definitively lost.

3 A prelude to a critique?

3.1 Sraffa's radical project

The above results have been inspired by Sraffa's approach. However, we have already mentioned certain differences between the analyses. These divergences are neither insignificant nor accidental. Their ground lies in Sraffa's conception of the classical theory as a radical alternative to the dominant theory. One may not share the project but one cannot deny its existence. The subtitle of *PCMC* ('Prelude to a Critique of Economic Theory') and the preface eloquently bespeak this ambition. Two notions which are intimately linked to the marginalist theory are subjected to a conceptual critique:

- *The returns to scale.* The preface of *PCMC* begins as follows:

  > Anyone accustomed to think in terms of the equilibrium of demand and supply may be inclined, on reading these pages, to suppose that the argument rests on a tacit assumption of constant returns in all industries . . . In fact, no such assumption is made. No changes in output and [at least when switch in methods is not considered] no changes in the proportions in which different means of production are used by an industry are considered, so that no question arises as to the variation or constancy of returns.

  If the warning is followed, the concept of returns to scale is foreign to the theory of prices. The observation disqualifies any theory that relies on return-based hypotheses, whose typical example is the marginalist theory. The critique is a radical one.

- *Demand.* The very term 'demand' appears only twice in *PCMC*. Once in the first sentence of the preface quoted above. The second time it is stated that:

  > One might be tempted, but it would be misleading, to say that [the exchange ratio between basic products] depends as much on the Demand side as on the Supply side. (*PCMC*, §7)

The most instructive clue to Sraffa's position is found in the chapter entitled 'Land'. Sraffa writes that 'the scarcity of land provides the background from which rent arises'. By referring to the scarcity of an input rather than the high level of demand (which is found in Ricardo's text), Sraffa clarifies his point of view: demand matters because it imposes a constraint on the actual productive system. This very constraint is elsewhere designated 'requirements for use'. The idea is to discard a direct analysis of demand and consider it indirectly through its effects on production. The standpoint privileges production while taking into account constraints external to the productive system. Sraffa thus formulates the premises of his own construction in opposition to those of the marginalist theory. The latter is identified before being disqualified because of its internal logical contradictions. In one sentence, just as a few times suffice for the Queen of Night's fall, '*any* notion of capital as a measurable quantity independent of distribution and prices' (§ 48) is destroyed.

One must take account of this critique without blunting its ambition. What type of economic analysis can it help to develop? Certain weaknesses of *PCMC* indicate that there is no immediate answer. The post-Sraffian stream is itself divided between a critical objective and a positive one, whose coexistence becomes problematic when certain hypotheses attacked in the critical section are adopted in the analytical part. These contradictions are rarely faced openly. We will successively examine, with diverse standpoints, the questions of demand, returns and the theory of capital.

3.2 Requirements for use versus demand

For the sake of clarity, the constant returns hypothesis is retained here. The production costs increased by the ruling rate of profit appear on the left-hand side of the price equations, the value of production on the right-hand side. The equality between the two members makes sense if the produced quantities are indeed sold, otherwise the effective rate of profit would differ from the normal rate. Thus, the very writing of the prices of production presupposes the equality between 'supply' and 'demand' on the market. The question raised here is not the repudiation of demand, but that of its status within the conceptual apparatus of the theory of prices. In a letter to the French translator of *PCMC* (concerning the translation of the terms 'replacement' and 'self-replacement'), Sraffa wrote: 'In general it seems to me that when a term has become strongly associated with one particular technical sense, one may be forced to use a neologism if one wants to introduce a different technical term, in order to avoid confusion.' This quote might apply to the neologism 'requirements for use' that Sraffa introduces so as to avoid the term 'demand' which is commonly associated with the marginalist theory.

The conceptual and methodological work must be subjected to a close examination of its analytical conclusions. In single production (more precisely on the hypotheses of the non-substitution theorem) the quantities matter for the determination of the activity levels but the prices depend only on the distribution and the conditions of production. The notion of 'requirements for use' is introduced in *PCMC* in conjunction with joint production. Yet, Sraffa himself experiences difficulties with this concept, which is absent in his analytical developments! It is of significance that certain conclusions are grounded on what turns out to be an abusive analogy with single production. In our reconstruction of the theory of choice of techniques (chapter 19), we have endeavoured to combine analytical rigour with methodological fidelity to the posited principles: the requirements for use are taken into consideration only through the constraints that they impose on the productive system. The existence, uniqueness and convergence results show that this standpoint is neither arbitrary nor sterile. Their weakness is not due to the introduction of restrictive axioms, which is inherent to any construction of this type. It lies in the presupposition that systems of production are square: the employed methods are numerous enough to infer the prices, which then become 'prices of production'. Nevertheless, it is easy to construct examples in a classical framework in which the productive systems are rectangular because of either substitution or income effects. A direct knowledge of the demanded quantities, and not simply that of their effect on the operated methods, is then required to determine the prices. Is this phenomenon, characteristic of pure joint production, minor? No, since the question is not the degree of the extension of the 'complication' but that of the analysis of production considered as a theoretical object and a critical instrument. The aim is that of defining general principles and not merely convenient rules that are used in some configurations and not others. The fact that the squareness axiom may be unacceptable challenges the notion of price of production.

By stressing that the requirements for use are given, Sraffa's intention is that of breaking the symmetry between supply and demand that characterizes the marginalist theory of value. But even the expression 'given requirements' is ambiguous since one can interpret it as 'given function' or 'given vector'. Lippi's formalization retains the second interpretation (a given net product). This reading is faithful to Sraffa's approach but incompatible with the classical hypotheses concerning the demand behaviour of different classes: assuming that the net product vector as well as the structures of the capitalists' and the workers' demands are given amounts to defining distribution in physical terms and, therefore, is contradictory with an alternative analysis based on an exogenously given wage or rate of profit. These examples show that great precision is required in the definition of concepts and the list of data. The *a priori* choices are open but their nature is checked by their analytical consistency.

3.3 The returns

While we have tried to define the content of the concept of 'requirements for use' in the sense most adequate to Sraffa's analysis, we do not pursue the same path when probing into the question of returns, since this would lead us too far from our convictions. The question posed by the preface of *PCMC* is that of examining the very possibility of constructing a price system without reference to returns. The price of production equations express the uniformity of the profit rates across industries. The reference to this state can be justified by an argument that is made explicit in the classical economic literature: if the profitabilities differ, the capital flees industries with a low rate of profit and is invested in the more profitable sectors. In order to avoid complications related to dynamics, let us define the state of reference in static terms: when the rates of profit are uniform, no force pushes for a displacement of capital.

Is that reason acceptable? Only if it is developed in more detail. Whatever the profitability of the previously invested capital, the last euro will go into the industry that offers the highest profitability. The state of rest is thus characterized by the equality of the *marginal* rates of profit. In order for the price of production equations, which refer to the *average* or *total* profitability, to make economic sense, one must posit the identity of the marginal and average conditions, that is, the constancy of returns. This is why the notion of price of production in which the technical coefficients reflect the average magnitudes is economically indissociable from the constancy of returns, even though from a formal standpoint it is not. The same conclusion is reached when prices are interpreted as absolute prices which reflect the difficulty of production: they will be stable throughout if the conditions remain the same, up to the scale of production.

Sraffa suggests that the notion of returns to scale has no place in his construction so long as technical choices are not introduced, since no finite or infinitesimal variation is envisaged. However, in the presence of nonconstant returns, the arbitrage condition is the equality of the marginal rates of return: it is expressed by equations similar to the prices of production in which, however, the technical coefficients reflect marginal magnitudes and not average ones. The prices are thus determined by the last methods employed. Therein the reader will have recognized a basis of the rent theory. The refusal to introduce an hypothesis on returns also reflects another of Sraffa's presuppositions according to which analysis must proceed from the study of a given system to choice of techniques and the comparison of systems. This seductive idea is practicable in the case of single production but its application is often impossible when joint production is concerned.

3.4 *The theory of capital*

Sraffa's critique concerning the notion of capital is of a different nature from those on returns and demand. The analytical arguments mentioned in *PCMC* prove that the heterogeneity of capital goods forbids us to conceive capital as a factor of production. It is mainly over this theme that debates with the proponents of the neoclassical approach have crystallized. After having initially rejected the critique, the neoclassicals have come to acknowledge its validity.

Chapter 21, in which we have dealt with some aspects of these questions, is unfair to the work done by Sraffa and the post-Sraffians. Once the debate is over, one might be tempted to say that the Cambridge (US) camp had been obviously wrong from the very outset and this makes the success of Cambridge (UK) look too easily achieved. The argument forgets the initial difficulty of resisting the established modes of thought: the fact that the demand for capital is not necessarily decreasing with the interest rate remains hardly credible. The phenomenon implies, no doubt, that something in the conventional approach must be rejected. The question is: what? Those theories for which capital is conceived as a homogeneous magnitude and which introduce the notion of aggregate production function are deeply affected. But no rejection of those theories which do not require such concepts is inferred. It is not on the reswitching phenomenon itself, but on the consequences drawn from it that we disagree with radical conclusions.

On which side is 'the' marginalist school located? On the wrong one, if one considers its 'American' (Clark) or 'Austrian' (Böhm-Bawerk) versions; on the right one, for the Walrasian and post-Walrasian theories. The logical point of view that is adhered to here must be clearly distinguished from the historical one. The historians of economic thought may well consider that the changes that occurred in the last quarter of the nineteenth century proceed from a unique intellectual move, with the same principles applied to different aspects of economic theory. However, each of these constructions has a logical value of its own, and the critiques addressed to the American and Austrian variants do not apply to Walras' work that does not consider capital as a homogeneous magnitude. Whoever considers that the classical approach resists the contradictions of the labour theory of value should not claim that a critique of the Austrian theory is a sufficient argument against the general equilibrium theory. Chapter 21 examines the degree of relevance of various critiques regarding the theory of capital. To do so, the discussion of marginal equalities has been dissociated from the concept of capital.

The former, when adequately constructed (notably, they must be defined so as to have a sense independent of the numéraire), are valid: is it so surprising that the entrepreneurs' optimization behaviour finds a mathematical expression in form of marginal equalities?

Because our approach avoids the identification of the question of marginal equalities with that of capital, its assertions ('yes' to the marginal equalities, 'no' to aggregate capital and the macroeconomic production function) are more complex than clear-cut positions which either completely accept or reject the whole set of propositions. We consider that the post-Sraffian formulations which discard all formal conclusions associated with 'neoclassical theory' are inspired by a wrong strategic choice and are misleading.

4 The temptation of general equilibrium

The distinction between the neoclassical approach and the classical one governs the content of a renewed classical economy. The principle upheld in this study is twofold: on the one hand the only possible comparison term is the general equilibrium; on the other, that comparison requires one to respect the intellectual identity of each theory.

4.1 A necessary reference

A review of the state of economic theory in the 1920s and the 1930s is necessary to understand the nature of Sraffa's project and its major references. The weaknesses of the dominant economic discourse of the time are analysed in the articles of 1925 and 1926. The 'same' theory still dominates today but our reading of it has been modified. Indeed, it is the construction developed by Walras, not the one by Marshall, that is considered hardcore: the *ceteris paribus* clause no longer appears necessary. This hierarchical reversal has considerable importance for the relevance of critiques. This is why contemporary theorists can acknowledge the validity of the critiques of 1925 and 1926 without concluding that a substantial modification of analysis would be necessary today: these critiques concern the interdependence of the markets and are compatible with a general equilibrium framework.

In a context of generalized interdependence it is remarkable that the existence of an equilibrium can be established. This result was, however, only the first stage in the initial agenda of neoclassical theory, which also comprised discussions of spontaneous convergence towards equilibrium. It is now recognized that, except under specific hypotheses, such a law cannot be stated. This is why economists live in anguish, torn between their desire for rigour and an efficiency principle which ordains the introduction of simple hypotheses that cannot be totally justified, so as to lead to operational statements.

We have underscored some formal similarities between post-Sraffian theory and general equilibrium theory. It turns out that the tools elaborated by post-Walrasian economists, such as the GND lemma, are useful in the study of joint production. Their efficiency within the context of post-Sraffian theory is not a sufficient argument to conclude on matters specific to economic theory. However, it draws our attention to the parallels that exist among the retained hypotheses. It is an established fact that the law is adopted implicitly by post-Sraffian theory, perhaps because it is required for all price theories. This limit of the divergence with neoclassical theory constitutes an obstacle to the projects whose ambition is that of rapprochement with the Keynesian theory (we have in mind the 'old' version of the Keynes' theory which relies on the notion of effective demand and disequilibria between investment and savings; after Lucas . . .). A question is whether the affinity with general equilibrium surpasses formal similarity.

4.2 Apparent oppositions

Different conceptions of demand and production seem to characterize neoclassical and classical theories. A preliminary analysis aims at determining whether or not there exist insuperable divergences:

- The *concept of demand.* The marginalist theory of value is 'symmetrical': the price results from supply and demand, supply being determined by the maximization of profit and demand by maximization of utility. The concept of utility is philosophically significant, for two reasons. At the microeconomic level, it expresses the consumer's freedom. At the global level, it founds the notion of optimum and enables us to reflect on the rationality and the efficiency of the economic system. The version which we have retained of the marginalist theory discards this construction of demand based on utility and does not consider the service provided to the sovereign consumer as the ultimate economic goal. Demand is directly given as function of prices and income (or wealth). Can this presentation be thought of as having significantly deformed the theory? It is used in order to facilitate comparisons with the classical approach. There is no doubt that Sraffa rejects the notion of utility. Nevertheless, nothing in the critique expounded in *PCMC* relates to this issue, that is, the critique holds *independently* of any objection to the concept of utility. This is why a discussion of this notion is of secondary importance. We have duly underlined is that it is easy to prune away the notion of utility from the general equilibrium theory.

- The *conception of production.* It is in the opposition between two conceptions of production that Sraffa situates the core of the distinction between classical and marginalist approaches as well as the root of the marginalists' mistakes. The idea of reproduction is central to the classical approach. It leaves its imprint on the theory of value itself, whether in terms of labour value or prices of production. On the contrary the neoclassical theory is usually formulated in the framework described by Sraffa: production is conceived as 'a one-way avenue that leads from "Factors of production" to "Consumption goods"' (*PCMC*, appendix *D*), whence the role of the initial endowments and the interpretation of prices as scarcity indicators. However the neoclassical theory cannot be reduced to that representation. Thus all growth models, including that of Solow (1956), are centred on the reproduction of capital: this observation is independent of the critiques that may otherwise be made of the conception of capital.

Sraffa's description has the merit of informing us of the usual ways of thinking, not of the intrinsic limits of marginalist analysis. As soon as the debate comes to grips with the logic of the model and not its dominant mode of use, it cannot be based on the opposition between endowments and production. Scarcity and reproduction are dual aspects whose relative importance depends on the length of the temporal horizon: in the short run, endowments constitute a determining factor but their importance wanes in the long run.

4.3 *Post-Sraffian ambiguities*

These brief indications suffice to highlight the specificity of our interpretation with regard to other points of view defended by post-Sraffian economists. Thus, Garegnani reduces the theoretical core to a small number of relations among economic variables whose actual level depends on social and historical factors. All rapprochement with the long-term general equilibrium is excluded for different reasons: sometimes, this theory is perceived as a sophisticated variant of an aggregate capital model which is ultimately subjected to the same critiques as the American or Austrian versions. The link with the perspective of Malinvaud and that of the turnpike theory is either challenged or ignored. The notion of utility is considered as a necessary component of the marginalist approach. But the post-Sraffian researches adapt themselves with great difficulty to such a minimalist vision.

The debate is of crucial importance for economic analysis. Let us reiterate that it is on the analytical ground that the ideas are checked. Post-Sraffian conceptions are reflected in a specific practice and the exploration of a privileged formalization. A fundamental question concerns the domain of extension of the prices of production, considered as invariable relative prices. Is the regular growth hypothesis an accessory to the permanence of prices? Or is it crucial to it, as understood by the theory of intertemporal equilibrium (relative prices are invariant because marginal productivities are invariant as well)? It is because the consideration of exhaustible resources is the simplest manner of excluding regular growth that this theory possesses the character of a test and deserves particular attention. The failures of post-Sraffian efforts in the treatment of this problem also reflect a widespread incomprehension of the intertemporal equilibrium theory.

5 A fruitful standpoint

5.1 Which exogenous variables?

The neoclassical model which we retain as a reference is disaggregated, intertemporal and eliminates utility. There remains a significant divergence with the classical theory – the choice of exogenous variables.

The neoclassical theory assumes given initial endowments. The prices and the quantities are determined endogenously under the hypothesis that all markets are cleared. Notably, the wage is the full-employment price on the labour market. In a long-term perspective, the regular growth hypothesis leads to the modification of these data since it assumes that the endowments are in the right proportions. If certain goods are not produced and belong to the endowments on each date, the general rate of growth is that of these endowments. This is the case when labour is the only non-produced good: the rate of growth is that of the population, corrected by an efficiency coefficient. The initial equilibrium repeats itself in the future with increased quantities and unchanged relative prices. There is permanently maintained full employment and the real wage per unit of effective labour is constant. On the contrary, the classical theory does not treat labour in the same way as it considers the other commodities. Surely enough, the tensions in the labour market do have an impact on the wage, but mainly because they modify the force relations between workers and capitalists. The full employment hypothesis is not retained and a positive wage is compatible with the coexistence of unemployment. Wage is thus considered as an exogenous variable whose level is determined by socio-historical conditions.

This divergence in the treatment of labour is of little importance in a formal sense and yet significant as far as economic interpretation is concerned:

- Formally speaking, under the simple assumption that the wage basket is given, each labour unit can be replaced by this basket. With the disappearance of labour, employment and wage, the main differences between the formalizations vanish and the same results hold for both models. This possibility explains why some results have sprung up within the standard theory, then transferred and adopted by post-Sraffian theory: the inventors of the non-substitution theorem were intrigued by the non-influence of demand; the truncation theory has its roots in the Austrian hinterland.
- It is because distribution is considered exogenous that the classical authors emphasize the trade-off between wage and profits or between wages, profits and rents. A direct link is thus established between an exogenous variable and one or more endogenous variable(s). Many results of the present study are inspired by this standpoint and consider a (re)productive system with an exogenous distribution variable. The alternative that consists in attributing a nil wage in case of underemployment is seductive to neither the practitioners nor the contemporary theorists who attempt to find reasons that justify the wage rigidity.

5.2 *The equilibrium paths*

Regular growth constitutes a natural reference for the study of intertemporal paths. The abandonment of the corresponding hypotheses introduces effective dynamics. We uphold the principle of the fundamental unity of the theory of competitive equilibria: the latter can only give rise to variants according to the hypotheses and the reading angle relied upon. With constant returns, the fundamental law is that of the absence of pure profits. When, as in single production, the number of active methods is sufficient, this law establishes an induction relationship between prices from one period to the next. Successive intertemporal prices are linked, even if the relative prices are not constant.

The non-arbitrage condition in the quest for maximum profit is the uniformity of marginal rates of profitability. However, the measure of the level of rate of profit sets a problem: with changing relative prices, the result depends on the chosen standard and remains partly conventional. This difficulty is a small one when one reasons within a Walrasian framework or when the real wage is given, since it is limited to an *ex post* calculation on a trajectory. On the contrary, when the rate of profit is taken as the exogenous parameter, the choice of the standard has an influence on the intertemporal trajectory itself. The theory of exhaustible resources defines a simple frame designed to test these ideas. Since a consistent post-Sraffian alternative to the construction developed in chapter 23 would undermine our interpretation, refutability is possible and we expect critiques with comparable coherence.

5.3 The disequilibrium paths

The overall picture that we have provided of the post-Sraffian experience acknowledges the originality and the fecundity of the adopted standpoint. But the dimension of radical critique which had been assigned for the initial project has not convincingly materialized. In our view, the approach's chief limitation lies in the equilibrium postulate which underlies the price theory. As far as the long-term aspects are concerned, it would be unreasonable to assume that the markets would never clear or that the rates of profit would differ structurally. In this respect, the prices of production are guides and the exploration of their properties is useful. However, this is only a part of the classical theory's heritage.

A major divergence with the Walrasian intertemporal model can be introduced only by abandoning the equilibrium hypotheses. A possibility would consist in admitting effective disequilibria in the existing markets or in assuming that the agents are not coordinated. These propositions have already been explored as alternatives to the restrictive axioms that have been retained. Yet, a re-reading of the classical authors should instil a few new ideas on the mode of functioning of a capitalist economy outside equilibrium. The simplest is that the rate of profit (whatever the theoretical difficulty in defining this concept may be) constitutes an essential indicator in guiding the movements of capital. If we have not studied the question of disequilibrium thus far, it is because the hypotheses required (behaviours, expectations, reaction time, etc.) entail a certain degree of arbitrariness that influences the qualitative properties of the dynamics. Our first aim was that of scrutinizing an already completed research field and its interpretations. It is on the basis of agreement on the validity of the foregoing review that a research programme may be elaborated.

6 Omega

Dear Piero: Off the beaten track, the programme you defined deals with some profound questions in economic theory. Intellectual curiosity and pleasure have illuminated twenty years of research devoted to this fascinating project.

Mathematical appendix: Elements of combinatorial geometry

1 A combinatorial problem

Let there be q given points $M_1, \ldots, M_q$ in general position in R^n ($q \geq n$). Any n of these points constitute an n-set. We consider two families $\boldsymbol{C}$ and $\boldsymbol{T}$ of n-sets. The family $\boldsymbol{C}$ (the candidates) is made of the facets of the convex hull of $M_1, \ldots, M_q$. The family $\boldsymbol{T}$ (the techniques) satisfies a combinatorial condition of the type: given a technique T and an arbitrary point M_i, M_i can be substituted for exactly one point M_j in T in such a way that the new n-set also belongs to $\boldsymbol{T}$ (several variants of this 'insertion axiom' will be considered, therefore the precise meaning of the word 'technique' varies from one section to another). The problem is to study $\boldsymbol{C} \cap \boldsymbol{T}$ (existence, numbering, orientation, convergence of algorithms).

The problem is tackled in two ways. In sections 2 and 3, the 'points' M_i represent any mathematical object (not necessarily points in R^n) and the family $\boldsymbol{C}$ itself is defined by a combinatorial condition, not as the collection of facets. This purely combinatorial approach is based on an abstract, or 'naked', version of the Sperner lemma. Some applications are proposed in section 4. The second approach, developed in sections 5 and 6, stems from an interpretation of Sraffa's theory of choice of technique and makes use of kinetic arguments, half geometrical and half combinatorial.

These questions do not seem to have been studied before in their general form. This appendix being fairly self-contained, a few repetitions of the previous chapters cannot be avoided. The reading requires the knowledge of some geometrical notions (facet, hyperplane, simplicial decomposition and . . . point). An acquaintance with the economic problems encountered in the book is useful.

2 Candidates and techniques

Let there be a given set $\{1, \ldots, q\}$ of q 'figures' which are abstract mathematical objects. The figures are also called 'points' or 'vertices'

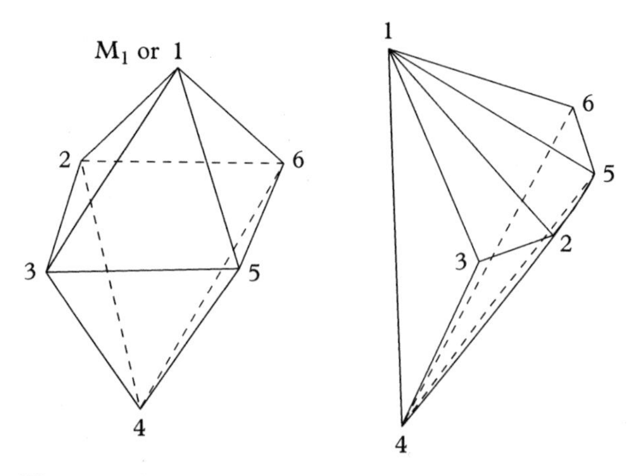

Figure A.1 Two polytopes with six vertices

(we will refer to 'figure i' for the abstract definitions and to 'point M_i', or 'vertex M_i', when there is a geometrical support). A 'number', also called an n-set, is a non-ordered set of n distinct figures. Neighbouring numbers are two numbers that differ by one figure.

Definition 1. Let there be q figures and a family $\boldsymbol{C}$ of numbers with n distinct figures (n given, $n \leq q$). $\boldsymbol{C}$ is called a family of candidates if the *replacement property* holds: given a number in $\boldsymbol{C}$, each figure ('old' figure) in this number ('old' candidate) can be replaced by exactly one other figure ('new' figure) in order that the new number also belongs to $\boldsymbol{C}$.

The members of $\boldsymbol{C}$ are called the candidates. For $n = 3$, an edge ij which belongs to some candidate belongs to exactly two candidates. For $n = 3$ and $q = 6$, examples of families of candidates are:

$$C_1 = \{123, 126, 153, 156, 423, 426, 453, 456\} \quad \text{eight candidates}$$
$$C_2 = \{123, 125, 165, 146, 465, 425, 423, 413\} \quad \text{eight candidates}$$
$$C_3 = \{123, 126, 146, 145, 245, 243, 436, 536, 526, 153\} \quad \text{ten candidates.}$$

A simple way to construct a family of candidates is to use a geometrical support: a triangulation, with q vertices, of a $(n - 1)$-dimensional manifold satisfies the replacement property and, therefore, defines a family of candidates. The construction is illustrated by figure A.1 representing two polytopes in R^3 with $q =$ six vertices: every vertex of a facet can be replaced by exactly one other vertex so as to obtain a new facet. Families $\boldsymbol{C}_1$ and $\boldsymbol{C}_2$ are the facets of the polytopes drawn in figure A.1.

For $n = 3$ and $q = 6$, the Euler relationship between the number of facets, edges and vertices shows that only those families with eight candidates can be represented as the facets of a polytope (a polytope is a compact polyhedron). A purely combinatorial approach is therefore required to obtain exhaustive lists. Since a permutation on figures $\{1, \ldots, q\}$ transforms a family of candidates into another, these families are defined up to permutations. For $n = 3$ and $q = 6$, it can be shown that the lists $\boldsymbol{C}_1$, $\boldsymbol{C}_2$, $\boldsymbol{C}_3$ are exhaustive (*Hint*: first consider the families of candidates which have the additional property that no figure can be inserted in two distinct ways into a candidate: $\boldsymbol{C}_1$ and $\boldsymbol{C}_3$ are obtained; second, consider the families which do not have the additional property: they are reduced to $\boldsymbol{C}_2$). Incidentally, this shows that the only polytopes in R^3 with six vertices are those represented in figure A.1.

Definition 2. A family $\boldsymbol{T}$ of distinct numbers (n given, $n \leq q$) is called a family of techniques if the *insertion property* holds: given any figure ('new' figure) and any number ('old' number) in $\boldsymbol{T}$, there is precisely one way to substitute the new figure for an old one in order that the new number belongs to $\boldsymbol{T}$.

The members of $\boldsymbol{T}$ are called the techniques. Given a family of techniques with q figures, a family with $q-1$ figures is obtained by 'killing' all numbers containing figure q. This property is used to build exhaustive lists of techniques by induction on q. For $n = 3$ and $q = 6$, and up to permutations on figures, the families of techniques are:

$$\boldsymbol{T}_1 = \{123, 124, 125, 126\}$$
$$\boldsymbol{T}_2 = \{123, 124, 153, 154, 126, 156\}$$
$$\boldsymbol{T}_3 = \{135, 136, 145, 146, 235, 236, 245, 246\}$$
$$\boldsymbol{T}_4 = \{123, 234, 345, 451, 512, 623, 456, 562\}$$
$$\boldsymbol{T}_5 = \{123, 234, 345, 451, 512, 613, 635, 652, 624, 641\}.$$

There exist three simple ways to build families of techniques. The first one is combinatorial, the other two geometrical:

- Consider a partition of $\{1, \ldots, q\}$ into n non-empty subsets $I_1, \ldots, I_n$. Then the collection of numbers $i_1 \ldots i_n$ such that $i_1 \in I_1, \ldots, i_n \in I_n$ is a family of techniques ('Jim techniques'). $\boldsymbol{T}_1$, $\boldsymbol{T}_2$ and $\boldsymbol{T}_3$ are Jim families.
- Let every figure i in $\{1, \ldots, q\}$ be represented by a point M_i in R^n and consider an arbitrary line (d) which cuts the convex hull of these points. The data are in the general position. Then the collection of n-sets $(i_1, \ldots, i_n)$ such that the line (d) intersects the convex hull

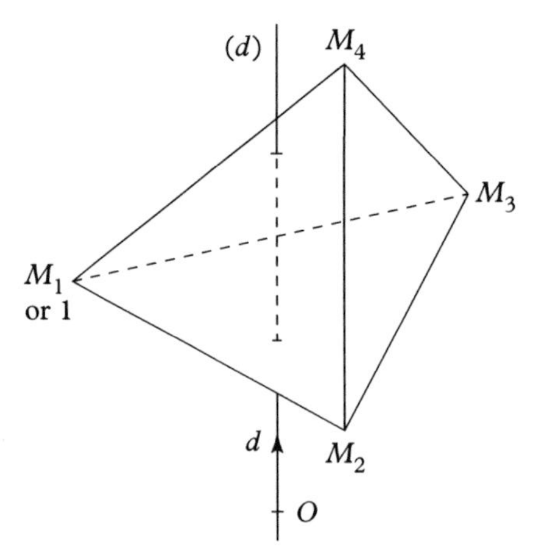

Figure A.2 Julius techniques

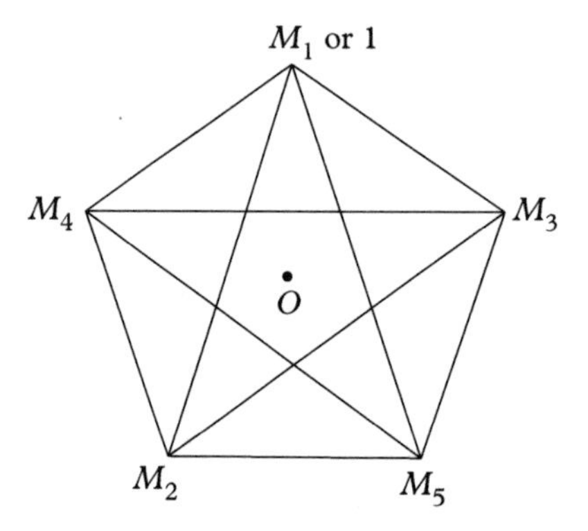

Figure A.3 Joseph techniques

$[M_{i_1} \ldots M_{i_n}]$ is a family of techniques (the 'Julius techniques'). The argument is apparent in figure A.2: Let (d) intersect triangle $[M_1M_2M_3]$ and consider another point M_4. Since (d) intersects one and only one of the three triangles $[M_1M_2M_4]$, $[M_1M_3M_4]$ or $[M_2M_3M_4]$, the new figure 4 can be inserted in a unique way into the old technique 123.

- A simpler device is derived from the above construction by projection on a vectoral hyperplane according to direction (d). Let every figure be represented by a point in R^{n-1}. An n-set is called a 'Joseph technique' if the origin belongs to the convex hull of its n vertices. The insertion property holds. For $Q = 5$, figure A.3 exhibits a geometrical embedding of a Joseph family $T = (123, 234, 345, 451, 512)$. With 3D-glasses, figure A.3 looks like a diamond and $\boldsymbol{T}$ turns out to be also a Julius family.

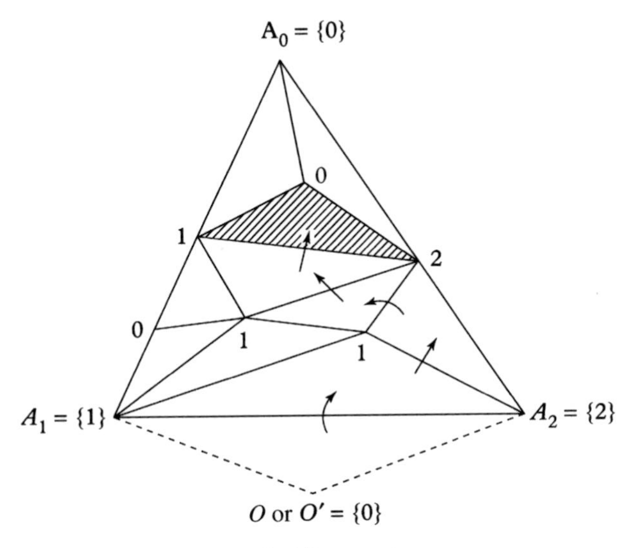

Figure A.4 The geometrical Sperner lemma

3 The naked Sperner lemma

3.1 The simplicial model

We intend to state a result concerning the intersection of a family of candidates and a family of techniques. The property might remain unclear if the reader is not aware of its origin, that is the geometrical Sperner (1928) lemma. We therefore remind (a particular case of) this lemma, sketch its algorithmic proof and stress the combinatorial aspects. Let $A_0A_1A_2$ be a triangle identified with the unit simplex in R^3. A finite number of points are introduced in $A_0A_1A_2$ and are the vertices of a simplicial decomposition: a simplicial decomposition is a set of 'small' triangles such that two non-disjoint triangles have either a vertex or a whole edge in common. By hypothesis, the edge A_1A_2 is not decomposed. Moreover, let every vertex of the decomposition receive a label 0, 1 or 2 (from now on, the figures are denoted from 0 to $q-1$ instead of 1 to q) obeying the only rule: a vertex belonging to the side of $A_0A_1A_2$ opposite to A_i does not receive label i. The rule implies that A_i receives label i. A triangle is said to be completely labelled when its vertices receive the complete set of labels 0, 1 and 2. The genuine Sperner lemma states the existence of at least one completely labelled small triangle. More precisely, the number of such triangles is odd (figure A.4).

We reinterpret the lemma as a property concerning two families of 3-sets. The first family is the collection $\boldsymbol{T}^*$ of completely labelled 3-sets (e.g. $A_0A_1A_2$ itself). The second family is the collection $\boldsymbol{C}^*$ of small triangles. The Sperner lemma states that $\boldsymbol{C}^* \cap \boldsymbol{T}^*$ admits an odd number of elements.

Family $\boldsymbol{T}^*$ satisfies the insertion property: given a completely labelled 3-set, any new vertex can be inserted in a unique way (it replaces the vertex with the same label). Therefore, $\boldsymbol{T}^*$ is a family of techniques of the Jim type. As for family $\boldsymbol{C}^*$, any edge *inside* the simplex is common to two triangles exactly, so that $\boldsymbol{C}^*$ is 'almost' a family of candidates. In order to extend the properties to all edges, we consider the 'skin' of the tetrahedron $OA_1A_2A_3$, where O is the origin in R^3 and receives label 0. The triangle OA_0A_1 is decomposed into small triangles $OA_0M_1, \ldots,$ OM_pA_1; similarly for OA_0A_2, but not for OA_1A_2 since the edge A_1A_2 is not decomposed by hypothesis. After adjunction of these new triangles to $\boldsymbol{T}^*$ and $\boldsymbol{C}^*$, extended families $\boldsymbol{T}$ and $\boldsymbol{C}$ are obtained and, now, the replacement property holds for $\boldsymbol{C}$. OA_1A_2 is the only completely labelled new triangle introduced in the extension. Therefore, proving the Sperner lemma amounts to showing that the intersection of the family $\boldsymbol{C}$ of candidates and the family $\boldsymbol{T}$ of techniques has an even number of elements. Scarf's algorithm proposes a constructive proof of the result. The algorithm starts from OA_1A_2, then defines a path from a small triangle to a neighbouring triangle inside the simplex. The path, which follows the arrows in figure A.4, retains labels 1 and 2 in the new triangle and stops when the third vertex has label 0. The existence of at least one completely labelled small triangle is obtained if it can be shown that the path has no cycle. The logical core of the proof is the 'house argument': consider a house (simplex $A_0A_1A_2$) and an entrance door (A_1A_2) which opens in a first room. From here, one enters into successive new rooms by means of successive doors labelled (1, 2). As there are at most two doors of this type in every room, the path is uniquely defined. If it had a cycle, a contradiction would be obtained by considering the *first* room where one returns (during the first visit, its two doors have already been opened and its two neighbouring rooms already visited). Since the house has no exit door distinct from the entrance door (a unique edge on the frontier of the simplex is labelled (1, 2)), the path must end up in a room with a unique door. This room is completely labelled, hence the existence result.

3.2 *The combinatorial lemma*

We claim that the construction needs no geometrical support and is purely combinatorial. This naked version of the Sperner lemma holds for abstract elements, independently of the simplicial model. We consider q

figures and two families of numbers which are respectively candidates and techniques according to Definitions 1 and 2.

Theorem 1 (naked Sperner lemma). The intersection of a family $\boldsymbol{C}$ of candidates and a family $\boldsymbol{T}$ of techniques admits an even number of elements.

Proof. Let us isolate the figure 0. Consider a candidate $R = (x_1, \ldots, x_n)$ and a 'marked' figure in it, say x_n, such that property (P) holds: the candidate R becomes a technique after substitution of 0 for x_n. (R, x_n) is called a room. The proof is constructive and based on an algorithm which associates a following room with the present room. (For its understanding, follow the arrows in figure A.4, starting from $R_0 = A_1A_2O$, with O as the marked point; in the notation of a room, the marked point is the one which will disappear at the next step of the algorithm.) The arguments are:

(a) *Initialization.* Let $R_0 = (a_1, \ldots, a_n)$ belong to $\boldsymbol{C} \cap \boldsymbol{T}$, if the intersection is non-void. By the insertion property applied to technique R_0, figure 0 can be inserted in a unique way into R_0 and is substituted for, say, a_n. (R_0, a_n) is a room, which is uniquely defined by R_0.

(b) *From a room to the next.* Let (R, x_n), with $R = (x_1, \ldots, x_{n-1}, x_n) \in \boldsymbol{C}$, be a room. By the replacement axiom applied to candidate R, x_n can be replaced in a unique way by some figure x_{n+1}, $x_{n+1} \neq x_n$, such that $R^+ = (x_1, \ldots, x_{n-1}, x_{n+1})$ is a candidate. By the insertion axiom applied to technique $T = (x_1, \ldots, x_{n-1}, O)$, x_{n+1} can be inserted in a unique way into T in order to obtain a technique:

  (i) If x_{n+1} replaces O, then R^+ belongs to $\boldsymbol{C} \cap \boldsymbol{T}$.

  (ii) If x_{n+1} replaces another figure, say x_{n-1}, then $T^+ = (x_1, \ldots, x_{n-2}, x_{n+1}, O)$ is a technique. Therefore (R^+, x_{n-1}) is a room, which is determined in a unique way by (R, x_n) and is dubbed the new room. In this case, R^+ is not a technique, because the coexistence of the two techniques T and T^+ would be contradictory with the uniqueness of the insertion of O within R^+.

(c) *Properties.* Let us show that the procedure is reversible. Let (R, x_n) be a room:

  (i) Let R belong to $\boldsymbol{T}$. By the replacement axiom applied to R, x_n can be replaced in a unique way by some x, $x \neq x_n$, such that $R^- = (x_1, \ldots, x_{n-1}, x)$ is a candidate. Then (R^-, x) is a uniquely defined room.

  (ii) Let R not belong to $\boldsymbol{T}$. By the insertion axiom applied to $\boldsymbol{T}$, x_n can be inserted in a unique way into T in order to obtain a technique: x_n takes the place of x_1 ($x_1 \neq O$ since $R \notin \boldsymbol{T}$) and $T^- = (x_2, \ldots, x_n, x, O)$ is a technique. By the replacement axiom applied to candidate R, x_1 can be replaced by a unique figure x_0 such that $R^- = (x_0, x_2, \ldots, x_n)$ is candidate. Then (R^-, x_0) is a uniquely defined room.

The applications defined in points (b) and (c) are reciprocal from each other. They have three more properties:

- The next room differs from the present room (they differ by the marked point of the present room);
- If R belongs to $\boldsymbol{C} \cap \boldsymbol{T}$, the previous and the next rooms coincide;
- If R does not belong to $\boldsymbol{C} \cap \boldsymbol{T}$, the previous and the next rooms differ.

(d) *The algorithm*. Given an element R_0 of $\boldsymbol{C} \cap \boldsymbol{T}$, its associated room (R_0, a_n) is defined in a unique way (point (a)). The application considered in point (b) transforms this room into another and, by repeating the operation, defines an algorithm in the set of marked candidates. Let us stop the algorithm when a technique is reached. Given the properties mentioned in point (c), the path does not admit a loop, because a contradiction would be obtained by considering the first room into which it comes back. A final room exists and this is another element of $\boldsymbol{C} \cap \boldsymbol{T}$. Since two distinct paths have no element in common, the paths link the elements of $\boldsymbol{C} \cap \boldsymbol{T}$ two by two. Hence, the conclusion. ■

3.3 *Orientations*

From now on, the order of the figures in a number matters and, when the replacement or the insertion axiom applies, the new figure takes the place of the old. The notions of an oriented candidate and an oriented technique are first illustrated by the geometrical model. The general definitions for the abstract model and its related properties follow.

An orientation of the candidates can be introduced in the geometrical model. Let us take the origin of R^3 *inside* the polytopes represented in figure A.1. Point M_i is the extremity of the vector denoted m_i. Let the orientation of candidate $M_iM_jM_k$ be the sign of $det(m_i, m_j, m_k)$. The orientation has two properties: (*i*) a permutation of the vertices alters the orientation according to the signature of the permutation, and (*ii*) neighbouring candidates have opposite orientations because the facets are separated by the vectoral hyperplane spanned by their common edge.

As for the orientation of techniques, consider first a family of Joseph techniques (figure A.3). Let the orientation of an ordered Joseph technique $M_iM_jM_k$ be positive or negative according as (m_i, m_j, m_k) turns clockwise or counter-clockwise. The properties of the orientation are: (*i*) a permutation of the vertices alters the orientation according to its signature, and (*ii*) neighbouring techniques have the same orientation. Second, consider a family of Julius techniques (figure A.2). Let us choose an origin O on (d) and an orientation by means of a vector d. The orientation of an ordered Julius technique $M_iM_jM_k$ is defined by the sign of ε $sign\ det(m_i, m_j, m_k)$, with $\varepsilon = +1$ or $\varepsilon = -1$ according to whether $[M_iM_jM_k]$ cuts the positive or the negative part of (d). With this convention, the same two properties as for the Joseph techniques hold (distinguish according as the origin on (d) is inside or outside the tetrahedron $M_1M_2M_3M_4$).

The idea explored below is to eliminate the geometrical support and define an orientation on candidates and techniques on the sole basis of their combinatorial properties. The orientation, or 'colour', of an element of $\boldsymbol{C} \cap \boldsymbol{T}$ is obtained by comparing its orientation as a candidate with its orientation as a technique. We consider abstract numbers but, now, the figures within a number are ordered (hence the notations $\vec{C}$ and $\vec{T}$) and the order is maintained when the replacement or the insertion property applies. The signature of a permutation σ is denoted $sign(\sigma)$.

Definition 3. A family $\boldsymbol{C}_{or}$ of candidates is orientable if, when the set of figures of a candidate is globally preserved after a sequence of replacements, the signature of the permutation on the figures is the parity of the number of replacements. Then family $\boldsymbol{C}_{or}$ is oriented, i.e. there exists a function sgc: $\boldsymbol{C}_{or} \rightarrow \{-1, +1\}$ such that:

- For any permutation σ on the figures of a candidate $\vec{C}$

$$sgc(\sigma(\vec{C})) = sign(\sigma)\ sgc(\vec{C}).$$

- The function *sgc* assigns opposite values to neighbouring candidates.

For $n = 3$ and $q = 6$, the families $\boldsymbol{C}_1$ and $\boldsymbol{C}_2$ are oriented since they are represented by a geometrical model. As for $\boldsymbol{C}_3$, consider the loop 123–153–154–254–234–231 which preserves globally the figures 1, 2, 3. Since the parity of the number (five) of replacements is not that of the permutation 123–231, $\boldsymbol{C}_3$ is not orientable.

Definition 4. A family $\boldsymbol{T}_{or}$ of techniques is orientable if, when the set of figures of a technique is globally preserved after a sequence of insertions, the signature of the permutation on the figures is even. Then family $\boldsymbol{T}_{or}$ is oriented, i.e. there exists a function sgt: $\boldsymbol{T}_{or} \rightarrow \{-1, +1\}$ such that:

- For any permutation σ on the figures of a technique $\vec{T}$

$$sgt\ (\sigma(\vec{T})) = sign(\sigma)\ sgt(\vec{T}).$$

- The function *sgt* assigns the same value to neighbouring techniques.

For $n = 3$ and $q = 6$, five families of techniques have been identified. The first four families are represented as Joseph techniques and, therefore, admit an orientation. In the last family, the loop 123–125–625–624–324–321 preserves 123 globally but does not satisfy the condition on the effect of a permutation: $\boldsymbol{T}_5$ is not orientable.

Definition 5. Let $\boldsymbol{C} = \boldsymbol{C}_{or}$ and $\boldsymbol{T} = \boldsymbol{T}_{or}$ be two oriented families of candidates and techniques, respectively. For an element E of $\boldsymbol{C} \cap \boldsymbol{T}$, the product $sgc(\vec{E})\ sgt(\vec{E})$ is independent of the order of the figures in $\vec{E}$ and defines the colour, white (if $+1$) or black (if -1), of the element.

Theorem 2. $\boldsymbol{C} \cap \boldsymbol{T}$ admits as many white as black elements.

Proof. The proof of Theorem 1 shows that the elements of $\boldsymbol{C} \cap \boldsymbol{T}$ appear in pairs at the extremities of a path. The idea is to show that the extreme elements have opposite colours. We follow the proof of Theorem 1 but modify slightly the description of the procedure. After a number of steps, the situation is characterized by a pair $(\vec{C}, \vec{T})$ made of an ordered candidate and an ordered technique: $\vec{C}$ is written $\vec{C} = (x_1, \ldots, x_{n-1}, x)$ with the last element x as marked figure, and $\vec{T}$ is written $\vec{T} = (x_1, \ldots, x_{n-1}, O)$. Let x be replaced by y into $\vec{C}$ and y be inserted into $\vec{T}$. If y takes the ith position in the new technique $\vec{T}^+$, with $i \neq n$, then $x_i = z$ becomes the new marked figure. After permutation of the ith and the nth figures in $\vec{C}$, the new pair is: $\vec{C}^+ = (x_1, \ldots, y, \ldots, x_{n-1}, z)$ with z as marked figure, and $\vec{T}^+ = (x_1, \ldots, y, \ldots, O)$. We have $sgc(\vec{C}^+) = sgc(\vec{C})$ (one replacement and one transposition) and $sgt(\vec{T}^+) = sgt(\vec{T})$ (one insertion), therefore the product $sgc(\vec{C})\ sgt(\vec{T})$ is unchanged along the trajectory. However, at the very last step, y is inserted in the nth position and an element of $\boldsymbol{C} \cap \boldsymbol{T}$ is reached by means of one replacement and no transposition. The sign changes at this step, so that the colours of the two extremities are opposite. ■

Once the notion of colour has been introduced, the surprising fact is that the evenness of the solutions (Theorem 1) is not linked to the notion of orientation, since the property also holds for non-orientable families. The result is not apparent in the geometrical model which is automatically oriented.

4 Two applications

The naked Sperner lemma does not exclude that the intersection $\boldsymbol{C} \cap \boldsymbol{T}$ is void. An existence result is obtained when the problem concerns two families $\boldsymbol{C}^*$ and $\boldsymbol{T}^*$ which are extended to a family $\boldsymbol{C}$ of candidates and a family $\boldsymbol{T}$ of techniques, with an odd number of elements in $\boldsymbol{C} \cap \boldsymbol{T}$ belonging to the extension. We apply the strategy to the geometrical Sperner lemma, then to the notion of a pre-technology and an economic model.

4.1 The geometrical Sperner lemma

Let there be a simplicial decomposition of the unit simplex $S_{n-1} = A_0A_1 \ldots A_{n-1}$ in R^n. Every vertex of the decomposition receives a label in $\{0, \ldots, n-1\}$, with the restriction that a vertex belonging to a face opposed to A_i does not receive label i. In the oriented version, the vertices of a completely labelled simplex are considered in the order $0, 1, 2, \ldots, n-1$, and this orientation is compared to that of $A_0A_1 \ldots A_{n-1}$, with $det(A_0, A_1, \ldots, A_{n-1}) > 0$.

Theorem 3. (Sperner lemma). In a simplicial decomposition of the unit simplex, the number of completely labelled simplices is odd. More precisely, the number of positively oriented simplices exceeds by one those of the opposite orientation.

Proof. Let us introduce a supplementary point O' with negative components in R^n (therefore the origin belongs to the interior of $O'A_0 \ldots A_{n-1}$) and which receives label 0, as in figure A.4. The families $\boldsymbol{C}^*$ and $\boldsymbol{T}^*$ defined in Section 3.1 are completed as explained there, with O' instead of O, and become $\boldsymbol{C}$ and $\boldsymbol{T}$ (it is no longer assumed that the sub-simplex S_{n-2} opposed to A_0 is not decomposed). $\boldsymbol{T}$ is a family of Jim techniques, $\boldsymbol{C}$ a geometrical family of candidates. The oriented naked lemma applied to the extended families $\boldsymbol{C}$ and $\boldsymbol{T}$ can be stated as follows: the difference Δ_n between the number of white and black elements in $\boldsymbol{C}^* \cap \boldsymbol{T}^*$ is the opposite of the same difference, calculated on the elements belonging to the extension. By construction, these last elements are written $(O', M_1, \ldots, M_{n-1})$, where the points $M_1, \ldots, M_{n-1}$ belong to the sub-simplex S_{n-2} opposed to A_0. It follows from the three facts:

- (*i*) the trace on S_{n-2} of a simplicial decomposition of S_{n-1} is a decomposition of S_{n-2},
- (*ii*) the $(n-1)$-sets $(M_1, \ldots, M_{n-1})$ we are considering are those labelled $1, \ldots, n-1$,
- (*iii*) $sign\ det_n(O', m_1, \ldots, m_{n-1}) = -sign\ det_{n-1}(m_1, \ldots, m_{n-1})$,

that $\Delta_n = \Delta_{n-1}$. By induction on the dimension, we have $\Delta_n = \Delta_1 = 1$. ■

The Brouwer–Kakutani (1941) Theorem and the GND lemma are classical applications of the Sperner lemma.

4.2 *Pre-technology and the Colour Theorem*

Let A and B be given semi-positive $q \times n$ matrices satisfying the strict r-productivity hypothesis ($r \geq 0$)

$$\exists y_0 > 0 \qquad y_0(B - (1+r)A) \gg 0 \tag{1}$$

and l be a positive vector in R^q_{++} (the positivity assumption can be weakened, but we may alternatively assume $l_i = 1$ without restriction). The data are in general position. In the economic interpretation, the ith row of (A, l, B) is considered as a method of production, i.e. the vector b_i is produced by means of the input vector a_i and the amount l_i of labour. Let us stack n additional rows, from $i = q+1$ to $q+n$, with $a_i = (0, \ldots, 1, \ldots, 0), l_i = 0, b_i = (0, \ldots, 0)$, to the original data (the name remains (A, l, B)). The family of dominant n-sets $(i_1, \ldots, i_n)$, which are such that

$$\exists p > 0 \;\; [B - (1+r)A]p \leq l \text{ with equality for the components } i_1, \ldots, i_n \tag{2}$$

coincides with the facets $\boldsymbol{F}^*$ of the convex set $P = \{c; c \leq \Sigma^q_{i=l} \lambda_i((b_i - (1+r)a_i)/l_i)\}$, where $(\lambda_i, \ldots, \lambda_q)$ belongs to the unit simplex. P is not a polyhedron, but the replacement property holds after completion of $\boldsymbol{F}^*$ by the freak n-set made of the free disposal methods: $\boldsymbol{F} = \boldsymbol{F}^* \cup (i_{q+1}, \ldots, i_{q+n})$ (the freak n-set being associated with a zero price vector, note that it does not satisfy condition (2)).

Definition 6. Let there be a collection of methods. A pre-technology is a family $\boldsymbol{T}$ of n-sets, including the n-set made of the free disposal methods, that satisfies the insertion condition retained in Definition 2.

Theorem 4. A pre-technology admits an odd number of dominant n-sets.

Proof. The dominant n-sets in $\boldsymbol{T}$ are the n-sets belonging to $\boldsymbol{T} \cap \boldsymbol{F}$, except the freak n-set. The result follows from the naked Sperner lemma. ■

The oriented lemma applies if $\boldsymbol{T}$ itself is oriented, as in the following result. Let d be a given row-vector in R^n_+. We consider the system (3)–(5):

$$y(B - A) \geq d \qquad [p] \tag{3}$$

$$[B - (1+r)A]p \leq l \quad [y] \tag{4}$$

$$y > 0, \; p > 0 \tag{5}$$

where (y, p) are the unknowns. In the economic interpretation, relation (3) means that the given net basket d is produced, with a zero price for over-produced commodities. Relation (4) means that the operated methods yield the normal rate of profit r, while the non-operated methods do not yield more (details are given in chapter 11).

Theorem 5 (Colour Theorem). Let $(\overline{A}, \overline{B})$ refer to the active part of a solution to (3)–(5), i.e. we retain the rows corresponding to the positive components of y. Then, generically:

- Any solution $(\overline{A}, \overline{l}, \overline{B})$ to (3)–(5) is square;
- There is one more solution with $det(\overline{B} - \overline{A})$ and $det(\overline{B} - (1+r)\overline{A})$ having the same sign (white solutions) than with opposite signs (black solutions).

Proof. Since the free disposal methods are explicitly taken into account, inequality (3) can be replaced by the equivalent equality

$$y(B - A) = d \tag{6}$$

Consider the system (4)–(6). Flukes apart, at least n vectors $b_i - a_i$ are required to generate a given vector d in R^n, therefore the number of positive components of y in equality (6), including the free disposal methods, is at least equal to n. Flukes apart, any vector p satisfies at most n equalities of the type (2), therefore the positive components of y in the complementarity relationships (4) is at most equal to n. On the whole, the number of positive components of y in a solution to (4)–(6) is generally equal to n. When condition (3) or (6) is temporarily replaced by

$$\exists \overline{y} >> 0 \quad \exists \lambda \quad \overline{y}(\overline{B} - \overline{A}) = \lambda d \tag{7}$$

for some positive or negative scalar λ, it turns out that the n-sets of methods $(i_1, \ldots, i_n)$ satisfying (7) constitute a Julius family and, therefore, the strong insertion axiom holds. Moreover, the freak n-set belongs to the family since it generates $-d$: This family is a pre-technology. According to Theorem 4, there exists an odd number of solutions to (4)–(5)–(7). For any solution we have $\lambda dp = \overline{y}(\overline{B} - \overline{A})p \geq \overline{y}(B - (1+r)\overline{A})\overline{p} = \overline{y}\overline{l} > 0$, therefore λ is positive and $(\overline{y}/\lambda, \overline{p})$ is a solution to (4)–(6). In conclusion, the number of solutions to (4)–(6) is generically odd. Moreover, an orientation for the Julius techniques is defined as explained on p. 317, by $sgt(i_1, \ldots, i_n) = \varepsilon\ sign\ det(b_{i_l} - a_{i_l}, \ldots, b_{i_n} - a_{i_n})$ whereas the candidates are oriented by means of function $sgc(i_1, \ldots, i_n) = sign\ det(b_{i_1} - (1+r)a_{i_1}, \ldots, b_{i_n} - (1+r)a_{i_n})$. For the freak n-set ($b_{i_j} = 0$, a_{i_j} unit vector), the two determinants have the same sign and ε is negative (negative production of d), therefore this element is black. After its elimination, there remains an excess of one white solution. The same conclusion holds if the active part excludes the free disposal methods and the overproduced commodities. ■

A continuity argument shows that a solution exists even if the data are not in general position (Lippi's Theorem). Note that the constructive proof of Theorem 1 proceeds from a room to a neighbouring room, i.e. in its applications to Theorems 4 and 5, from a facet to a facet. The algorithm stops when a facet with an intersection with (d) is found. Condition (4) is satisfied at every step of the algorithm and the objective is to meet equality (6). As illustrated by figure 11.5, the dual 'market algorithm', for which equality (6) is always satisfied and which stops when condition (4) is met, may fail to converge.

5 An algorithm for techniques

5.1 An alternative approach

We now explore another way to tackle the same type of problems. This alternative approach is closer to (our interpretation of) Sraffa's theory of choice of technique. From a mathematical standpoint, one can start from the specific model made of (2) and (7). The profitability constraints expressed by the conditions (2) will be maintained throughout. The n-sets that satisfy (2), or dominant n-sets, are represented by the facets of a polytope and their structure is that of a family of candidates. The n-sets satisfying (7) constitute a family of Julius techniques. What happens if (7) is replaced by another condition, which however is such that the family of sets satisfying the new requirements meets the insertion axiom or some of its variants? The existence of a dominant technique is unclear since the naked Sperner lemma is not an existence result. We take the opportunity of a new start to think about the 'market algorithm' suggested by Sraffa and described in chapter 9, section 2. This algorithm goes from a technique to a neighbouring technique and stops when a candidate is reached.

From an economic standpoint, the questions studied concern the existence and uniqueness of a dominant technique and the convergence of the market algorithm. The approach is partly geometrical and partly combinatorial:

- Method $i = 1, \ldots, q$ is geometrically represented by its r-net product per worker (vector $c_i = (b_i - (1 + r)a_i)/l_i$ or point C_i). The c_is are in general position in R^n. Let $[H] = [C_{i_1}, \ldots, C_{i_n}]$ denote the affine hyperplane associated with the n-set $I = (i_1, \ldots, i_n)$ (notation [...] is used

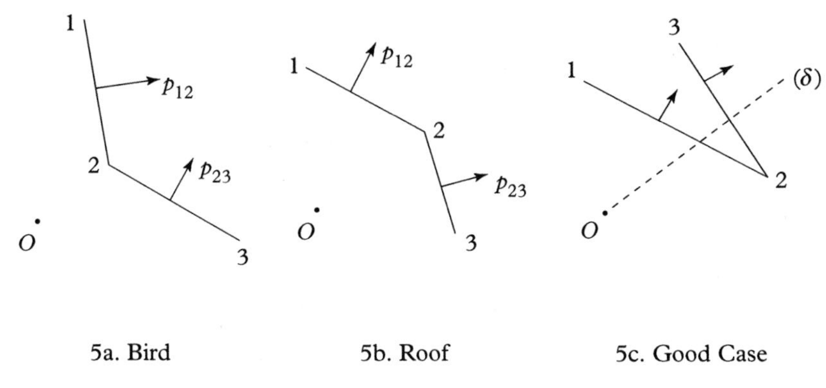

Figure A.5 Comparison of neighbouring n-sets (r-space)

for hyperplanes and (. . .) for n-sets). The associated price vector p is defined by the n equalities $c_i p = 1$, $i \in I$: it is uniquely defined and orthogonal to $[H]$ (since free disposal is no longer assumed, condition $p > 0$ is ignored). Method j yields extra profits at these prices if C_j is located above $[H]$, i.e. in the half-space not containing the origin. A dominant n-set is such that no method yields extra profit: it is geometrically represented by a facet of the convex hull of the C_ks. This configuration is hopefully reached at the last step of the market algorithm.

- The combinatorial aspects come from the definition of the family of techniques. A family of techniques is now defined by an insertion condition and a consistency condition, with some variants according to the problem studied (though the same term 'technique' is used everywhere). The insertion condition is a variant of the property assumed in Definition 2. The consistency condition ensures a link between the combinatorial and the geometrical aspects. For $n = 2$ goods, assume that method 3 can be inserted in place of method 1 in the 2-set (1, 2). Figure A.5 represents the r-space with three possible configurations for the 'old' n-set (1, 2) and 'new' n-set (2, 3).

We compare the profitability of the 2-sets (1, 2) and (2, 3):

- In the bird case 5a, method 3 yields extra profits at prices p_{12} but, after a switch to the new technique (2, 3), the old method 1 also yields extra profits at prices p_{23}. The market algorithm oscillates perpetually between two techniques. The bird configuration must be eliminated for the existence and convergence problem.
- In the roof case 5b, techniques (2, 1) and (2, 3) are simultaneously dominant. This configuration must be eliminated for the uniqueness problem.

- Case 5*c* is the only one in which the strong consistency property holds: method 3 yields extra profits at prices p_{12} and method 1 pays extra costs at prices p_{23}, so that 3 is unambiguously preferred to 1. This configuration is easily characterized:

Lemma 1 (strong consistency). Let I and J be neighbouring n-sets in R^n, which differ by one vector c_n and c_n' (points C_n and C_n'). The strong consistency property means that C_n' is above the affine hyperplane $[I]$ spanned by the points of I if and only if C_n is below the affine hyperplane $[J]$ spanned by the points of J. It holds if and only if one of the equivalent properties is met:

(*i*) $det(c_i, i \in I)$ and $det(c_j, j \in J)$ have the same sign;

(*ii*) The c_is $(i \in I)$ and the c_js $(j \in J)$ generate positively some common vector.

Proof. For given vectors $(c_1, \ldots, c_n)$, the set of vectors c_n' satisfying condition (*i*) is the half-space delimited by the linear hyperplane $[c_1, \ldots, c_{n-1}]$ and containing c_n. By the separation theorem between convex cones, the set of vectors c_n' which do not satisfy condition (*ii*) is the opposite half-space, therefore conditions (*i*) and (*ii*) are equivalent. Let p and p' be the price vectors in terms of wage ($w = 1$) associated with I and J, i.e. $c_1p = c_2p = \ldots = c_np = 1 = c_1p' = c_2p' = \ldots = c_n'p'$. One of the n-sets is unambiguously preferred to the other if either ($c_n'p > 1$ and $c_np' < 1$) or ($c_n'p < 1$ and $c_np' > 1$) holds, i.e. if $c_n'p - 1$ and $c_np' - 1$ have opposite signs. Consider the decomposition $c_n' = \sum_{i \in I} \gamma_i c_i$. Since $c_n'p - 1 = \sum_i \gamma_i - 1$ and $c_np' - 1 = \gamma_n^{-1}(c_n' - \sum_{i \neq n} \gamma_i c_i)p' - 1 = \gamma_n^{-1}(1 - \sum_{i \neq n} \gamma_i) - 1 = \gamma_n^{-1}(1 - \sum_{i \in I} \gamma_i)$, the strong consistency condition is written $\gamma_n > 0$. This is equivalent to $det(c_1, c_2, \ldots, c_n')/det(c_1, c_2, \ldots, c_n) = \gamma_n > 0$, therefore to condition (*i*). ■

5.2 *Quasi-technology and existence*

Once a geometrical interpretation has been given, the economic meaning of the C_is can be forgotten and the problem stated in purely geometrical terms. The notion of a dominant n-set refers to that of a facet (Definition 7). The family of techniques is defined by an insertion condition, which is combinatorial, and a non-bird property which is geometrical but weaker than the strong consistency property (Definition 8):

Definition 7. Let there be q points in R^n ($q \geq n$). The n-set $I = (C_{i_1}, \ldots, C_{i_n})$ is called dominant if no point C_i ($i = 1, \ldots, q$) is above the affine hyperplane $[I]$.

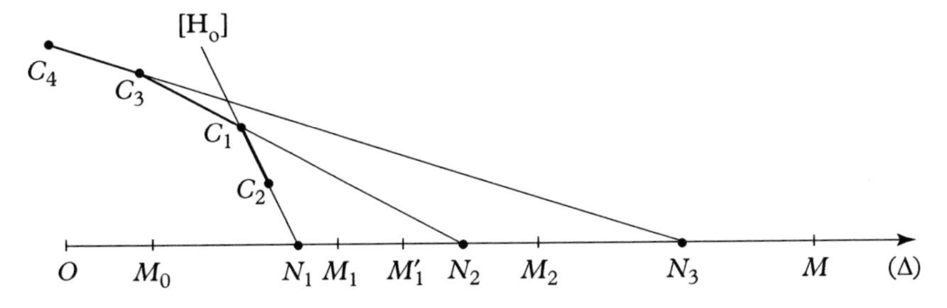

Figure A.6 An argument of kinetic geometry

Definition 8. A *quasi-technology* is a non-empty family $\boldsymbol{T}$ of n-sets, called techniques, satisfying the property: given a technique T_1, any point M_2 above the affine hyperplane $[T_1]$ can be substituted for some point M_1 in T_1 in such a way that: (*i*) (insertion property) the new n-set T_2 belongs to $\boldsymbol{T}$, and (*ii*) (non-bird property) M_1 is below hyperplane $[T_2]$.

Definition 8 eliminates the bird case. Compared with Definition 2, it is no longer assumed that the insertion is unique. We intend to prove the existence of a dominant technique and the convergence of the market algorithm for quasi-technologies. The property retained in Definition 8 being local since it concerns neighbouring n-sets, it is not clear that it suffices to ensure global convergence.

Theorem 6 (existence). A quasi-technology admits one dominant technique at least.

Proof. The proof is by induction on the number q ($q \geq n$) of points. (Figure A.6 illustrates the construction for $n = 2$.) We take the result for q points denoted C_i: let $T_0 = (C_1, \ldots, C_n)$ be a then dominant technique. An additional point M is now introduced. The idea of the proof is to replace M by a moving point μ which 'grows' from O to M along the half-line (Δ) and takes the successive positions $M_0, M_1, \ldots, M_{\mathcal{J}} = M$ on (Δ). By definition, a j-technique is an n-set built with points $C_1, \ldots, C_q$ and M_j and which becomes a technique once M_j is replaced by M, and a j-technique is dominant if it is a facet of the convex hull of $O, C_1, \ldots, C_q, M_j$. We intend to show the existence of a dominant j-technique by induction on j from $j = 0$ to $j = \mathcal{J}$. If the induction works, the result holds for $M_{\mathcal{J}} = M$ and the strategy succeeds in establishing the existence of a dominant technique for $q + 1$ methods. The point M_j ($j = 0, \ldots, \mathcal{J}$) is located in the jth cell defined below:

(i) *The 0-cell.* By the induction hypothesis on q, there exists a dominant technique $T_0 = (C_1, \ldots, C_n)$ before the introduction of M. Consider the intersection N_1 of (Δ) with $[H_0] = [C_1, \ldots, C_n]$. The 0-cell is the segment ON_1 (if several dominant techniques coexist, choose N_1 at the farthest intersection with (Δ); if (Δ) is entirely below the hyperplane, consider that N_1 is at infinity on (Δ)). Then, for any point M_0 in the 0-cell, $(C_1, \ldots, C_n)$ is a dominant 0-technique. The inequalities $c_i p_0 \leq 1$ $(i = 1, \ldots, q)$ and $m_0 p_0 < 1$ hold, with n equalities.

(ii) *The 1-cell.* Let μ peep out of the 0-cell and be located slightly after N_1 on (Δ) (position $\mu = M_1$ in figure A.6). The sequence of arguments is:

(a) M_1 is above $[H_0]$, therefore so is M.

(b) By the insertion and the non-bird properties, M can be inserted into $(C_1, \ldots, C_n)$ – say, M replaces the old point C_n–, in such a way that $(C_1, \ldots, C_{n-1}, M)$ is a technique and C_n is below $[C_1, \ldots, C_{n-1}, M]$.

(c) Since C_n is below $[C_1, \ldots, C_{n-1}, M]$ and on $[C_1, \ldots, C_{n-1}, N_1]$, it is below $[C_1, \ldots, C_{n-1}, M_1]$ since $M_1 \in N_1 M$ ('boundary argument').

(d) The partial conclusion is: $(C_1, \ldots, C_{n-1}, M_1)$ is a 1-technique and C_n is below its associated hyperplane: if p_1 denotes the associated vector, we have

$$c_n p_1 < 1. \tag{8}$$

(e) Consider now the points C_i $(i \neq 1, \ldots, n)$. Since they are strictly below $[C_1 \ldots C_{n-1}, N_1]$, they remain below $[C_1, \ldots, C_{n-1}, M_1]$ when M_1 is close enough to N_1:

$$m_1 p_1 = c_1 p_1 = \ldots = c_{n-1} p_1 = 1 > c_i p_1 (i \neq 1, \ldots, n). \tag{9}$$

(f) Let us be more precise on the domain of validity of (8) and (9). Inequality (8) holds for any point μ located after N_1 on (Δ). As for (9), the $(n-1)$-set $(C_1, \ldots, C_{n-1})$ is common to two facets, one of them being $(C_1, \ldots, C_{n-1}, C_n)$. Let the other be denoted $(C_1, \ldots, C_{n-1}, C_{n+1})$, and N_2 be the intersection of $[C_1, \ldots, C_{n-1}, C_{n+1}]$ with (Δ) (consider that N_2 is at infinity on (Δ) if there is no intersection). By definition, the 1-cell is the segment $N_1 N_2$ on (Δ). For a point μ in the 1-cell, let p be the vector such that $\mu p = \ldots = c_{n-1} p = 1$. The inequalities $c_i p < 1$ $(i \neq 1, \ldots, n)$, which hold for $\mu = M_1$ close enough to N_1, continue to hold as long as one of them is transformed into an equality, that occurs for $\mu = N_1$ and $\mu = N_2$. Therefore the inequalities (9) hold for any μ in the 1-cell. (Since M_1 is located after N_1 and belongs to the 1-cell, N_2 is located after N_1.)

(g) The conclusion is that, for any point M_1 in the 1-cell N_1N_2, $(C_1, \ldots, C_{n-1}, M_1)$ is a dominant 1-technique.

(*iii*) *Next cells.* Let μ move out of the 1-cell and reach position M_2 slightly after N_2. The same sequence of arguments as for the 1-cell applies, with minor modifications. Point C_{n+1} is above $[C_1, \ldots, C_{n-1}, M_2]$ and, therefore, above $[C_1, \ldots, C_{n-1}, M]$ by a boundary argument. By the insertion axiom, C_{n+1} can be inserted into technique $(C_1, \ldots, C_{n-1}, M)$. It does not take the place of M (otherwise a dominant technique on the q initial methods would be obtained and a contradiction would appear with the definition of N_1). Let it replace C_{n-1}. $(C_1, \ldots, C_{n-2}, C_{n+1})$ is an $(n-1)$-set common to two facets, one of them being $(C_1, \ldots, C_{n-2}, C_{n-1}, C_{n+1})$. Let the other be $(C_1, \ldots, C_{n-2}, C_{n+1}, C_{n+2})$. By definition, N_3 is the intersection of $[C_1, \ldots, C_{n-2}, C_{n+1}, C_{n+2}]$ with (Δ) and the 2-cell is the segment N_2N_3 on (Δ). The same arguments as above show that $(C_1, \ldots, C_{n-2}, C_{n+1}, M_2)$ is a dominant 2-technique for any M_2 in the 2-cell. By induction, the existence of a dominant j-technique is established for any j. Since there are finitely many cells, the actual position M on (Δ) is reached for $j = \mathcal{J}$ and the existence of a dominant technique is established for $q + 1$ methods. Hence, the result. ■

Notation $T_i \rightarrow T_j$ (T_j is preferred to T_i) means that T_i and T_j are neighbouring techniques which meet the strong consistency condition (figure A.5c), with point M_j above $[T_i]$ and M_i below $[T_j]$. We now study the convergence of the market algorithm.

Theorem 7 (convergence). Given an arbitrary technique T_0 in a quasi-technology $\boldsymbol{T}$, there exists a sequence $T_0 \rightarrow T_1 \rightarrow \ldots \rightarrow T_r$ of successively preferred neighbouring techniques such that the final technique T_r is dominant.

Proof. Let $\boldsymbol{T}' \subset \boldsymbol{T}$ be the subset of techniques for which the conclusion of Theorem 7 does not hold. Assume $T_0 \in \boldsymbol{T}' \neq \emptyset$. For M above $[T_0]$, a technique T_1 obtained by inserting M into T_0 also belongs to $\boldsymbol{T}'$ (if not, there would exist a chain $T_1 \rightarrow \ldots \rightarrow T_r$, hence a chain $T_0 \rightarrow T_1 \rightarrow \ldots \rightarrow T_r$ with T_r dominant, therefore $T_0 \notin \boldsymbol{T}'$). Therefore $\boldsymbol{T}'$ is a quasi-technology and, by Theorem 6, admits a dominant technique T_h. A contradiction is obtained for T_h, whether T_h is dominant in $\boldsymbol{T}$ or not: in the second case, there exists a preferred neighbouring technique $T_{h+1} \notin \boldsymbol{T}'$, and a chain $T_h \rightarrow T_{h+1} \rightarrow \ldots \rightarrow T_r$ is built. Therefore $\boldsymbol{T}' = \emptyset$. ■

Note that the existence result has been established first and that convergence is obtained as a consequence of existence. Moreover, Theorem 7 is compatible with the coexistence of a cycle $T_0 \to T_1 \to \ldots \to T_5 \to T_0 \to \ldots$ as exemplified in chapter 19, section 7.

5.3 *Pseudo-technology and uniqueness*

For uniqueness results the roof case must be eliminated, hence the version of the insertion condition retained below:

Definition 9. A *pseudo-technology* is a family $\boldsymbol{T}$ of n-sets, called techniques, satisfying the property: given a technique $T_1 \in \boldsymbol{T}$ and a point C_2 below $[T_1]$, C_2 can be substituted for some C_1 in T_1 in such a way that (*i*) (insertion) the new n-set T_2 belongs to $\boldsymbol{T}$, and (*ii*) (non-roof) C_1 is above $[T_2]$.

Because of the symmetry between Definitions 8 and 9 and the existence results for quasi-technologies, a uniqueness result (up to indifference between techniques associated with the same price vector) is expected for pseudo-technologies. A counter-example is illustrated by figure A.7, which represents five points C_i in R^3 ($n = 3$, $q = 5$). When the family of techniques is $\boldsymbol{T} = \{123, 234, 345, 451, 512\}$, the insertion property holds. Moreover, in figure A.7, any two neighbouring techniques have a non-roof configuration because they have a common intersection. Therefore, $\boldsymbol{T}$ is a pseudo-technology. However, techniques $C_5C_1C_2$ and $C_3C_4C_5$ are both dominant. An additional property must be introduced to ensure uniqueness.

Definition 10. A point C_i is *non-compulsory* if it does not belong to all techniques. A pseudo-technology is *soft* if, given a non-compulsory point C_i in technique $T = (C_{-i}, C_i)$, there exists a point C_j ($C_j \neq C_i$) such that T and the neighbouring n-set (C_{-i}, C_j) are comparable, i.e. the strong consistency property holds. (It is not required that (C_{-i}, C_j) is a technique.)

The family $\boldsymbol{T}$ is not soft: in figure A.7, consider method 2 in the technique $T = (123)$; the strong consistency property does not hold when T is compared with either (143) or (153).

Theorem 8 (uniqueness). A soft pseudo-technology admits one dominant technique (up to indifference) at most.

Proof. The proof is by induction on the number q of points and is symmetrical to that of Theorem 6. Let us admit the result for q points. For $q + 1$

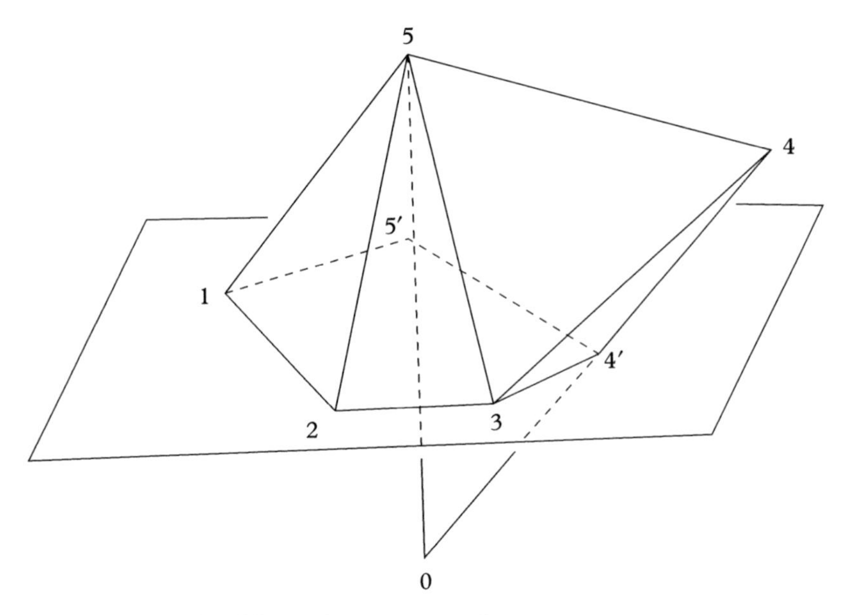

Figure A.7 Non-uniqueness example

points, assume the existence of two dominant techniques $T = (C_1, \ldots, C_{n-1}, M)$ and $\overline{T}$, which differ at least by one non-compulsory point M ($M \notin \overline{T}$). As in the proof of Theorem 6, let M vary along a half-line (Δ) but, this time, M takes successive positions $M_J, \ldots, M_j, M_{j-1}, \ldots$ closer to the origin. The notion of dominant j-technique is the same as in the proof of Theorem 6. A dominant j-technique $T_j = (C'_1, \ldots, C'_{n-1}, M_j)$ gives birth to a dominant $(j-1)$-technique as follows: after a jump from M_j to M_{j-1}, a point C'_n which was below $[T_j]$ is now above $[C'_1, \ldots, C'_{n-1}, M_{j-1}]$. By a boundary argument, C'_n is below $[C'_1, \ldots, C'_{n-1}, M]$ and, by the insertion axiom, it can be inserted into the technique $(C'_1, \ldots, C'_{n-1}, M)$. When M is replaced by M_{j-1}, a $(j-1)$-technique T_{j-1} is obtained. Similar arguments as in the proof of Theorem 6 show that T_{j-1} is dominant on $\{C_1, \ldots, C_q, M_{j-1}\}$.

Assume that, at some stage of the procedure, C'_n is substituted for M_j. Then a dominant technique $(C'_1, \ldots, C'_{n-1}, C'_n)$ on the q points $\{C_1, \ldots, C_q\}$ is obtained. By the induction hypothesis on uniqueness for q methods, this technique coincides with $\overline{T}$. At the previous stage, C'_n was below the j-dominant hyperplane $[C'_1, \ldots, C'_{n-1}, M_j]$, therefore below $[C'_1, \ldots, C'_{n-1}, M]$ by a boundary argument. By the non-roof axiom, M is above $[\overline{T}]$. A contradiction is obtained with the hypothesis that $\overline{T}$ is a dominant technique on the $q + 1$ points.

Therefore, a dominant 0-technique $T_0' = (C_1', \ldots, C_{n-1}', M_0)$ is finally reached, with M_0 as close as desired to the origin (the 0-cell as defined in the proof of Theorem 6 may be too large, but its definition can be easily adapted to the following argument). By the softness axiom, point M in technique $(C_1', \ldots, C_{n-1}', M)$ can be replaced by some point C_j in such a way these two n-sets have the strong consistency property. The determinant criterion (Lemma 1) shows that the n-sets $(C_1', \ldots, C_{n-1}', M_0)$ and $(C_1', \ldots, C_{n-1}', C_j)$ are also comparable. As T_0' is a dominant 0-technique, C_j is below $[T_0']$. Strong consistency implies that M_0 is above $[C_1', \ldots, C_{n-1}', C_j]$, which is not the case when M_0 is very close to the origin. A contradiction is obtained: the induction hypothesis on the number of methods works. Hence, the uniqueness result. ■

Finally, let us draw attention to an implicit restriction imposed by the definition of a pseudo-technology. Definition 9 assumes that *any* point below $[T]$ can be inserted into a given technique T. Consider a point M *foreign* to T, i.e. the vector m is negatively generated by the vectors of T. Then, as a geometrical representation shows, any n-set obtained after insertion of M violates the non-roof condition with T. Therefore, Definition 9 requires that no method is foreign to a technique. A sufficient condition is that all points are located in the same half-space. Otherwise, the definition of the insertion property and the results must be adapted.

5.4 *Technology*

Definition 11. A *technology* is a family $\boldsymbol{T}$ of n-sets, called techniques, satisfying the property: given a technique $T_1 \in \boldsymbol{T}$ and a point C_2, C_2 can be substituted for some C_1 in T_1 in such a way that: (*i*) (insertion) the new n-set T_2 belongs to $\boldsymbol{T}$; (*ii*) (strong consistency) T_1 and T_2 are comparable.

Theorem 9. In a technology, there is a unique way to insert a point into a technique.

Proof. If a point M can replace C_1 as well as C_2, the three determinants $det(c_1, c_2, \ldots, c_n)$, $det(m, c_2, \ldots, c_n)$ and $det(c_1, m, \ldots, c_n)$ have the same sign by Lemma 1. Then the neighbouring techniques $(M, C_2, C_3, \ldots, C_n)$ and $(M, C_1, C_3, \ldots, C_n)$ have determinants of opposite signs, and the consistency condition is violated. ■

Definition 12. A technology is *robust* if any two techniques $T = (C_i, i \in I)$ and $T' = (C_j, j \in \mathcal{J})$ can positively generate some common vector:

$$\exists \alpha \gg 0 \quad \exists \beta \gg 0 \quad \sum_{i \in I} \alpha_i c_i = \sum_{j \in \mathcal{J}} \beta_j c_j.$$

Since two facets have no interior common point, two robust techniques cannot be simultaneously dominant: robustness implies uniqueness. What are the relationships between robustness and softness? An apparent difference is that the softness axiom is 'local' (it compares neighbouring n-sets) whereas the robustness axiom is global. Theorem 10 states that softness is the local version of robustness.

Theorem 10. For technologies, robustness and softness are equivalent properties.

Proof. Let us first assume that the technology is robust. We isolate a non-compulsory point C_i in $T = (C_1, \ldots, C_i, \ldots, C_n)$. The vectoral hyperplane spanned by $\{c_1, \ldots, c_{i-1}, c_{i+1} \ldots, c_n\}$ separates R^n into two half-spaces. If all points C_j ($C_j \neq C_i$) were located in the half-space not containing C_i, the robustness hypothesis would be violated. Therefore, there exists some C_j in the same half-space as C_i, and the softness property is met.

Assume now that the technology is soft. Once a technology $\boldsymbol{T}$ is given on $\{c_1, \ldots, c_q\}$, a technology $\boldsymbol{T}'$ is defined on $\{\lambda_1 c_1, \ldots, \lambda_q c_q\}$ for any $\lambda_i > 0$ by the condition: $(c_i, i \in I) \in \boldsymbol{T} \Leftrightarrow (\lambda_i c_i, i \in I) \in \boldsymbol{T}'$. Softness and robustness are preserved by this operation. Therefore the length of vectors c_i can be modified at will.

Let $(C_1, \ldots, C_r, C_{r+1}, \ldots, C_n)$ and $(C_1, \ldots, C_r, \overline{C}_{r+1}, \ldots, \overline{C}_n)$ be two techniques in $\boldsymbol{T}$ which have r common points ($r \leq n - 1$). If they have no common positive linear combination (non-robustness), the two positive cones spanned respectively by their n vectors are separated by a vectoral hyperplane $xp = 0$ containing $c_1, \ldots, c_r$. We may assume, by modifying the lengths of the vectors, that $||c_1|| = \ldots = ||c_r|| = L$, $c_{r+1}p = \ldots = c_n p = 1$, $\bar{c}_{r+1}p = \ldots = \bar{c}_n p = -1$ and $|c_i p| < 1$ for all other vectors. If $r = 0$, these two techniques are dominant; if $r \geq 1$, this is also the case if L is great enough. A contradiction is obtained with Theorem 8. Therefore, softness implies robustness. ■

6 Application and comparisons

Let us give a simple algebraic application of Theorem 10. By definition, a Stiemke matrix is a square matrix T which transforms some positive row vector into a positive row vector.

Definition 13. A family $\boldsymbol{T}$ of square regular matrices is called a Stiemke family if $T_1 T_2^{-1}$ is a Stiemke matrix for any pair of matrices in $\boldsymbol{T}$.

Theorem 11. Let $\{c_1, \ldots, c_q\}$ be q vectors in R^n $(q \geq n)$ such that any n vectors are linearly independent. Let there be a family $\boldsymbol{T}$ of square matrices whose n rows are extracted from $\{c_1, \ldots, c_q\}$ and such that:

- For any matrix $T_1 \in \boldsymbol{T}$ and any c_i, there exists a matrix T_2 in $\boldsymbol{T}$ obtained by substituting c_i for some row of T_1, without changing the sign of the determinant.
- Let c be a vector that does not belong to all matrices in $\boldsymbol{T}$. When c belongs to a matrix in $\boldsymbol{T}$, it is possible to substitute some c_j $(c_j \neq c)$ for it without changing the sign of the determinant.

Then $\boldsymbol{T}$ is a Stiemke family of matrices.

Proof. The assumptions imply that $\boldsymbol{T}$ is a soft technology (Definitions 10 and 11). According to Theorem 11, it is robust. Robustness means that, for any pair (T_1, T_2) of matrices, there exists positive row vectors α and β such that $\alpha T_1 = \beta T_2$, hence the Stiemke property. ■

Corollary. A square matrix M whose all principal minors are positive is a Stiemke matrix.

Proof. Consider the family $\boldsymbol{T}$ of square matrices in which the ith row is either the ith row of M or that of the identity matrix. Since the condition on the principal minors implies that $\boldsymbol{T}$ satisfies the assumptions of Theorem 11, the result follows by applying the theorem to $T_1 = M$ and $T_2 = I$. ■

A comparison of the results relative to the Sperner lemma (sections 2, 3 and 4) and the market algorithm (section 5) shows a number of differences and similarities:

- Uniqueness of insertion is required in the Sperner lemma in order to obtain a well-defined path with a reversibility property to which the house argument applies.
- The non-bird property required for the convergence of the market algorithm has no equivalent in the Sperner-type results.
- Figure A.7 suggests that the oddity results are specific to a certain type of problem.
- The existence proof for quasi-technologies is close to that of the Sperner Lemma: it consists in finding a corridor leading from an old candidate (the dominant technique before the introduction of the new point) to a dominant candidate (after the introduction of the new point). The

corridor is a sequence of neighbouring candidates, the last one being a technique.

One may wonder if the construction presented in section 5 can be rid of its geometrical medium and stated in purely combinatorial terms for adequately chosen axioms.

7 Sources

Von Neumann (1937) generalized the Brouwer Theorem and introduced the use of fixed-point theorems in economics. Arrow and Debreu (1954) adapted this innovation to solve the eighty-year-old problem of the existence of a general equilibrium. But the Brouwer–Kakutani fixed-point theorem was then considered as a non-constructive result. Scarf (1960) exhibited a simple example for which the tâtonnement process does not converge. Lemke and Howson (1964) and Lemke (1965) defined an algorithm that converges towards the solution of a bimatrix game. Scarf (1967) reinterpreted the procedure as the construction of a fixed point or, in its economic application, of an equilibrium. The finding, illustrated by the constructive proof of the geometrical Sperner lemma, initiated a host of researches at the border between economics and applied mathematics. Gould and Tolle (1974), Todd (1974) and Tuy (1979) aimed at unifying them by defining a more abstract framework that, in its purest form, we now identify with the naked Sperner lemma.

The starting point of our own work is Sraffa's theory of choice of technique (chapter 19). Its steps have been: definition and properties of the Jim techniques (Bidard 1984b), combinatorial definition of techniques (Bidard 1984c), existence and uniqueness results on technologies (Bidard 1990a). These results correspond to the content of section 5, which mixes combinatorial and geometrical considerations. The purely combinatorial approach developed in sections 2 and 3 is posterior: the hand-crafted method used by Bidard and Erreygers (1998a) to count the equilibria of the Lippi model drew attention on the replacement property of the facets of a polytope. The naked Sperner lemma came from an endeavour to simplify and extend that construction. The axioms improve upon Bidard (1998c): they renounce the existence result and interpret the Sperner lemma as an evenness property.

References

BOOKS AND ARTICLES

Abraham-Frois, G. and Berrebi, E. (1980), *Rentes, rareté, surprofits* (Paris, Economica)

Agata, A. d' (1983), The Existence and Unicity of Cost-Minimizing Systems in Intensive Rent Theory, *Metroeconomica*, 35, 147–58.

Åkerman, J. G. (1923–4), *Realkapital und Kapitalzins*, 2 vols. (Stockholm, Centraltryckeriet)

Allais, M. (1947), *Economie et intérêt* (Paris, Imprimerie Nationale)

Anderson, J. (1777 [1968]), *An Inquiry into the Nature of the Corn Laws* (Edinburgh, C. Elliot); reprint (1968) (New York, A. M. Kelley)

Arena, R. *et al.* (1982), *Etudes d'economie classique et néo-ricardienne* (Grenoble, Presses Universitaires de France)

Arrow, K. J. (1951), Alternative Proof of the Substitution Theorem for Leontief Models in the General Case, in Koopmans (ed.) (1951a), 155–64

(1983), *Collected Papers* (Oxford, Blackwell)

Arrow, K. J. and Debreu, G. (1954), Existence of an Equilibrium for a Competitive Economy, *Econometrica*, 22, 265–90

Arrow, K. J. and Hahn, F. H. (1971), *General Competitive Analysis* (San Francisco, Holden-Day)

Arrow, K. J. and Intriligator, M. D. (eds.) (1981–6), *Handbook of Mathematical Economics*, 3 vols. (Amsterdam, North-Holland)

Arrow, K. J. and Levhari D. (1969), Uniqueness of the Internal Rate of Return with Variable Life of Investment, *Economic Journal*, 79, 560–66

Atsumi, H. (1991), On the Rate of Interest in a Neo-Austrian Theory of Capital, in McKenzie and Zamagni (eds.) (1991), 393–409

Autume, A. d' (1982), L'introduction du temps dans la théorie de l'équilibre général, *Cahiers d'Economie Politique*, 7, 93–127

(1988), La production jointe: le point de vue de la théorie de l'équilibre général, *Revue Economique*, 39, 325–47

Baldone, S. (1974), II capitale fisso nello schema teorico di Piero Sraffa, *Studi Economici*, 29, 45–106; trans. as Fixed Capital in Sraffa's Theoretical Scheme, in Pasinetti (1980), 88–137

Bellino, E. (1993), Continuous Switching of Techniques in Linear Production Models, *The Manchester School*, 61, 185–201

Bellman, R. E. (1957), *Dynamic Programming* (Princeton, Princeton University Press)
Benveniste, L. (1976), Two Notes on the Malinvaud Condition for Efficiency of Infinite Horizon Programs, *Journal of Economic Theory*, 12, 338–46
Benveniste, L. and Gale, D. (1975), An Extension of Cass' Characterization of Infinite Efficient Production Programs, *Journal of Economic Theory*, 10, 229–38
Bewley, T. F. (1972), Existence of Equilibria in Economies with Infinitely Many Commodities, *Journal of Economic Theory*, 4, 514–40
(1982), An Integration of Equilibrium Theory and Turnpike Theory, *Journal of Mathematical Economics*, 10, 233–67
Bharadwaj, K. (1970), On the Maximum Number of Switches between Two Production Systems, *Schweizerische Zeitschrift für Volkswirtschaft und Statistik*, 106, 409–29
Bharadwaj, K. and Schefold, B. (eds.) (1990), *Essays on Piero Sraffa* (London, Unwin Hyman)
Bidard, C. (1978), The Extended Perron–Frobenius Theorem and Joint Production, University of Lyon II, mimeo
(1981), Travail et salaire chez Sraffa, *Revue Economique*, 33, 448–67
(ed.) (1984a), *La production jointe. Nouveaux débats* (Paris, Economica)
(1984b), Choix techniques en production jointe, in Bidard (ed.) (1984a), 186–207
(1984c), Jules et Jim, in Bidard (ed.) (1984a), 208–10
(1984d), Irreducibility, Indecomposability and Imprimitivity of Endomorphisms, University of Paris X-Nanterre, mimeo
(1986a), Is von Neumann Square?, *Journal of Economics*, 46, 407–19
(1986b), The Maximum Rate of Profit in Joint Production, *Metroeconomica*, 38, 53–66
(ed.) (1987), *La rente* (Paris, Economica)
(1988), The Falling Rate of Profit and Joint Production, *Cambridge Journal of Economics*, 12, 355–60
(1989), Equilibrium with a Qualitative Walras' Law, *Journal of Economic Theory*, 47, 203–5
(1990a), An Algorithmic Theory of the Choice of Techniques, *Econometrica*, 58, 839–59
(1990b), From Arrow–Debreu to Sraffa, *Political Economy, Studies in the Surplus Approach*, 6, 125–38
(1991), *Prix, reproduction, rareté* (Paris, Dunod)
(1996), All-Engaging Systems, *Economic Systems Research*, 8, 323–40
(1997a), Fixed Capital and 'Finished' Goods: Critique of a Concept, *Studi Economici*, 61, 5–10
(1997b), Pure Joint Production, *Cambridge Journal of Economics*, 21, 685–701
(1998a), The Maximum Rate of Profit in a Fixed Capital Model, *Studi Economici*, 63, 5–14
(1998b), Laws on Long-Term Prices, *The Manchester School*, 66, 453–65
(1998c), Le lemme de Sperner nu, *Recherche Opérationnelle*, 32, 193–210

(1999a), Fixed Capital and Internal Rate of Return, *Journal of Mathematical Economics*, 31, 523–41

(1999b), Linear Programming and the von Neumann Model, *Metroeconomica*, 51, 122–25

(1999c), Competition without Far Sight is Nothing, University of Paris X-Nanterre, mimeo.

(2000), Wicksell and Douglas on Distribution and Marginal Productivity, in Kurz (ed.) (2000), 315–22

(2003), Revealed Intertemporal Inefficiency, University of Paris X-Nanterre, mimeo

Bidard, C. and Ehrbar, H. (1996), Relative Prices in the Classical Theory: Facts and Figures, Universities of Paris X-Nanterre and Salt Lake City, mimeo

Bidard, C. and Erreygers G. (1998a), The Number and Type of Long-Term Equilibria, *Journal of Economics*, 67, 181–205

(1998b), The Adjustment Property, *Economic Systems Research*, 10, 3–17

(1998c), Sraffa and Leontief on Joint Production, *Review of Political Economy*, 10, 427–46

(1999), The Concept of a Sector, Universities of Paris X-Nanterre and Antwerp, mimeo

(2001a), The Corn–Guano Model, *Metroeconomica*, 52, 243–53

(2001b), Further Reflections on the Corn–Guano Model, *Metroeconomica*, 52, 254–67

Bidard, C. and Franke, R. (1987a), On the Existence of Long-Term Equilibria in the Two-Class Pasinetti–Morishima Model, *Ricerche Economiche*, 41, 3–21

(1987b), On Walras' Model of General Equilibrium: A Simpler Way to Demonstrate Existence, *Journal of Economics*, 47, 315–19

Bidard, C., Hendaoui, A. and Poulon, F. (eds.) (1998), *Keynes et Sraffa. Recherches de passerelles* (Paris, Cujas)

Bidard, C. and Hosoda, E. (1987), On Consumption Baskets in a Generalized von Neumann Model, *International Economic Review*, 28, 509–19

Bidard, C. and Klimovsky, E. (2004), Switches and Fake Switches in Methods of Production, *Cambridge Journal of Economics*, 28 (1), 89–97

Bidard, C. and Krause, U. (1996), A Monotonicity Law for Relative Prices, *Economic Theory*, 7, 51–6

Bidard, C. and Salvadori, N. (1995), Relationships between Prices and Techniques, *European Journal of Political Economy*, 11, 379–89

(1998), Solutions to Linear Equations Depending on a Parameter, *Rivista di Matematica per la Scienze Economiche e Sociale*, 19, 103–12

Bidard, C. and Schatteman, T. (2001), The Spectrum of Random Matrices, *Economic Systems Research*, 13, 289–98

Bidard, C. and Steedman, I. (1996), Monotonic Movements of Price Vectors, *Economic Issues*, 1, 41–4 (and: Editor's corrections in *Economic Issues*, 2, 85–6)

(2001), Monotone Price Movements, *International Journal of Applied Economics and Econometrics*, 9 (2), 229–40

Bidard, C. and Woods, J. E. (1989), Taxes, Lands and Non-Basics in Joint Production, *Oxford Economic Papers*, 41, 802–12

Bidard, C. and Zerner, M. (1990), Positivité en théorie spectrale relative, *Comptes rendus de l'Académie des Sciences*, 310, série *I*, 709–12

(1991), The Perron–Frobenius Theorem in Relative Spectral Theory, *Mathematische Annalen*, 289, 451–64

Böhm-Bawerk, E. von (1889 [1959]), *Kapital und Kapitalzins* (Innsbruck, Wagner); 4th edn. trans. as *Capital and Interest*, 2 vols., 1959 (South Holland, Illinois, Libertarian Press)

(1986 [1949]), Zum Abschluss des Marxschen System, in H. E. Boenig (ed.) *Staatwissenschaftliche Arbeiten: Festgaben für Karl Knies* (Berlin); trans. as Karl Marx and the Close of his System, in Sweezy (ed.) (1949), 3–118

Bortkiewicz, L. von (1906–7 [1952]), Wertrechnung und Preisrechnung im Marxschen System, *Archiv für Sozialwissenschaft und Sozialpolitik*, 23, 1–50 and 25, 10–51; trans. as Value and Price in the Marxian System, in A. T. Peacock *et al.* (eds.), *International Economic Papers* (London, Macmillan, 1952), 2, 5–61

(1907 [1949]), Zur Berechtigung der grundlegenden theoretischen Konstruktionen von Marx im dritten Band des 'Kapital', *Jahrbücher für Nationalökonomie und Statistik*, 34, 370–85; English trans. as On the Correction of Marx's Fundamental Theoretical Construction in the Third Volume of Capital, in Sweezy (ed.) (1949).

Bródy, A. (1997), The Second Eigenvalue of the Leontief Matrix, *Economic Systems Research*, 9, 253–8

Brouwer, L. E. J. (1912), Über Abbildungen von Mannigfaltigkeiten, *Mathematische Annalen*, 71, 97–115

Brown, M., Sato, K. and Zaremba, P. (eds.) (1976), *Essays in Modern Capital Theory* (Amsterdam, North-Holland)

Bruno, M., Burmeister, E. and Sheshinski, E. (1966), The Nature and Implications of the Reswitching of Techniques, *Quarterly Journal of Economics*, 80, 526–53

Burmeister, E. (1974), Synthesizing the Neo-Austrian and Alternative Approaches to Capital Theory: A Survey, *Journal of Economic Literature*, 12, 413–56

Cantor, D. G. and Lippman, S. A. (1983), Investment Selection with Imperfect Capital Markets, *Econometrica*, 51, 1121–44

(1995), Optimal Investment with a Multitude of Projects, *Econometrica*, 63, 1231–40

Cass, D. (1972a), On Capital Overaccumulation in the Aggregative Neoclassical Model of Economic Growth: A Complete Characterization, *Journal of Economic Theory*, 4, 200–23

(1972b), Distinguishing Inefficient Competitive Growth Paths, *Journal of Economic Theory*, 4, 224–40

Champernowne, D. G. (1953–4), The Production Function and the Theory of Capital: A Comment, *Review of Economic Studies*, 21, 112–35

Clark, J. B. (1899), *The Distribution of Wealth: A Theory of Wages, Interest and Profits* (New York, Macmillan)

Cottle, R. W., Pang, J.-S. and Stone, R. E. (1992), *The Linear Complementarity Problem* (New York, Academic Press)

Dana, R. A., Florenzano, M., Le Van, C. and Lévy, D. (1989a), Production Prices and General Equilibrium Prices: A Long Run Property of a Leontief Economy, *Journal of Mathematical Economics*, 18, 263–80

(1989b), Asymptotic Properties of a Leontief Economy, *Journal of Economic Dynamics and Control*, 13, 553–68

Dantzig, G. B. and Manne, A. S. (1974), A Complementarity Algorithm for an Optimal Capital Path with Invariant Proportions, *Journal of Economic Theory*, 9, 312–23

Debreu, G. (1956), Market Equilibrium, *Proceedings of the National Academy of Sciences of the USA*, 38, 886–93

(1959), *Theory of Value* (New York, Wiley)

(1970), Economies with a Finite Set of Equilibria, *Econometrica*, 38, 387–92

(1974), Excess Demand Functions, *Journal of Mathematical Economics*, 1, 15–21

Desrousseaux, J. (1961), Expansion stable et taux d'intérêt optimal, *Annales des Mines*, Paris

Deutsch, E. and Neumann, M. (1985), On the First and Second Order Derivatives of the Perron Vector, *Linear Algebra and its Applications*, 71, 57–76

Dierker, E. (1972), Two Remarks on the Number of Equilibria of an Economy, *Econometrica*, 40, 951–53

Dietzenbacher, E. (1988), Perturbations of Matrices: A Theorem on the Perron Vector and its Applications to Input–Output Models, *Journal of Economics*, 48, 389–412

Dore, M., Chakravarty S. and Goodwin R. (eds.) (1989), *John von Neumann and Modern Economics* (Oxford, Clarendon Press)

Dorfman, R., Samuelson, P. A. and Solow, R. M. (1958), *Linear Programming and Economic Analysis* (New York, McGraw-Hill)

Duménil, G. and Lévy, D. (1984), The Unifying Formalism of Domination: Value, Price, Distribution and Growth in Joint Production, *Journal of Economics*, 44, 349–71

(1985), The Classicals and the Neoclassicals: A Rejoinder to Frank Hahn, *Cambridge Journal of Economics*, 9, 327–45

(1987a), Value and Natural Prices Trapped in Joint Production Pitfalls, *Journal of Economics*, 47, 15–46

(1987b), The Dynamics of Competition: A Restoration of the Classical Analysis, *Cambridge Journal of Economics*, 11, 133–64

(1991), Les classiques après Walras, *Economie Appliquée*, 44, 107–30

(1993), *The Economics of the Profit Rate* (Aldershot, Edward Elgar)

Eatwell, J. (1987), Walras's Theory of Capital, in Eatwell, Milgate and Newman (eds.) (1987), IV, 868–72

Eatwell, J., Milgate, M. and Newman, P. (eds.) (1987), *The New Palgrave. A Dictionary of Economics*, 4 vols. (London, Macmillan)

Eatwell, J. and Panico, C. (1987), *Sraffa, Piero (1898–1983)*, in Eatwell, Milgate and Newman (eds.) (1987), IV, 445–52

Eilenberg, S. and Montgomery, D. (1946), Fixed Point Theorems for Multivalued Transformations, *American Journal of Mathematics*, 68, 214–22

Erreygers, C. (1989), On Indirect Taxation and Weakly Basic Commodities, *Journal of Economics*, 50, 139–56

(1990), *Terre, rente et choix de techniques. Une étude sur la théorie néo-ricardienne*, PhD thesis, University of Paris X-Nanterre

(1991), Production of Commodities without Commodities: Ricardo on Profit and Rent in the 'Principles', *Recherches Economiques de Louvain*, 57, 349–60.

(1992), Marchandises non fondamentales et système étalon en présence de terres, *Revue d'Economie Politique*, 102, 687–702

(1994a), Non-Substitution, Quantum Numbers and Sectors, UFSIA-SESO, University of Antwerp, mimeo

(1994b), The Impossibility of a Comparison of Techniques: A Comment, *Jahrbücher für Nationalökonomie und Statistik*, 213, 95–9

(1994c), Heterogeneous Labour, Scarcity, and Choice of Techniques, *Metroeconomica*, 45, 47–66

(1995a), On the Uniqueness of Square Cost-Minimizing Techniques, *The Manchester School*, 63, 145–66

(1995b), Ricardo's Theory of Tax Incidence: A Comment, *Cambridge Journal of Economics*, 19, 819–25

(1996a), The Hotelling Rule in a Multi-Commodity Economy, University of Antwerp, mimeo

(1996b), Sustainability and Stability in a Classical Model of Production, in S. Faucheux, D. Pearce and J. L. R. Proops (eds.), *Models of Sustainable Development* (Cheltenham, Edward Elgar), 345–62

(1998), 'Natural Resources', in H. D. Kurz and N. Salvadori (eds.), *The Elgar Companion to Classical Economics* (Cheltenham, Edward Elgar), II, 149–56

Faustmann, M. (1849), Berechnung des Werthes, welchen Walboden sowie nicht hauptbare Holzbestande für die Waldwirtschaft besitzen, *Allgemeine Forst und Jagd Zeitung*, 15, 441–5; trans. as On the Determination of the Value which Forest Land and Immature Stands Possess for Forestry, in M. Gane, Martin Faustmann and the Evolution of Discounted Cash Flow, *Oxford Institute Papers*, 42, 1968.

Filippini, C. (1977), Positività dei prezzi e produzione congiunta, *Giornale degli Economisti e Annali di Economia*, 36, 91–9

Filippini, C. and Filippini, L. (1982), Two Theorems on Joint Production, *Economic Journal*, 92, 386–90

Fisher, I. (1907), *The Rate of Interest* (New York, Macmillan).

(1930 [1986]), *The Theory of Interest* (New York, A. M. Kelley)

Flaschel, P. (1982), On Two Concepts of Basic Commodities for Joint Production Systems, *Journal of Economics*, 42, 259–80

Flemming, J. S. and Wright, J. F. (1971), Uniqueness of the Internal Rate of Return: A Generalisation, *Economic Journal*, 81, 256–63

Franke, R. (1986), Some Problems Concerning the Notion of Cost-Minimizing Systems in the Framework of Joint Production, *The Manchester School*, 52, 298–307

Frobenius, G. (1908), Über Matrizen aus positiven Elementen, I, *Sitzungsberichte der Königlichen preussischen Akademie der Wissenschaften*, 471–6

(1909), Über Matrizen aus positiven Elementen, II, *Sitzungsberichte der Königlichen preussischen Akademie der Wissenschaften*, 514–18

(1912), Über Matrizen aus nicht negativen Elementen, *Sitzungsberichte der Königlichen preussischen Akademie der Wissenschaften*, 456–77

Gale, D. (1955), The Law of Supply and Demand, *Mathematica Scandinavia*, 3, 155–69

Gale, D. and Nikaido, H. (1965), The Jacobian Matrix and Global Univalence of Mappings, *Mathematische Annalen*, 159, 81–93

Garegnani, P. (1960), *Il capitale nelle teorie della distribuzione* (Milan, A. Giuffrè)

(1966), Switching of Techniques, *Quarterly Journal of Economics*, 80, 555–67

(1970), Heterogeneous Capital, the Production Function and the Theory of Distribution, *Review of Economic Studies*, 37, 407–36

(1976), On a Change in the Notion of Equilibrium in Recent Work on Value and Distribution: A Comment on Samuelson, in Brown, Sato and Zaremba (eds.) (1976), 25–45

(1987), Surplus Approach to Value and Distribution, in Eatwell, Milgate and Newman (eds.) (1987), IV, 560–74

Georgescu-Roegen, N. (1951), Some Properties of a Generalized Leontief Model, in Koopmans (ed.) (1951a), 155–64

Gould, F. J. and Tolle, J. W. (1974), A Unified Approach to Complementarity in Optimisation, *Discrete Mathematics*, 7, 225–72

Grandmont, J. M. (1982), Temporary General Equilibrium Theory, in Arrow and Intriligator (eds.) (1981–6), II, 879–922

Groenewegen, P. D. (1977), *The Economics of A. R. J. Turgot* (The Hague, Martinus Nijhoff)

Guichard, J. P. (1979), *Rente foncière et dynamique sociale*, PhD thesis, University of Nice

Hagemann, H. (1987), Internal Rate of Return, in Eatwell, Milgate and Newman (eds.) (1987), II, 892–94

Hagemann, H. and Kurz, H. D. (1976), The Return of the Same Truncation Period and Reswitching of Techniques in Neo-Austrian and More General Models, *Kyklos*, 29, 678–708

Hahn, F. H. (1982), The Neo-Ricardians, *Cambridge Journal of Economics*, 6, 353–74

Harcourt, G. (1972), *Some Cambridge Controversies in the Theory of Capital* (Cambridge, Cambridge University Press)

Harrod, R. F. (1948), *Towards a Dynamic Economics* (London, Macmillan)

Hawkins, D. and Simon, H. A. (1949), Note: Some Conditions of Macroeconomic Stability, *Econometrica*, 17, 245–48

Hayek, F. A. von (1931), *Prices and Production* (London, Routledge & Kegan Paul)

Herrero, C. and Villar, A. (1988), A Characterization of Economies with the Non-Substitution Property, *Economics Letters*, 261, 147–52

Hicks, J. R. (1939), *Value and Capital* (Oxford, Clarendon Press)

(1970), A Neo-Austrian Growth Theory, *Economic Journal*, 80, 257–81

(1973), *Capital and Time. A Neo-Austrian Theory* (Oxford, Clarendon Press)

Horn, R. A. and Johnson, C. R. (1990), *Matrix Analysis* (Cambridge, Cambridge University Press)

Hosoda, E. (1993), Negative Surplus Value and Inferior Processes, *Metroeconomica*, 45, 29–42
(2001), Recycling and Landfilling in a Dynamic Sraffian Model: Application of the Corn–Guano Model to a Waste Treatment Problem, *Metroeconomica*, 52, 268–81
Hotelling, H. (1931), The Economics of Exhaustible Resources, *Journal of Political Economy*, 39, 137–75
Jevons, W. S. (1871 [1965]), *The Theory of Political Economy*; reprint (1965) (New York, A. M. Kelley).
Johansen, L. (1972), Simple and General Non-Substitution Theorem for Input–Output Models, *Journal of Economic Theory*, 5, 383–94
Kakutani, S. (1941), A Generalization of Brouwer's Fixed Point Theorem, *Duke Mathematical Journal*, 8, 416–27
Kaldor, N. (1955–6), Alternative Theories of Distribution, *Review of Economic Studies*, 23, 83–100
(1989), John von Neumann: A Personal Recollection; foreword in Dore, Chakravarty and Goodwin (1989), vii–xi
Karmel, P. H. (1959), The Marginal Efficiency of Capital, *Economic Record*, 35, 429–34
Kemeny, J. G., Morgenstern, O. and Thompson, G. L. (1956), A Generalization of von Neumann's Model of an Expanding Economy, *Econometrica*, 24, 115–35
Keynes, J. M. (1936), *The General Theory of Employment, Interest and Money* (London, Macmillan)
Klimovsky, E. (1985), *Renta y ganancia en la economia politica clasica*, Universidad Autónoma Metropolitana, Mexico
Koopmans, T. C. (ed.) (1951), *Activity Analysis of Production and Allocation* (New York, Wiley)
(1957), *Three Essays on the State of Economic Science* (New York, McGraw-Hill)
Kregel, J. A. (ed.) (1983), *Distribution, Effective Demand and International Economic Relations* (London, Macmillan)
Kurz, H. D. (1978), Rent Theory in a Multisectoral Model, *Oxford Economic Papers*, 30, 16–37
(1986), Classical and Early Neoclassical Economists on Joint Production, *Metroeconomica*, 38, 1–37
(1987), Capital Theory: Debates, in Eatwell, Milgate and Newman (eds.), 1, (1987), 357–63
(ed.) (2000), *Critical Essays on Piero Sraffa's Legacy in Economics* (Cambridge, Cambridge University Press)
Kurz, H. D. and Salvadori, N. (1993), Von Neumann's Growth Model and the 'Classical' Tradition, *European Journal of Economic Thought*, 1, 129–60
(1994), Choice of Technique in a Model with Fixed Capital, *European Journal of Political Economy*, 10, 545–69
(1995), *Theory of Production. A Long-Period Analysis* (Cambridge, Cambridge University Press)
(1997), Exhaustible Resources in a Dynamic Input–Output Model with 'Classical' Features, *Economic Systems Research*, 9, 235–51

(2000), Economic Dynamics in a Simple Model with Exhaustible Resources and a Given Real Wage Rate, *Structural Change and Economic Dynamics*, 11, 167–79

(2001), Classical Economists and the Problem of Exhaustible Resources, *Metroeconomica*, 52, 282–96

Lemke, C. E. (1965), Bimatrix Equilibrium Points and Mathematical Programming, *Management Science*, 11, 681–89

Lemke, C. E. and Howson, J. T. (1964), Equilibrium Points of Bimatrix Games, *SIAM Journal on Applied Mathematics*, 12, 413–23

Leontief, W. (1941), *The Structure of the American Economy* (Cambridge, Mass., Harvard University Press)

Levhari, D. (1965), A Non Substitution Theorem and Switching of Techniques, *Quarterly Journal of Economics*, 79, 98–105

Levhari, D. and Samuelson, P. A. (1966), The Nonswitching Theorem is False, *Quarterly Journal of Economics*, 80, 518–19

Lévy, D. (1984), Le formalisme unificateur du surclassement: valeur, prix, répartition et croissance en production jointe, in Bidard (ed.) (1984a), 37–51

Lippi, M. (1979), *I prezzi di produzione. Un saggio sulla teoria di Sraffa* (Bologna, Il Mulino).

Lyapunov, A. (1907), Problème général de la stabilité du mouvement, *Annales de Toulouse*, 9, 2

Majumbar, M. (1974), Efficient Programs in Infinite Dimensional Spaces: A Complete Characterization, *Journal of Economic Theory*, 7, 355–69

Malinvaud, E. (1953), Capital Accumulation and the Efficient Allocation of Resources, *Econometrica*, 21, 233–68

(1962), Efficient Capital Accumulation: A Corrigendum, *Econometrica*, 30, 570–3

Malthus, T. R. (1815), *An Inquiry into the Nature and Progress of Rent* (London, John Murray)

(1820 [1951]), *Principles of Political Economy* (London, John Murray); reprint in Sraffa (ed.) (1951–73), II

Manara, C. F. (1968), Il modello di Piero Sraffa per la produzione conjiunta di merci a mezzo di merci, *L'Industria*, 1, 3–18, trans. in Pasinetti (1980), 1–15

Mantel, R. (1974), On the Characterization of Aggregate Excess Demand, *Journal of Economic Theory*, 7, 348–53

Marx, K. (1894 [1972]), *Capital*, vol. III; reprint (London, Lawrence & Wishart, 1972)

McKenzie, L. W. (1954), On Equilibrium in Graham's Model of World Trade and Other Competitive Systems, *Econometrica*, 22, 147–61

(1959), On the Existence of General Equilibrium for a Competitive Market, *Econometrica*, 27, 54–71

(1987), Turnpike Theory, in Eatwell, Milgate and Newman (eds.) (1987), IV, 712–20

(1991), Comment, in McKenzie, and Zamagni (eds.) (1991), 410–20

McKenzie, L. W. and Zamagni, S. (eds.), (1991), *Value and Capital: Fifty Years Later* (New York, New York University Press)

Mirrlees, J. A. (1969), The Dynamic Nonsubstitution Theorem, *Review of Economic Studies*, 36, 67–76

Montani, G. (1972), La teoria ricardiana della rendita, *L'Industria*, 3–4, 221–43

(1975), Scarce Natural Resources and Income Distribution, *Metroeconomica*, 27, 68–101

Morishima, M. (1960), Existence of Solution to the Walrasian System of Capital Formation and Credit, *Journal of Economics*, 12, 238–43

(1964), *Equilibrium, Stability and Growth. A Multisectoral Analysis* (Oxford, Clarendon Press)

(1996), Refutation of the Nonswitching Theorem, *Quarterly Journal of Economics*, 80, 520–25

(1969), *Theory of Economic Growth* (Oxford, Clarendon Press)

(1973), *Marx's Economics. A Dual Theory of Value and Growth* (Cambridge, Cambridge University Press)

(1974), Marx in the Light of Modern Economic Theory, *Econometrica*, 42, 611–32

(1977), *Walras' Economics. A Pure Theory of Capital and Money* (Cambridge, Cambridge University Press)

Neumann, J. von (1937), Über ein ökonomisches Gleichungssystem und eine Verallgemeinerung des Brouwerschen Fixpunktsatzes, in K. Menger (ed.), *Ergebnisse eines mathematischen Kolloquiums*, 8, 73–83 (Leipzig, Franz Deuticke); trans. as A Model of General Equilibrium, *Review of Economic Studies* (1945–6), 13, 1–9

Newman, P. (1962), Production of Commodities by Means of Commodities, *Schweizerische Zeitschrift für Volkswirtschaft und Statistik*, 98, 58–75

Nikaido, H. (1956), On the Classical Multilateral Exchange Problem, *Metroeconomica*, 8, 135–45

Nuti, D. M. (1973), On the Truncation of Production Flows, *Kyklos*, 26, 485–96

Okishio, N. (1961), Technical Change and the Rate of Profit, *Kobe University Economic Review*, 7, 85–99

Parrinello, S. (1983), Exhaustible Natural Resources and the Classical Method of Long-Period Equilibrium, in Kregel (ed.) (1983), 186–99

(2001), The Price of Exhaustible Resources, *Metroeconomica*, 52, 301–15

Pasinetti, L. L. (1962), Rate of Profit and Income Distribution in Relation to the Rate of Economic Growth, *Review of Economic Studies*, 29, 267–79

(1966), Changes in the Rate of Profit and Switches of Technique, *Quarterly Journal of Economics*, 80, 503–17

(1973), The Notion of Vertical Integration in Economic Analysis, *Metroeconomica*, 25, 1–29; reprint in Pasinetti (ed.) (1980), 16–43

(ed.) (1977a), *Contributi alla teoria della produzione congiunta* (Bologne, II Mulino)

(1977b), *Lectures on the Theory of Production* (London, Macmillan)

(ed.) (1980), *Essays on the Theory of Joint Production* (London, Macmillan), trans. of Pasinetti (ed.) (1977a)

(1988), Growing Sub-Systems, Vertically Hyper-Integrated Sectors and the Labour Theory of Value, *Cambridge Journal of Economics*, 12, 125–34

Perron, O. (1907), Über Matrizen, *Mathematische Annalen*, 64, 248–63
Petri, F. (2000), *The Long-Period and the Very Short: An Essay in Clarification on Equilibrium, Capital, and the Microfoundations of Macroeconomics*, University of Siena, mimeo
Phelps, E. (1961), The Golden Rule of Capital Accumulation, *American Economic Review*, 51, 638–42
Piccioni, M. and Ravagnani, F. (2002), Absolute Rent and the 'Normal Price' of Exhaustible Resources, Centro di Ricerche e Documentazione 'Piero Sraffa', Quaderno di Ricerca, 2, mimeo
Pitchford, J. D. and Hagger, A. J. (1958), A Note on the Marginal Efficiency of Capital, *Economic Journal*, 68, 597–600
Pollitt, B. H. (1990), Clearing the Path for 'Production of Commodities by Means of Commodities': Notes on the Collaboration of Maurice Dobb in Piero's Sraffa's Edition of 'Works and Correspondence of David Ricardo', in Bharadwaj and Schefold (eds.) (1990), 516–28
Quadrio-Curzio, A. (1966), *Rentita e distribuzione in un modello economica plurisettoriale* (Milan, Giuffrè).
Quint, T. and Shubik, M. (1997), A Theorem on the Number of Nash Equilibria in a Bimatrix Game, *Game Theory*, 26, 353–9
Radner, R. (1961), Paths of Economic Growth That are Optimal with Regard only to Final States: A Turnpike Theorem, *Review of Economic Studies*, 28, 98–104
(1967), Efficiency Prices for Infinite Horizon Production Programs, *Review of Economic Studies*, 34, 51–66
Ramsey, F. (1928), A Mathematical Theory of Saving, *Economic Journal*, 38, 543–59
Raneda, I. J. and Reus, J. A. S. (1985), Irregular Leontief–Sraffa Systems and Price-Vector Behaviour, University of Alicante, mimeo
Ricardo, D. (1809 [1951]), The Price of Gold, A Reply, in Sraffa (ed.) (1951–73), III, 36–46
(1810a [1951]), *The High Price of Bullion, a Proof of the Depreciation of Bank Notes*, in Sraffa (ed.) (1951–73), III, 47–127
(1810b [1951]), First Letter on the Bullion Report to the *Morning Chronicle*, in Sraffa (ed.) (1951–73), III, 131–9
(1815 [1951]), *An Essay on the Influence of a Low Price of Corn on the Profits of Stocks*, in Sraffa (ed.) (1951–73), IV, 9–41
(1817 [1951]), *On the Principles of Political Economy, and Taxation*, in Sraffa (ed.) (1951–73), I
(1820 [1951]), Notes on Malthus' *Principles*; reprint in Sraffa (ed.), (1951–73), II
(1823a [1951]), Absolute Value and Exchangeable Value (A Rough Draft), in Sraffa (ed.) (1951–73), IV, 361–97
(1923b [1951]), Absolute Value and Exchangeable Value (Later Version, Unfinished), in Sraffa (ed.) (1951–73), IV, 398–412
Robinson J. V. (1953–4), The Production Function and the Theory of Capital, *Review of Economic Studies*, 21, 81–106
Roncaglia, A. (1978), *Sraffa and the Theory of Prices* (Chichester, Wiley); trans. of *Sraffa e la teoria dei prezzi* (Rome, Laterza, 1975)

Salvadori, N. (1981), Falling Rate of Profit with a Constant Real Wage: An Example, *Cambridge Journal of Economics*, 5, 59–66

(1982), Existence of Cost-Minimizing Systems within the Sraffa Framework, *Journal of Economics*, 42, 281–98

(1985), Switching in Methods of Production and Joint Production, *The Manchester School*, 53, 156–78

(1986), Land and Choice of Techniques within the Sraffa Framework, *Australian Economic Papers*, 25, 94–105

(1987), Les ressources naturelles rares dans la théorie de Sraffa, in Bidard (ed.) (1987), 161–76

(1988a), Fixed Capital within a von Neumann–Morishima Model of Growth and Distribution, *International Economic Review*, 29, 341–51

(1988b), Fixed Capital within the Sraffa Framework, *Journal of Economics*, 48, 1–17

Salvadori, N. and Steedman, I. (1988), Joint Production Analysis in a Sraffian Framework, *Bulletin of Economic Research*, 40, 165–95.

Samuelson, P. A. (1951), Abstract of a Theorem Concerning Substitutability in Open Leontief Models, in Koopmans (ed.) (1951a), 155–64.

(1961), A New Theorem on Nonsubstitution, in H. E. Hegeland (ed.), *Money, Growth and Methodology*, published in honour of Johan Åkerman (Lund, Club Geerup)

(1962), Parable and Realism in Capital Theory: The Surrogate Production Function, *Review of Economic Studies*, 29, 193–206

(1966), A Summing Up, *Quarterly Journal of Economics*, 80, 568–83

(1979), Paul Douglas's Measurement of Production Functions and Marginal Productivities, *Journal of Political Economy*, 87 (5), 923–39

Samuelson, P. A. and Modigliani, F. (1966), The Pasinetti Paradox in Neoclassical and More General Models, *Review of Economic Studies*, 33, 269–301

Sato, K. (1974), The Neoclassical Postulate and the Technology Frontier in Capital Theory, *Quarterly Journal of Economics*, 88, 353–84

Saucier, Ph. (1981), *Le choix des techniques en situation de limitation des ressources*, PhD thesis, University of Paris II, mimeo

Scarf, H. E. (1960), Some Examples of Global Instability of the Competitive Equilibrium, *International Economic Review*, 1, 157–72

(1967), The Approximation of Fixed Points of a Continuous Mapping, *SIAM Journal of Applied Mathematics*, 15, 1328–43

Schefold, B. (1971), *Piero Sraffas Theorie der Kuppelproduktion, des Kapitals und der Rente* (*Mr. Sraffa on Joint Production*), PhD thesis, University of Basle, mimeo

(1974), Fixed Capital as a Joint Product and the Analysis of Accumulation with Different Forms of Technical Progress, in Pasinetti (ed.) (1980), 138–217

(1976), Relative Prices as a Function of the Rate of Profit: A Mathematical Note, *Journal of Economics*, 36, 21–48

(1978a), On Counting Equations, *Journal of Economics*, 38, 253–85

(1978b), Fixed Capital as a Joint Product, *Jahrbücher für Nationalökonomie und Statistik*, 192, 415–39

(1978c), Multiple Product Techniques with Properties of Single Product Systems, *Journal of Economics*, 38, 29–53

(1980), Von Neumann and Sraffa: Mathematical Equivalence and Conceptual Difference, *Economic Journal*, 90, 140–56

(1985), Ecological Problems as a Challenge to Classical and Keynesian Economics, *Metroeconomica*, 37, 21–61

(1988), The Dominant Technique in Joint Production Systems, *Cambridge Journal of Economics*, 12, 97–123

(1989a), *Mr. Sraffa on Joint Production and Other Essays* (London, Unwin Hyman)

(1989b), A Digression on Exhaustible Resources, in Schefold (1997), 278–91

(1997), *Normal Prices, Technical Change and Accumulation* (London, Macmillan)

(2001), Critique of the Corn–Guano Model, *Metroeconomica*, 52, 316–28

Silcock, T. H. (1959), Complementarity and Future Time: A Note on the Marginal Efficiency of Capital, *Economic Journal*, 69, 816–19

Smith, A. (1776 [1976]), *An Inquiry into the Nature and Causes of the Wealth of Nations*, reprinted as vol. II of R. H. Campbell, A. S. Skinner and W. B. Todd (eds.), The Glasgow Edition of the Works and Correspondence of Adam Smith (Oxford, Oxford University Press)

Solow, R. (1956), A Contribution to the Theory of Economic Growth, *Quarterly Journal of Economics*, 70, 65–94

Sonin, I. M. (1995), Growth Rate, Internal Rates of Return and Turnpikes in an Investment Model, *Economic Theory*, 5, 383–400

Sonnenschein, H. (1973), Do Walras' Identity and Continuity Characterize the Class of Community Excess Demand Functions?, *Journal of Economic Theory*, 6, 345–54

Soper, C. S. (1959), The Marginal Efficiency of Capital: A Further Note, *Economic Journal*, 69, 174–77

Sperner, E. (1928), Neuer Beweis für die Invarianz des Dimensionszahl und des Gebietes, *Abhandlungen aus dem Mathematischen Seminar der Hamburgischen Universität*, Hamburg, 6, 265–72

Sraffa, P. (1925), Sulle relazioni fra costo e quantità prodotta, *Annali di Economia*, 2, 277–328

(1926), The Laws of Returns under Competitive Conditions, *Economic Journal*, 36, 535–50

(1951), Introduction, in *The Works and Correspondence of David Ricardo*, I (Cambridge, Cambridge University Press), xiii–lxii

(ed.) (1951–73), *The Works and Correspondence of David Ricardo*, 11 vols., I–IX, 1952, X, 1955, XI, 1973 (Cambridge, Cambridge University Press)

(1960), *Production of Commodities by Means of Commodities. Prelude to a Critique of Economic Theory* (Cambridge, Cambridge University Press)

(1962 [1970]), Correspondence with P. Newman, edited in Bharadwaj (1970)

Starrett, D. A. (1970), The Efficiency of Competitive Programs, *Econometrica*, 38, 704–11

Steedman, I. (1975), Positive Profits with Negative Surplus Value, *Economic Journal*, 85, 114–23

(1976), Positive Profits with Negative Surplus Value: A Reply to Mr. Wolfstetter, *Economic Journal*, 86, 873–6

(1977), *Marx after Sraffa* (London, New Left Books)
(1984), L'importance empirique de la production jointe, in Bidard (ed.) (1984a), 5–20
(ed.) (1988), *Sraffian Economics*, 2 vols. (Aldershot, Edward Elgar)
(1994), 'Perverse' Behaviour in a 'One-Commodity' Model, *Cambridge Journal of Economics*, 18, 299–311
(1997), Price Scheme Cones, in A. Simonovits and A. Steenge (eds.), *Prices, Growth and Cycles* (London, Macmillion), 270–79
Stiglitz, J. E. (1970), Non-Substitution Theorems with Durable Capital Goods, *Review of Economic Studies*, 37, 543–53
Sweezy, P. M. (ed.) (1949), *Karl Marx and the Close of his System by Eugen von Böhm-Bawerk, and Böhm-Bawerk's Criticism of Marx by Rudolf Hilferding* (New York, A. M. Kelley)
Todd, M. J. (1974), A Generalized Complementary Pivoting Algorithm, *Mathematical Programming*, 6, 243–63
Torrens, R. (1821) *An Essay on the Production of Wealth*, reprint in Dorfman (ed.) (1821 [1965]) (New York, A. M. Kelley), 1965
Turgot, A. R. J. (1766), *Réflexions sur la formation et la distribution des richesses*; trans. as Reflections on the Production and Distribution of Wealth, in Groenewegen (1977)
Tuy, H. (1979), Pivotal Methods for Computing Equilibrium Points: Unified Approach and New Restart Algorithm, *Mathematical Programming*, 16, 210–77
Varri, P. (1974), Prezzi, saggio del profitto e durata del capitale fisso nello schema teorico di Piero Sraffa, *Studi Economici*, 29, 5–44; transl. as Prices, Rate of Profit and Life of Machines in Sraffa's Fixed Capital Model, in Pasinetti (ed.) (1980), 55–87
Walras L. (1874 [1988]), *Eléments d'économie politique pure ou théorie de la richesse sociale* (Paris, Guillaumin); reprint in *Auguste et Léon Walras, Oeuvres Economiques Complètes*, VIII (Paris, Economica), 1988
Wicksell, K. (1901 [1934]), *Vorlesungen über Nationalökonomie*; trans. as Lectures on Political Economy, I (London, Routledge & Kegan Paul), 1934
Wicksell, K. (1923 [1934]), A Review and a Mathematical Elucidation of the Analysis in Åkerman's Doctoral Dissertation, *Realkapital und Kapitalzins* (Lund, Swiden); reprint in Wicksell (1934 [1901]), 274–99
Woods, J. E. (1990), *The Production of Commodities: An Introduction to Sraffa* (London, Macmillan)
Wright, J. F. (1959), The Maximal Efficiency of Capital, *Economic Journal*, 69, 813–16

JOURNAL SYMPOSIA

Quarterly Journal of Economics (1966), Symposium on Paradoxes in Capital Theory, 80 (4)
Metroeconomica (2001), Symposium on Exhaustible Natural Resources and Sraffian Analysis, 52 (3)

Author index

Subject index